Russia's Air Power in Crisis

Smithsonian History of Aviation Series

Von Hardesty, Series Editor

On December 17, 1903, human flight became a reality when Orville Wright piloted the *Wright Flyer* across a 120-foot course above the sands at Kitty Hawk, North Carolina. That awe-inspiring twelve seconds of powered flight inaugurated a new era. The airplane quickly evolved as a means of transportation and a weapon of war. Flying faster, farther, and higher, airplanes soon encircled the globe, dramatically altering human perceptions of time and space. The dream of flight appeared to be without bounds. Having conquered the skies, the heirs of the Wrights eventually orbited the Earth and landed on the Moon.

Aerospace history is punctuated with extraordinary feats of heroism and technological achievement. But that same history also showcases the devastating impact of aviation technology in modern warfare. The airplane—as with many other important technological breakthroughs—has provided safe, reliable, and inexpensive travel for millions. Vertical flight continues to play a key role in rescue and communications.

International in scope, this scholarly series includes original monographs, biographies, reprints of out-of-print classics, translations, and reference works. Both civil and military themes are included, along with studies related to the cultural impact of the airplane. Together, these diverse titles contribute to our overall understanding of aeronautical technology and its evolution.

Associate Series Editor: Michael Gorn, historian

Advisory Board: Horst Boog, historian, Germany; Tom D. Crouch, National Air and Space Museum; Carl-Fredrik Geust, independent scholar, Finland; John T. Greenwood, Center for Military History; R. Cargill Hall, NRO Historian; Roger D. Launius, chief historian, National Aeronautics and Space Administration; Felix Lowe, publisher, South Carolina; Howard McCurdy, American University; Stephen McFarland, Auburn University; John H. Morrow Jr., University of Georgia; Richard J. Overy, King's College, London; Dominick Pisano, National Air and Space Museum; Robert van der Linden, National Air and Space Museum; Kenneth Werrell, Radford University; Christine White, Pennsylvania State University; Robert Wohl, University of California at Los Angeles

RUSSIA'S AIR POWER IN CRISIS

BENJAMIN S. LAMBETH

• • • • **A RAND Research Study** • • • •

SMITHSONIAN INSTITUTION PRESS • WASHINGTON AND LONDON

For Kathy and Rob

Copy editor: D. Teddy Diggs
Production editor: Ruth G. Thomson
Designer: Janice Wheeler

Library of Congress Cataloging-in-Publication Data
Lambeth, Benjamin S.
　Russia's air power in crisis / Benjamin Lambeth.
　　　p.　　cm. — (Smithsonian history of aviation series)
　　Includes bibliographical references and index.
　　ISBN 1-56098-991-2 (alk. paper)
　　1. Russia (Federation). Voenno-Vozdushnye Sily.　2. Air power—Russia (Federation)
　3. Chechnia (Russia)—History—Civil War, 1994–1996—Aerial operations.　I. Title.
　II. Series.
　UG635.R9L1823　1999
　359′.00947′09049—dc21　　　　　　　　　　　　　　　　　　　98-53121

British Library Cataloguing-in-Publication Data available

Manufactured in the United States of America
06 05 04 03 02 01 00 99　5 4 3 2 1

∞　The paper used in this publication meets the minimum requirements of the American National Standard for Information Sciences—Permanence of Paper for Printed Library Materials ANSI Z39.48-1984.

For permission to reproduce illustrations appearing in this book, please correspond directly with the owners of the works, as listed in the individual captions. The Smithsonian Institution Press does not retain reproduction rights for these illustrations individually, or maintain a file of addresses for photo sources.

Contents

Abbreviations

AWACS	airborne warning and control system
CIS	Commonwealth of Independent States
GCI	ground-controlled intercept
KFA	Frontal Aviation Command (*Komandovanie frontovoi aviatsii*)
LRA	Long-Range Aviation
NATO	North Atlantic Treaty Organization
RAF	Royal Air Force
R&D	research and development
RTU	replacement training unit
SAM	surface-to-air missile
UPT	undergraduate pilot training
USAF	U.S. Air Force
VPVO	Air Defense Forces (*Voiska protivovozdushnoi oborony*)
VTA	Military Transport Aviation (*Voyenno-transportnaya aviatsia*)
VVAUL	Higher Military Aviation School for Pilots (*Vyssheye voyennoye aviatsionnoye uchilishche letchikov*)
VVS	Military Air Force (*Voyenno-vozdushniye sily*)

Preface

This book summarizes more than two decades of research into Soviet and, since 1992, Russian air doctrine, air force modernization, and flight training. Its origins date back to 1976, when I first began exploring at RAND, under U.S. Air Force (USAF) sponsorship, how conventional air power related to Soviet concepts for theater war in Europe and what that relationship implied for U.S. defense planning. The book, begun as an inquiry into what the revelations of glasnost in the late 1980s indicated about the real strengths and weaknesses of Soviet air power, has since evolved into a portrait of decline as military aviation in Russia, like most everything else about the Soviet might that commanded such Western respect throughout the cold war, has progressively wasted away during the eight years since the USSR's collapse.

My interest in Soviet air power was first sparked by the rare opportunity I had to fly with the USAF's 64th Fighter Weapons Squadron at Nellis Air Force Base, Nevada, in early 1976 to gain firsthand exposure to a new program called Red Flag, which had just been activated to provide U.S. and allied aircrews with the most realistic training possible short of actual combat. The 64th was one of four recently established USAF "Aggressor squadrons" (two at Nellis and one each in Europe and the Pacific) that operated the T-38 supersonic jet trainer and, later, the F-5E lightweight fighter to simulate the MiG-21, the Soviet Air Force's best air-combat fighter at the time. The intent of the Aggressor program was to replicate as closely as possible what was then known about Soviet style and practice in air combat so that U.S. aircrews could gain hands-on experience with what they might encounter should they ever have to confront their Soviet opposites in a shooting war.

As the USAF's designated experts on Soviet fighter weapons and tactics, the instructors who flew in the Aggressor squadrons were avid consumers of any insights that might enhance their appreciation of how their Soviet counterparts trained and operated. For my part, as a longtime student of Soviet affairs and a recently licensed private pilot, I came away from my own first exposure to the Aggressors and Red Flag determined to find an avenue that might allow me to combine my professional background in Soviet military matters with my avocational interest in flying in a way that might help better inform both the Aggressors and the broader USAF leadership, which had long looked to RAND for analytic support on a wide spectrum of issues.

That determination led over time to an ever-closer working relationship with airmen and threat assessors at all levels, not only in the U.S. Air Force but also in the U.S. Navy, U.S. Marine Corps, and several allied air forces. Those connections, in turn, opened up a cornucopia of opportunities for me to further broaden my exposure to the world of air operations by gaining firsthand flying experience on tactical training missions in nearly three dozen different types of high-performance military aircraft worldwide over the course of two decades. They also created numerous occasions for me to take part in some highly instructive joint-service and multinational looks at Soviet fighter training and tactics. Most important, they offered me a chance at RAND to write extensively, under USAF sponsorship, on a variety of trends and issues related to Soviet and, later, Russian air power. This book, which draws heavily on the Soviet and Russian defense literature produced since the onset of glasnost in 1986, including a rich reportage on air power, represents the capstone of that effort.

If there was a single event that ultimately led to this book, it was the opportunity I had to get to know Valery Menitsky, the chief test pilot of the Mikoyan Design Bureau, at the 1988 Farnborough Air Show in Great Britain after the first flight demonstration of the MiG-29, with great fanfare, to a Western audience. Thanks to that initial contact and several more that followed over the ensuing year, in December 1989 at the Soviet Air Force's showcase Kubinka air base near Moscow, I became, at Menitsky's behest, the first American to fly the MiG-29 (in a two-seat trainer version with Menitsky in the front cockpit) and, by the account of a subsequent Soviet press report, the first Westerner invited to fly a combat aircraft of any type inside Soviet airspace since the end of World War II. In short order, that experience opened further doors into the once-closed world of Soviet military aviation, including the opportunity I had in December 1991 to meet at length with the commander in chief of the Soviet Air Force, Colonel General Pyotr S. Deinekin, at his Moscow headquarters on the day before the heads of the Soviet republics announced the dissolution of the USSR.

The warmth and candor of that meeting with General Deinekin encouraged me to seek USAF sponsorship of a RAND research effort that would enable me to document the evolution of post-Soviet Russian air power in a manner that might actually draw on Russian Air Force cooperation. My hope was to provide Western specialists with an assessment that transcended the usual dry facts and figures to impart an informed feel for the Russian Air Force as a living institution. Ultimately, that sought-after cooperation from the Russian Air Force proved to be too ambitious a goal to elicit from the higher echelons of the Russian military in the still halting process of post-Soviet Russian reform. Nevertheless, as an experiment in professional outreach, the attempt was not a total failure. I met three times thereafter with General Deinekin during subsequent trips to Moscow to discuss my research plan and its progress. I also had several conversations with Major General Vasily Aleksandrov, the commander of the Russian Air Force's Central Research Institute. Finally, I was able to gain further insights into the operational side of Russian fighter aviation through an invitational Su-27 flight with the Gromov Flight Research Institute and two front-seat advanced-handling flights in a MiG-21 and MiG-23 with the Mikoyan Design Bureau, all at the Zhukovsky Flight Test Center near Moscow.

For whatever value this book may offer as a contribution toward a better Western understanding of Russian air power, I am indebted first and foremost to the late Colonel Moody Suter, USAF (Ret.), the creator of Red Flag and a fighter pilot's fighter pilot who was the first to lend a clear direction to my nascent interest in Soviet military aviation in 1976. I am grateful also for the early influence of Andrew Marshall, Director of Net Assessment in the U.S. Department of Defense, and Major General Jasper A. Welch Jr., USAF (Ret.), former Assistant Chief of Staff for Studies and Analysis, Headquarters U.S. Air Force, in sharpening my appreciation of the importance of conducting honest vulnerability analysis in addition to focusing on obvious military strengths in the study of Soviet combat capability. Finally, I am beholden to a succession of managers in RAND's Project AIR FORCE research division, and particularly to James A. Thomson, now RAND's president and chief executive officer, for having provided me with the needed support to do most of the research, travel, and writing that made this book possible.

As for those kind enough to offer me critical feedback on earlier iterations of this study over the course of its evolution, I wish to acknowledge the following: Lieutenant Colonel Barry Watts, USAF (Ret.), now head of the Northrop Grumman Analysis Center; Lieutenant General Heikki Nikunen, former commander of the Finnish Air Force; General Richard Hawley, USAF, commander, Air Combat Command; Lieutenant Generals Stephen Croker, USAF (Ret.), Bradley Hosmer, USAF (Ret.), Ronald Iverson, USAF (Ret.), and Joseph Redden, USAF; Brigadier General John Reppert, U.S. Army, and Major David Johnson, USAF, former defense attaché and assistant air attaché at the U.S. Embassy in Moscow; Air Chief Marshal Sir Michael Armitage, RAF (Ret.); Air Marshal Sir John Walker, RAF (Ret.); Air Vice Marshal Tony Mason, RAF (Ret.); Professor John Erickson, University of Edinburgh; Major Randy Mayer, USAF (Ret.); Steve

Dunn, Headquarters Air Combat Command; Colonel Samuel Clovis, USAF (Ret.); the late Major Allen Clovis, USAF (Ret.); my RAND colleagues Abraham Becker, Tim Bonds, the late Carl Builder, Jeff Hagen, William O'Malley, Donald Stevens, and Milton Weiner; and a former Soviet fighter pilot now residing in the United States. I am grateful as well to my RAND colleague Ashley Tellis and to Rose Gottemoeller, former deputy director of the International Institute for Strategic Studies, for their critiques of an earlier version of this book; to Malcolm Palmatier, my RAND editor, for his usual keen eye; to Judy Lewis and Emily Rogers at RAND for their help in the final preparation of the manuscript; to my editors at the Smithsonian Institution Press, Von Hardesty and Mark Hirsch, for their good counsel in converting what was initially a technical report written for defense professionals into a book aimed at a more general readership; and to Teddy Diggs, for her deft finishing touches in bringing this book to fruition. I also owe a word of acknowledgment to the Rockefeller Foundation for having granted me a five-week residency at its Study and Conference Center in Bellagio on Lake Como, Italy, where the initial drafting of the book was done in September-October 1991.

Finally, I would like to express my special thanks to General Deinekin and Major General Aleksandrov of the Russian Air Force for meeting with me numerous times during my trips to Moscow between 1991 and 1995. I am likewise indebted to four top-ranked Russian test pilots with whom I was privileged to fly in Russian airspace—Valery Menitsky, Vladimir Gorbunov, and Pavel Vlasov of the Mikoyan Design Bureau and Anatoly Kvochur of the Gromov Flight Research Institute—as well as to Rostislav Belyakov, the since-retired head of Mikoyan; Anatoly Belosvet, the deputy general designer at Mikoyan; Grigory Sedov, Mikoyan's former chief test pilot; and Mikoyan pilots Roman Taskayev, Boris Orlov, and Marat Alykov for helping me to gain a closer feel for the human side of military aviation in Russia. Out of respect for lingering cold war sensitivities, I did not ask to interview on the record any of these Russian air power principals, and none are responsible in any way for the observations and conclusions in this book. That said, my contacts with them greatly contributed to eradicating any remaining doubt, in my mind, that Russian airmen stand both tall and proudly among their peers worldwide as genuine aviation professionals.

1.   Introduction

Russian air power, long a proud symbol of Soviet military might, has fallen on hard times in recent years. In the wake of the USSR's collapse in 1991, what was once a world-class air force (*Voyenno-vozdushniye sily,* literally "military air forces," or VVS) plunged almost overnight from 20,000 pilots and 13,000 aircraft to 13,000 pilots and 5,000 aircraft, mostly of obsolescent design. The disintegration of the Warsaw Pact and the ensuing end of the East-West confrontation further deprived the Russian VVS of a clear threat to guide the equipping and training of its forces. That, in turn, prompted a near-instantaneous loss of its familiar roles and missions beyond the most basic one of homeland defense. On top of that, the fact that the nation's defense was now obliged to begin at Russia's western edge saddled the VVS with new responsibilities for which it was ill-configured and poorly prepared. Foremost among its new challenges was adjusting to a radically changed external security environment at a time of mounting financial difficulty on the home front.

Even before the traumatic fall, there were gathering signs that the Soviet VVS, like the other Soviet services, was entering its most turbulent time since its wartime trials during the early 1940s. Since then, largely because of reduced funding, the leadership of the VVS has been forced to cope with a staggering array of headaches: frozen force modernization; truncated flight training and a consequent rise in the accident rate; appalling living conditions for aircrews and their families; and hard questions about how to retain and grow the next generation of leaders. The Russian VVS now routinely cannibalizes some aircraft to keep others flying, even though that violates long-standing safety rules. Starved for cash, it also is barely meeting officers' payrolls. Since 1991, it has undergone a massive drawdown, has consolidated many functions, and has sought to develop new operational concepts appropriate to Russia's post–cold war security needs. Yet efforts to build on such steps have been repeatedly thwarted by a budget crunch that not only has prevented the most basic improvements but also has continued to reduce the number of serviceable aircraft in all commands.

Russian airmen, however, have successfully endured more apocalyptic crises, most notably the surprise attack by Nazi Germany in the summer of 1941. In his masterly account of the epic rise of the Soviet VVS from near disaster following the Nazi onslaught to its recovery four years later as the world's largest tactical air arm, Von Hardesty ably described how that trial by fire had the ironic effect of providing Soviet combat aviation with "an accelerated passage to moderniza-tion and power."[1] Although the problems inherited by the post-Soviet VVS were less ominous as far as the long-term survival of the Russian state was concerned, they were no less threatening to the nearer-term vitality of Russian air power. For the Russian VVS leaders, as for their predecessors in 1941, the preeminent ques-tion was whether the blend of crisis and opportunity imposed by the watershed events of 1991 portended a fate of inexorable decline or, in Hardesty's formula-tion, a situation from which they might yet again conjure up "an accelerated pas-sage to modernization and power."

Lending faith to Russian airmen at all levels as they struggle to cope with their travails is their awareness that aviation, especially military aviation, has enjoyed a rich tradition in Russia. Indeed it predates the seventy-four-year intercession of Soviet communism. To note some of the high points, the world's first loop ma-neuver was performed by Major Pyotr Nesterov in 1913. Russia developed and successfully flew the world's first four-engine strategic bomber, Igor Sikorsky's *Ilya Muromets,* over the Eastern Front in World War I. Valery Chkalov com-manded a pioneering flight in 1937 from Moscow to Vancouver via the North Pole.[2] And Soviet airmen fought valiantly in World War II and played a key role in the defeat of Nazi Germany.[3]

The USSR led the way in jet aviation as well, with the introduction of the MiG-15 fighter in 1948. This was the world's first high-performance combat air-craft by modern standards, and it proved to be a technical match for the U.S. F-86 in the skies over Korea.[4] In 1961 cosmonaut Yury Gagarin, a former Soviet fighter pilot, became the first human to orbit the earth. Throughout the cold war, the So-viet VVS was widely regarded by Western defense officials as a formidable fight-ing force. By any measure, the VVS and the Soviet aircraft industry, from their austere beginnings in the early 1920s to the enthralling flight demonstrations of the MiG-29 during its Western debut at the 1988 Farnborough Air Show in Great Britain, earned the USSR—and later Russia—legitimate pride of place as an avia-tion giant.

Despite that rich background, most Westerners were able to follow develop-ments in Soviet aviation only from a distance because of the Soviet leadership's obsession with secrecy and societal closure. Like the rest of the Soviet military, the VVS was a denied area, a central component of the Soviet threat and thus an object, first and foremost, of Western intelligence concern. Other observers of the VVS were able to catch only glimpses beneath the often tantalizing, but rarely satisfying, appearances provided by the Soviet press and by Western threat assessments that periodically made their way into the public domain.

Because of that indistinctness, two British aviation experts noted in 1986: "Any attempt to describe the way aircraft are incorporated into the Soviet Air Forces, how they train, how they contribute to Soviet operational doctrine, and above all, how militarily effective they are, must be circumscribed again and again by conditions that apply in few other areas of military study." Those analysts offered four good reasons why any bold assertions about the VVS needed to be advanced with studied care: "First, Russia goes to great lengths to conceal evidence of a kind which in the West may be found in technical journals, obtained from conversations, and observed on airfields. Second, much of the evidence which does become available is fragmented, sometimes contradictory, and frequently open to varying interpretations. Third, interpretation of that evidence, like any other, is susceptible to the preconceptions of the analyst. Finally, even if the evidence was comprehensive and the analysis always well judged and objective, the factors making up the equation of Soviet military effectiveness are so variable that a wide range of solutions would still be possible."[5]

That was sound counsel at the time it was written. Once the cold war began winding down, however, such obstructions to analysis largely faded away. The collapse of the USSR and the opening up of post-Soviet Russia made tracking the development of military aviation far easier than it had been during the darkest years of the Soviet-U.S. standoff. The Russian media, notably including the military and technical press, for the first time became purveyors of real facts instead of merely veiled hints in need of interpretation. More important, Russia's military and industry leaders became ever more accessible to outsiders and showed a heightened willingness to engage in serious give-and-take with their Western counterparts. The result of such welcome developments was the possibility of an unprecedented look at Russian air power as it really was.

There remained limits, of course, which rendered the Russian military less than a completely open book. For example, in 1993 Russia's defense minister, Army General Pavel Grachev, noted that although already fielded military equipment was generally no longer treated as classified, future models and developments remained "state secrets."[6] Nevertheless, Russian military aviation was no longer a denied area or part of a declared threat to Western security. More and more, as contacts between Russian and Western aviation professionals, including air chiefs, continued to grow, Westerners were able to study Russian air power much as one would study military aviation in any other country. That more open and permissive climate revealed a VVS in the throes of a painful metamorphosis, unmistakably embarked on a course of reform yet uncertain in outlook as it strove to enter the twenty-first century as a renewed institution.

One might ask: so what? Why should anyone care now about an air force that not only has ceased being a threat to Western security but, indeed, finds itself operating in virtually a survival mode? The answer, simply put, is that the tribulations of the VVS since the USSR's collapse have been emblematic of similar problems affecting the other Russian armed forces.[7] Even before the costly misadventure in Chechnya, signs of privation were prevalent enough to warrant a characterization of Russia's military as a crumbling giant. In the years since, the situation has only worsened. The surface navy rarely puts to sea any more because of insufficient funds for fuel, and most of Russia's submarine fleet is likewise rusting away in home port. There have been no ground force exercises at the divisional level or higher since 1992. Not even the best army units are fully manned and equipped. In brief, more than just the VVS suffered a body blow in the wake of the disintegration of the Soviet state. One and all, Russia's armed services became but faint shadows of the Soviet leviathan that had towered over the North Atlantic Treaty Organization (NATO) across the Fulda gap in Germany for more than two generations.

How did the cutting edge of what President Ronald Reagan in 1983 ominously called the "evil empire" find itself reduced to such decrepitude in the space of barely a decade? The chapters that follow will offer one perspective on the saga of Russia's military decline by chronicling the devolution of Soviet and Russian air power from roughly the mid-1980s, when the disintegration of the USSR first began, through the Soviet collapse and the ensuing retrenchment of the VVS, to today's budget crisis, which threatens to set back Russian air power for as much as a generation.[8] Although all aspects of Russian air power, including strategic aviation and airlift, will be addressed, the main focus will be on theater air power, and on fighter aviation in particular, since those adjuncts of Soviet and Warsaw Pact planning for a possible conventional showdown against NATO were of greatest concern and controversy among Western analysts throughout the later years of the cold war. The aim in part is to close the books on that controversy once and for all, using as evidence the cornucopia of firsthand testimony that has been provided in the open press by VVS officers at all levels since the beginning of former Soviet President Mikhail Gorbachev's policy of glasnost, or openness.

What can we learn from such an effort, and why is it worth undertaking? To begin with, the frank admissions of Russia's pilots and commanders up and down the rank hierarchy since the onset of glasnost have given Western students of Russian air power an unprecedented chance to update and, where necessary, correct past impressions of the VVS. By clarifying a number of operations and training issues that had long simmered but had remained largely suppressed by the Communist Party's intolerance of dissent, that spontaneous outpouring of information has helped break down much of the mystery that once shrouded all but the broadest outlines of VVS practice. Questions that were hotly debated, without resolution, among Western analysts throughout the 1980s have finally been put to rest, confirming earlier suspicions that Soviet fighter aviation was severely shackled by top-down restrictions on pilot initiative and independence, sharply limiting the flexibility of what otherwise appeared to be a well-endowed fighting force.

Beyond that, better knowledge of where the air arm of the former Soviet Union stands today can shed useful light on the course it may take once the continuing post-Soviet reform effort gets past its current troubles and assumes a more even keel. Whatever transition pains the Russian VVS may be experiencing today, there is little doubt that Russia will eventually emerge from the USSR's collapse as a nation to be reckoned with. There also is little doubt that the VVS, for better or worse, will constitute an important part of Russia's future military capability.

For the moment, however, the story of Russian air power since the USSR's demise has been mainly one of decline and lost effectiveness. In August 1992, in what soon afterward became his signature refrain, the commander in chief of the VVS, Colonel General Pyotr S. Deinekin, poignantly insisted: "A Russia without wings is not Russia. It has had, does have, and will have them."[9] Yet however well the VVS leaders may have sized up their predicament and come to grips with it intellectually, any return of Russian air power to even a rough approximation of its glory days of the cold war is unlikely, at least in the near term. Russia may indeed still have wings, in General Deinekin's formulation. But those wings have become severely weakened—a far cry indeed from the Soviet air juggernaut that once gave Western defense planners such legitimate and serious pause.

2. The Soviet Legacy

The abortive coup attempt of August 1991 that started the clock ticking toward the fall of Soviet communism four months later affected the VVS much as it did the other Soviet services—and Soviet society across the board. With the old order discredited and stripped of any lingering claim to legitimacy, the path was cleared for a new look at all the VVS's aspects that had been driven by the idiosyncrasies of the Soviet state. At the same time, most remaining strictures against freedom of expression within the military were lifted. As the VVS monthly magazine later commented, "Glasnost continues to uncover an interminable stream of problems that used to be kept silent in the life of our armed forces."[1]

The first consequence of note for the VVS in the wake of the failed coup attempt would be a change in leadership. In July of the previous year Colonel General Yevgeny Shaposhnikov had been appointed VVS commander in chief to replace retiring Marshal of Aviation Aleksandr Yefimov, a World War II veteran who had commanded the VVS since 1984. That appointment marked a generational shift in the VVS leadership. Considering that Shaposhnikov was picked over a large number of more senior officers, his appointment seemed to reflect a higher-level determination by Mikhail Gorbachev's government to infuse the VVS with new blood. In contrast to the previous succession of commanders of Yefimov's vintage, Shaposhnikov typified a new breed of more technically minded officers who lacked the ideological and historical baggage of their predecessors. Age forty-eight at the time of his selection, he was (and remains) the youngest man to have commanded the VVS at any time in its postwar history.

From his first days as commander in chief, General Shaposhnikov showed ample signs of being a reform-minded leader with little patience for the hidebound ways of the Soviet military bureaucracy. A fighter pilot by upbringing, he had commanded a MiG-23 regiment in the Group of Soviet Forces in Germany (GSFG) in

1975 as a lieutenant colonel at the young age of thirty-four.[2] He subsequently climbed the VVS career ladder rapidly, advancing to the position of air commander for the GSFG in 1987 before being tapped to become first deputy VVS commander in chief the following year. Even Alexander Zuyev, the former VVS captain who defected to the United States via Turkey by flying a stolen MiG-29 from his base in Soviet Georgia to Trabzon on the Black Sea in May 1989, attested that Shaposhnikov was well regarded among squadron pilots. Commenting on Shaposhnikov's role in putting down the 1991 coup attempt and his subsequent elevation to the position of defense minister, Zuyev characterized the VVS chief as "a real reformer, a patriotic professional officer who knew where his true loyalties lay."[3]

Shaposhnikov drew a line forcefully against those Soviet military chiefs who had supported or otherwise sympathized with the plotters of the coup attempt.[4] For refusing to abide the attempt, Shaposhnikov was selected to replace the disgraced General Dmitry Yazov as defense minister once the back of the putsch was broken.[5] Shortly thereafter, he was elevated to the rank of marshal of aviation. Choosing a successor to take over his vacated post as VVS commander in chief, he selected his first deputy, Colonel General Pyotr Deinekin.[6] In the immediate aftermath of the coup, both he and Deinekin resigned their memberships in the Communist Party of the Soviet Union.[7]

Unlike many previous VVS commanders, whose past operational experience had been as fighter pilots, Deinekin had risen instead through the ranks of the bomber community. The son of a fighter pilot who died in 1943 while flying a LaGG-3 during the Great Patriotic War, Deinekin attended the Balashov Higher Military Aviation School for Pilots and eventually earned his wings as a bomber pilot, later serving on squadron duty and, in time, commanding a Tu-22M Backfire regiment. After that, he commanded an air division, an air army, and ultimately the VVS bomber command, known as Long-Range Aviation (LRA), before being tapped by Shaposhnikov to become first deputy VVS commander in chief in 1990. During his career progression, he attended the Gagarin Air Academy and later graduated with honors from the General Staff Academy. At the time of his appointment, he had accumulated more than 5,000 hours of flying time, including an initial qualification checkout in the Tu-160 Blackjack supersonic bomber, the VVS counterpart to the U.S. B-1B. In June 1996, along with the four other Russian service chiefs, he was promoted to four-star rank by President Boris Yeltsin in Yeltsin's bid for the chiefs' support just four days before the closely run presidential election.

Initial Responses to the Failed Coup

Not long after his appointment as defense minister, General Shaposhnikov remarked that the events of August 1991 had occasioned a "moment of truth for reviving the prestige of military service." He declared that the time had come to cast away, once and for all, the pervasive suspicion and distrust that had undermined the pursuit of combat readiness throughout the Soviet era. He added that the abortive coup had prompted long-overdue decisions regarding the conduct of military life, and he promised sweeping changes based on the principles of professionalization, quality, democratization, and sufficiency.[8]

The first new measure announced by Shaposhnikov was the dismantling of the political control apparatus that had long plagued the full maturation of military professionalism in the Soviet armed forces.[9] That disestablishment of the military's Main Political Administration had immediate consequences for a large contingent of political officers in the VVS. Before the coup, the VVS had 8,500 such officers, many of whom were pilots. Among them, 29 were generals.[10]

Shaposhnikov made departyization of the military a matter of professional pride. "It is a very important task," he declared, "and not just a sign of the times or of fashion. In a multiparty system, the military could become an object of contention. We need to be above that." Once the political officers were defrocked, Shaposhnikov said his next priority would be to professionalize the armed forces. He cautioned that such reform—"a major controversy until recently"—would not be attended to before the proper social-impact studies and cost analyses were done. He did promise, however, that the problem would finally "get the attention it deserves."[11]

Other reform goals declared by Shaposhnikov included redoubling efforts to address the gaping welfare needs of the armed forces, retiring a surfeit of unneeded generals, and easing restrictions on military secrecy. On the first count, Shaposhnikov warned that the most imposing problems, notably those pertaining to training and social needs, could not be righted instantly. A more pressing concern, he said, was to "revive the concept of the honor of an officer and give it living content." Shaposhnikov reiterated his earlier charge that the rejected Soviet system had been responsible for maintaining "strife, distrust, and confrontational relations" throughout the armed forces, leading to a pernicious atmosphere that was "ruinous to the interests of combat readiness."[12]

As for accumulated deadwood, Shaposhnikov spoke of "hundreds" of generals who had remained on the payroll too long. He suggested that perhaps only 15 to 20 percent of those would ultimately be retained. He further called for a reduction of obligatory service from two years to eighteen months and for the gradual displacement of mandatory conscription by a volunteer system. Finally, with respect to dismantling the despised machinery of Soviet censorship, he declared a presumption of openness in all activities that did not entail legitimate state secrets.[13]

For his part, the new VVS commander in chief, General Deinekin, left no room for doubt about where he laid the blame for the many years of stagnation in

VVS practice. He said: "The processes of departyization and depoliticization . . . that have been initiated actively reflect the long-standing attitude of most military flyers. The party political structures that [previously] existed interfered constantly and quite persistently in the conduct of virtually all aspects of our combat training, tying the hands of commanders and specialists."[14] Asked later what he felt the effects would be on the VVS as a result of the dismantling of those structures, General Deinekin replied: "Regardless of the final shape the reform will take, the air force will benefit from it. This country's air force suffered the burden of communism for 74 years. Now that burden has finally ceased to exist."[15]

Immediate Consequences of the Breakup of the USSR

Shaposhnikov highlighted a number of destabilizing by-products of the disintegration of the Soviet Union, including an epidemic of nationalism in some former republics, territorial claims due to past arbitrary determination of borders between republics, a desire among many former republics to eliminate the "imperial center," friction aggravated by the incomplete division of the spoils of the former USSR among the former republics, an absence of economic stability, and the presence of Russian forces outside of Russia.[16] In the face of those disruptions and dislocations, the newly installed government of Russian President Yeltsin took determined steps to supplant the USSR with a Commonwealth of Independent States (CIS) that might preserve at least a semblance of the former union's integrated defenses. A CIS Joint Armed Forces Command was created, and Shaposhnikov was named its commander in chief. At best, the CIS faced an uphill climb from the beginning because of the refusal of most former Soviet republics, notably Ukraine, to sacrifice their recently gained sovereignty to that new and suspect entity.

Problems with Air Defense

The collapse of the Soviet multinational state posed an immediate challenge to the air defense of the former USSR's territorial space. Almost alone among modern military powers, the Soviet Union—and, after its disintegration, Russia—vested that critical function in a separate service, the Air Defense Forces (*Voiska protivovozdushnoi oborony,* or VPVO). Even before the disintegration of the union, the newly appointed VPVO commander in chief, Colonel General Viktor Prudnikov, conceded that the echeloned and multitiered Soviet air defense system was overdue for a top-to-bottom review now that the cold war was over and the NATO threat ceased to exist.[17] He stressed, however, that the system must remain unified regardless of changes that might be put into effect. Anticipating the USSR's impending breakup, he rightly cautioned that no single state in a renewed confederation would possess the needed wherewithal to create such a system independently. "Any fragmentation of aerospace defense forces," he pointed out, "whether in terms of republics or in terms of branches of the armed services," would inevitably result in "considerable expenditure toward developing parallel command structures."[18]

In a clear challenge to the idea of Russia's retaining VPVO as a separate service despite the end of the cold war, Army General Vladimir Lobov, who had been appointed chief of the General Staff following the failed August coup, raised an eyebrow at "whole clusters of duplicative parallel military structures," singling out in particular "air units in the VVS and VPVO that perform similar, if not identical, functions."[19] Later, General Prudnikov conceded that a reassessment of VPVO's existing organization might be warranted, although he insistently clung to the rock-bottom need to maintain its separate and distinct command and control system.[20]

The chief of the VPVO headquarters staff, Colonel General Viktor Sinitsyn, amplified on that need, citing various reorganization proposals that had come to light, including the distribution of VPVO assets among other branches of the military. He said that this option harked back to the attempted reforms of 1980, which had prompted a reduction in the combat capability of VPVO units and a dilution of accountability for executing the air defense mission. Sinitsyn added that in 1986, "having realized that this imposed decision was in error," the military was "forced to return to a unified VPVO command, having wasted considerable resources and lost some personnel during the interim." In light of that, Sinitsyn continued, it was curious that some people were yet again proposing to abolish the unified aerospace defense system: "Such a move would cause serious problems for the command of VPVO forces and personnel. The air defense system that has been built up, consisting of an array of interdependent, truly unique, and very costly systems, will fall apart." Sinitsyn volunteered that VPVO's leadership had developed a plan that included integrating elements of VPVO into a new service to be called the Strategic Deterrent Force. That, he suggested, "would help preserve the unified air defense system that was formed over a period of decades and would prove its value in the new political conditions."[21]

General Prudnikov was even more explicit regarding the need for a unified air defense net for the embryonic CIS. He pointed out that air defense of the CIS's western portion had "substantially worsened" as a result of the collapse of the Warsaw Pact. That meant the loss of a forward radar zone covering a depth of 800–1,000 kilometers, to say nothing of a changed disposition of alert VPVO interceptors and surface-to-air missiles (SAMs). Prudnikov warned that the problem would become even more critical following the withdrawal of VPVO units from the Baltic republics. He spoke with guarded hope about the prospects for coordinating CIS air defenses with the national systems of Eastern Europe on a bilateral basis, citing a protocol signed with Romania as a promising step in the right direction. But he added, "We really need to rely on our own forces."[22]

The head of VPVO's Center for Operational and Tactical Research likewise remarked that the Soviet High Command had spent years building a layered air defense with the best equipment and technical experts, only to be confronted in 1991 with a major breach in its former front line: Ukrainian leaders demanding that former Soviet VPVO assets on Ukrainian soil be handed over for their own sovereign use. Security problems could arise unless such "anarchy" was soon brought under the guiding control of common sense, he warned. "Things may reach a point where it will not be just Rust who will fly in."[23] (The reference was to Matthias Rust, the West German teenager who scandalized the Soviet defense establishment in 1988 when he penetrated the USSR's western frontier in a Cessna 172 and landed unmolested in Red Square.)

What seemed at first to be a step toward retaining at least a modicum of integration occurred on May 26, 1992, when the first deputy Ukrainian defense minister signed an agreement in Moscow ensuring Ukrainian participation in a joint system of antimissile defense and in a coordination of air defense.[24] That cooperation proved to be short-lived, however. The following October the CIS military leaders were said to be "making desperate efforts . . . if not to preserve the air defense system in its old form, at least to organize reliable cooperation among its republics in this sphere."[25] At a conference of CIS defense ministers, Shaposhnikov stressed the urgency of an agreement on unified air defense, but the idea never got past the talking stage.

In mid-1992 General Prudnikov reported that at least some of the unified air defense architecture of the former USSR had been preserved, although efforts by various CIS member states to nationalize their portions threatened to undermine the whole system. "Practically every day," he complained, "we experience bans on the movement of our units, or a disruption in the regular flow of trains to be offloaded of equipment, or problems with pay. . . . These are not isolated cases." On the plus side, Prudnikov noted that although the VPVO defense environment had lost some of its westernmost borders as a result of the union's collapse, radar coverage remained multiecheloned and effective.[26]

The commander of the Moscow Air Defense District, Colonel General Anatoly Kornukov, also stressed that the idea of an echeloned and perimeter defense must remain central to VPVO's concept of operations. He said he was not particularly worried about the loss of the all-union unified system, although he admitted that the loss of the forward area had had a deleterious impact on early detection and warning. In effect the Moscow Air Defense District had now become a frontier command, obliging its personnel to abandon any complacent notions of still being safely in "the rear."[27]

By the end of the year, Prudnikov was no longer skirting the issue of the effect of the union's collapse on the air defense of Russia. Asked how things had changed during the preceding year, he answered: "For the worse. The process of sovereignization has deprived the integrated air defense system of many of the components that ensured its reliable functioning." He also had little good to say about the gathering calls to "reform" VPVO: "As I recall, and I have over 32 years of service in VPVO, there is always someone bent on transferring and splitting up the forces. The most recent attempts of this kind took place in the 1980s, when air defense units were transferred to the [military] districts. Analysis showed that aside from damaging national security and causing problems, this 'reform' produced nothing. On the contrary, the prestige of VPVO was undermined and, along with it, its combat potential." Prudnikov argued that such moves invariably produced additional layers of management, with the net result that each new tier meant lost time: "If that happens, it means either a wrong decision is made, or the decision is made too late." Citing as a case in point the September 1983 Soviet downing of Korean Airlines Flight 007, he said: "We should have straightened things out the very moment the aircraft penetrated our air border, not at the last minute. Perhaps then the tragedy could have been averted." Prudnikov further disclosed that only some 70 percent of VPVO's original assets remained on Russian soil and that it would take time to get Russian air defense integrity back to an acceptable level. Despite lip service from other republics for an integrated surveillance and monitoring system, those same republics declined to recognize the operational control of Shaposhnikov's CIS joint command. In some cases, notably in Transcaucasia, the new republics also lacked the trained manpower needed to operate the radar stations.[28]

Thus a strong initial Russian hope that a unified CIS air defense might be preserved eventually proved to be unfounded. On the eve of the breakup of the USSR, General Prudnikov had warned that any fragmentation of air defenses among the CIS republics would impose considerable costs on Russia to create new command structures in their place.[29] In short order, that was exactly what happened. The result was an almost overnight disappearance of what Shaposhnikov called "a single military-strategic area" developed over a seventy-year span of Soviet history.[30]

Following the breakup of the USSR, Russia's air sovereignty found itself protected mainly by the surviving remnants of the former Soviet VPVO, with some of the resultant slack taken up by the fighter arm of the Russian VVS.[31] The Defense Ministry's declared plans for the third stage of an ongoing military reorganization implied that VPVO might eventually be disestablished, with its core assets being absorbed into the VVS and a newly constituted Strategic Deterrent Force. With the announced plan of President Yeltsin to merge VPVO's fighters with the VVS on efficiency and cost-savings grounds (see Chapters 3 and 10), the days of VPVO as a separate service appeared to be numbered. Throughout most of the 1990s, however, it remained an active part of Russia's military aviation complex, and its operational training continued despite resource restrictions, undermanning, and "chronically belated funding."[32]

Impact on the Defense Industry

Serious problems were portended as well by the dispersion of the Soviet aircraft industry as a result of the USSR's dissolution. Early on, General Deinekin warned that the aviation industry had become "so interwoven with the VVS" that splitting the industry up among different republics "could endanger the very existence of the armed forces." The good news was that about 85 percent of the plants of the former Soviet military aircraft industry remained on Russian soil. Nevertheless, in the interest of maintaining an integrated CIS air capability, Deinekin said he was hoping to negotiate effective horizontal ties between various regions and republics, notably Ukraine, the second-most-important republic after Russia for aircraft production and the main supplier of transport aircraft and engines of all types.[33]

The VVS also inherited serious supply problems as a result of the collapse of the USSR. Colonel General Anatoly Malyukov, the chief of the VVS headquarters staff, reported that even in late 1991 the situation had already become very serious. Among other things, he said, the VVS had been forced to make do without new batteries for a time because all aircraft batteries were manufactured in Ukraine.[34] The Lugansk factory ceased shipping batteries, and the Baltic states halted the production and shipment of aircraft radios.

In commenting on Ukraine's claim to all former Soviet assets deployed on its territory, Shaposhnikov pointed out that Ukraine lacked even a single combat aircraft production facility. In light of that, he predicted that aircraft stationed in Ukraine would cease flying within six months at the outside: "There will be no engines, spare parts, or tires. At the same time, there is no mechanism through which these commodities can be supplied from Russia, either by barter or for hard currency."[35] General Deinekin described the situation as the inevitable outgrowth of a conscious Soviet decision, harking back to Joseph Stalin's time, to set up aircraft design bureaus in some republics, manufacturing plants in others, and engine factories in still others—all to advance the goal of ensuring the economic integration of the multinational Soviet state.[36]

As CIS joint forces commander, Shaposhnikov expressed Russia's readiness to help member states set up their own indigenous armed forces, including a system for acquiring weapons, equipment, spare parts, repair systems, and the required training. He predicted in early 1992 that without this help, efforts by members to break up the integrated VVS would inevitably lead to a shortage of fuel and spares for republican air forces, since aircraft were assembled and spares were manufactured largely in Russia and since there was no mechanism for selling spare parts to the republics should they establish their own air forces.[37]

On the domestic front, the VVS deputy commander for logistics, Lieutenant General Stanislav Ivanov, indicated growing concern over the potential loss of "responsibility, discipline, and order" in relations with the VVS's Russian suppliers. In particular, he complained that the flow of supplies was being disrupted by "new economic relations" and that deliveries were no longer being provided in an orderly manner through Gosplan but rather on the basis of contracts negotiated with individual producer plants. "Not all suppliers," he said, "will meet us halfway. We frankly don't know which is better—for the state to maintain a monster like Gosplan, which prescribed everything for everybody, or for VVS rear services and enterprises to keep a special staff that travels around the country scrounging whatever they need." As for the impact of the "new business conditions" inspired by Gorbachev's economic reforms, Ivanov lamented: "We are not feeling any advantages whatsoever in anything."[38]

From the CIS to Russian Unilateralism

In May 1992 the Russian armed forces were born for a second time on the heels of a failed effort by the Yeltsin government to establish a viable CIS military organization. As early as two weeks after the breakup of the USSR, there was speculation in Moscow that should negotiations toward a unified CIS prove unsuccessful, there would be every reason for Russia's leadership to declare Russia the USSR's successor in military matters.[39] Not long afterward, the February accords signed by each CIS member in Minsk gave each republic the right to create its own armed forces.[40]

On assuming his role as commander in chief of the CIS Joint Armed Forces, Shaposhnikov rued the fact that the military profession in the USSR had been forced to endure "the grief of the Afghan war, the pain of internal feuds, and an insulting lack of understanding by society, along with undeserved reproaches, instant poverty, and a lack of social prospects."[41] A priority goal of the new Russian leadership, he said, was to undo those corrosive influences as quickly as possible. Ultimately, that challenge would fall to Yeltsin's new defense minister, Army General Pavel Grachev. However, Shaposhnikov did much to pave the way in the immediate aftermath of the failed August coup. During his four months as the USSR's last defense minister, he eliminated Communist Party influence from the armed forces, abolished party control structures in the military, disestablished the "paradise group" of inspectors in the Defense Ministry—a sinecure for semiretired marshals—and discharged some seven hundred unneeded generals into the reserve.[42]

Troubled Relations with Ukraine

Russia's dealings with Ukraine soured almost from the first moments following the disintegration of the Soviet state, resulting in considerable part from an ownership dispute over the plenitude of front-line military hardware that Ukraine inherited from the former Soviet Union. Because of the USSR's western strategic orientation, much of its best and most modern combat equipment had been fielded on Ukrainian soil. As a result, Ukraine emerged from the union's collapse as, among other things, the possessor of over one thousand military aircraft, including between one-quarter and one-third of the VVS's MiG-29s and Su-27s, half of its forty Il-78 tankers, almost half of its Il-76 transports, and all but three of its serviceable Tu-160 Blackjack bombers. Those assets instantly endowed Ukraine with an air force considerably larger, at least on paper, than that of any West European country, including Britain, France, and Germany.

The Ukrainians proved to be touchy about their claimed proprietary rights to the VVS equities left on their territory. In response to General Deinekin's warning that the Tu-160s based at Priluki would become inoperable if Ukraine did not promptly release them to Russia, a Ukrainian Defense Ministry press release countered that the aircraft were "in working condition and completely ready" and that Ukrainian pilots were flying them and were "not losing their skills." That implausible claim added that there was no disputing Ukraine's "privatization" of the aircraft, since it was "a matter for a sovereign state to decide how, when, and what it will do with its property."[43]

The first outright sign of a gathering standoff between the two new countries occurred in early February 1992, when six Su-24 tactical bombers were secretly flown from their base in Ukraine to Russia by defecting Russian aircrews who refused to swear an oath of allegiance to Ukraine. Shaposhnikov, CIS armed forces commander, rejected a demand from Ukraine's president at the time, Leonid Kravchuk, that the aircraft be handed back to Ukraine and that the aircrews be returned to stand trial for desertion.

As a result of that episode, Ukraine unilaterally announced on February 17 that it was nationalizing the CIS air division at Uzin, which consisted of a regiment of 22 Tu-95 bombers, an Il-78 tanker regiment, and a support transport squadron. Two days earlier, with Shaposhnikov's blessing, the commander in chief of the CIS LRA, Colonel General Igor Kalugin, had fired the division's commander, Major General Bashkirov, for having sworn an oath of allegiance to Ukraine. Bashkirov was promptly reinstated by Ukraine's defense minister (and General Deinekin's former Soviet VVS colleague), Colonel General Konstantin Morozov. That contretemps followed earlier bad feelings triggered by an effort by Moscow to order a number of Il-78 tanker crews based at Uzin to deploy with their aircraft on a CIS "training mission" to Russia. Suspecting a Russian ploy to regain physical possession of the aircraft and thus claim ownership of them, the crews refused and were backed by Bashkirov.

Earlier, the division in question had become riven with controversy over whether to yield to a demand by Kiev that its officers swear an oath of allegiance to Ukraine. The tanker regiment's aircrews took the oath hastily, at night, and under duress. Most of the bomber crews refused, with the predictable result that the division became split. Without tanker support, the operational reach of the bomber division was considerably reduced. As General Deinekin later commented wryly, "Pardon my unparliamentary language, but bombers without tankers are like eunuchs."[44]

Ukraine's insistence on Russian respect for Ukrainian sovereignty escalated sharply on March 21, 1992, when General Deinekin, in his role as CIS air forces commander, sought to fly to Ukraine to inspect CIS strategic flying units. The flare-up began when Deinekin sent a coded message to General Morozov stating his intended route plan and visit schedule for five stops in Ukraine beginning on March 24. Kiev, in turn, dispatched an icy reply forbidding Deinekin to "fly over the airfields of a neighboring state." Its message added that since Moscow had not reached an agreement with Ukraine on the status of CIS strategic nuclear forces on Ukrainian soil, Deinekin's presence in Ukraine's armed forces was "not expedient."[45] In yet a further escalation Shaposhnikov, CIS commander, fired off an angry démarche that accused the Ukrainian Defense Ministry of violating CIS accords and upbraided Kiev for obstructing Deinekin in the legitimate performance of his CIS duties. The denouement, on March 25, saw Kiev finally rescind its initial denial and grant approval for Deinekin to visit Ukraine as planned.

General Deinekin later received a group of LRA pilgrims from Ukraine who had declined to repudiate their allegiance to the former Soviet Union.[46] The Russians had been given an ultimatum either to sign an oath of loyalty to Ukraine or to vacate the republic's territory. Deinekin assured them that Russia needed their experience and devotion to flying. He said that in total, 690 Russian airmen had returned from Ukraine after having been forcibly removed from flight status and deprived of living accommodations.

If anything, Ukraine's air force was in even worse straits than Russia's after the disintegration of the union because of rampant supply problems. Only two days of flight operations were generated at the LRA base at Uzin for two full months in early 1992. Some pilots had gone three or four months without flying.[47] At the fighter base at Voznesensk, a MiG-29 regiment commander reported that his rate of training was "substantially less" than the two or three times a week he had flown in the Soviet VVS.[48]

Shortly after assuming command of the newly independent Ukrainian VVS, Lieutenant General Valery Vasilyev declared that problems with access to fuel, engines, spare parts, and repair were not tied to Ukraine's declaration of independence or to any troubled political dealings with Russia.[49] Rather, he insisted, they were the result of broken economic ties between the now separated production entities, along with an associated drop in production. Vasilyev claimed that the operational status of the Ukrainian VVS was on a rough par with that of the Russian VVS. He added that because of some regiment and squadron commanders' decisions to return to Russia, vacancies had opened up, especially for squadron commanders. He noted that the Ukrainian VVS would continue to experience a drawdown in units. He also announced the establishment of four new operational headquarters: one on the western sector, in Lvov; another on the southwestern sector, in Odessa; and a headquarters each for transport aviation and for reserves and training.[50]

A subsequent report sounded considerably less upbeat. A Ukrainian VVS captain complained that deliveries of jet fuel had recently been reduced to a minimum, with the result that aircrews were "seizing any chance to fly to forestall a break in their training and to avoid losing their proficiency." The captain added that cannibalization (the use of parts from one aircraft to keep others flying) had become common, owing to a "chronic" shortage of spare parts, even though the maintenance experts knew "full well" that, for reasons of flight safety, "they should not remove equipment from one aircraft to another." He pointed to the common U.S. rule of thumb that a military aviator should fly no fewer than 200 hours a year to maintain an acceptable level of proficiency. In sharp contrast, he said: "Our pilots will soon not be able to fly at all due to the general shortage. . . . They are still managing to perform their assigned missions by using old reserves and resorting to barter deals. But what will it be like for Ukrainian airmen tomorrow?"[51]

After the USSR's collapse, a debate unfolded in Ukraine over merging the VVS and VPVO into a single service, with some espousing that such a move should be made on efficiency grounds and others countering that since air defense was paramount, all air operations should be subordinated to VPVO. The commander of Ukraine's VPVO, Lieutenant General Lopatin, advocated a go-slow approach. Not surprisingly, he also left little doubt about his commitment to a separate VPVO service, on the ground that "blind emulation of the structures of the West and the United States," where air defense was an organic component of the U.S. Air Force (USAF), "was not suitable for Ukraine and would be a major mistake."[52]

Not long afterward, a Ukrainian Defense Ministry collegium endorsed a proposal to create a new branch of the Ukrainian armed forces by merging the VVS and VPVO into an integrated Air Defense Force.[53] This left unanswered the question of where Ukraine's air-combat and ground-attack fighters would be lodged, to say nothing of the many other aircraft that Ukraine had inherited from the USSR. The final resolution came in February 1993, with a reversal that brought Ukraine's VPVO and VVS assets into a Ukrainian VVS under the command of Lieutenant General Vladimir Antonets. Vasilyev and Lopatin were named deputy commanders in chief.[54]

The development of an independent air force by Belarus was plagued by many of the same problems that afflicted Russia and Ukraine. The commander of the Belarus VVS, Lieutenant General Sergei Sedov, confirmed a serious shortage of fuel and spare parts, which had limited Belarus pilots to no more than 40–45 flying hours a year (as opposed to what he said was a reasonable norm of 70–80 hours). General Sedov voiced special concern over the mass outflow of skilled personnel from his air force, in sharp contrast to Russia's surplus of such personnel. He added that if the process was not soon halted, his air force would be "unable to scrape together even one crew per aircraft" and, in short order, would lose its "entire 'golden generation'—those who fly." He also noted that Belarus lacked a flight school for training replacement pilots and that Belarus, unlike Russia, had inherited "a sufficient amount, even *too* much, of the most modern aviation equipment."[55]

The decisive rout of the reform element—led by President Stanislav Shushke-vich—in the January 1994 Belarus elections and the replacement of this element by a more stolid leadership of old-school communists inclined toward reestablishing closer economic and military ties with Russia raised the prospect that the considerable front-line assets lost to Belarus by the Soviet VVS might eventually be formally resubordinated in some fashion to the Russian VVS.[56] Since Belarus subsequently signed an integration treaty with Russia, this remains a possibility that bears watching.[57]

New Priorities and Concerns

On assuming the helm as the Russian VVS commander in chief, General Deinekin inherited a near-total inversion of the priorities that typically concern a peacetime military aviation establishment. Such matters as force modernization, training and tactics, and similar mission-related preoccupations took an instant backseat to the more pressing needs of housing and caring for badly deprived personnel at a time when the VVS was already reeling from the depredations of communism and the breakup of the USSR. Among other vexations, Deinekin found himself saddled with a severely curtailed procurement and operations budget, a fuel shortage of crisis dimensions, a bloated pilot-to-aircraft ratio further aggravating the insufficiency of available flying hours for Russian aircrews, widespread maintenance problems caused by a dearth of spare parts and the breakdown of military conscription, and an impacted and antiquated air traffic control system. Those problems, in turn, occasioned a heightened aircraft accident rate, as well as a precipitous drop in the former prestige and respectability of VVS service, with potentially grave implications for future officer recruitment.

The Collapse of State Financing for Defense

During the final days of its existence in late 1991, the Soviet Defense Ministry reported that outlays for weapons and associated procurement had fallen by 23 percent from the previous level in 1990. Ministry spokesmen anticipated that a comparable reduction would occur in 1992, meaning that defense production would be effectively halved from the baseline 1989 level.[58] In the end the Russian VVS received only 15 percent of the research and development (R&D) and procurement allocations that it was expecting for 1992. That forced it to buy equipment at the barest minimum level required to ensure that Russia's aircraft industry would not become completely moribund. Even such elementary provisions as flight suits and helmets were said to be in critically short supply.[59]

The head of the Central Finance Directorate of the CIS joint command reaffirmed the trend toward diminished spending for equipment, offset by a commensurate growth in support for the quartering and welfare needs of Russian officers and their families. He estimated that some 70 percent of Russia's total defense expenditure for the first quarter of 1992 approved by the Supreme Soviet would be funneled into the social sector.[60] About 70 percent of the Defense Ministry's capital construction outlays in 1993 went to housing for military families.

Shortly before his appointment as first deputy minister of defense, Andrei Kokoshin, then deputy director of the USA and Canada Institute, predicted that Russia's defense industry would receive virtually *no* production orders in 1992, since all available funds had to be used to clothe and house military personnel.[61] Among Russia's airmen, an understandable concern emanating from that prompt reversal of spending priorities was that the VVS might eventually be gutted as a fighting force, much as had occurred a generation earlier when, as General Malyukov put it, "many futures in aviation were destroyed at the end of the 1950s because of [Premier Nikita] Khrushchev's excessive fascination with missiles."[62] By late 1993, promised funding allotments from the Ministry of Finance had fallen so far behind, complained Kokoshin, that the Defense Ministry was a full one trillion rubles in arrears to the defense industry for goods and services already delivered.[63] (That number increased to 2.2 trillion in 1994.) Indeed, added the chief of the ministry's Main Budget and Finance Directorate, the Russian civilian airline Aeroflot had ceased honoring military transportation orders as of summer 1993 because of the enormous debt the Defense Ministry had piled up.[64]

The inertia of the old Soviet system, which routinely favored strategic missiles and armor, proved slow to die. In 1992, according to General Deinekin, aviation equipment accounted for only 12–15 percent of Russia's arms purchases, as contrasted to an asserted 25–30 percent in the United States. After the USSR's collapse, the Russian VVS found itself forced to cancel any further purchases of the MiG-29 and to defer the development and procurement of several variants of the Su-27, which had been designated by the VVS as the intended mainstays of Russia's fighter inventory for at least the remainder of the twentieth century.

Galloping inflation since President Yeltsin's elimination of state price controls in January 1992 astronomically drove up the cost of new aircraft. As a direct result research, development, test, and evaluation (RDT&E) on new platforms were largely frozen, and the financing of several promising prototype programs was reportedly halted (see Chapter 9). In the United States, according to General Deinekin, the USAF received 34–37 percent of all R&D funds budgeted in the 1991–93 defense appropriation; the comparable figure for Russia was only around 15 percent.

As a stopgap measure, the VVS sought nonbudgetary funding from domestic and foreign investors. To clear the way for that novel arrangement, a decree signed by President Yeltsin in February 1992 authorized the VVS to sell up to sixteen hundred of its older aircraft to foreign buyers for hard currency. The idea was that any ensuing revenue would be channeled toward the production and operation of military aircraft in Russia, with the VVS acting as "chief client and guarantor." By one account, it was expected (quite unrealistically) that the VVS might collect up to $9 billion from such sales through the year 2000.[65] It was further hoped that such sales would, in addition to funding priority aviation programs, yield tax-exempt proceeds that might help the VVS build more housing and supplement officers' salaries.

Before the beginning of summer, however, there were reports that contraband weapons were falling into the hands of rebels and gunmen in bordering former republics, ultimately leading Defense Minister Grachev to concede that criminal proceedings had been initiated against some suspected perpetrators.[66] Several months later, Grachev reported that as a result of the military's authorization to engage in commercial activities, "some servicemen failed the independent business test." He added, "In our pseudomarket atmosphere, many went astray and couldn't resist abusing their official positions." A number of generals were fired outright as a result of such abuses. Others were reported to be under criminal investigation.[67] Retired VVS Major General Aleksandr Tsalko noted with disgust how this "approved" sale of military equipment to private buyers had become corrupted to the point that few of the proceeds had actually reached the armed forces.[68]

Understandably, General Deinekin was reluctant to take on the embarrassing question of alleged corruption by unnamed VVS colleagues in the commercial sale of military equipment. He would concede only that in July 1992 President Yeltsin's decree authorizing aircraft sales had been rescinded, and he would neither confirm nor deny press allegations of corruption on a vast scale in the Ministry of Foreign Economic Relations in the sale of Russian arms and military hardware.

A Growing Pilot Surplus

The Russian VVS's crew ratio, or the number of line pilots per operational aircraft, more than doubled after the collapse of the USSR. General Deinekin stated in early 1992 that the ratio had risen to three pilots for each flyable aircraft because of force reductions and accelerated unit withdrawals from Eastern Europe and the former Baltic republics.[69] He later remarked that in some units the crew ratio had become as severe as *five* pilots per aircraft.[70]

This pilot glut was especially pronounced in fighter and ground-attack units. According to the head of the VVS Training and Assignment Directorate, Lieutenant General Aleksandr Osipenko, voluntary withdrawals of VVS aircrews from active flight status at the end of 1992 posed no threat to projected pilot needs. On the contrary, there was a requirement to *reduce* overall pilot strength by at least 25 percent merely to stay abreast of continuing unit deactivations and force reductions.[71]

At VVS headquarters one approach suggested for grappling with the pilot surplus problem was to encourage fighter pilots who wanted to remain on flight status to volunteer for other aviation branches or to accept navigator assignments. As a triage technique for managing its aircrew-reduction plans, the VVS treated those pilots who had served three to four years in a given assignment as a "reserve" pool for potential selection to higher positions. Those who had five or more years in the same posting and who were considered poor prospects for promotion were typically released into the reserve.

Because of the pronounced shortage of available cockpits, General Osipenko conceded that there was "no chance" that every 1993 flight school graduate would be guaranteed a flying assignment. A sizable number of freshly minted pilots were banked in temporary jobs on headquarters staffs, in command posts, or as technicians, with the understanding that they would eventually be moved on to a flying assignment once one became available. As a matter of policy, the VVS stated that it would not force a flight school graduate to serve in a nonflying assignment outside his specialty. Accordingly, those newly winged pilots who declined banked assignment options were graduated with the rank of lieutenant and summarily discharged into the reserve.[72]

Shortly after the USSR's collapse, the Russian VVS established a goal of reducing its crew ratio to a stabilized norm of three pilots for every two aircraft in an effort to ease the burden on day-to-day training in operational squadrons. A case in point was offered by a senior lieutenant who described taxiing out for a long-awaited flight to a weapons range to maintain his mission currency, only to experience an avionics system failure immediately before takeoff. The result was a noneffective sortie. The lieutenant later remarked: "The aircraft situation here is really like a free-for-all. You should see how emotions flare up when we are preparing our little 'plan.' Each pilot and flight commander thinks that his problems are the most important. What happens is that everyone keeps pulling the blanket over to his side. . . . All these gyrations are prompted by the growing number of pilots arriving from VVS units undergoing reductions and, for other reasons, from various areas of the former USSR. But the aircraft pool remains the same."[73]

The Crisis in Flying Hours

Following President Yeltsin's lifting of price controls in January 1992, fuel costs escalated by 2,000 percent during the remainder of that year.[74] The first deputy head of the Defense Ministry's Main Budget and Finance Directorate reported that because of reduced appropriations for fuel, pilots were typically getting less than one-third of their annual flying norm.[75] One article noted that because of an excess of flight personnel and the severe shortage of petroleum, oil, and lubricants (POL) and spares, the average flight time accrued by Russian fighter pilots during the first ten months of 1991 was less than 40 hours and that, not surprisingly, regiments were experiencing more accidents. The authors of this article proposed that the VVS, with no realistic prospect for operational aircrews to meet even their minimal mission-currency requirements, should suspend its published training norms, at least for the time being. Keeping the norms on the books merely encouraged unit commanders to engage in dishonest reporting. The authors further remarked that many VVS pilots were accidents waiting to happen: "Pilots are still languishing while awaiting their chance to fly. Once they do get airborne, their commanders worry—will their pilot, having such limited proficiency, make it back to his base in one piece?"[76]

Even before the USSR's collapse, a senior pilot wrote of casually perusing several squadron-mates' flight logs and noting that in one month, one pilot had flown ten sorties for seven hours, in the next month seven sorties (six day and one night) for four hours, and the next month only two sorties for barely more than an hour. That partly reflected, he said, the effects of a self-inflicted VVS "prohibition mania," whereby fighter units were forced to suspend *all* flight activity in the wake of an accident until the causes were determined—even if the accident occurred in a helicopter or transport squadron! The result, he added, was merely to aggravate the existing safety problems, since noncurrent pilots were, by definition, more accident-prone than proficient ones. Worse yet was the reflexive tendency of many unit commanders to impose a determined "back to basics" approach in the wake of an accident. Because this policy erred in imposing blanket bans on experienced and junior pilots indiscriminately, even the most proficient pilots would "slip willy-nilly back to the level of average ones."[77]

General Deinekin confirmed in early 1993 that largely because of the fuel shortage, Russian VVS fighter pilots were averaging 40 flying hours a year, bomber pilots 80 hours, and pilots in Military Transport Aviation (*Voyenno-transportnaya aviatsia,* or VTA) 150 hours (the differences reflected variations in mission type, with LRA and transport crews flying fewer sorties of longer duration).[78] Deinekin further reported that the VVS at the time had roughly two assigned pilots for each single-seat aircraft, since several thousand fighter pilots stationed in the former republics had returned home following the collapse of the union.[79] In most cases the fuel shortage required regiment commanders to preclude their staff officers from flying altogether, so as to ensure the most rational distribution of their meager fuel allotments to their neediest line pilots.

Conditions were scarcely better in 1992 for VVS fighter units awaiting final withdrawal from eastern Germany. The air commander for the Western Group of Forces (WGF), Lieutenant General Anatoly Tarasenko, remarked that to give each pilot an equal chance to fly in such circumstances would be tantamount to providing an opportunity to no one, since "letting everyone fly, but no more than once or twice a month, would mean taking everyone to the brink of losing his professional skills."[80]

While awaiting the planned withdrawal of one WGF regiment from Germany in 1993, a deputy commander reported that his unit was being allotted only 100 tons of jet fuel a month, the amount previously apportioned for the training schedule for a *single day.* With approximately 3 tons of fuel consumed on a typical 30-minute fighter training sortie, the result, said Colonel A. Novikov, was predictable: "Figure it out yourself. You come up with 33 flights for sixty aircrews." A regiment commander, Colonel Borisyuk, added, "It pains the soul to think of the fate of our pilots, [since] in every civilized nation aircrews are regarded as a real treasure." Borisyuk noted, "A true pilot will never, of course, actually forget how to fly." However, he stressed, a minimum of three flights a month was "the lower threshold that must not be crossed."[81]

A later account of WGF training indicated similar currency and proficiency concerns as forward-based VVS units approached the midpoint of their three-year phased withdrawal from former East German territory. The deputy commander of Russian forces in Germany, Major General Nikolai Seliverstov, reported that available flight time for WGF pilots had been cut to the bone and that tactical training missions had grown progressively more rudimentary as a result of the disappearance of any operational purpose behind the lingering Russian presence in Germany. A Third-Class pilot stationed at Finow remarked that he anticipated flying no more than 40 to 50 hours in 1993.[82]

The fuel shortage affected more than Russia's fighter pilots. General Kalugin, commander in chief of LRA, reported that flying time for his bomber crews had also fallen to crisis levels because of fuel limitations and the declining service life of many LRA aircraft. Kalugin added that he had been forced to limit his bomber crews to flying combat aircraft only along fixed navigational routes and to using the Tu-134 jet transport as a bomber surrogate for most routine proficiency training.[83]

Colonel General Anatoly Borsuk, head of the VVS Combat Training Directorate, noted that the availability of engines and spare parts had fallen off dramatically in recent years. He lamented the poor reliability both of new equipment and of older aircraft that had long been in squadron service. He further complained of a shortage of flight simulators, a growing dearth of engineering and technical support personnel, and an excess of aircrews resulting from unit shutdowns within Russia and the continuing withdrawal of VVS regiments from Eastern Europe as mandated by the Conventional Forces in Europe (CFE) Treaty. In 1992, said Borsuk, a VVS fighter pilot's annual flying allotment was two and a half times less than the ideally desired amount and three to four times less than that said to be provided for U.S. military pilots. Some VVS pilots, he said, went without flying for two and a half to three months. By that time, even in LRA, they no longer met flight currency standards and had to be retrained.[84]

In a revealing snapshot of where things stood a year later, a military reporter provided an arresting account of VVS flight activity during a typical day in the fall of 1993. A conversation with Major General Aleksandr Slukhai, senior duty officer in the central command post at VVS headquarters, indicated that VVS flight schools and fighter aviation recorded 845 sorties that day for a total of 459 flying hours, with LRA registering 183 sorties for 115 hours and VTA logging 117 sorties at training centers for 58 hours in the air. The total came to slightly more than 1,000 VVS flights. The reporter tried hard to put the best-possible spin on those figures: "There is no basis for the idle conjectures of certain mass media that the VVS has neglected combat training. . . . A total of 1145 training flights in a 24-hour period—is that not combat training?" The bitter truth, however, was laid bare in General Slukhai's more disquieting observation: "Some days the flying time for the entire VVS adds up to the number of hours the regiment I previously commanded would have flown in a 24-hour period."[85] In a telling contrast, General Deinekin earlier reported that on a typical flying day in August of the preceding year, the VVS had registered 6,798 sorties.[86]

Maintenance Shortcomings
Like the USAF, the Russian VVS operates a three-tiered aircraft-servicing system that includes routine flight-line, as-needed base-level, and periodic depot maintenance.[87] Base-level maintenance (the equivalent of USAF intermediate

maintenance) is performed by the regimental Technical Maintenance Unit (*Tekhnicheskaya ekspluatatsionnaya chast,* or TECh), which additionally conducts scheduled inspections every 600 and 1,200 flight hours on an airframe.

Problems with quality control, long a plague on VVS maintenance, grew considerably after the USSR's collapse. General Shaposhnikov reported that the Soviet VVS had managed to sustain a 90 percent aircraft-in-commission rate during 1990.[88] Less than a year later, however, to cite a representative example, one regiment of the Russian VVS reported that only 25–30 percent of its Tu-22M bombers were serviceable, with the rest out of commission because of engine or other problems. The general in charge of acquisition in the Defense Ministry attributed the maintenance problems to a lag in manufacturing technology and poor quality control at the production line, along with a shortage of modern production tooling and poor discipline at aircraft and engine factories.[89] This, however, was only part of the explanation.

VVS maintenance manning in 1991 was one-third below assigned strength, with only half the needed number of replacement personnel provided by the various training schools.[90] That was in considerable part a consequence of the failed conscription system. In 1993, largely owing to the generous student-deferment provisions (since withdrawn) approved by the Russian parliament and the refusal of most other draft-age males to honor their call-up notices, Defense Minister Grachev predicted that only 26 percent of the anticipated number of draftees nationwide would report for induction.[91] In the important Moscow Military District, the expected number was as low as 3 percent.

As a result, noncommissioned manning fell to the 50 percent level or below in many VVS and VPVO units. That was an "alarming indicator," said General Prudnikov, VPVO commander in chief. He added: "It was always felt that a unit was not operationally ready if it dropped below 70 percent. We have now crossed that line."[92] Even before the August 1991 coup, the VVS deputy commander for logistics complained that maintenance manning remained well below its mandated strength. He said that as a result, the VVS was able to provide only some 60 percent of its required rear-service support for training and readiness.[93]

In the face of their acute manpower shortage, regiment commanders often arbitrarily cut the number of maintenance personnel assigned to flying squadrons, without first weighing the likely effects on maintenance delivery.[94] The shortage of skilled manpower further obliged unit-level maintenance sections to assign barely trained conscripts to serve as aircraft mechanics.[95] For good reason, VVS maintenance professionals complained: "The soldier in aviation [was] of little help to the officer technician." Even in the best of times, the VVS maintenance schools for conscripts yielded poorly trained graduates, few of whom developed any significant skills by the end of their obligatory twenty-four-month service period. Most ended up merely performing guard duty and attending to housekeeping chores. Zuyev, the VVS MiG-29 pilot who defected in 1989, recalled that many of those conscript mechanics could barely read Russian and had to be instructed using the same rote techniques one would use with a child. For that reason, fighter regiments were forced to rely on a small core of trained maintenance officers, supported by warrant officers who supervised the conscripts and bent every effort to prevent them from "destroying the aircraft."[96]

Today, because of the scarcity of fuel, functional check flights (FCFs) following routine maintenance are no longer performed. That departure from sound practice naturally has engendered an indifferent attitude on the part of maintenance personnel toward aircrew write-ups and, in turn, has lowered aircrew confidence in their equipment. A TECh officer complained that maintenance understaffing was causing minor write-ups to go unattended until the next scheduled intermediate maintenance, in the blind hope that the TECh might discover and fix the identified problems.

VVS fighter squadrons also do not routinely require formal postflight maintenance debriefs by the pilot. Nor, apparently, do they maintain detailed logs for recording and tracking avionics anomalies. Among suggested interim fixes for these problems have been the use of flight recorders to monitor the performance of the fire-control system to aid in postflight troubleshooting and the conduct of postmaintenance system checks during scheduled training sorties (in effect, an FCF on the run), on the premise that any such checks, however haphazard, are better than none.[97]

Since the introduction of latest-generation aircraft like the MiG-29 and Su-27 into its inventory, the VVS has encountered recurrent problems with fault isolation in avionic systems capable of multiple failure modes, much as the USAF experienced with the F-15 during its first years of operational service. "At the outset," complained one Russian officer in a refrain familiar to USAF avionics technicians, "everything is fine. Then an anomaly occurs. By the end of the flight, everything is back to normal again. It is extremely difficult to detect such a stray defect on the ground."[98]

Adding to that problem considerably, much of the VVS maintenance support equipment is rudimentary. Setting up a diagnostic system at the regiment level often calls for artful and aggressive scrounging skills, plus complete reliance on the unit's own resources. Because of the widespread unavailability of computers, it is particularly difficult to monitor avionics status and predict failures. Accordingly, some navigation and weapons delivery modes are not used at all because of their poor accuracy and reliability.

Cannibalization of parts from some aircraft to keep others flying has become common in many fighter units, even though the practice is in direct contravention of hallowed safety regulations. Such reliance on "donor aircraft" (a polite term for hangar queens) was bound to occur sooner or later as a result of the steadily declining availability of assemblies and spare parts. The impetus behind this flouting of published rules and good judgment has been to keep the greatest-possible number of aircraft flyable at any cost, since flying hours are meted out according to the number of serviceable aircraft in a given unit. Even *with* cannibalization, some units have lost considerable flight time as a result of delays in the delivery of tires, POL, and other consumables. One officer wrote: "We will find a way out of this situation by hook or by crook, including by cannibalizing aircraft. But what about tomorrow?"[99]

A shift to contract maintenance has been widely portrayed as the only workable solution over the long haul, since such an arrangement would "nurture a work environment conducive to the development of an incentive in each technician to become a bona fide professional." The situation has been further aggravated by forbidding work conditions in many cases. One navigator assigned to the Transbaikal Military District complained: "We are flying on scrap metal. The equipment is old. There are virtually no spares, nor any facilities for repair. People in the squadron often say: 'Jet fuel and blood are mixed together with us.' Imagine forty degrees below freezing. An exposed flight line. People working with bare hands. Their fingers split. So you have blood and kerosene. Of course we are unhappy. But we serve. Someone has to defend the country."[100]

Safety and the Accident Situation

All of this has had a predictable impact on flying safety in the VVS. Shortly after becoming commander in chief, General Shaposhnikov admitted to "several dozen" aircraft accidents in 1990, with 60 percent involving equipment in good working order. Shaposhnikov conceded that any improvement of the situation would require the prior solution of "a whole host of problems associated with VVS life and activity."[101]

The Russian VVS showed an increase in the number of major mishaps in 1992, the first year following the collapse of the USSR. However, the head of the Flight Safety Service (*Sluzhba bezopasnosti poletov,* or SBP), Major General Aleksei Alekseyev, insisted that the increase did not constitute grounds for immediate alarm, since "even in the most favorable years for the country, the state of safety was only a bit better." Alekseyev confirmed that for decades, the proportion of flight mishaps due to pilot error had exceeded 60 percent. The big difference by that time—1993—was that recurrent failures to implement effective preventive measures had been amplified by new plagues affecting the health of the flying community, including a lack of adequate fuel allocations, flight simulators, support equipment, and pay.[102]

A report in June 1992 declared that the aircraft accident rate was "threatening to shift from isolated instances to a landslide." It noted twenty-six major mishaps in VVS operating units in 1991 and eight during the first three months of 1992 alone. The article added that in some regiments, pilots were not getting even a minimal allocation of 40 flying hours a year and that those were the units in which the accident rate was most disturbingly on the rise. The report implored the VVS to take a hard look at proven foreign aviation safety practices in search of a better way to ramp down the incidence of flight mishaps. It also stated that in 1968 the VVS roughly matched the USAF in the number of accidents per 100,000 hours, whereas by 1992 the VVS exceeded the USAF's rate by a factor of two, even with "many times" fewer flying hours.[103]

In 1993 General Deinekin disclosed that the VVS was suffering some fifty fatalities and upward of one hundred aircraft losses per year in routine training accidents. The majority of those were caused not by equipment failure but by pilot error, with most occurring to experienced aviators holding the topmost aeronautical rating of Pilot First Class.[104] Deinekin went on to report that there was an increase in the number of aviation-related fatalities in 1992 because of several mishaps involving transports and that the flight safety environment had worsened notably. One of the chief reasons, he said, was the collapse of stable financing for fuel purchases. Deinekin reported that in 1992 the VVS was granted only half the fuel allotment that it had received in 1991 and that because of irregular deliveries the supply for that year was effectively down 20 percent more.[105]

Several years earlier, Marshal of Aviation Pavel Kirsanov, then deputy commander of the Soviet VVS, had faulted the VVS's tendency to focus on ferreting out the most proximate cause of an accident as a basis for parceling out blame, without probing deeper for associated causes that might have been more pertinent as root explanations for the accident.[106] He also singled out the burdensome collateral duties levied on squadron pilots as a hindrance to the maintenance of an adequate level of aircrew proficiency.[107] Such distracting claims on a young pilot's time, he said, were an invitation not only to catastrophic accidents but, worse yet, to a calculated compromise of integrity, as reflected in such dishonest actions as "redoing flight planning tables or falsifying write-ups on the plans and logs," a practice commonly disparaged throughout the U.S. armed forces as "pencil-whipping." He said that commanders who tolerated, or themselves indulged in, such shortcuts instilled in their subordinates a habit of "merely processing the paperwork properly and getting away with a violation."[108]

In a similar expression of high-level candor, Lieutenant General Vladimir Andreyev, the respected commander of VPVO fighter aviation, conceded that Soviet efforts to grapple with the safety problem had for thirty years consisted mainly of idle talk. He added that the problem would never be fixed merely by "words and threatening directives." To illustrate the extent to which the system had lost sight of the big picture, he recalled once asking his subordinates at VPVO headquarters, just as an experiment, to come up with a list of questions to which a MiG-31 pilot needed to know the answers. "And they produced . . . a

900-page book! Nobody can assimilate that much detail. And the pilot does not need it! You need to give a pilot the minimal amount of knowledge necessary to allow him to fly his aircraft responsibly. And then—let him improve himself. With that, there is no limit." Continuing, Andreyev said: "If a pilot has mastered the minimal amount of knowledge, we won't torture him with more theory. We'll clear him for three months and let him fly with God. Later, we'll check to see whether he has grown or stagnated. As a rule, self-improvement occurs." However, Andreyev added, for any such system to work, a culture change would be needed in the flying community. "If we wish to be called professionals," he said, "we in the military first of all must put a decisive end to formalism, bureaucratism, dishonesty, and cooking the figures in every conceivable way."[109]

In a related argument, a senior navigator in late 1991 chided both the Combat Training Directorate and the SBP, whose leaders he portrayed as sometimes being "more zealous about faulting each other than about finding constructive solutions." The price of concentrating solely on apportioning blame rather than on understanding the cause of accidents and developing appropriate measures for preventing recurrences, he added, was "the papering over of dangerous situations that will surely recur."[110]

Arbitrariness in accident investigations, however, remains a continuing problem in Russian military aviation. A case in point followed a MiG-31 mishap in which the aircraft experienced violent uncommanded pitch and roll oscillations shortly after takeoff. The crew finally ejected successfully only moments before the aircraft struck the ground. The ensuing debrief of the pilot and eyewitness accounts of the mishap both confirmed a mechanical failure on the aircraft. Nevertheless, the accident board reported the cause to have been the pilot's attempt of a mission "beyond his capabilities." That finding was rejected by all aircrews in the parent regiment as patently bogus. Yet the only "preventive measures" implemented in the wake of the investigation were to relieve the two crew members of their squadron duties and to ground the pilot.[111]

A related example of how the fuel crisis and resultant reduced flying hours left their mark on the accident rate was a fatal mishap involving a Su-24 following a failure of the left afterburner to light during takeoff. The resultant asymmetric thrust caused by the loss of power on the affected engine reportedly produced an uncommanded roll into the ground immediately following a takeoff that should have been aborted. An assessment of the accident afterward concluded that the lapsed pilot proficiency underlying that particular mishap represented "the chief risk factor in conditions of a sharp reduction in flying hours."[112]

Problems with Air Traffic Control

The Russian VVS inherited a Byzantine air traffic control (ATC) and flight clearance system from the former Soviet Union. To secure approval for a scheduled flight from one military airfield to another in a different center's jurisdiction, a pilot must submit an airspace reservation request to the controller at his home airfield two hours before his planned departure. After that, the request moves in sequence through the home unit's command post to the military sector of the regional civilian ATC center, to the zonal center, to the ATC center at the destination airfield, and finally to the individual controller at the destination airfield. Only then, with the home regiment commander's approval, can the flight be cleared to depart.[113]

Controllers with transit approval authority have little incentive to facilitate the movement of air traffic through their jurisdictions. Pilots still joke about one controller said to have never authorized a single aircraft to pass through his assigned airspace throughout his entire career as a duty officer! Seasoned pilots do not even bother wasting their time submitting a cross-country flight request during the last hour before a controller shift change, during mealtime, or at any time on the day before a holiday. One pilot complained: "The fewer that are flying, the less the resultant hassle. As they say, God forbid that anything should happen." He recounted a nightmare experience during which he was forced to lay over at a civilian airfield for two days in the course of a cross-country flight. First, he could not get fuel. After he finally scrounged the fuel, the weather deteriorated. "But typically," he said, "for some reason it only deteriorated for us military fliers. Cross-country civilian crews at that point were still not being delayed. . . . I'm surprised the VVS leadership hasn't yet figured out why aircrews from various ministries and agencies seek in every conceivable manner to avoid landing at military airfields." He added, "The time has come to review the current structure of air traffic control points, eliminate redundant echelons, and make the 'unified' ATC system truly unified." Since the main responsibility for coordinating flights, including military flights, resides within the civilian component of the ATC system, he noted, it makes no sense to retain military ATC centers other than where they are needed because of unusually dense local military traffic. He suggested that this would minimize friction between the military and civilian components of the ATC system. He also contrasted the hidebound Russian system with that of the United States, "where they only control rather than command air traffic" and where flight clearances can routinely be processed in minutes.[114]

Post-Soviet Russia is only now beginning to modernize that encrusted system. Even before the breakup of the USSR, there was an acknowledged problem of artificial jurisdictional barriers. The commander of VPVO communications reported that the VVS, the navy, and the ground forces each monitored their own portion of Soviet airspace alongside the civilian ATC system. VPVO also maintained its own radar surveillance, controlling up to 12,000 flights a day through a mere 150-kilometer strip of airspace. A move toward a reconfigured Unified

Air Traffic Control System (*Yedinaya sistema upravlenia vozdushnovo dvizhenia,* or YeS UVD) was finally prompted by the realization that it made no sense for controllers of those overlapping jurisdictions to be sitting often literally side by side yet receiving only that information pertinent to their own operational concerns.[115] A portion of the new system was slated to be tested in 1995, but a subsequent lack of funding slowed its implementation to a crawl.

The Declining Quality of VVS Life

Three years before the collapse of Soviet communism, a former VVS officer (now associated with the influential Russian Council on Foreign and Defense Policy) offered a rare glimpse behind the myth of privileged life in the officer corps when he suggested that if unit commanders could only gain state permission to use the government funds that they had managed to save through frugal spending to build housing, kindergartens, and other social facilities for VVS personnel, they could inspire a major savings campaign and elicit widespread support from below.[116]

In a similar vein, six months before the August 1991 coup General Shaposhnikov, VVS commander, complained about the inadequate provision of housing and social amenities for the families of VVS officers. Some of the problem he blamed on the return of Soviet units from Eastern Europe at an unexpectedly rapid rate. However, Shaposhnikov added that responsibility for the VVS's housing conundrum lay primarily with local civilian councils, which had failed to make good on their pledges to provide housing for the VVS. To take up at least part of the slack, the VVS committed 80 percent of its capital construction funds in 1991 for family housing. It also established a Main Engineering Administration to accelerate the resolution of the housing problem.[117] Yet the following year, some 22,000 VVS families remained without living quarters. Over 3,500 of those were families of pilots.

Even for VVS families lucky enough to be blessed with adequate living accommodations, daily existence is all too often bleak. Shortly before the coup, the VVS chief political officer noted that about half of all officers' wives possessed special work qualifications yet lacked any realistic chance of finding gainful employment in the often remote parts of the country where their husbands were stationed.[118] Such deprivation has had a predictable impact on morale. Acknowledging that many officers had remained hard-working and devoted professionals in the face of mounting adversity, the deputy commander of the flight school at Chernigov confessed that he felt "frankly ashamed to reproach people for their deficiencies" when they sat at their work stations on air bases for up to twelve to fourteen hours a day.[119] Much the same sentiment was reflected in a Defense Ministry poll of eleven hundred officers in all of Russia's services, including the

VVS and VPVO. The poll indicated that many were "losing their social and moral reference points and values, and their confidence in tomorrow [was] dying away."[120]

At the time of the 1991 coup, a Moscow bus driver typically was paid more than a trained Soviet fighter pilot. Since then, the economy has degenerated to a level where line pilots have to work the fields on weekends to help bring in the crop. Many VVS officers have been forced to harvest their own agricultural produce, with base commanders cultivating plots and maintaining subsidiary farms on their airfields. The chief of logistics, Lieutenant General Ivanov, remarked caustically: "We get nothing but extra headaches for this."[121]

Even at prestigious Kubinka, the showcase VVS fighter base located in the southwestern outskirts of Moscow, fighter pilots often spend their spring and summer weekends weeding and hoeing. The former commander of the VVS's Su-27 flight-demonstration team, Colonel Vladimir Basov, said: "All of us are forced to tend our kitchen gardens because we don't have any other source of food." He added: "It's a shame our pilots get lower pay than a plumber or a mechanic."[122] General Deinekin himself commented that cadets at the Barnaul flight school lived in such austere conditions that they were forced to use parachutes as blankets during the wintertime.[123]

Again, such problems have not been limited to fighter aviation. General Kalugin spoke candidly of the grim living conditions of Russia's bomber crews. "I visited the flight mess—a very, very poor table. And the families of the fliers? They can barely make ends meet." Kalugin freely acknowledged complaints about social injustice and a lack of legal protection, about nothing to look forward to after being discharged or retired, and about the persistent "grains of mutual distrust" that had taken root and accumulated over the years.[124]

Sad to say, Russia's pilots have watched their professional pride slowly drain away as a result of such pernicious influences. Smoking is said to be the rule among them, and drinking to excess has become more and more prevalent. "The whole country drinks, after all, and do they ever!" wrote one disgusted pilot. "Why should aviation be any better?"[125] Only a few officers reportedly take part in regular physical exercise, and many work out only enough to get ready to pass their semiannual evaluation—if it is given. Even those tests are typically a charade because of the widespread prevalence of cheating.

Faltering Service Prestige and Pilot Recruitment

During the banner years of the Soviet Union, appeals to patriotism and the romance of high-performance flight were all that was needed to entice the best of Soviet youths to seek a VVS career. Today, squalid living conditions and rapidly dwindling opportunities for pilots to fly have become barriers to VVS recruitment.

Consistently low pay for officers and the badly tarnished image of a military career in post-Soviet Russia, set against the precipitous decline in the quality of service life, have resulted in a virtual disappearance of competition for pilot-training slots in both the VVS and VPVO. Even before the USSR's collapse, the commandant of the flight school at Kharkov reported that the influx of new cadets had fallen "drastically." He noted that 790 applicants were accepted to Kharkov in 1989, whereas only 312 entered the program in 1990. He added: "There was practically no competition after the medical board's findings. In some cases, we were even forced to reexamine those who received 'twos.'"[126]

During the early 1970s, six to eight applicants typically vied for each available pilot-training slot nationwide. More recently, the VVS has been forced "to accept adolescents who have shown only fair knowledge on the entrance exams. The criterion for their enrollment is just good health, and even that with certain allowances." One colonel complained: "There is essentially no weeding out after psychological testing. There is no one to choose from!"[127] Another pilot cynically joked that flight school acceptance standards had fallen to such a low state that there were now only two criteria: "The applicant must be able to hear thunder and see lightning—and one of those is waiverable!"[128]

Many junior officers simply quit out of disillusionment. In July 1992, for example, all forty-eight graduates of the flight school at Barnaul declined to honor their service commitments because of "no prestige and no prospects." After being awarded their commissions and aeronautical ratings, they were immediately released into the reserve.[129] In trying to come to grips with that disturbing trend, the VVS chief of education, Major General Yakim Yanakov, frankly conceded: "Today's youths have begun looking harder and deeper into life's questions. They can no longer be won over simply by slogans and appeals. Firm assurances of a dignified social status of officership are now required."[130]

3.   Evolving Organization, Doctrine, and Forces

Seemingly undaunted by adversity, the Russian VVS lost little time in stepping out aggressively to cope with its many challenges prompted by the demise of the USSR. To begin with, it managed an unprecedented drawdown of forces in just four years. That drawdown included completion of the return of all forward-deployed Soviet VVS assets in the Baltic states and former Warsaw Pact countries of Eastern Europe, a reduction in deployed combat aircraft to well below the Conventional Forces in Europe (CFE) Treaty ceilings, and a summary retirement of many obsolescent and obsolete aircraft.

At the same time, the Russian VVS moved with dispatch to consolidate its organization and functions, increase the quality of its equipment, and attend to the needs of its people. It sought a new image to help restore the attractiveness of VVS service, including adoption of a new uniform, with air force blue replacing the old army green. It today continues to search for new operational concepts appropriate to Russia's still-undefined security needs in the post–cold war era. And it is pursuing a measured force-modernization effort in the face of almost preclusive funding constraints.

The following discussion draws extensively on a remarkable document compiled in 1994 by the VVS Central Research Institute and edited for publication in the West by the respected civilian defense expert Aleksei Arbatov, formerly of the Institute of World Economy and International Relations and now deputy head of the Committee on Defense of the Russian State Duma.[1] That document, referred to hereafter as "the VVS analysis," was unprecedented in Russian practice. Both in breadth and in depth, it came close to being the Russian equivalent of a U.S. military posture statement. It was astonishingly frank in describing the VVS's roles and missions, organizational status, and force-development plans up to the year 2015, as well as the many problems that threaten to obstruct the implementation of those plans. Even in the recent past, such information would have been treated by the Russian defense bureaucracy as highly sensitive.

Post-Soviet Retrenchment and Reform Plans

In the immediate aftermath of the USSR's collapse, Russia strove to maintain an integrated military posture throughout the newly created CIS. Once that goal proved evanescent, Marshal Yevgeny Shaposhnikov, in his new role as commander in chief of the CIS Joint Armed Forces, continued to plead, without success, for the preservation of at least joint CIS air and air defense forces, since those had been fielded with the former USSR's strategic defense needs in mind rather than with regard for the new borders that had appeared as a result of the union's collapse.[2] Shaposhnikov also pled, likewise to no avail, for five or six CIS core states to form an alliance modeled on NATO.[3]

Once the CIS heads of state failed to agree on defense integration at their crucial meeting in Minsk on February 14, 1992, it was only a matter of time before an independent Russian military, including a Russian VVS, would be created from the detritus of the USSR. As the outgoing chief of the Soviet General Staff, General Vladimir Lobov, observed: "The process of disintegration of a once-unified organism is becoming more and more irreversible, [occasioning] an insistent necessity . . . of forming and putting into action a Ministry of Defense and a General (or Main) Staff for a Russian military in the near future."[4]

As early as January 1992, a decree by Boris Yeltsin anticipating the creation of a Russian Defense Ministry had been drafted.[5] Soon thereafter, efforts to proceed with developing an independent Russian defense establishment gained momentum.[6] Yeltsin's newly appointed defense minister, Army General Pavel Grachev, conceded that it might take as long as ten years for Russians "to be able to speak with full confidence about the establishment of Russian Federation armed forces in a new guise," more or less the same length of time he felt would be needed for Russia's new statehood to reach maturity.[7] Four major hurdles cited by Grachev included establishing a new and smaller force "consistent with the times," making a smooth transition to new hardware based on modern technology, fundamentally reforming existing concepts of training and force employment, and creating a new image for the Russian serviceman.

The Formation of a Russian Military

The decree setting up the Russian armed forces was signed by President Yeltsin on May 7, 1992. Three months later, the service chiefs and other senior officials of the Russian Defense Ministry and armed forces were announced: Colonel General Vladimir Semenov, commander in chief of the Ground Forces; Colonel General Igor Sergeyev, commander in chief of the Strategic Missile Forces; Admiral Feliks Gromov, commander in chief of the navy; and Colonel General Viktor Prudnikov, commander in chief of VPVO.[8] Colonel General Pyotr Deinekin was named commander in chief of the new Russian VVS less than two months thereafter.[9]

As a first item of business, Grachev reported that the decline in readiness of Russia's forces had been arrested, that command and control had been restored, and that an initial inventory of the equipment inherited by the new Russian military had been conducted. His immediate plan was to start reducing the size of the Russian military by one-quarter, to three million troops, in compliance with the negotiated terms of the CFE Treaty.[10]

In June 1992, Grachev announced a military reform program that would proceed in three phases. The first phase, to be completed in 1993, included establishing a Russian Defense Ministry; laying a legal foundation for the creation of Russian Federation armed forces; taking initial steps toward defining the organization, structure, and force levels of the Russian armed forces; withdrawing troops under Russian jurisdiction from the former Soviet republics; and developing a command and control structure for the Russian armed forces. The second phase, to be completed in 1994, would close out the withdrawal of Russian troops from the former republics; further reduce and restructure Russia's remaining forces; establish a system of social safeguards for servicemen and their families; and shift to a mixed conscript and voluntary base of recruitment, with provisions for alternative national service. Grachev indicated that throughout this second phase of reform, the existing arrangement of five military services (Strategic Missile Forces, Ground Forces, VPVO, VVS, and navy) would be retained. For the third phase, beginning in 1995, Grachev allowed for the possibility of reorganizing and combining various services. He stressed, however, that any such changes would be carried out in an evolutionary manner, since breaking up existing structures over the following two to three years, while Russia remained in the grips of a severe economic crisis, could trigger a breakdown of order and discipline, a lowering of readiness, and perhaps even "the utter disintegration of the military."[11]

The third and final stage of Grachev's planned reforms, to continue until the end of 1999, envisaged a reduction in troops by 1.3 million, bringing the military down to 1.5 million overall, with defense expenditures ideally stabilized at around 5–6 percent of gross national product.[12] Also for this third stage, open season was promised regarding the existing five-service arrangement, including the possibility of much realignment and consolidation of assets and perhaps some services disappearing altogether, with VPVO's fighters going to the VVS and with the rest of VPVO's assets moving to a new Strategic Deterrent Force. Ground force organization would then shift from an army/division focus to a corps/brigade focus, with ensuing implications for air support needs.[13]

Grachev openly chafed at the understandable difficulty of conducting rational defense planning "in the absence of an elaborated, officially adopted Russian military doctrine."[14] No doubt in part to help alleviate that concern, and after much anticipation both in Moscow and in the West, such a doctrine was finally promulgated by the Ministry of Defense in November 1993.[15] It contained numerous warmed-over elements of the old Soviet doctrine for conventional warfare, with appropriate amendments at the margins to account for Russia's new regional security preoccupations. Quite unlike the former Soviet doctrine, it was prefaced by a formal declaration that Russia had no enemies.

Shaposhnikov was among the first to criticize the issuance of such a doctrine when some important prior questions remained unanswered. "We still do not know," he complained, "what we are, where we are going, and what our ultimate goals are. . . . Our blueprint for national security should follow from a blueprint for the development of the Russian state. . . . We have to say: These are our interests, these are the possible dangers and threats to our interests, and from that you get a blueprint, a doctrine."[16] He had a valid point.

Toward a Mobile Force Concept

Grachev's reform plan further envisaged a new Russian military structure consisting primarily of a rapid-reaction force made up of airborne units, lightly armored and air-transportable motorized rifle formations, Mi-26 helicopters, and military transport aircraft, plus marines and logistic support units.[17] Amplifying on that planned mobile force concept, Grachev said that the biggest structural changes would affect the ground forces, to include the creation—in each military district—of several divisions at full readiness, with the rest being considered reserve divisions.[18]

Shortly before his selection to become first deputy minister of defense, Andrei Kokoshin observed that the long-dominant armored component of the Soviet armed forces had become "an anachronism, a dinosaur from World War II." He suggested that the new Russia needed to rebuild its military with primary emphasis on the high-technology services (the VVS and VPVO, the Strategic Missile Forces, and the navy) and with "significantly reduced and restructured ground forces" configured for rapid deployment to any area where an outside threat to Russia's security might arise. Kokoshin added that Russia should "not rely too much on a nuclear shield" but rather should concentrate its attention and resources on building up small but efficient general-purpose forces.[19]

One of the first hints of official thinking about the likely composition and character of Russia's mobile forces came in a Defense Ministry announcement in November 1992 that such forces would begin as an interbranch, or joint *(mezhvidovoy),* combat formation and might later become an autonomous component of the armed forces. The forces would center on the inland Volga and Ural Military Districts. With the collapse of the Soviet war machine and the persistence of lengthy Russian borders, it was deemed no longer possible to guard those borders with permanent garrisons. The core of the new peacekeeping forces, envisaged as operating under CIS and United Nations auspices, would be made up of Russian airborne troops. During its formative stages, that core was envisaged by Grachev as including two airborne divisions and three airborne brigades, backstopped by several army helicopter regiments, three marine battalions, and some VPVO and communications units, along with subordinated VVS fighter and ground-attack squadrons—all of which would begin to take shape in concrete form sometime in 1995. Ultimately, the VVS component of Russia's rapid-deployment force would comprise five or six fighter regiments, five bomber regiments, two ground-attack regiments, and four airlift divisions. This was, of course, before Russia's invasion of Chechnya in December 1994, with the ensuing costs and complications that indefinitely postponed any serious thoughts of further reform along such lines.

The restructured Ural and Volga Military Districts were elevated in importance from rear to second-echelon operating areas as a direct result of the USSR's disintegration. They were chosen to provide a realistic setting in which the Russian High Command might validate its sought-after shift from the large battle formations of classic Soviet military practice to more highly mobile, rapid-reaction forces. The first echelon of those newly configured forces was scheduled to be based in the North Caucasus Military District, which was said to confront the main threat of ethnic rivalries to the south. As it turned out, that was a prescient call, since the Russian invasion of Chechnya two years later drew heavily on the military forces, particularly the combat aircraft assets, that had recently been relocated to the North Caucasus Military District.

New Looks for the Russian VVS

Today's Russian VVS is but a fragment of the former Soviet VVS that General Deinekin inherited from Shaposhnikov four months before the USSR's collapse in December 1991. As noted earlier, most of the latest-generation combat aircraft of the Soviet VVS, as well as its best-developed airfields, had been positioned beyond the westernmost borders of the Russian Federation. Those assets were lost to other newly independent states after the former union ceased to exist. Russia retained a large number of jet trainers and earlier-generation combat aircraft, along with their associated bases. However, the Russian VVS lost 37 percent of the former Soviet Union's MiG-29s, 23 percent of its Su-27s, 43 percent of its most modern Il-76 jet transports, and the overwhelming majority of its Tu-160 and Tu-95 strategic bombers. In all, barely 60 percent of the aircraft and 50 percent of the air bases of the former Soviet VVS were left on Russian soil.[20]

About 40 percent of the Soviet VVS's depot-level maintenance and repair facilities were also lost to other newly independent states. Its air-to-ground missiles had been inspected and maintained solely in Estonia. More than half its Su-24s had undergone depot maintenance in Lithuania. Its Su-25s had been serviced only at depots in Lithuania and Georgia, and its Tu-95s had been overhauled exclusively in Ukraine. Because of the severe shortage of assemblies and spare parts in Russia, the Russian VVS was left with no near-term solution to the problem created by those losses. Among the Soviet VVS's most modern bases, 44 were in Eastern Europe and 94 in the former Soviet republics, leaving Russia with some 90 major airfields in total, only half of which were considered to be of top quality. Even the latter were in need of enhancement through the construction of aircraft shelters and better maintenance and support facilities, neither of which the Russian VVS's bare-bones budget could even remotely support.[21]

Force Reductions and Consolidation

With no funding to underwrite the purchase of new aircraft, General Deinekin's options for replenishing the Russian VVS's losses occasioned by the breakup of the Soviet Union were limited to withdrawing the small amount of current-generation equipment the Soviet VVS had deployed in the Baltic states, Poland, East Germany, and Transcaucasia. That withdrawal did not begin with the USSR's demise, however. On the contrary, the Soviet VVS had initiated a planned pullback of forward-based regiments, divisions, and air armies from Czechoslovakia and Hungary as early as 1990. In 1991 it commenced a withdrawal of aircraft and units from Poland, the Baltic states, and Transcaucasia and in 1992 from East Germany. In total, some 300 operating units, more than 30,000 personnel, and 700 combat aircraft were brought home to Russian territory during this period, with more than half of those units and over 500 aircraft redeployed to the air forces of the Moscow Military District alone.

In 1992 the Russian VVS withdrew 36 air regiments from Eastern Europe and former Soviet republics.[22] In 1993 it further withdrew its 40 MiG-23s and its ground support personnel deployed at the Burevestnik airfield on Iturup, one of several islands in the Kuril chain that Japan claims as its territory. That move left Russia with no remaining air bases in the disputed region.[23] By late 1994, 40 regiments had been withdrawn from former forward-operating locations.[24]

Russia's aviation manpower also underwent a significant decline from its former Soviet level. From a total of a little over one million men in the Soviet VVS, VPVO, and naval aviation in 1989, the combined number for the three Russian air arms by 1998 was down to 335,000.[25] Furthermore, as a result of the failure of conscription, the three services became abnormally top-heavy with officers. In 1989 conscripts formed 69 percent of the VVS and 60 percent of VPVO. In 1996, by contrast, officers and career noncommissioned officers in both services outnumbered conscripts two-to-one.

Employment Concepts and Air Doctrine

In traditional Soviet military doctrine, the army-dominated General Staff relegated air power to a secondary role as a supporting element in a combined-arms approach to war fought and won mainly by massive infantry and armored forces. Almost overnight, however, the operational focus of the Russian armed forces shifted from a stress on theater offensive warfare to regional power projection, which naturally played to the VVS's greatest strengths. Increasingly since the success of coalition air operations against Iraq in the 1991 Persian Gulf War, Russian military experts, and not just airmen, have come to recognize and acknowledge the new capabilities of air power, properly used, in determining joint-force combat outcomes.[26]

Tacitly acknowledging the example of Desert Storm, the VVS analysis cited at the beginning of this chapter held: "The success of ground operations increasingly depends on air force missions, from achieving air supremacy until the moment the enemy surrenders." It further echoed the well-known refrain of Western airmen that the essence of air power is flexibility, calling such flexibility "crucial for the defense of Russian territory, with its vast expanse, decreasing inventory of combat aircraft, urgent need to allocate economic resources to support and maintenance facilities, and uncertainty about the potential origins and combinations of future threats."

The analysis conceded that the likelihood of major war had diminished greatly with the ending of the cold war and that both Russian and American planners now believed the chief near-term danger entailed wars of low and medium intensity. Revealingly, however, it added that the chance of high-intensity conflict could not be ruled out altogether, since "low-intensity conflicts are not sufficiently demanding to define the size or technology of the Russian Air Force." That reservation testified unabashedly to the persistent determination of the VVS to continue pressing the state of the art in aviation technology, even though Russia confronts no near-term threats that would even remotely warrant new systems going beyond the capability of the weapons that Russia already possesses, let alone the expenditure of the scarce funds that would be needed to pay for such systems. In a discerning comment on that aspect of the analysis, Arbatov noted that its assessment of the strategic landscape and the more implausible contingencies cited as a basis for Russian force planning reflected the natural tendency of any military organization "to retain as much as possible of its traditional strategic roles and operational missions, giving only lip service to the new post–cold war security realities."[27]

The VVS analysis sketched out five scenarios that, it said, constituted the core of the planning assumptions assigned to the VVS by the Defense Ministry through the early years of the twenty-first century.

The Northwestern and Western Strategic Salient. In an apparent reach for the one "high-intensity" scenario needed to justify continuing with a robust R&D and force-development program, the analysis cited the possibility that "NATO might try to employ force to settle Russian internal conflicts, to deny Russia its legitimate interests, or even to seize parts of its territory to undercut strategic positions or for post-conflict bargaining." That fanciful scenario postulated that NATO would begin any such offensive with intense air and naval bombardment aimed at seizing the Kaliningrad region and then would press to Russia's western frontier through Belarus and Ukraine, employing both air attacks and deep ground-force penetration into the Leningrad and Moscow Military Districts. Such a possibility, according to the analysis, called for a VVS capability to repel enemy air operations, prevent amphibious landings, and conduct offensive and defensive counterair operations over enemy territory.

The Southwestern Strategic Salient. Somewhat more plausibly, the analysis visualized subtle efforts by Turkey and Iran to weaken Russia's position in Transcaucasia and to win over the largely Muslim populations of Azerbaijan, the North Caucasus, and several other conflicted areas in the region. That second scenario suggested that an escalation of fighting between Armenia and Azerbaijan, or the complete disintegration of Georgia, might lead to large-scale military intervention by Russia, Turkey, and Iran. Such a possibility could harbor all sorts of escalatory potential, including a Turkish attack supported indirectly by NATO.[28] The latter threat, suggested the analysis, would necessitate prompt counteroffensive operations by the North Caucasus air group and, later, by Russian combined-arms formations. (Perhaps revealingly, the analysis anticipated no operations such as those subsequently carried out by Russian forces against Chechnya.)

The Southern Strategic Salient. Similarly, the analysis conjured up the prospect that Turkey, Iran, Afghanistan, and Pakistan might seek to play on Muslim sympathies in Central Asia and Kazakhstan and seize strategically important areas and assets in the region. Such a scenario would require an opposing coalition of Tadzhikistan, Uzbekistan, Kazakhstan, and Russia, spearheaded by VVS aircraft from the Caucasus and Volga-Ural Military Districts, to provide air cover, tactical reconnaissance, and interdiction of enemy lines of communication.

The Far Eastern Strategic Salient. A fourth scenario reflected continued Japanese claims on the Southern Kuril Islands and a stated concern that Russia's nearly complete demilitarization of the Southern Kurils might embolden Japan to solve its "northern territories" problem by force. The analysis compounded that extreme implausibility by envisaging Japan as conducting such an operation with active U.S. complicity. It then erected guaranteed preconditions for a self-fulfilling prophecy by suggesting that the VVS would be obliged to engage U.S. aircraft carriers in support of any Russian counteroffensive.

The East Siberian Strategic Salient. In what came perhaps closest to being a valid worst-case situation that Russia might have plausible grounds to worry about, the analysis contemplated a possible Russo-Chinese war triggered by unrenounced Chinese territorial claims against portions of Kazakhstan, Kirgizstan, Tadzhikistan, and Russia. This last scenario acknowledged that Russia's long border, insufficient ground forces, lack of strategic depth, and exposed regional infrastructure and lines of communication would put a special premium on early and intense VVS counterattacks against high-value Chinese military, command and control, and industrial targets.[29]

In considering the force requirements for those scenarios, the analysis pointed out that the VVS would perform numerous functions generic to all circumstances yet that each scenario presented unique demands as well, considering the wide variations in the respective climates and topographies, basing and maintenance infrastructures, prospects for prompt reinforcement and resupply, and likely opposing forces. General Deinekin almost surely had such variations in mind when he said, "We are working out definite views on waging armed conflict depending on the theater of military operations and the forces situated there." He added as an example that if the hypothetical enemy was in the Far East, then "one must take into account the concept of enormous space." Different looks, he went on to note, would be required for operations in mountainous areas.[30]

The analysis was candid in conceding VVS limitations. In the Far Eastern scenario, it acknowledged the small number of airfields in the region as a major constraint on dispersal, redeployment, and reinforcement. It further conceded that any Russian air operations against Japan would be of "quite limited effectiveness," considering the sophistication of Japanese and U.S. air defenses and the VVS's shortage of combat aircraft with sufficient range.

As for the "high-intensity" case of Eastern Europe, the analysis frankly admitted that the VVS "would be at a disadvantage." NATO's air forces, it noted, would be able to deploy quickly to forward bases in Eastern Europe, and NATO "generally has longer-range and better air-to-surface missile attack capabilities." To accommodate any such contingency, the VVS would mainly use fighters in conjunction with VPVO to protect Russia, since the VVS's ground-attack aircraft suffer from short ranges and limited in-flight refueling capability. The analysis further acknowledged that any use of Russian medium- and long-range bombers would result in "unacceptable" attrition, since NATO's air defenses are dense and Russia's fighter escorts lack sufficient endurance to accompany the bombers to their targets.

The analysis concluded that the VVS's existing force structure, aircraft, and weapons mix, its industrial support, its deployment pattern, its basing and maintenance infrastructure, its command, control, and communications and intelligence (C3I), and its redeployment capability were all "woefully inadequate to respond to the regional contingencies of the new [Russian] military doctrine." The commendable candor of the analysis was not matched, unfortunately, by an awareness that its insistence on clinging to outmoded threat constructs in the interest of justifying its more ambitious force-modernization goals could only work to postpone both the VVS's recovery to good health and the broader gains to be had from a cooperative security relationship between Russia and the West.

New Commands and Organizational Arrangements

General Deinekin touted the VVS as the chief provider of mobility for Russia's armed forces and declared that the main goal of its restructuring through the year 2000 would be to create, from existing formations, "a separate, highly mobile branch of the armed forces" featuring an appropriate mix of personnel, platforms, and weapons able to perform the full spectrum of combat missions, either jointly or independently.[31] In keeping with that declared goal, he moved in 1993 to consolidate the operational components of the VVS into four major commands: LRA; VTA; a new Frontal Aviation Command (*Komandovanie frontovoi aviatsii,* or KFA); and a new Reserve and Training Command. The first two were familiar holdovers from the Soviet era. The latter two represented an attempt to gain greater coherence and efficiencies in VVS organization.

According to General Deinekin, that move was undertaken in part to help the VVS reduce the size of its educational and training establishment and its management superstructure.[32] More important, however, was the firmer grip the new KFA gave the VVS over its fighter and ground-attack assets. Previously, Russia's tactical air power had been subordinated to the regional military districts under the immediate operational control of the ground forces. The new command set up to rectify that situation was inaugurated in February 1994 under Colonel General Nikolai Antoshkin, who for the preceding five years had been the air commander for the Moscow Military District.

Deinekin also moved to eliminate four former district directorates in an attempt to cut back on the VVS's administrative overhead. In its new incarnation, the scaled-down VVS would have only 170 generals instead of the former 300 or more, with numerous former officer billets being remanded to civilians. Deinekin said that this reorganization would be carried out in several stages en route to its completion at the end of 1995, with a view toward making the VVS "the most important constituent of Russia's armed forces, as is happening in all the world's developed countries."[33] Russia's subsequent rude awakening in Chechnya, however, indicated that the VVS had a way to go yet before it could even remotely lay credible claim to being "the most important constituent" of the Russian military (see Chapter 8).

According to General Deinekin, the VVS and VPVO, while still independent services, made a concerted effort to retain in the post-Soviet era the interactivity that had existed between them throughout the Soviet period since VPVO's establishment as a separate service in 1954. Deinekin added that gaps in the coverage of Russia's SAM defenses created by the breakup of the USSR had increased the burden on VVS fighter aviation, which would consequently use its capabilities "to the maximum" in support of the home-defense mission. On the sensitive issue of VPVO's future as a separate service, Deinekin granted that the imperatives of reform could indeed "require, at a certain stage, combining the forces and means of the VVS and VPVO into a single service branch." He added diplomatically, however, that any such move would be a "complex and painful process" involving diverse pros and cons. On the plus side, Deinekin rightly observed, such a merger would permit more centralized command and control of air defense operations, along with greater efficiencies and resultant economies from consolidating duplicative airfields and maintenance and logistics systems. The problems associated with any such merger, he suggested, would stem mainly from the fact that the two services had traditionally been separate, necessarily implying difficult changes in institutional practices and habit patterns. He added that considerable financial problems would also be created by any such consolidation during the transition period. Accordingly, Deinekin suggested that neither the Yeltsin government nor the Defense Ministry was yet ready to proceed with combining the two services, if only because of the additional burden such a merger would impose on state funds in the short run. Subsequently, Grachev indicated that VPVO would be retained, at least for the near term, as a separate service.[34]

New Basing Approaches
A particularly acute problem for the VVS in the wake of the USSR's breakup involved rationalizing its inherited deployment and basing infrastructure. That network of assets wholly reflected what Russia was left with after the USSR fell apart and bore little relationship to subsequent VVS contingency planning, intended reforms, or operational doctrine. The VVS analysis noted that around 70 percent of the VVS aircraft were based in the European part of Russia: 15 percent located in the northwestern direction, 25 percent in the western direction, and 30 percent in the southwestern direction. Of the remaining 30 percent east of the Urals, 20 percent faced the Far East and only 10 percent faced China. The analysis properly called that inherited deployment pattern "distorted" and

pointed out that the VVS needed fewer aircraft in the northwestern and Far East salients and more in the North Caucasus Military District opposite Transcaucasia, Turkey, and Iran.

The analysis further stated that two-thirds of all VVS aircraft in European Russia were based only 200–300 kilometers from Russia's western borders and that bombers and transports were concentrated on an "unacceptably small" number of bases. The VVS faced a severe ramp-space problem owing to the massive withdrawal of former Soviet aircraft from the Warsaw Pact's forward area since 1991. According to the VVS analysis, only half of KFA's fighters remained revetted or protected in hardened shelters. Russian analysts noted with interest the USAF's idea of composite wings and its application of the composite-wing concept during the 1991 Persian Gulf War.[35] It remains to be seen whether the VVS will eventually adopt an analogous approach.[36]

For the interim, the VVS analysis advocated a less radical approach, which it called "aircraft basing regions," aimed at providing a fully equipped operations and maintenance infrastructure for all aircraft permanently based in the region, as well as for any additional aircraft that might be deployed to a given direction during mobility exercises or actual crises. Those bases were to be established at existing KFA, LRA, and VTA major airfields located more than 300 kilometers inside Russia's new borders. According to the analysis, they would be configured to maintain and support all aircraft types earmarked for operational roles in their assigned regions. They also would be designed to accommodate five or six permanently based fighter squadrons and to serve as hubs for outlying airfields attached to them. Realistically speaking, the analysis conceded that the biggest obstacle threatening the realization of this concept was the government's lack of funds.

Force Structure and Force Development Plans

The baseline for the Soviet planned air strength before the USSR's dissolution was set down in the CFE Treaty signed in November 1990. To comply with the treaty, the Soviet Union was obliged to reduce the number of its combat aircraft west of the Urals to 5,150. That ceiling included tactical and air-defense fighters, LRA medium bombers (heavy bombers were regulated by the separate Strategic Arms Reduction Treaty), and combat-capable trainers of the VVS and VPVO. The L-29 and L-39 basic jet trainers were excluded.

During the CFE negotiations, the USSR had reported its overall number of combat aircraft west of the Urals to be 6,611, including 4,323 VVS aircraft and 1,338 attack helicopters (225 in the VVS inventory and the remainder assigned to army aviation). After ratification of the treaty, the VVS was to retain 3,590 combat aircraft, including 300 medium bombers and 440 combat-capable trainers, with 1,560 combat aircraft remaining in VPVO, including 60 combat-capable trainers. That would have left the USSR with 1,461 surplus combat aircraft, divided almost equally between the VVS and VPVO, to be destroyed or used as static displays, maintenance training aids, or target drones. The plan for the VVS aircraft on the eve of the USSR's collapse was for 290 to be cut up for scrap, 208 reclassified as unarmed trainers, 160 used for targets, 15 assigned as maintenance trainers, and 36 earmarked for static displays.[37]

Those numbers were soon overtaken by events as Russia's continuing unilateral military drawdown brought VVS force levels well below the mandated CFE ceiling. General Deinekin announced VVS plans to scrap 2,000 aircraft in 1993 alone, with a view toward ultimately retaining only latest-generation aircraft in the operational inventory.[38] He later stated that the VVS inventory would be reduced by yet another third in 1994.[39] Colonel General Anatoly Malyukov indicated that the VVS had ordered "literally a few" Tu-160s, Su-24s, and Su-27s just to keep the military aircraft industry from dying. He said that no further Su-25s or MiG-29s had been ordered and that the MiG-21, Su-7, and Su-17 had been retired from active service. A similar fate later befell the MiG-23, MiG-27, and Su-17M, as well as bombers built in the 1960s (the Tu-22, Tu-95M, and Tu-95K), which were slated to be removed from the active inventory well before the end of the 1990s.[40]

A major headache afflicting the VVS was the great diversity of its aircraft types. Kokoshin admitted that the long-established, costly Soviet acquisition practices had resulted, even in the best of times, in needless difficulties in the realm of operations and maintenance. He added that it would take years for the VVS to rid itself of this burden, since it was no easy matter to write off all the dubious "riches" the Soviet military had accumulated over several generations of aircraft development thanks to such acquisition overkill. He further predicted that the Defense Ministry would, in the future, radically reduce the number of aircraft types in its inventory, "concentrating on the best items of equipment and saying a resolute *nyet* to those that fail to demonstrate the requisite quality."[41]

Even as the twenty-first century nears, it remains hard to say what the VVS's force structure will look like once the continuing round of post-Soviet retrenchment is completed. General Malyukov frankly admitted in 1993 that he could not offer a firm projection of the VVS's expected strength, since any figures he might provide could be rendered invalid at a moment's notice. He indicated that through a combination of radical downsizing and the introduction of latest-generation technologies, the hoped-for combat potential of the Russian VVS would be about 50 percent greater than that of the former Soviet VVS. He was careful to add, however, that this forecast was based wholly on paper plans and that its realization would depend entirely on the outlook for state funding.

Government allocations for the procurement of new equipment by the VVS dropped precipitously after the breakup of the USSR. According to the VVS analysis, outlays for the development of new platforms fell 70 percent during the first three years following the end of the cold war. In 1991 aircraft procurement was cut 46 percent for frontal air and 41 percent for bombers and transports. In 1992 procurement of tactical aircraft was only 21 percent of the 1991 level, with that of bombers and transports down to 36 percent of the preceding year's figure. Procurement funds were cut again by 31 percent for frontal air in 1993, with another cut of 23 percent in 1994.

The effects of those cuts were strikingly apparent in the contrast between the numbers of military aircraft acquired in 1984 and 1994. During the early 1980s, to take a typical annual Soviet figure, the USSR produced an average of 400–450 fighters and 100 bombers and transports a year. Yet in 1993–94 only 23 fighters were procured by the VVS, VPVO, and navy combined. By the end of 1994, production of the Su-24, Su-25, and MiG-29 had been halted; annual production of the MiG-31 for VPVO was down to "single numbers"; procurement of developmental variants of the Su-27 was anticipated to decline to below 14–16 aircraft a year; and production of the Tu-160, Tu-142, and Tu-95 was terminated. According to the VVS analysis, funds allotted to the VVS for procurement in 1993–94 were insufficient even to pay for the replacement of aircraft lost in accidents. The analysis warned that if the trend continued into the late 1990s, Russia's military aviation industry could begin to collapse, causing the country to lose its competitive edge as a global aerospace power for decades to come.

On that last score, the VVS analysis grimly conceded that VVS force structure goals mandated by the new military doctrine could not be met with projected state funding. Merely to sustain an active inventory of 2,000 fighter and attack aircraft while replacing the MiG-23, MiG-27, Su-17, and older Su-25s with new equipment, Russia would have to produce 110 to 115 new aircraft a year to the year 2000. The analysis pointed out that the Yeltsin government's current and likely future defense budget would not support those production rates. As a result, curtailed procurement would cause the VVS's tactical aircraft inventory to decline from the mandated goal of 2,000 aircraft to around 1,440 by the year 2000. Once that occurred, even a full economic recovery by the year 2010 would not enable the VVS to build back up to its mandated level. Furthermore, such calculations excluded the added cost associated with the concurrent need to modernize LRA, VTA, VPVO, and the navy. The analysis concluded that those problems were "insoluble by any VVS planning or budgeting" and were "fundamentally a matter of national priorities [to be] addressed at the highest levels of the Ministry of Defense, and by the president, the Security Council, and Federal Assembly of the Russian Federation."

KFA

The VVS's new KFA, instituted in 1993, embraced all fighter and ground-attack aircraft in the VVS inventory. Its establishment withdrew Russian fighter aviation from the immediate control of the regional military district commanders, long the practice throughout the Soviet era, and resubordinated it directly to VVS headquarters. Like the USAF's Air Combat Command, KFA had as its declared purpose the organization, training, and equipping of Russia's tactical air forces for operational commitment as necessary to joint commands such as the mobile forces that were concurrently being set up.

Like all other VVS components, fighter aviation shrank considerably from a high of over 5,000 combat aircraft in 1989 to less than half that number in 1996. By then the centerpiece of a much-reduced VVS that had become, in effect, a tactical air arm with airlift and bomber backup, KFA maintained an inventory of some 2,300 combat aircraft. Of those, about one-third were fourth-generation MiG-29s and Su-27s. The remainder were older aircraft slated to be retired before the end of the 1990s.[42]

According to the VVS analysis, KFA in 1994 listed on its roster of assets 450 MiG-29s, 190 Su-27s, 490 Su-24s, 170 Su-25s, and 480 MiG-27s, plus an assortment of MiG-23s, MiG-25s, and Su-17s slated for imminent retirement. The command was made up of five air armies, each including three divisions containing three regiments of three squadrons each. (A KFA division typically operated 90–120 aircraft depending on type and mission.) KFA also assumed control of two operational conversion centers equipped with a total of some 300 MiG-29s, Su-24s, Su-25s, and Su-27s for transitioning new undergraduate pilot training (UPT) graduates onto the equipment they would fly on squadron service. In addition it acquired the advanced combat training center at Lipetsk some 400 miles south of Moscow, which developed KFA training and readiness standards, produced fighter weapons instructors, and offered mission-employment training to experienced aircrews.

The VVS analysis anticipated that if existing budget trends continued, KFA's combat aircraft holdings would decline from 2,280 to 1,670 aircraft in 1997; to 1,440 in 2000; to 1,330 in 2005; to 1,140 in 2010; and to 870 by 2015. That projection, moreover, did not reflect anticipated peacetime attrition, which at the time was running at about 1.2 percent annually for latest-generation aircraft and 2 percent a year for all remaining aircraft. By the year 2000, according to the analysis, normal attrition through routine operations and training accidents could result in a loss of up to 60 third-generation aircraft. By 2015 normal attrition could occasion a loss of up to 215 fourth- and fifth-generation aircraft.

The increasingly dim outlook for a new Russian air-combat fighter to replace the MiG-29 and the Su-27 will be deferred for more detailed consideration in Chapter 9. It should be noted here, however, that the VVS is facing an uphill struggle even to gain the needed funding to support its desired modernization of existing systems, let alone underwrite the acquisition of a next-generation fighter. The VVS analysis anticipated that a new multirole close-support fighter with low-observable (or "stealth") features could come on line after the year 2000 to replace the Su-25. It made no reference whatever in its force projections, however, to any MiG-29 or Su-27 follow-on.

The VVS decided as far back as 1993 to forgo acquiring more MiG-29s and to base its future fighter force, at least for the near term, on air-to-air, ground-attack, and reconnaissance and electronic countermeasures (ECM) upgrades of the basic Su-27 airframe. The chief of the VVS Operations Directorate pointed out that the Su-27 was designed from the outset with a view toward preplanned product improvement.[43] The two-seat, all-weather ground-attack improvement of the aircraft has been redesignated the Su-32. The single-seat air-combat upgrade equipped with three-dimensional thrust vectoring and canard control surfaces will be called the Su-37. Both aircraft have been flying in demonstrator form for several years at the Zhukovsky Flight Test Center and on the international air show circuit. Interestingly, and perhaps revealingly, the VVS analysis described these as Russia's impending "fifth-generation" fighters. Neither, however, has yet been funded for series production.

LRA

Previously the Soviet counterpart to the bomber portion of the USAF's Strategic Air Command and a core component of Moscow's nuclear deterrent force, LRA has shed much, though not all, of its former intercontinental nuclear attack role since the end of the cold war, substituting a new mission of providing extended strategic "reach" in support of Russia's newly emerging regional power projection needs. It also has experienced a significant drawdown in deployed forces since the late 1980s as a result of arms-reduction agreements and the USSR's collapse.

Reduced to a single air army in the wake of the USSR's demise, LRA in 1994 listed on its roster of assets 145 Tu-95s, 170 Tu-22Ms, and 4 Tu-160s, plus 40-odd Mya-4 and Il-78 tankers and assorted transports, for a total inventory of some 400 aircraft. Myriad ownership questions arose in the immediate aftermath of the USSR's collapse, when LRA lost many of its strategic bombers to other newly independent states. More than half of the aviation complement of the former USSR's strategic nuclear forces ended up in Ukraine and Kazakhstan. Of the 160 LRA strategic bombers that had been based on non-Russian Soviet territory, 70 percent were modern Tu-95s and Tu-160s.[44]

The government of newly independent Kazakhstan was reasonable enough with Moscow, agreeing to return those inherited Soviet bombers for which it had no legitimate use. The last 4 of a total of 40 late-model Tu-95MS cruise-missile

carriers were returned to Russia from their base near Semipalatinsk in Kazakhstan in February 1994.[45] (Some older Tu-95s were left in Kazakhstan for the
Kazakh VVS.) The story with Ukraine, however, was something else. The sole
operational unit of Soviet Tu-160s, the 184th Heavy Bomber Regiment, had been
based at Priluki in Ukraine. On the USSR's dissolution, those aircraft immediately fell into Ukrainian hands and triggered a testy contretemps between
Moscow and Kiev over their return to Russia as a part of the CIS's strategic
forces. Only three serviceable Tu-160s were retained in Russia, with a fourth
subsequently delivered by the manufacturer to the LRA base at Engels, which
had been intended to be the VVS's master Tu-160 base on completion of its construction.[46] In April 1994 production of the Tu-160 at the Tupolev plant in Kazan
was brought to a close by a personal order from President Yeltsin.[47]

For a time, the Ukrainian government was demanding upward of two billion
rubles from Russia for each Tu-160 it might return, a price tantamount to extor-
tion, considering that the aircraft were wholly a windfall acquisition by
Ukraine.[48] After much hard bargaining on both sides, the Russian VVS finally
negotiated the reacquisition of ten of the aircraft at a more equitable price.[49] Undoubtedly the aircraft were in need of extensive refurbishment, however, since
they were all but nonflyable for five years as a result of inadequate fuel provisions, maintenance, and spare parts.[50]

Like KFA, LRA in 1994 anticipated a drawdown through the first decade of
the twenty-first century from its current force of some 400 bombers and tankers
to an inventory roughly half that size. Declared plans were to retire all Tu-16,
Tu-22, Tu-95M, and Tu-95K aircraft, leaving a bomber force made up of
Tu-22M, Tu-95MS, and Tu-160 aircraft, supported by Il-78 tankers.

VTA

By far the most painful aircraft loss suffered by Russia in the wake of the
USSR's disintegration was felt in VTA. The largest group of late-model Il-76 jet
transports, and those with the longest remaining service life (200 aircraft out of
the 450 possessed by the USSR), were based in Ukraine.[51] Their loss was doubly
disturbing in light of Russia's newly emergent regional peacekeeping challenges
and the consequent power projection needs they engendered, an operational challenge that was sorely tested by the airlift demands of the war in Chechnya three
years later.

General Malyukov, the chief of the Russian VVS headquarters staff and a career fighter pilot, admitted in 1993 that the VVS's single biggest shortfall was in
the realm of air transport. The VVS analysis likewise observed that mobility was
the highest priority for the Russian armed forces, adding that the missions assigned to VTA by Russia's new military doctrine "far exceed present capabilities." By way of example, the analysis noted that all of VTA would be required

to move just a single airborne division in two sorties and that VTA's capabilities would have to be increased at least threefold if it was to provide the mobility envisaged by the new doctrine.

VTA in 1996 consisted of three air divisions, each made up of three regiments possessing some 30 transport aircraft apiece. There also were several independent airlift regiments assigned to the command. The combined inventory included some 350 Il-76, An-12, An-22, and An-124 airlifters.[52] To triple its lift capacity as recommended by the VVS analysis, VTA would have to produce 28 to 30 new Il-106 transports after the year 2000, when that follow-on aircraft, now in development, is expected to be ready for production. According to the VVS analysis, however, achievement of that goal would completely deprive the VVS of any funds to modernize its other force components. Compounding the problem for VTA was that most aircraft production facilities were located outside of Russia. The plants that produced the Il-76 and the An-124, along with those that made their engines, were lost to Uzbekistan and Ukraine, respectively.

Reserve and Training Command

The Reserve and Training Command was set up, among other things, to manage the VVS's four UPT schools and several additional schools for training navigators, air traffic controllers, and foreign students. It also took over the VVS's "boneyard," where surplus aircraft are held in nonflyable storage. At the time of its establishment in 1993, the command operated some 1,000 L-39 basic jet trainers distributed among the Kacha, Barnaul, Tambov, and Balashov flight schools, as well as some 300 Tu-134 jet transports.

When first activated, the Reserve and Training Command had ambitious plans to form, in the near future, a "first-line reserve" made up of units withdrawn from the Warsaw Pact countries and former republics and of obsolescent aircraft kept in flyable storage from decommissioned units. A "second-line" reserve, according to the VVS analysis, would be equipped with older combat aircraft retained in nonflyable storage. The command anticipated that once the second-line reserve system was established and activated, the VVS would be able to reconstitute enough aircraft within about one week to equip a single fighter regiment. A serious problem, however, was that many of the VVS's stored aircraft were rapidly deteriorating beyond the point of further serviceability as a result of exposure to harsh elements. Another complication was that vital components and subsystems of many stored aircraft were being looted on a massive scale because of inadequate security and accounting.

The VVS badly needs a new basic trainer and reported a requirement in 1994 for 800 aircraft.[53] Its aging L-39s manufactured in Czechoslovakia and procured by the Soviet VVS as a "burden-sharing" gesture to its then–Warsaw Pact ally had become a maintenance nightmare, with spare parts reportedly in "catastrophically" short supply. Requests for replacement parts went routinely unful-filled, leaving supplies so scarce that, according to one complaint, "you couldn't find the simplest 3.5 volt light bulb in an entire regiment, even in daylight and with a flashlight."[54] Currently in competition to replace the Czech-built L-39 are Mikoyan's MiG-AT and Yakovlev's Yak-130, with a VVS source selection and production decision still pending after years of being reported as "imminent."[55]

VPVO

In the immediate aftermath of the USSR's disintegration, Russia's VPVO oper-ated all homeland SAMs, early-warning radars, ground-controlled intercept (GCI) sites, and fighter-interceptors. The fighter portion of the force experienced a rate of decline much like that of the other combat air arms between the late 1980s and mid-1990s. From a high of some 2,300 operational interceptors on the eve of the USSR's collapse in December 1991, the number was down by roughly half in 1994.[56] Organized into five air defense armies, mostly concentrated in western and far eastern Russia, the command at that time operated some 325 Su-27s, 425 MiG-31s, 20 A-50 AWACS (airborne warning and control system) aircraft, and a residual number of MiG-23s that were awaiting retirement. It also maintained a UPT school at Armavir, which operated some 225 L-39s and 73 MiG-23s, a similar flight school at Stavropol, which also trained MiG-31 radar-intercept operators, and an advanced interceptor weapons training center at Savostleika.[57]

The VVS analysis pointed out that if the fighter branch of VPVO eventually merged with the VVS—a move said at the time to be under "intensive debate"—those assets would become an important part of the VVS's overall force posture and would significantly affect its operational planning and procurement needs. Force-modernization plans appeared limited to developing and producing an ad-vanced MiG-31M if and when procurement allocations might make that possible. Budget constraints promised a further decline in VPVO fighter strength over time, with the 1994 force of some 1,100 interceptors expected to fall to as low as 380 by 2010.

Naval Aviation

Although Russia's naval aviators belong to a separate service, they wear VVS uniforms, receive their training at VVS flight schools, and hold VVS rather than naval ranks.[58] They also are afflicted by post-Soviet constraints no less severe than those that have beset the VVS and VPVO. During its final days the Soviet Navy maintained over 1,000 aircraft, consisting of shore-based fighters and fighter-bombers, cruise-missile-carrying bombers, maritime patrol and recon-naissance aircraft, antisubmarine warfare (ASW) helicopters, and transports.

That number has since declined dramatically in consonance with Russia's post–cold war military drawdown. An increase had occurred in 1991 when the navy received a transfer of 290 "excess" Su-24, Su-25, MiG-27, and Su-17 fighter-bombers from the VVS. That almost certainly was the result of a Soviet ploy intended to help the VVS evade CFE Treaty limits by playing a clever shell game with its supposedly "excess" aircraft.

According to its first deputy commander, Major General Nikolai Rogov, naval aviation during the late Soviet era was responsible for protecting nuclear ballistic missile submarines (SSBNs) and submarine cruise-missile platforms, engaging enemy surface action groups, interdicting sea lines of communication, and aiding in maritime defensive and offensive operations. Those missions have since been scaled back from their former blue-water orientation to a continental focus, in keeping with the across-the-board retrenchment of Russia's military power and reach. In 1992 General Rogov acknowledged a 30 percent reduction in naval personnel and a 20 percent drawdown in the navy's aircraft inventory, with priority attention now being devoted to the air arms of the Northern and Pacific fleets.

Among many proposals for further consolidating Russia's radically trimmed-down military, the idea floated for a time to subordinate the navy's Tu-22M bombers to VVS operational control and to transfer its fighter and ground-attack aircraft directly to the VVS. Predictably, Rogov opposed that idea, on the ground that its implementation would, in his words, "deprive the navy of organic strike aviation to counter the threat of air and missile attack." Were the navy's combat aircraft to be taken over by the VVS, Rogov maintained, the fleet would then have to rely on VVS units untrained for air war at sea. Such an arrangement, he feared, would create new command and control problems. To the contrary, he suggested, the continuing decline in Russia's submarine and surface warfare strength demanded an offsetting "reinforcement" of naval aviation. With no compelling strategic rationale, Rogov's argument had an all-too-familiar ring of rote justification of existing roles and missions. Perhaps anticipating worse things to come, Rogov took care not to reject altogether the idea of combining LRA and the navy's cruise-missile aviation. He suggested, however, that considering the predominance of naval air's responsibilities in the maritime arena, it made more sense to subordinate naval aviation to the navy. He also found it more sensible, in light of Russia's diminished post–cold war maritime threat, to retain the long-range missile aircraft of the Northern and Pacific fleets but to reduce the navy's involvement in fighter-bomber, ASW, and reconnaissance aviation.[59]

The Russian Navy's first commander in chief, Admiral Feliks Gromov, reported in 1993 that naval aviation would be reduced further, by approximately 40 percent, with chief emphasis being given to the development of carrier-based fighters, cruise-missile carriers, and ASW aircraft. He frankly admitted, however, that because of the continuing funding crisis, there would be "serious difficulties in the practical attainment of these ideas."[60]

A more upbeat early assessment of Russian naval aviation's durability in the face of the funding crisis was offered by its commander, Colonel General V. Potapov, who stressed that even with reduced funding, fuel shortages, and maintenance deficiencies, continuation training in operational units would remain aimed at preserving mission readiness among enough aircrews that, "if necessary, every flying unit would be able to carry out its primary mission." Potapov acknowledged that dwindling aircraft service life was threatening to ground a considerable portion of the aircraft inventory. He added that the navy intended to press ahead in ASW, leaving unaddressed the hard question of where Russia's requirement for such a capability remained in the rank-ordering of its post–cold war military needs.[61]

Much as in the VVS, a significant rise in naval aviation's accident rate was prompted by the prolonged disruption of shipboard helicopter and aircraft operations due to insufficient funds in the navy's training account. One aviation colonel complained in 1993 that his pilots had not taken part in shipboard operations for more than a year. That, he said, jeopardized "not just the regiment's combat readiness but flight safety as well."[62]

The Soviet Navy's development of the first-generation ASW cruisers *Moskva* and *Kiev* during the late 1960s, and its later development of the second-generation heavy carrier *Admiral Kuznetsov,* had hardly given it a serious ship-based attack aviation capability. Nevertheless, the developments provided a feel for big-deck carrier aviation that could not have been acquired any other way. In 1992 General Rogov spoke optimistically about the Russian Navy's determination to stay involved in carrier-based fighter aviation. Unfortunately for these ambitions, the initial exposure to the complex demands of carrier aviation was acquired just as the funding crisis threatened the demise of carrier-based air power in Russia altogether.[63] One retired admiral and former deputy chief of the General Staff, Admiral Nikolai Amelko, even charged that the building of Russian carriers was a "wildcat scheme" all along and was totally at odds with the USSR's defensive military doctrine. He complained that aircraft carriers had nothing to contribute to the nation's defenses and merely promised to "eat up resources."[64]

In 1993 the navy selected the Su-27K over the MiG-29K as its preferred shipboard fighter, a choice that resulted in cancellation of further development of the MiG-29K. The carrier version of the Su-25 ground-attack aircraft also was terminated.[65] On becoming operational, the Su-27K was redesignated the Su-33.[66] The carrier *Admiral Kuznetsov* deployed with the Northern Fleet in 1993 sporting a squadron of 16 Su-33s, 8 Su-25s, and 10 Ka-27 helicopters. In August of that year no serving navy pilots had fully qualified for Su-33 carrier operations, although their training was in progress.[67] Concurrently, the navy phased out its inventory of plagued Yak-38 vertical takeoff and land (VTOL) fighters modeled on the British and U.S. Marine Corps Harrier jump-jet and canceled the big-deck carrier that had long been under construction at the Nikolayev shipyard.[68] The latter decision in particular raised fundamental questions about the long-term prospects for Russian carrier aviation.

4. Undergraduate Pilot Training

Throughout most of the cold war, the Soviet VVS operated a specialized undergraduate pilot training (UPT) program consisting of a dozen Higher Military Aviation Schools for Pilots (*Vysshiye voyenniye aviatsionniye uchilishcha letchikov,* or VVAULs) located in various Soviet republics. Each school trained cadets for conversion to a specific aircraft category, with curricula tailored variously toward fighters, ground-attack aircraft, strategic bombers, and transports, depending on the school. A full course lasted four years and combined training in officership, college-level science and engineering, and basic flying skills. Application to a VVAUL meant signing up for a twenty-five-year service commitment in the event of successful completion of the course, with service time commencing the year of enrollment. Graduates of the program at each school were commissioned with the rank of lieutenant, awarded a degree in engineering, and given an aeronautical rating of basic pilot.

Although the VVS and VPVO were separate services, their VVAULs offered virtually indistinguishable training programs. Captain Alexander Zuyev, the VVS MiG-29 pilot who defected to the United States in 1989, received his flight training at Armavir, a VPVO school, and subsequently was assigned to the VVS.[1] Fighter-oriented schools used the Czech-produced L-29 and, later, L-39 jet trainers for primary and basic instruction, after which cadets would receive an initial qualification checkout on the aircraft they would fly on their first operational assignment (generally the MiG-21 or the MiG-23 for air-to-air pilots and the Su-17 or the MiG-27 for pilots headed for ground-attack units). That transition took place during the final year of the VVAUL course.

Acceptance to fighter VVAULs was highly competitive. Lieutenant Viktor Belenko, the VPVO MiG-25 pilot who defected with his aircraft to Japan in 1976, stated that of some 4,000 applicants for slots in his pilot-training class at Armavir, only 360 were selected and that about 100 of those were washed out before completion of the program.[2] The most popular schools were more difficult to get into. For example, Zuyev reported that the Kacha VVAUL for fighter pilots was all but inaccessible without inside connections or other pull. Zuyev added that in the year he applied, 100,000 tenth-year high school aspirants nationwide had applied for all twelve VVS and VPVO flight schools, with as many as 20,000 applying to Armavir alone. Only about 2,000 of the latter passed the rigorous physical and aptitude tests, with 300 ultimately selected for the Armavir class beginning in September 1978.

Screening and Selection

Because of the Soviet military's pervasive secrecy, little was published about the VVAUL system or the nature of a flying career in the VVS, apart from pamphlets that mainly played up the romance and patriotic appeal of military aviation.[3] As a result, in marked contrast to Western military pilot-recruiting practice, most information for interested Soviet youths was passed along by word of mouth, with family acquaintances from the retired pilot community often playing an important part.

Applications were solicited from civilian high school students, serving conscripts and career noncommissioned officers, reservists who had completed their compulsory service obligation, active-duty warrant officers, military construction personnel, and secondary school cadets in the Suvorov military and Nakhimov naval boarding schools.[4] The enrollment age window for civilian youths was 17–21 years, with age 23 being the cap for all other applicants. Interested high school students obtained information on available flight schools and application procedures from their town or regional military commissariat *(voyenkomat),* the Soviet equivalent of a U.S. draft board. Military personnel were directed to apply through their unit commander by April 1 of the desired year of entry. Civilians could apply to their *voyenkomat* up to May 1. In all cases, application was to a specifically requested VVAUL.

Initial screening tests were administered by the applicant's local *voyenkomat.* Those were followed by a series of three increasingly exacting medical examinations. Candidates were also screened for political rectitude and reliability, with especially close looks given to religious family members or any relatives who had traveled abroad. The successful applicant had to produce a strong character and political suitability recommendation from his paramilitary unit or high school military instructor.

Voyenkomat staffs would complete their prescreening by May 15 and forward their recommendations to the VVAULs by June 5. By June 30, the VVAULs would inform those applicants who had been selected when to arrive at the school for further testing. Admission of non-Russian or non-Slav candidates into either VVS or VPVO VVAULs was the exception to the rule, although such candidates often became outstanding and respected pilots.[5]

Those surviving the first cut proceeded by train to the VVAUL to which they had applied, where they lived under tents for four weeks of further physical, psychological, and academic testing. Throughout the evaluation and screening phase, all applicants were treated as conscripts and served standard conscript meals. Between examinations, they would do routine conscript work, such as unloading bricks from flatbeds, digging ditches, weeding fields, and laying concrete slabs for runways. During that time, they were closely observed and rank-ordered by the school staff.[6]

Medical standards were uncompromising, with qualifying applicants expected to meet the cosmonaut criteria of a Category 1 health certificate. In practice, most line MiG-29 and Su-27 pilots held a Category 2 certificate, which was only slightly less demanding. However, they had to maintain 20/20 vision (called "one-by-one" in the Soviet system). No pilots who wore glasses flew fighters in the VVS.[7]

The VVAUL written exam covered secondary school subjects, including mathematics and physics, Russian language and composition, and the history of the USSR. A special waiver was allowed for graduates of the Suvorov and Nakhimov military boarding schools and, in rare cases, for military applicants who had received the Hero of the Soviet Union award for valor. Those candidates were accepted without testing in general subjects, assuming that all other standards had been successfully met. The demanding mathematics and physics tests weeded out rural-area applicants whose high school preparation was substandard.

The physical fitness test included bar chin-ups, a timed 100-meter dash, a 3,000-meter cross-country run, and a 100-meter swim. The psychological exam consisted of a diagnostic questionnaire and other analytic tests. Applicants were also screened for motor skills, with the hand-eye coordination test being administered by means of a crude control stick and "gunsight" apparatus.

The evaluation process divided the candidates into three groups, ranging from qualified (Group One) through borderline (Group Two) to unqualified (Group Three). Those who made the final cut entered the fall course as beginning fourth-class cadets *(kursanty)*. Special amenities promised to cadets as aspiring career aviators included free meals seven days a week, forty-five days of paid leave annually, travel anywhere in the USSR on Aeroflot for a modest fee, and retirement at age forty with two-thirds pay for the rest of one's life. The best medical care in the USSR was also available, along with enormous social prestige and other privileges.[8]

The UPT Syllabus

At Armavir in 1978, according to Zuyev, the 1,100 cadets who made up the school's complement of pilot trainees were divided into four sections. The school followed an instruction plan that had half the cadets at any given time on deployment to outlying airfields for flight instruction on the L-29 or the MiG-21 and the other half at the school for academics or additional flying. Auxiliary training fields were remote from the school, often as far as 100 miles away.

During the first year, the daily schedule began with a 6:00 A.M. wake-up and forty-five seconds to dress for running and calisthenics, followed by wash-up and preparation of the barracks for inspection. Academic instruction began at 7:30 and continued for twelve hours, until 7:30 P.M., six days a week, with lights out at 10:00 P.M. Sunday was not free but involved cleanup duties, as well as mandatory lectures by the school's political officer *(zampolit)*. Zuyev remarked that the cadets hated those lectures and would often slip a flight manual inside their Marxist-Leninist texts to gain some value from what they otherwise considered a waste of time.[9]

Evidently there was little or no systematic hazing. Zuyev noted that VVAUL *kursanty* were aware that first-year cadets at U.S. military academies were regularly harassed by upperclassmen. He added: "We found that a totally alien concept. Here we needed mutual support to survive the rigorous work load."[10] However, there was an abundance of snitches *(stukachi)* among one's classmates and the staff who would readily tattle to the school's commander or, worse yet, to its KGB "special section" *(osoby otdel)* for any observed political indiscretions or other malfeasance. Cadets had to be wary at all times against these omnipresent spies.

Cadets were taught that U.S. pilots were able and courageous and would stay and fight rather than turn and run if confronted in the air. They also were briefed that the USAF used special psychological screening tests to identify and single out applicants with the greatest aptitude for combat flying.[11] Cadets were given security clearances and were allowed to read periodic intelligence reports on the U.S. and NATO air threat. Those writings were said to be straightforward, objective, and devoid of sermonizing.

Parachute training was mandatory and involved initial qualifying jumps from an An-2, with a minimum of two static-line jumps annually thereafter. Remarkably, the Soviets did not use altitude chambers, either in VVAULs or in operational units, to instruct aircrews to recognize their hypoxia symptoms, despite the Soviet awareness that foreign air forces routinely used such chambers for high-altitude indoctrination. The VVS did operate altitude chambers to conduct aeromedical research and, on occasion, to test aircrews for hypoxia susceptibility. But to this day, it does not conduct a regular physiological training program, even though aircrews and medical personnel have more than once called for one.[12] There also is no routine provision for aircrew G-awareness orientation and G-tolerance training on a centrifuge.[13]

Preflight instruction on the L-29 or the L-39 began at the end of the second semester of the first year of academics, with six months of flying commencing at the start of the second year after a summer vacation break. During the flight-training phase, wake-up was at 4:00 A.M. for an early breakfast, followed by as many as three sorties a day, with additional classroom academics in the afternoon. Short sorties were the rule, and it was common for cadets not to be cleared for solo flight until after thirty-six or more dual instruction rides. The L-29/L-39 primary phase included basic aircraft handling, navigation, formation, and aerobatics, with each training flight capped by a return to base on the automatic direction-finding (ADF) needle. Toward the end of basic training, cadets participated in a judged maneuver competition. The last year of the VVAUL program was devoted entirely to flying.

The flying program at Armavir during the early 1970s included 100 hours on the L-29 and 200 hours on the MiG-17, for a total of 300 dual and solo hours. A decade later, Zuyev completed the program with only 230 hours, all on the L-29. He was one of fifty top-graduating cadets in his class who converted from the L-29 directly to the MiG-23. Other cadets upgraded first to the MiG-21. The conversion syllabus began with an extensive ground school on aircraft systems and procedures, followed by initial flights in a two-seater. Later, as the L-29 was phased out and replaced by the more modern L-39, primary flight training in the VVS consisted of 60 hours, with basic training adding another 90 hours, the latter concentrating on air-to-air maneuvering, air-to-ground gunnery, two-ship tactical formation, and squadron-level flight activities.

Operational Conversion

Through the mid-1980s the VVS provided its prospective fighter pilots with initial qualification training on their assigned operational aircraft during the final year of the VVAUL course. Cadets graduated as basic pilots cleared to fly the MiG-21 or the MiG-23 only within a narrow band of operations, to include clear-weather takeoffs and landings, formation flight, and basic ground-attack and aerial maneuvering. They would then report to their assigned unit for upgrade training to full mission-ready status. Zuyev reported that agents from line regiments would visit Armavir and other VVAULs, much like U.S. professional sports coaches conduct college scouting tours for the most promising players.

The first squadron in a line fighter regiment accommodated the most seasoned pilots and was a dedicated air-to-air unit. The second squadron was made up of less-experienced pilots and performed the regiment's assigned secondary missions. New pilots out of the VVAULs reported to the third squadron, which was, in effect, a full-time top-off training unit. Regiment commanders found themselves saddled with as many as twenty-five new pilots at any given moment, facing the long road to mission readiness in an upgrade program that might continue for three years or more. That meant that at least one-third of any fighter regiment would be constantly operating in a requalification mode.[14]

That approach to operational conversion entailed a grossly inefficient division of regimental supervisory attention, for it meant that every commander was responsible not only for his unit's combat readiness but also for the dictates of a rudimentary upgrade program that typically worked at cross-purposes with his mission-readiness needs. The approach naturally fed a certain cynicism among the more hard-bitten senior pilots, who understandably were more interested in attending to their mission-employment concerns than nursemaiding wet-behind-the-ears newcomers from the VVAUL system. At a gathering of instructors in a converting MiG-23 unit convened to hear a briefing on the MiG-29's vaunted resistance to spinning and departures from controlled flight, one jaded colonel sitting in the back of the room gave vent to such impatience when he muttered skeptically: "Let some nonrated lieutenants fly it. *They* will find a way to spin it."[15]

To this day, the VVS pilot-upgrade syllabus is embedded in a document called the Combat Training Course (*Kurs boyevoi podgotovki,* or KBP). This document features a measured progression through the following aeronautical rating levels:

> *Pilot Third Class.* This bottom-rung rating typically requires a year of training after VVAUL graduation. It calls for 600 sorties overall, for about 350–400 hours of total flying time. On receiving this rating, the upgrading pilot is cleared to fly day-only training missions with weather minimums of a 750-foot ceiling and a half-mile visibility and in formations ranging from a four-ship flight to a full squadron of sixteen aircraft. The rating typically means the pilot has completed the first fifty-two syllabus "exercises" (each ranging from one to eight or more sorties) in the day portion of the KBP.

> *Pilot Second Class.* The next rating may take as many as three to four years after graduation. It requires 770 sorties, for around 450–500 hours of total flight time. Those pilots earning this rating are cleared to pull both day and night alert duty, are fully instrument flight rules (IFR) qualified, and are authorized to fly supervised ground-attack and air-combat training missions. They are allotted the same weather minimums as Third-Class pilots, with additional night minimums of a 3-mile visibility and a 1,500-foot ceiling. Second-class pilots are cleared for all conventional air-to-ground

mission events. Zuyev observed that getting past the written and practical instrument flight exams and night-formation qualification made the Second-Class rating the military pilot's toughest hurdle.

Pilot First Class. This rating requires 1,200 sorties, for a minimum of 550 hours of total flight time. Achieving it often took six to seven years beyond VVAUL graduation.[16] (A USAF pilot typically reaches this same experience level within two years or less.) First-Class pilots are fully IFR rated and are cleared to perform any standard mission event. Weather minimums are a 0.9-mile visibility and a 450-foot ceiling. The minimum currency requirement for maintaining a First-Class rating is 50 hours of total flying time a year, including 10 hours of day IFR flight.

Beyond the First-Class rating is a designation called "sniper pilot," said to be reserved for a few "highly experienced leaders."[17] It is not a formal aeronautical rating but rather is more akin to a VVS seal of approval for demonstrated professionalism, experience, and incident-free flying. Sniper pilots must have a First-Class rating and a minimum of 1,500 hours of total time. They are not necessarily the best pilots in the VVS but rather are those favored by the system or otherwise commanding either special pull or longevity. One VVS general told me that the designation is meaningless as far as formally evaluated airmanship is concerned and that the highest proficiency level recognized by the KBP is the First-Class pilot rating.

At the pinnacle of the VVS pilot hierarchy is yet another rating (or, more correctly, decoration) called "Honored Military Pilot." The few bearers of this coveted honorific typically include the commander in chief, his principal deputies, the commanders in chief of the major commands, and a scattering of fast-burner regiment commanders marked for a rapid climb up the career ladder. It is awarded for special aeronautical and professional accomplishment.

Post-Soviet Changes in the UPT System

One of the most serious weaknesses in the Soviet approach to military pilot selection was its provision that allowed each aspirant to pick the aircraft and mission type for which he would compete. That shortcoming was spotlighted in a comment made in 1993 by the chief of the Russian VVS's Cadres Training and Assignment Directorate, who noted that applicants were expected to indicate to their *voyenkomat* the name of the VVAUL they "wished to attend."[18] Such an approach may well have ensured that only the most promising and capable cadets accepted into any VVAUL would successfully complete the training program and earn wings. However, because it did nothing to stream the right *kinds* of candidates to those schools where they would be best suited by temperament and abilities to begin with, there was no way of guaranteeing that the best young men in the country for fighter pilot training, for example, would be properly identified and vectored toward such training.

The Soviet approach to VVAUL training was sharply criticized in 1990 by Lieutenant General Nikolai Antoshkin, air commander for the Moscow Military District. Antoshkin complained that the program was churning out too many graduates who were "neither pilots nor engineers" and whose inadequate airmanship skills were putting an excess burden on line regiments, making the latter, in effect, basic training units to pick up the slack left by a deficient VVAUL syllabus.[19] A deputy VVAUL commander concurred, attributing the poor quality of VVAUL graduates to excessively low required performance levels and "rigid restrictions" on what was allowable in UPT training.[20] That, in his view, meant simply handing off unresolved problems to line regiments, leading to a situation that could be rectified only by the top VVS leadership.[21] Evidently the first deputy commander in chief of the Russian VVS, Colonel General Viktor Kot, agreed, since he said that the VVAUL course was "the weakest link" in the VVS military education system.[22]

A new approach to UPT training was first aired as early as 1988 by the VVS deputy commander for education and training, Colonel General A. Goryainov. Commenting on the high washout rate of cadets during the primary phase, Goryainov proposed a new look at VVAUL selection criteria, with greater emphasis on applicants' emotional stability and their ability to refocus attention quickly. Goryainov noted that many cadets who had been deselected shortly after their first solo flight could have been eliminated sooner, more economically, and with less emotional trauma had there been adequate screening criteria to detect their deficiency early on. He admitted frankly that VVAUL candidate-selection methods were "weak" and that the VVS needed more support from the human resources community.[23]

By the end of 1988 the VVS abandoned operational conversion in the VVAULs, whereby fourth-year cadets in the fighter pipeline completed an initial checkout on the MiG-21 or the MiG-23 before being handed off to line units for upgrading and final mission-qualification training. Partly as a cost-saving measure, the schools had already begun instructing on a single aircraft type (either the L-29 or the L-39), with graduates proceeding to the equivalent of a USAF replacement training unit (RTU) for initial qualification training on their assigned combat aircraft. During the RTU course, students concurrently earned a Third-Class pilot rating before proceeding to their assigned unit for top-off training.

The VVS's purpose in introducing this new RTU arrangement, called an Aviation Training Center (*Uchebno-aviatsionny tsentr*), was to relieve line unit commanders of much of their former conversion-training burden. It remains unclear, however, how well the new system has performed in that respect. One weapons instructor in a fighter regiment complained as early as 1990 that the UPT and RTU phases were still not satisfactorily attending to the full spectrum of training needs, since "a significant portion of the workload for aircrew training" was still being passed on to line units. Consequently, he observed, operational squadrons still resembled flying school units and were "stretched to the limit just to upgrade and certify their pilots." He added, "Because of this, there can be no advanced training in the intended sense of the term." His implied message seemed to be that the VVAULs and RTUs needed to work on sending a better product to line units so that squadron commanders could pursue an orderly aircrew mission-certification plan without feeling constantly driven to dedicate extra sorties toward remedial instruction of their new pilots.[24]

Shortly after the MiG-29 entered service in 1987, the VVS conducted an experiment in which the best graduates from the Chernigov VVAUL were selected to convert directly to the new fighter in the guards regiment at Kubinka.[25] In earlier times, the standard practice had been to upgrade only experienced pilots onto new equipment in the initial cadre. The MiG-29, however, proved uniquely forgiving to new VVAUL graduates. Initial conversion was provided by the advanced tactical training and evaluation center at Lipetsk, the VVS's main fighter weapons and tactics facility. In a precursor to that approach, Zuyev participated in the third MiG-29 checkout course at Lipetsk, during which he received a month of academics on aircraft systems but no flight training. Afterward, he returned to his new unit and was given a local-area checkout, from initial qualification to full mission readiness, entailing 46 sorties.

Since those early efforts toward VVAUL reform during the USSR's final years, UPT in the VVS has undergone a top-to-bottom change. Under the previous system, an aspiring pilot would receive initial flight orientation in a paramilitary club during his secondary school years. He would then enter the four-year VVAUL regime, which combined officer, engineering, and flight training through initial conversion to a combat aircraft type. In contrast, the new system approved in 1992 by Colonel General Pyotr Deinekin entailed initial flight orientation in secondary boarding schools, followed by screening and selection for a *five*-year VVAUL program, with flight training solely on the L-39.[26] Entering cadets under this new arrangement received three years of full-time classroom instruction and officership training. Only afterward would it be determined whether they would continue on from academics to the flying phase, which was now compressed into two years rather than spread out over three as before.

Those cadets cleared to continue in the flying program receive generic flight instruction on the L-39 and then transition to their assigned operational aircraft at an RTU following UPT graduation and commissioning. One goal of those changes, said General Deinekin, was to ensure that cadets entering the primary flying phase would be intellectually mature young men rather than "17-year old greenhorns incapable of controlling not only an aircraft but themselves." General Antoshkin added that the VVS had begun "looking toward an RAF [Royal Air Force]–style streaming system." If a fast-jet student failed to make the grade, even at a late stage of training, he would have "no opportunity of flying any type of aircraft."[27]

The first two boarding schools, collocated at the Yeisk and Barnaul VVAULs, opened their doors to aspiring high school students in September 1990. They were not VVS schools but rather were operated as a part of the national educational system. Male students between fifteen and sixteen years old who had completed junior high school and were physically qualified for pilot training were eligible for admission, with preference going to those who had received initial flight orientation in paramilitary flying clubs.[28] Early, optimistic portrayals of the boarding school system envisaged tenth-grade students receiving 25 hours of screening instruction in the L-39, with eleventh-grade students logging an additional 15 hours, plus the initial portions of pre-VVAUL ground school training.

Whatever the underlying rationale, offering callow high school youths such extensive exposure to a complex jet aircraft like the L-39 in a mere flight familiarization and screening program made little sense from either a training or a cost perspective. If that idea ever got past the talking stage in the paramilitary training system before the latter folded in 1991, it almost surely failed to survive the deep budget cuts that later afflicted Russian military aviation across the board. Even in the best of circumstances, Western aviation professionals would have faulted it as a needlessly expensive and counterproductive extravagance.

The Russian VVS's roster of schools for pilot and other officer specialty training has been trimmed considerably from that of the former Soviet VVS. Of the twelve original VVAULs, the VVS has been left with only four: the Kacha VVAUL, near Volgograd and named for A. F. Myasnikov, for fighter pilots; the Tambov VVAUL, named for M. M. Raskovoi, for bomber pilots; the Barnaul VVAUL, named for Marshal of Aviation K. A. Vershinin, for ground-attack pilots; and the Balashov VVAUL, named for Chief Marshal of Aviation A. A. Novikov, for transport pilots.[29] Navigators are trained at the Chelyabinsk flight school. Military air traffic controllers get their training at the former VVAUL at Yeisk.[30] The Zhukovsky Air Force Engineering Academy in Moscow trains maintenance officers in aircraft and power plant, armament, avionics, and electrical systems. The VVS lost the Chernigov and Kharkov VVAULs and the Lugansk navigator school to other republics in the wake of the USSR's breakup. The Sysansk and Saratov VVAULs for helicopter pilots were transferred to the ground forces when the latter took over all rotary-wing aviation. Two former Soviet VVAULs were combined into a single school at Tambov for prospective multiengine naval and VTA pilots.

At the outset of that scaled-back approach, General Goryainov indicated that there was no shortage of VVAUL applicants, that annual vacancies were being filled, and that the schools were operating at full capacity. Yet he conceded a need to raise the level of competition and to improve initial screening in the interest of getting stronger candidates. In 1995 there were five applicants for each vacancy at Barnaul, where prospective Su-24 and Su-25 pilots receive introductory flight training. However, cadets by that time were receiving only 150 hours of primary and basic instruction on the L-39, as contrasted with 220 to 230 hours during the Soviet period and with a planned 200 hours when the post-Soviet VVAUL system was first inaugurated. The fuel shortage and lack of spares further undermined the intensity and tempo of VVAUL training. In 1995 there were 300 students in three training units at Barnaul, but typically no more than 12 of the 80 L-39s at the Kamen-on-Ob auxiliary airfield were mission-capable at any given time.[31]

Instructor Pilot Selection and Training

The VVS maintains three categories of instructor pilots (IPs): flight examiners in operational squadrons, RTU instructors, and basic flight instructors in the VVAULs. In line units, flight commanders and senior supervisors typically maintain IP status on their assigned aircraft type. Each regiment offers an IP upgrade course, and IPs in operational units are all First-Class pilots.[32] Those in RTUs have all had previous operational experience. Instructors in the VVAULs occupy the lowest rung on the ladder and are more often than not stuck in a dead-end job. A majority of VVAUL instructors are "plowbacks"—VVAUL graduates assigned directly to UPT training duty with no operational experience.

Before the USSR's collapse, General Goryainov conceded that VVAUL instructors led a bleak existence, typically working ten to twelve hours each day and living in cramped quarters offering no privacy to themselves or their families. He further confirmed that IP status in the VVAUL system offered few career prospects. Sorry living conditions at auxiliary airfields drove officers away from any interest in serving as flight instructors. Another disincentive was rotating temporary-duty assignments at remote training airfields, which forced pilots to remain separated from their wives and families often for months on end. Belenko called being a VVAUL instructor "the worst duty conceivable."[33]

The commander of the Kharkov VVAUL stated, shortly before the USSR collapsed, that VVAUL instructors should be selected competitively from among Second- or First-Class pilots in line units.[34] General Goryainov, however, announced the inauguration of a new system in which potential VVAUL instructors would be selected from among those graduating cadets found to possess a "special talent" for instruction, thus confirming that primary reliance on plowbacks would continue. As for whether cadets with their hearts set on operational flying would ever consent to enter such a program voluntarily, Goryainov acknowledged that the belief "those who can't do, teach" remained widespread. He further conceded that only "dire circumstances" would impel a line combat pilot to request assignment as a VVAUL instructor. Goryainov disagreed that only operationally experienced pilots would make good VVAUL instructors. He did, however, insist that only First-Class pilots should serve as IPs in the VVAULs. He also rejected the idea that VVAUL IPs picked from line units should continue to fly their former operational aircraft, since their combat proficiency could never be maintained at the level required by published VVS mission-readiness standards.[35]

In 1991 one VVAUL instructor complained that the system that had been allowed to devolve over the past decades had produced a sharp decline in the professionalism of Soviet military flight instruction: "The old is forgotten, and anything new that goes beyond the bounds of what is officially allowed is proscribed." He noted that IPs searched in vain for a legendary instructional techniques manual written in 1953 by one G. Golubev. Nothing had since been issued to replace it. The teaching of instructional techniques, moreover, was derided by experienced instructors as comparable "only to the antiliteracy campaign at the beginning of the 1920s." The IP career track itself was portrayed as the ultimate explanation for its lack of professional appeal. As one disaffected flyer put it: "What combat pilot would agree to abandon his line unit for a VVAUL, his combat aircraft for a trainer, his higher pay for low pay, and his agreeable work schedule for the exhausting duty of a training regiment?"[36]

Toward the end of the Soviet era VVAUL instructors, acting much in the manner of combined big brother and watchdog, handled up to six students at a time. They often flew up to nine instructional sorties in a day that began with a pickup at 4:00 A.M. The flying was typically unchallenging (Belenko commented from his own experience that after the fortieth loop of the day, "a loop was not so interesting.")[37] Like most line units, VVAUL squadrons lacked computers to facilitate record-keeping by instructors. As a result, the squadron commander and his deputy were obliged to spend a minimum of three to four hours out of a fourteen-to-sixteen-hour workday building the next day's training schedule by hand.

The individual IP was only a cog in the wheel of that encrusted system, with his every step monitored and "with no initiative permitted in any case."[38] Commanders and other supervisors routinely did the thinking for instructors and second-guessed their every suggestion, particularly regarding the elimination of failing cadets. According to Zuyev, the school's leadership placed considerable pressure on instructors to shepherd slow learners through the syllabus. VVAUL commanders were reluctant to wash out a marginal performer because of the

Communist Party's requirement that VVS pilot-production norms be unwaveringly met.

For their part, IPs were "gripped in a vise of documents regulating flight operations" and were allowed little freedom to decide how to teach, what methods to use, or even what subjects to emphasize. Inevitably, a pronounced morale problem arose. One bitter instructor explained: "Working with one eye constantly on one's superior officers instills a feeling of fear, never mind any inclination toward showing initiative or creativity. This fear, in turn, engenders a lack of confidence in one's actions. I see this as the reason for the pessimistic and dispirited mood among pilots in many regiments."[39]

Issues in Training Philosophy

With the onset of glasnost, Soviet pilots grew increasingly voluble about the self-imposed deficiencies of the VVS's hypercautious approach to flight training at all levels. A case in point was the discontent over the VVS's summary abandonment of a spin-recovery training program. Shortly after the introduction of the L-39 into the VVAUL system, the aircraft showed resistance to entering a spin and an inability to recover from a spin once forced into one in some conditions of flight. Subsequently, the previously mandatory spin-training portion of the VVAUL syllabus was eliminated. As of the spring of 1990, spin training in the L-39 remained prohibited.

A VVS colonel questioned the sense of that approach, noting that one could teach a student to handle an aircraft to its full maneuver capabilities either by instilling habits that would never produce stall and spin conditions or by actually demonstrating stalls and spins so that students would truly know their aircraft and the recovery techniques that worked best. The VVAULs, he noted, still followed the former approach. Yet that hypercautiousness did not prevent students from flying into unusual situations that resulted in departures from controlled flight. Citing a confidential survey of MiG-21 instructors, the colonel noted that many instructors did not fly their aircraft into heavy buffet, even though they might remain well short of the aircraft's threshold of departure from controlled flight. Because of such arrested training, he said, pilots were consistently failing to extract the full extent of the aircraft's maneuver and performance capabilities.[40]

Not long afterward, an experienced test pilot and two Mikoyan Design Bureau engineers wrote an article in which they concurred with the VVS colonel. They explained how the ban on spin training in the L-39 had been a result both of "subjective views of individuals" and, even more, of the "concepts for air power application that had taken shape" during the 1960s and 1970s. They further noted that during the years when spin training had been routine, the loss rate of aircraft to departures from controlled flight was low and that line pilots entered maneuvering engagements with confidence in their ability to handle the aircraft. Spin-recovery training in the MiG-15 was standard until the VVS commander in chief banned it, purportedly because the loss rate in the VVAULs was exceeding the loss rate in line MiG-15 squadrons. The authors attributed that negative attitude to the changed VVS and VPVO training approach, which had begun during the early 1960s when the main air-to-air mission profile consisted of a single-pass missile attack against a high-speed, high-altitude target and required no hard maneuvering.[41]

With the renewed emphasis on maneuvering air combat in the 1970s, a resurgent premium was placed on the importance of advanced aircraft-handling skills. Since aggressively flying to angle-of-attack (AOA) limits is intrinsic to close-in maneuvering air combat, pilots needed to gain full confidence in their aircraft's handling characteristics by experiencing those characteristics firsthand through spin training. Without such confidence, they would never extract the most out of their aircraft's performance, owing to a constant fear of departing from controlled flight.[42] As a first step toward a remedy, the authors of the article recommended establishing a nucleus of instructors in a setting such as the civilian test pilot school at the Gromov Flight Research Institute at Zhukovsky to develop a syllabus for safe spin training for VVAUL cadets.

Another input into this debate was an article noting that full operational leverage could be attained only by flying an airplane to its limits and that this remained all but impossible because of "tight restrictions," in the interest of safety, on such flight parameters as G and AOA. The writer of the article, a retired colonel, stated that VVAUL and RTU students were not being systematically exposed to flying aircraft to their aerodynamic limits, with the result that inadvertently approaching the edge of the performance envelope could cause them to aggravate rather than correct an incipient problem. He insisted that mastering "prohibited" flight regimes was dictated not only because pilots could inadvertently enter them but also because in combat (such as Soviet pilots had repeatedly seen in Afghanistan) the instinct for survival will inevitably force pilots into flight regimes that go beyond published restrictions.[43]

The colonel added, "The existing system for determining restrictions is imperfect and in serious need of correction." He cited the inherent tension between peacetime concerns for maintaining safety and wartime concerns for ensuring maximum combat effectiveness, with the former calling for tighter restrictions and the latter for looser ones. He argued that since pilots in combat will surely exceed published limits in the interest of winning—or surviving—they must learn during peacetime what to expect at all corners of the flight envelope. Revealingly, he noted that after the introduction of the MiG-21 into operational service, there had not been a single case of a pilot recovering successfully from an inadvertent spin. Naturally, because of the great altitude loss involved and the uncertainty of recovery, he did not advocate spin training in high-performance aircraft. He did, however, call for hands-on familiarization with aircraft handling and performance characteristics in the stall and post-stall regions of flight in the interest of spin-entry recognition and prevention.[44]

Mikoyan MiG-21MF. *Top:* The world's most prolific jet fighter, with more than ten thousand produced since it first flew in 1955, this definitive version of the classic MiG-21 lifts off for an air-to-ground range mission carrying a pod of high-velocity rockets under each wing. The aircraft was retired from Russian VVS service in 1993 but continues to soldier on in many other air forces around the world. (Reprinted by permission from *Russian Aircraft.* Copyright © Mashinostroyeniye Publishers)

Mikoyan MiG-29. *Above:* Shown here with a load of two R-60, two R- 27, and two R-33 air-to-air missiles (NATO-designated AA-8 Aphid, AA-10 Alamo, and AA-11 Archer, respectively), the Mikoyan Design Bureau's most acclaimed product is unmatched in instantaneous turn rate and overall agility, although it suffers limited engagement time compared with its Western counterparts due to its lower internal fuel capacity. The latest versions have been provided with extra internal fuel, as well as with improved ground-attack systems to give the aircraft a better multirole capability. (Reprinted by permission from *Russian Aircraft.* Copyright © Mashinostroyeniye Publishers)

Mikoyan MiG-31. *Top:* A development of the MiG-25 featuring a second crew station for a radar-intercept officer and trading off the former's Mach 2.8 top speed for greater endurance and a lower-altitude supersonic capability, the MiG-31, shown here over the Kamchatka Peninsula in the far east of Russia, mounts a radar with a search range of greater than 120 miles and a track-while-scan capability that can handle up to fourteen targets simultaneously. The aircraft is a mainstay of the VPVO interceptor inventory today. (Photo courtesy AviaData/Arms Communications)

Sukhoi Su-24. *Above:* Called a "tactical bomber" in VVS parlance, this Soviet counterpart to the USAF's swing-wing F-111 carries a pilot and navigator and mounts a terrain-following radar enabling night and all-weather penetration of enemy airspace at low level. The supersonic jet was the VVS's primary weapon for deep interdiction and airfield attack in NATO's rear from the mid-1970s until the end of the cold war. A reconnaissance variant was used for gathering target intelligence during the 1994–95 war in Chechnya. (Photo courtesy Hans Halberstadt/Military Stock Photography)

Sukhoi Su-25UB. *Top:* This two-seat trainer version of the VVS's premier close-support aircraft is directed to parking after a tactical range mission to fire high-velocity rockets. The heavily armored jet, seemingly built of angle-iron and with an ungainly appearance to match, was inspired by the USAF's A-10 tank killer and was similarly designed for survivability. Although subsonic, it reportedly suffered only twenty-three losses to enemy ground fire out of some sixty thousand combat missions in Afghanistan. (Photo courtesy Hans Halberstadt/Military Stock Photography)

Tupolev Tu-95. *Above:* LRA's sole surviving strategic bomber first flew in 1952 and served nearly four decades in the intercontinental nuclear attack role. Like this carcass languishing at the Engels heavy bomber base 520 miles southeast of Moscow, many were cut up in compliance with the START I agreement. The sixty-odd Tu-95MS versions remaining in service are expected to motor on for twenty more years as long-range conventional cruise-missile carriers. (Photo courtesy U.S. Department of Defense)

Ilyushin Il-76. *Top:* The main workhorse of VTA since the early 1970s, the Il-76 is most closely comparable to the USAF's C-141 in size and mission. Although nearly half of the Soviet VTA inventory of these aircraft went to the non-Russian newly independent states when the USSR fell apart, the remaining three hundred, although stretched to the limit, provided commendable support to Russia's otherwise failed attempt, in 1994–95, to suppress the Chechen rebellion. (Photo courtesy Hans Halberstadt/Military Stock Photography)

Antonov An-124. *Above:* This mammoth airlifter is Russia's counterpart to the USAF's C-5A Galaxy and is the world's largest production aircraft, with some twenty-five having been manufactured to support VTA's lift requirements for oversize and outsize cargo. Most now fly with civil registrations and Aeroflot livery and are used for private-contract deliveries to raise much-needed nonbudget revenue for the VVS. (Photo courtesy Hans Halberstadt/Military Stock Photography)

The morning brief. *Left:* Lieutenant Colonel Vladimir Basov, an Honored Military Pilot and leader of the VVS's Su-27 flight-demonstration team, outlines the day's operations plan to assembled aircrews at the VVS fighter base at Kubinka southwest of Moscow. Before Russia's financial crisis put a stranglehold on VVS training, each flying day began with an all-hands overview of planned events and ended with a mass debrief. (Photo courtesy Hans Halberstadt/Military Stock Photography)

Mission planning. *Above:* During the cold war, Soviet fighter and ground-attack pilots alternated between flight-planning days and flying days. Like these pilots at the Kubinka fighter base, they would not only ensure that they had covered all the operational and safety-of-flight considerations pertinent to their upcoming sorties but also script out in advance every anticipated maneuver, from takeoff to landing. That process guaranteed a highly canned and stereotyped approach to mission employment, in contrast to the more free-form and adaptive Western style. (Photo courtesy Hans Halberstadt/Military Stock Photography)

Final acceptance. *Right:* A snow-dusted MiG-25 pilot at the Kotlas air base in northern Russia signs out his aircraft with the maintenance crew chief (always an officer in both the Soviet and Russian systems) after a last-minute walkaround inspection to verify that the aircraft is flightworthy. He has yet to don the hard protective shell and visor over his vintage leather helmet. (Carey Schofield, *Inside the Soviet Military,* New York: Abbeville Press, 1991. Photograph by Leonid Yakutin, reprinted here by kind permission of Calmann & King Ltd., London. Copyright © 1991 Calmann & King Ltd.)

"That's right . . . just like this." *Above:* Using one's hands to describe maneuvering flight has been a trademark of fighter pilots since the earliest days of military aviation. In the VVS, however, pilots like this Su-17M instructor and student were taught to perform maneuvers "by the book" to an extent that Western pilots would find devoid of room for improvisation or adaptability. Russian pilots have since acknowledged that this practice was one of the most serious weaknesses in their operational repertoire. (Reprinted by permission from *Russian Aircraft.* Copyright © Mashinostroyeniye Publishers)

Waiting in sequence. The crew of a Su-24, navigator on the left and pilot on the right, sit strapped in with their canopies open, standing by for clearance to start the engines. The navigator is wearing an earlier-generation helmet, with an externally mounted visor. The pilot sports the most recent model, with an internal visor and holes across the top to aid in helmet retention in case of a high-speed ejection. (Carey Schofield, *Inside the Soviet Military,* New York: Abbeville Press, 1991. Photograph by Leonid Yakutin, reprinted here by kind permission of Calmann & King Ltd., London. Copyright © 1991 Calmann & King Ltd.)

"Cleared for takeoff." *Top:* The ground-based supervisor of flying was the quarterback of Soviet VVS fighter training, especially when it came to air-to-air maneuvering. Serving not only as the principal controller but also, in effect, as the mission commander, he ensured that all major in-flight moves were directed by ground control. He also made many decisions, including emergency decisions, that would routinely be made by the pilot in Western practice. (Photo courtesy of Hans Halberstadt/Military Stock Photography)

Airborne and climbing. *Above:* This formation takeoff by two MiG-21UB two-seaters, with the wingman staggered as far back as 75 feet from his leader, reflects standard Soviet and Russian VVS practice and entails sufficient aircraft separation to amount almost to separate single-ship takeoffs in close proximity. The extended periscope apparent over the aft cockpit of the lead aircraft is a common Soviet design feature that allows the instructor visibility over the nose whenever the landing gear is extended. (Reprinted by permission from *Russian Aircraft.* Copyright © Mashinostroyeniye Publishers)

Crème de la crème à la Russe.
Left: Valery Menitsky, Mikoyan's chief test pilot, enters the headquarters building at Kubinka air base, after a short ferry mission from the Soviet flight-test center at Zhukovsky, for the author's MiG-29 flight in December 1989. The equivalent in rank of a VVS major general before his retirement from flying in 1993, Menitsky remains one of Russia's most experienced and honored pilots. In 1990, with the cold war winding down, he became the first Soviet aviator invited to address and accept membership in the U.S.-headquartered Society of Experimental Test Pilots. (Photo courtesy Benjamin S. Lambeth)

En route procedures. *Top:* The navigator of a Beriyev A-50 AWACS operating out of Pechora in northern Russia monitors mission progress using a slide rule. Even at this advanced stage of the computer age, slide rules remain standard equipment in today's cash-strapped VVS and VPVO. (Photo courtesy AviaData/Arms Communications)

Hail fellows well met. *Left photo:* Like their counterparts around the world, Russia's fighter pilots are professionals to the core yet are also relaxed and generally have a keen sense of humor. Against the backdrop of an Il-76, Lieutenant Colonel Vladimir Basov *(left)*, in camouflaged winter flight suit and jacket, and Lieutenant Colonel Aleksandr Kutuzov *(second from right)*, leader of the VVS's MiG-29 flight-demonstration team, share a moment of levity with two other officers at Kubinka air base. (Photo courtesy Hans Halberstadt/Military Stock Photography)

Russia's top fighter general. *Right photo:* Lieutenant General Nikolai Antoshkin *(right)* and another VVS pilot at Kubinka air base show off the latest fashion in Russian flight gear, including the cutaway G-suit normally worn by Russian aircrews underneath rather than over their flight suits. Air commander for the Moscow Military District at the time of the USSR's collapse, Antoshkin was later named commander of the Russian VVS's short-lived KFA until it was disestablished by a Defense Ministry decree in 1997. (Photo courtesy Hans Halberstadt/Military Stock Photography)

The commander in chief. *Left:* Colonel General Pyotr Deinekin, head of the VVS from the last months of the USSR until December 1997, sits in the cockpit of a USAF B-52 bomber during his visit to the United States in 1992 at the invitation of the USAF's chief of staff, General Merrill McPeak. Deinekin, a 5,000-hour bomber pilot who was qualified in the Tu-160, flew the USAF's B-1B from the aircraft commander's seat during that visit. (Photo courtesy U.S. Air Force)

Weather recce. *Above:* Day-to-day operations at Soviet fighter bases in East Germany would begin with an early-morning weather reconnaissance mission flown by a two-seat fighter carrying a regimental observer to ensure that local conditions met the required minimums for the day's planned training sorties. Here a MiG-23UB two-seater, its speed brakes extended for a pre-takeoff check, prepares to taxi past a toned-down and hardened bunker, which typified the Soviet VVS's spartan facilities in the Warsaw Pact forward area throughout most of the cold war. (Photo courtesy Stefan Petersen)

A farewell to Soviet arms. *Top:* Three pilots of the 19th Guards Fighter-Bomber Aviation Regiment at the Soviet VVS's Mirow air base in the former East Germany stand proudly in review as one of their unit's last MiG-27s taxies out to the runway for its return flight to Russia, bearing melancholy witness to the final chapter closed in the VVS's long history of forward operations in now-reunited Germany. (Photo courtesy Jan Jorgensen)

The look of tomorrow? *Above:* In January 1999 MiG-MAPO finally unveiled its long-awaited Article 1.42 fifth-generation fighter prototype, which Mikoyan spokesmen had been touting for years as Russia's answer to the USAF's F-22 stealth air-combat fighter. Alluded to by some VVS leaders as the MiG-37, the aircraft is indisputedly in a class ahead of Mikoyan's MiG-29, which it was designed to succeed. However, Western experts have questioned its stealth characteristics, and the continuing Russian financial crisis makes it almost certain that the aircraft will be flown as a technology demonstrator only. (Photo courtesy *Aviation Week and Space Technology*)

5.   Combat Training in Front-Line Units

Western analysts first began paying serious attention to Soviet air-combat train-ing and operational style during the mid-1970s, roughly coincident with the es-tablishment of the USAF's Aggressor program and realistic large-force training exercises like Red Flag, which had been designed and implemented to correct the aircrew training deficiencies unmasked by the surprisingly poor U.S. combat per-formance in Vietnam. For most of the decade that followed, Soviet tactical air training remained an object of intense interest, as well as extensive guesswork, throughout both the air intelligence and the fighter communities. Because con-clusive evidence about the character and quality of Soviet training was largely in-accessible, impressions of Soviet air-combat prowess were based heavily on ob-served practices of the air forces of Moscow's military client states, most notably North Vietnam, Egypt, and Syria. These impressions gained further reinforce-ment from the informed comments of occasional defectors and from various in-ferences drawn from a close reading of articles in the VVS monthly magazine and other Soviet military writings. From such fragmentary evidence, the Soviet pilot appeared to be bound by a heavily scripted repertoire that was almost com-pletely dominated by close control from the ground. That control, it was gener-ally thought, left him little room for exercising the free-form initiative and adapt-ability that had long been a hallmark of Western tactical air practice.

Analysts disagreed considerably, however, over the extent to which that as-sumed weakness was an inherent condition of Soviet fighter aviation and, even so, whether it mattered much in a military establishment that was widely be-lieved to be ready, as a matter of principle, to trade high loss rates for victory. In-tense debates ensued as protagonists for both schools of thought sought to justify their interpretations of the Soviet air challenge, with each side drawing sustenance from the inherent ambiguity surrounding much of the limited information on the Soviet fighter arm and its training activities.

Contrasting Western Views before the USSR's Collapse

Two stereotypes of the Soviet tactical air challenge vied for dominance in the West throughout the latter years of the cold war. One was the view typically propounded in official documents like the U.S. Defense Department's *Soviet Military Power* report and formal threat appraisals used to support the Pentagon's annual budget requests to Congress. That carefully hedged view was based largely on such known tangibles as aircraft and weapons capabilities, observed operational performance, force structure and size, and related quantifiables. In essence, it maintained that the Soviet VVS outnumbered NATO in fighter strength and was making steady advances in equipment, advances that promised to narrow, if not eradicate, the West's perceived edge in air-combat prowess.

This worst-case perspective tended to magnify the Soviet air threat by drawing linear inferences from such proven measurables as range-payload capability and radar and missile performance envelopes and extrapolating assumed operating attributes of Soviet equipment from those measurables, without much thought given to how that equipment might actually be used in a combat setting. For example, in stipulating that a Su-24 tactical bomber with a standard weapons load could fly, say, 700 nautical miles to a designated target deep inside NATO territory and return home, most analysts failed to consider whether a typical captain in a typical VVS Su-24 squadron had the required proficiency and adaptability actually to fly critical portions of that route at low altitude, in marginal weather, in the face of determined NATO opposition, and find the target and achieve the planned mission results.

A second, and very different, view predominated among U.S. and allied fighter pilots armed with the requisite security clearance and appropriate access to give informed consideration to the question. This view held that however impressive the VVS's equipment and order of battle might appear on paper, the Soviet pilot was poorly trained by Western standards and represented a weak link that could be exploited. He was seen as merely a cog in a wheel, as a rigid "by-the-book" aviator who deferred to his ground controller on all important decisions, and above all as the product of an operational culture that made a point of teaching him not to do much thinking for himself.

Typical of the latter view was the appraisal by a USAF Aggressor squadron commander who was as well versed in Soviet fighter tactics as any Westerner could be, given the constraints of the time. In 1981 this USAF officer asked: "Exactly how good is the enemy? Is he a ten-foot giant? Not exactly. In fact, without exaggerating, one could place him in the mediocre to poor category when it comes to air-combat capability. Certainly his equipment has not improved at nearly the rate ours has. Most important, however, Soviet training is so inferior to ours that this could well be the deciding factor in the outcome of the next conflict."[1] That appraisal was based in part on the poor Soviet showing a decade earlier, when five Soviet-flown MiG-21s were deftly dispatched by Israeli F-4s and Mirages in an intense five-minute engagement over Suez during the 1970 War of Attrition.[2] It was further supported by the known fact that Soviet air doctrine required most sorties to be flown under the constant control of a ground-based mission supervisor, with the added proviso that if contact with the controller was lost, the mission was to be aborted.[3]

A USAF threat analyst no less well informed on Soviet operational practice attempted to discredit this view by challenging its alleged tendency to dismiss the Soviet fighter pilot as "virtually a puppet, rigidly controlled by GCI and acting as little more than flying artillery." In her counterargument, she insisted: "The situation has changed considerably in the last few years. The Soviets have entered a period of intense study and discussion of their theory of tactics and are beginning to implement changes in their operational training."[4] A comparable claim was reflected in the U.S. Defense Department's 1983 edition of *Soviet Military Power,* which declared: "The Soviets have recently made significant changes in their air-combat tactics and training programs. Pilot independence and initiative are now stressed."[5]

Despite heated contention over such questions, however, the prevailing view among U.S. aircrews who paid close attention to the issue was that the typical Soviet fighter pilot was probably up to Western standards in his basic flying ability yet remained largely untutored in the maneuvering skills, situation awareness, and tactical mindset that made the crucial difference between winning and losing in a dynamic, multiparticipant aerial combat engagement. That image was reinforced by the heavily choreographed and clumsy manner in which Soviet interceptors engaged and shot down Korean Air Lines Flight 007 in September 1983. As indicated in detail by the published transcript of air-to-ground communications between the Su-15 pilot and his GCI controller, the intercept was a model of confusion and directed behavior from start to finish.[6] It took the Soviet pilot a full fourteen minutes to down the 747 after his initial reported visual contact. During that period, he was vectored all over the sky by his controller even as he had the aircraft in sight. At one point during the intercept, he closed to within 6,000 feet of the target. But he never positively identified it or showed any other sign of initiative in the situation.

Granted, that debacle was conducted by the separate VPVO rather than by VVS fighters, which operated under somewhat looser constraints during vectored intercepts. Nevertheless, it was characteristic of the Soviet military's tendency to deny its combat aircrews much room for exercising individual initiative or independent judgment. Almost up to the demise of the USSR, disagreements persisted over the ultimate meaning that this seemingly rigid operating style had for overall Soviet war-fighting capability. Yet most U.S. fighter pilots seemed ready to accept as axiomatic the following characterization offered by a U.S. Naval Reserve F-4 pilot: "I have found that asking two U.S. pilots for their tactics in a given situation elicits three different answers. By contrast, it is my understanding that three Russian fighter pilots will all give the same answer."[7]

That impression gained powerful backing from a British aviation writer's 1986 account based on interviews with Indian Air Force pilots, who spoke freely of their frustrations while undergoing MiG-21 conversion training in the USSR during the early 1970s.[8] Although those interviews reflected dated information, they dovetailed nicely with the picture offered by subsequent indicators, including line pilots' periodic veiled complaints voiced in the VVS monthly journal. The essence of that picture was that continuity had outweighed change during the intervening years.

According to that 1986 account, the VVS followed, throughout the service life of the MiG-21, a syllabus approach that assumed the student had an almost complete lack of understanding of fighter aircraft, as well as an entrenched incapacity to learn in any manner other than repetitive instruction over a prolonged period. The experienced Indian pilots who had enrolled in the Soviet course complained that it progressed at a snail's pace by Western standards and fixated at length on the most inconsequential matters, including proper head and hand movements for various procedures and functions in the cockpit. The operational conversion schools for foreign pilots at Tashkent and Lugovaya also enforced exaggerated operating restrictions, including a ban on instrument flight or entry into clouds, any display of individual initiative, or any other departure from strict and rigidly defined procedures. As an example, the Indian pilots stated that they were required to land out of a long, flat approach from a wide traffic pattern and were prohibited from making full-flap landings because of the MiG-21's allegedly excessive sink rate. Some instructors prohibited their students from generating roll rates in excess of 90 degrees per second, even though the MiG-21 had far greater roll responsiveness than that.

This was all most unsettling to the Indians, who were experienced pilots brought up in the manner of the British RAF. Although they did not buck the system, they were facing an imminent war with Pakistan and needed to know the MiG-21's full operational capability and performance spectrum. Yet they literally had to beg to try anything of tactical relevance or value. In addition to being saddled with excessively conservative rules, the Indian pilots found that the instructors frequently disagreed among themselves over what the rules were. In all, the Indians said, the Soviet approach was to instruct "rather in the way small children learn multiplication tables," with students frequently chanting the correct answers in unison. The report added, "Any deep thought about how to get the best out of one's aircraft, or even hack an unusual situation, was simply not part of the syllabus."[9]

Fortunately, the information explosion occasioned by Mikhail Gorbachev's glasnost and the subsequent collapse of the Soviet state made developments in the armed forces of the former USSR easier to understand in detail, as the preceding chapters have shown. Among other things, the VVS ranks issued an unprecedented venting of complaints that were highly revealing of long-suppressed deficiencies in VVS operating practice. Among the openly aired grievances with which the VVS leadership now had to contend were a growing recognition of severe shortcomings in approaches to training at all levels, mounting discontent over the mindless administrative detail and paperwork that dominated squadron and regiment life, a pervasive lack of honesty and integrity within flying units, the poor quality and reliability of much of the equipment provided by the aviation industry, and increasingly apparent inequalities between Soviet and Western equipment and operational capability.

Those criticisms hit especially hard on such perennial vexations as overly intrusive higher-headquarters meddling in day-to-day flight operations, seemingly endless bureaucratic proceduralism at the regiment level, and a continuing tension between the demands of flight safety and the often conflicting imperatives of realism in peacetime operational training. Russian pilots and commanders expressed unhappiness as well over more fundamental concerns, such as misplaced service priorities, rampant careerism and compromises of integrity by commanders looking mainly to "get ahead," and a consequent loss of vision and sense of purpose by the institution as a whole.

True enough, many such complaints that were aired by Russian pilots and commanders during the early years following the beginnings of glasnost sounded remarkably similar to those that had been voiced for decades by airmen the world over. Indeed they tended to bear out the widespread belief that some complaints simply go with the trade. As retired RAF Air Vice Marshal Tony Mason aptly remarked, "Anyone who has spent any time in a barracks or squadron crew room, or as a senior officer has stayed on late at a unit dinner night, will know that British servicemen can hold their own internationally when criticizing the system, their equipment, their personnel management, and especially their senior commanders." The same could be said of U.S. or any other allied airmen. Yet in the case of the VVS, as Mason noted, the grassroots criticism of established norms let loose by the floodgates of glasnost was "too extensive, too specific, too repetitive, and too similar from many rank levels" for any such cautionary note to carry much weight. Mason further pointed out that behind many such outcries from the ranks of VVS officers was "a sense of hurt pride, frustrated professionalism, and a genuine desire for reform, rather than rejection or destruction."[10]

Standardization Evaluation

VVS fighter regiments during the late Soviet period operated quite differently from their Western counterparts. Although comparably burdened by paperwork and reporting responsibilities, they were far less scrupulous about honoring published rules in day-to-day practice. VVS headquarters promulgated explicit and detailed training guidelines as a matter of routine. Yet the enforcement of those guidelines at the unit level was selective at best and capricious at worst and in either case strongly reflective of the personal inclinations of the regiment commander.

A squadron's normal operating routine was governed by the flight operations manual and by the Combat Training Course (*Kurs boyevoi podgotovki*, or KBP). The manual specified the number and type of sortie events to be performed by each pilot per training period in order for the pilot to be considered mission-ready. These events ranged from instrument approaches to various air-to-air and air-to-ground weapons delivery profiles. The KBP was a structured syllabus progression for new RTU graduates upgrading to full mission-ready status. It consisted of more than two hundred air-to-air and surface-attack instructional blocks, proceeding from initial qualification through two-ship and four-ship to regiment-level events. (As noted in Chapter 4, the first fifty-two of these "exercises" covered basic conversion to the aircraft and were completed during the RTU phase.) Each sortie profile specified carefully defined roles, with no allowance for any free play or role reversals in a formation.[11]

The main measure of a Soviet fighter squadron's effectiveness was its performance in upgrading new pilots to First-Class status and its maintenance of previously achieved First-Class pilot ratings.[12] Advancement by a pilot to First-Class status was conducted in accordance with the KBP, which was loosely analogous to the USAF's Graduated Combat Capability (GCC) evaluation system and was updated roughly every five years. In theory such training documents would enforce procedural standardization throughout the fighter force. In reality, however, regiment commanders routinely determined their own standards. As a result, one weapons instructor complained, there was no way to ascertain a pilot's ability to carry out a maneuver sequence short of taking him up for a check ride that included the maneuver sequence. That instructor implied that nothing in VVS fighter aviation practice allowed for "ensuring a steadily increasing complexity of mission assignments from one training sortie to the next."[13] By 1990 experienced pilots were complaining openly about shortcomings in the application of the training norms specified in the KBP. One lieutenant colonel flatly asserted that VVS fighter readiness existed "on paper only."[14]

While he was commander in chief of the Soviet VVS, Colonel General Yevgeny Shaposhnikov insisted that it was essential to provide a means of systematically tracking the mission events flown by each pilot during a training cycle in order to create a more substantiated basis for averting situations conducive to accidents. Citing a case in point from his own former regiment, he noted how the use of such an approach had revealed one pilot to have repeated the same mistake three times in a single month. That helped determine where remedial efforts needed to be concentrated to increase that pilot's proficiency.

Day-to-day Soviet fighter upgrade training was conducted in accordance with the syllabus progression laid out in the KBP, whereas a unit's performance during the operational readiness inspection (ORI) was assessed according to published criteria in the "Manual of Combat Procedures and Regulations." That inconsistency was said by Lieutenant Colonel A. Zhukov to have been directly responsible for one out of every four mishaps during inspections because of the exceptional pressure the inspections put on regiment commanders to succeed. Zhukov further reported that missions flown in accordance with the KBP did not automatically qualify pilots to carry out missions specified in the "Manual of Combat Procedures and Regulations."

Zhukov added that experienced pilots were convinced that the existing system had reached a dead end. Commanders, he said, knew implicitly that any deviation from the flight operations manual would result in administrative sanctions. They also understood that they could get by with paying only lip service to their tactical training obligations. Units were barraged incessantly with directives from higher headquarters about the need for improved proficiency. Yet because of the perverse incentives and conflicting pressures at work, those directives were routinely dismissed as empty declarations. Unit commanders paid little heed to the "Manual of Combat Procedures and Regulations" in their day-to-day training.

Zhukov's proposed solution was to integrate KBP and mission-employment training in such a way that new pilots could be systematically advanced toward mission-ready status in compliance with real tactical needs and a clear concept of operations. He noted how experiments had shown that, given an opportunity to think through their training needs themselves, upgrading pilots would quickly rise above "job-related infantilism" and gain a better appreciation of where they needed remedial work. Such an approach, he said, would end the dangerous situation whereby unit commanders temporarily suspended their normal square-filling (or pursuit of "gross numbers") as the ORI approached, only to revert to mindless practices once the stress of the inspection had passed. Zhukov insisted that it was past time to end such "shifting back and forth."[15]

Much of what passed for mission-certification training in Soviet fighter regiments was conducted at a fairly rudimentary level in comparison with Western practice. Even in 1988, before the beginning of the VVS's funding crisis, a senior training officer wrote that young upgraders had to be drilled in such simple tasks

as visual pilotage, navigation aids orientation, maintenance of position in formation, meeting assigned range times, and orderly recovery to a safe landing.

On assuming command of the VVS, General Shaposhnikov proposed a major
revamping of its operating practices at the unit level. "Long ago," he declared in
a 1990 interview, "I became convinced that much, much needs to be reexamined
in our system of combat training." For a while, he noted, VVS headquarters had
assumed that recurring performance deficiencies uncovered during annual inspections were simply testaments to the faulty leadership of unqualified regiment
commanders. Yet those commanders would be reprimanded and replaced time
and time again, with little discernible effect. Eventually, headquarters concluded
that the system itself was the culprit. In an uncharacteristic attempt to fix the
problem, Shaposhnikov claimed, the VVS reached way down into the ranks of
the flying community to solicit criticism and suggestions from below, on the
premise that "if reform is not to become a child of the apparatus, it must go both
up and down." In particular, Shaposhnikov noted a need to change the VVS approach to training so that the pilot could "continuously improve himself as a professional." As a first step toward that goal, the general proposed dividing pilots
into proficiency categories such as "A, B, C, and D." He noted: "When one
makes it into the last group, it will mean in fact, and not just on paper, that he
knows everything. . . . As it is, we all rush hastily to get pilots to the First-Class
rating, but we don't achieve a stable level of skill."[16]

A related innovation proposed by Shaposhnikov was a more rational apportionment of flying hours among pilots so that those on the low end of the annual
allocation could maintain at least enough proficiency to remain safe, if not fully
mission-ready. The general cited as an example a notional First-Class pilot on
regimental headquarters assignment who flew only 70 hours a year for several
years in a row and then somehow surprised everyone when he went to the range
and proved himself incapable of putting bombs on the target. Shaposhnikov further noted that such pilots caused 60 percent of the VVS mishaps.

Shaposhnikov implied that he had something in mind roughly comparable to
the USAF's approach to proficiency grading when he spoke of a need to "change
the whole system." The challenge, he said, was to "define the readiness categories" that pilots would have to go through and then to determine, "legally and
methodically," the permitted independence levels for pilots in each category.
Shaposhnikov seemed to be visualizing a system involving graduated levels of
certified aircrew capability and at least some mission specialization within units.
Under existing rules, he said, a pilot would typically fly to a weapons range a few
times and be declared competent to attack any ground target. That, he pointed
out, was a major part of the problem in that it tended to overlook the different
skills needed to execute progressively more demanding mission tasks. By way of
a better approach, he suggested: "If, in the future, we will have in a squadron, for

example, a flight of experts at disabling airfields, a flight for destroying Hawk antiaircraft missiles, and so on, then we can characterize its combat readiness without bias." To illustrate how such a classification scheme might work in practice, Shaposhnikov noted that area targets could be lumped together in group A, with smaller or harder-to-hit objectives assigned to progressively higher proficiency categories. Then, if a pilot was working at the performance level associated with, say, group D, he would truly and demonstrably be "capable of a lot." In all events, said Shaposhnikov, the goal must be "to get away from the practice of averaging everything out in our training."[17]

Operational Style

Soviet fighter-employment practices likewise contrasted sharply with the familiar training patterns of the U.S. Air Force, Navy, and Marine Corps. The biggest differences were an unbending top-down imposition of inhibiting rules for almost every circumstance of flight, a denial of any latitude for individual initiative on the part of pilots, and a dominant role played by the ground command post (*komandny punkt,* or KP) and the flight director (*rukovoditel poletov,* or RP) in overseeing both mission-qualification and line tactical training.[18]

In a striking testament to its rigid and stereotyped approach to mission preparation, the VVS used a practice called "dismounted training," whereby pilots took to the tarmac and, with model airplanes in hand, literally walked through each maneuver and event in an upcoming training mission. Such practice was even shown on Soviet television: pilots in full flight regalia actually lined up in echelon at the end of the "runway," walked forward to mimic the takeoff roll, selected afterburner, and then proceeded to climb out, depart to the work area, and execute each mission event in preplanned sequence. However useful that may have been in helping pilots visualize what they were about to perform in the air, it reflected a training philosophy based on scripted mission planning and rote memorization that was and remains fundamentally alien to Western practice.

Although the VVS began receiving its initial batches of the latest-generation MiG-29 and Su-27 fighters during the late 1980s, General Shaposhnikov confirmed that its operational style continued to rely heavily on direction from the ground. He admitted that the new equipment had enabled significant "adjustments in the training process and in flight operations control group (GRP) practices." However, he added: "The man at the console continues to play a deciding role." That statement spoke volumes about how far the VVS had yet to go before it could claim to have matched the independence that has long been routinely granted to Western fighter pilots.[19]

GRP is an abbreviation for *Gruppa rukovodstva poletov* (literally, "flight supervision group"). This is the approximate VVS analogue of a USAF fighter wing command post, but its role is far more intrusive and overbearing. It features a glassed-in control center with a clear view of the ramp, taxiway, and runway at each base. It is manned during flight operations by an RP (generally a senior pilot with the rank of major or higher), a radar controller, and a regiment-level supervisor. It combines the USAF functions of supervisor of flying (SOF), GCI, control tower, and runway supervisory officer (or mobile control). Most important, it makes for the airborne pilot many decisions that are typically made in the cockpit in Western practice.

Part of the reason for the arrested development of VVS tactical training and combat prowess has been this continued heavy reliance on the ground tactical control officer, whose responsibilities range from seeing to the successful completion of an intercept to making the key decision calls during in-flight emergencies. The ground controller also plays the dominant role when it comes to such elementary matters as deciding when to select afterburner during an intercept. In what would have been deemed an affront to aircrew professionalism by an unqualified outsider had it appeared in a Western military periodical, a junior VVS medical officer, of all people, once noted that Soviet pilots would typically get themselves into a tight predicament only to discover, to their relief, that in such "critical moments, the controller's calm, even voice and precise instructions [were there to] help [the] pilots maintain composure and successfully extricate themselves from their situation."[20]

By one informed Western account in mid-1991, free-form air-combat training remained the exception to the rule in Soviet fighter squadrons and generally consisted of visual setups in cases when GCI was overtasked. MiG-29 tactics differed little from MiG-23 tactics, and units rarely practiced intercepts against targets below 2,000 feet.[21] Command post controllers closely monitored and managed each training sortie. When one pilot en route to a weapons range wandered off his assigned heading only six minutes into the flight, the tactical control officer radioed him: "83, you're drifting right 25 degrees off course. Return to your proper heading!"[22] Typically, if the mission went well, the equipment was applauded. If something untoward occurred, the pilot received the blame.

The underdeveloped ability of VVS fighter pilots to respond quickly to changing conditions was borne out indirectly by the subsequent exposure of U.S. aircrews to former East German MiG-29 pilots, who were told, according to one firsthand account, "where to fly, when to turn on their radar, when to shoot, and when to come home."[23] This characteristic was further affirmed in 1992 by the West German Luftwaffe's commander in chief, Lieutenant General Hans-Jorg Kuebart, who noted that those East German MiG-29 pilots retained by the Luftwaffe following unification had to be requalified because of their differing tactical methods.[24]

Even when he was but a lieutenant colonel serving as a lowly regiment commander in 1975, Shaposhnikov cited several accidents that had occurred because of an inability of VVS pilots to adapt to a change in plans after the mission briefing.[25] By the time he had moved on to become air commander for the Group of Soviet Forces in Germany (GSFG) thirteen years later, Shaposhnikov noted how time-honored practices were hard to abandon, notwithstanding the new license apparently conferred by perestroika—Gorbachev's attempt at "restructuring" Soviet life. He said, "Born of the time of stagnation, such obstacles as oversimplification, formalism, overcautiousness, and fear of accepting responsibility for a demanding task remain almost insurmountable in the path toward accelerated progress in combat training."[26]

Shaposhnikov acknowledged the stultification and lack of initiative that largely accounted for the VVS's shortcomings in adaptability, and he stressed the need to get rid of those shackles on VVS effectiveness. As a case in point, he cited the decline in one unit's readiness level because of its leadership's mindless pursuit of "statistical indicators" of performance, which led it to oversimplify its mission tasking and eliminate the most challenging training events, all "masked by the excuse of flight safety." All too often, Shaposhnikov complained, "slogans and calls for restructuring" were used in place of what was truly needed to shake the VVS out of its complacency and bad habits, namely, "professional competence, purposefulness, activeness, responsibility, imagination, and a commander's boldness in making decisions."[27]

In 1993 two Ukrainian VVS officers confirmed what they called the "conservatism" of flight training in the former Soviet VVS. They noted, "Greater priority was placed on flight safety than on mission effectiveness." As a result, they said, the typical line pilot managed to master only about half the operational capability of his aircraft. The two former Soviet pilots charged that training in the Russian VVS continued to proceed "not like it does abroad, but rather by methods from a half-century ago." They confirmed stories of pilots "actually walking through an upcoming flight using a hand-held model airplane." They also acknowledged that Russia had "come to understand the erroneousness of this approach."[28]

Scheduling and Sortie Apportionment

Before the funding crisis so severely curtailed Russian tactical training, the types of sorties flown in day-to-day VVS operations were determined by the regiment's annual training plan. In preparing a day's flying schedule, the deputy squadron commander would assign each pilot appropriate mission profiles drawn from the KBP. Weather frequently dictated what complexity of sorties could be flown on any given day. Like Western air forces, the VVS maintains published pilot weather minimums for landing. These vary from pilot to pilot depending on aeronautical rating, often with further restrictions assigned by regimental instructors based on assessed instrument proficiency.[29]

General Shaposhnikov noted that event scheduling and sortie apportionment needed to be better informed ahead of time by such considerations as available flying hours, allowable fuel and training munitions, weapons range availability, and annual weather patterns to ensure "a constant and stable tempo of training and the avoidance of crash programs." For determining which pilots were qualified to fly which sortie profiles, he said that what was needed was not meaningless measures of aggregate activity but rather hard data on the "actual readiness of each pilot and navigator from each unit, from the two-ship element all the way up to the full squadron."[30]

Shaposhnikov more than once stressed the need for careful planning of a unit's training to eliminate problems otherwise created by frantic "last-minute and catch-up rush work." That statement implied that the VVS had standard procedures for the scheduling of training events but that individual regiment commanders frequently failed to make proper use of them. It was essential, Shaposhnikov said, "to make sure that each and every VVS officer knows what he will be doing today, tomorrow, next week, and next month." Furthermore, he added: "Once a plan or schedule has been agreed to, it should not be carved up on a daily basis just because of considerations driven by the multitude of things that need attending to that day."[31] Such concern often affects Western fighter unit commanders as well, who also feel periodic tension between the need to stick to an established training plan and recurrent pressures to modify the flying schedule at the eleventh hour so as to accommodate this or that need of the moment, whether it be a function of weather, maintenance delays, or other contingent circumstances.

Shaposhnikov deplored the tendency of supervisors to schedule pilots for mission events for which they were not qualified. He cited one case in which a First-Class pilot was cleared to fly a training sortie in a single-seat fighter, even though the pilot was not proficient enough to perform the scheduled events on the mission because of an excess of time away from the cockpit. The authorizing squadron commander had assumed that because of the pilot's seniority and experience, he "surely" was "able to carry out the task." The commander further figured that it would waste a valuable training asset to fly the pilot with an instructor in a two-seater that was badly needed elsewhere on the schedule for upgrading younger pilots. Indeed, Shaposhnikov said, the pilot himself knew that his upcoming flight was in violation of regulations. Yet he pressed ahead anyway out of misplaced self-confidence and flew a sortie for which he was unprepared, setting himself and others up for a potential mishap.[32]

Shaposhnikov went on to fault the shortsighted planning that allowed pilots to lose mission currency and the way in which some units shamelessly justified last-minute changes to previously settled flight schedules using the lame rationale of "reestablishing currency." Although that was an honest explanation as far as it went, it begged a more important question, in Shaposhnikov's view. "Who allowed you commanders," he would ask, "to organize your combat training so as to let your pilots lose their skills in the first place?" There was no more surefire way of flirting with accidents, he observed, than to be in a daily mode of constantly having to rearrange sorties and mission events in compensation for poor foresight.[33]

Shortly before the final withdrawal of Soviet forces from Germany, the air commander for the Western Group of Forces (WGF), Lieutenant General Anatoly Tarasenko, reported that German flight restrictions had kept his pilots from night flying for four months in 1991 and that they were to be similarly restricted for six months (from April 15 to October 15) in 1992. Scheduled day missions were directed to recover before 6:00 P.M. local time, almost two hours before official sunset. Because of those restrictions, WGF sorties in 1992 were apportioned at the regiment commander's discretion, such that the youngest pilots and those mission-ready aircrews representing the VVS's core talent pool were given the greatest amount of time. Other bandage fixes included reducing the average duration of scheduled sorties, eliminating repeat passes at the range, combining multiple mission events on a single sortie, curtailing afterburner use and flight into marginal weather to save fuel, and relying more on simulators, even though Russia's defense industry had radically curtailed their manufacture and technical support. In a nutshell, said General Tarasenko, WGF training had been reduced to mission scheduling "according to available fuel rather than operational need." Flight restrictions imposed by the German government were partly offset by periodic unit deployments back to Russia, with week-long detachments to Russian tactical ranges for live weapons training. Those deployments accounted for 37 percent of the WGF's total flight time and 50 percent of its night-flight time in 1992.[34]

A Typical Flying Day

In normal circumstances, before the funding crisis put VVS fighter training on indefinite hold, the daily flow pattern at a Russian fighter base differed substantially from that typically encountered at a counterpart Western base.[35] To begin with, regiments operated in two shifts six days a week rather than one shift five days a week, with individual squadrons alternating between flying days and maintenance down days. For a squadron working the second shift, flying days were Tuesday, Thursday, and Saturday, with routine aircraft maintenance and next-day mission planning conducted on Monday, Wednesday, and Friday.

Such a week at the squadron level would typically begin on Monday morning at 9:00 A.M., when the squadron commander, his deputy, and his flight commanders would meet to plan the upcoming week's maintenance and flying program. Once those details were blocked out, the squadron operations officer then prepared the next day's flying schedule, assigned sortie events for each pilot, and arranged for needed support services, such as air traffic control, navigation aids, and range control officers.[36]

Tactical control officers reviewed the flight schedule and determined which personnel would be needed in the command post during flight operations. They further attended to such administrative matters as determining takeoff and landing times, arranging for needed airspace reservations, and providing mission-planning guides listing preplanned maneuver sequences to be flown, airspeed restrictions, recovery fuel levels for each scheduled sortie, fuel consumption rates at different altitudes and for different mission profiles, alternate airfields, pertinent notices to airmen (NOTAMs), and so on.

Pilots then met with their flight commanders from 10:00 to 11:00 to review flight recorder tapes from the last flying period. At 11:00–11:30 the squadron commander announced mission areas to be emphasized, and the deputy commander assigned each pilot his next day's flight profiles from the KBP. From 11:30 to 1:00, pilots used those planning templates to develop highly scripted mission plans. The plans were handwritten in notebooks, to the point of actually diagramming the flight path and maneuver sequence to be flown, with every turn and airspeed at each critical point in the mission accounted for in advance. Depending on the sortie's complexity, those write-ups were approved by either the squadron commander or his deputy. Pilots were then asked to calculate their expected fuel-consumption specifics for each planned sortie, often under tight time constraints, submitting their results to be checked and approved by the tactical control officer.[37]

Lunch was taken from 1:00 to 3:00, after which mission planning resumed. At 4:00, pilots went through a cockpit familiarization review. From 4:30 to 5:00, they walked through their planned missions, from takeoff to landing. Fighter units also conducted regular classroom instruction in navigation and instrument flight procedures, often at a very basic level compared with Western practice. Each squadron had a "methods council," which vetted and approved suggestions from instructors and other supervisors and decided on training approaches and areas to be emphasized. The planning day ended with an all-officers' meeting at 5:00 with the regiment commander.[38]

On flying days, the squadron commander and flight commanders met at 5:40 A.M. to review the day's planned events. Aircraft scheduled to fly were towed from their shelters to the flight line by trucks, which also served as ground power units for the aircraft. This was followed by a fifteen- to twenty-minute regimental weather reconnaissance mission in a two-seat aircraft to check out conditions in the operating areas scheduled for use that day.

Aircrews arrived at the squadron by bus from their apartments between 6:00 and 7:00 and took breakfast at leisure in the officers' mess, followed by a mass briefing held from 7:30 to 8:00, during which the regiment commander announced his expectations and assigned broad tasking and safety reminders. Pilots then met with the meteorologist and the tactical control officer for a full weather briefing and overview of objectives for the day's planned sorties.[39]

Next came a GCI briefing and a squadron-wide review of safety and other rules of engagement. This was the only time that VVS pilots had any face-to-face contact with their radar controllers. With respect to the actual conduct of intercept missions, GCI could offer suggestions, but flight commanders had the last word. Most controllers were not trusted to give accurate target information and vectors. Contrary to widespread assumptions in the West, basic intercepts and maneuvering engagements using self-setups were frequently practiced without GCI support.[40]

Every pilot then mustered to the duty physician in a hangar dispensary for a routine medical check before being cleared to fly. Pilots were examined for blood pressure, temperature, pulse, respiration, and general suitability to fly. Among other things, this procedure offered a ready check for alcohol abuse, which at times was severe in the VVS, especially in remote areas.[41] Flight surgeons normally turned a blind eye if aftereffects of alcohol were detected, declaring the affected pilot down for duty not including flying (DNIF) that day for innocuous reasons, such as nasal congestion or an ear infection. However, if outright intoxication was suspected, the pilot would receive automatic grounding and possibly severe disciplinary action.[42] Following medical release, pilots scheduled for the first launch went through a final cockpit and emergency procedures review, after which they proceeded to the personal equipment room to draw their helmets and a 9-mm semiautomatic pistol to carry in the cockpit. That was followed by a walk-around inspection of the aircraft, a brief exchange with the aircraft's maintenance officer, and start, check-in, and taxi for a ritual 9:00 takeoff.

When fuel allocations were not a constraint, pilots typically flew three or four sorties each flying day.[43] That meant that pilots and maintenance personnel were constantly on the go, in a tempo of operations that a former Soviet pilot described to me as *sumasshedshy* ("crazy"). Because most Soviet fighters are fuel-limited, sorties generally lasted no more than 30 minutes from takeoff to landing.[44] Touch-and-go landings were infrequent. Maneuvering zones and weapons ranges were usually not far from the base, making for little wasted out-and-back time. An assigned zone for air-to-air work was normally situated within 15 to 20 nautical miles of the field.[45] VVS squadrons typically flew formed flights, with the same pilots in each flight of four aircraft. Pilot substitutions in those formed flights were rare.

The first sortie was normally down by 9:40 and was followed by a second meal and a short mission debrief with the flight leader and GCI. The scheduled takeoff for the second wave of the first cycle was at 10:20, with a third takeoff at 11:40. The first cycle ended at 1:00 P.M. with a mass debriefing with the regiment's training officer, followed by initial preparations for the next day's mission planning. A second flying cycle then took place from 1:00 to 7:00. Any pilot who demonstrated identified problems in need of attention on any of his sorties that day might then fly again with an instructor pilot (IP) in a two-seater for remedial work.

During peak flying periods at the height of the Soviet era, typically twenty-four aircraft were on a regiment's daily flying schedule. Single-seaters flew five or six times a day, with two-seaters flying more because of the greater demand on them, usually with a different upgrading pilot in the front cockpit on each successive sortie.[46] IPs flew more than line pilots because they were constantly upgrading newcomers from the VVAULs.[47] Each squadron maintained one spare for every three aircraft on the schedule, and a regiment might fly up to 180 short sorties in the course of a single routine training day. Today, to conserve fuel, commanders are encouraged to take every measure possible to minimize the hold time for aircraft awaiting takeoff and landing clearance. The fuel shortage has caused an increase in the scheduling of multievent sorties and, whenever practicable, in the shutting down of engines and towing of aircraft back to parking after landing.[48]

VVS fighter bases use designated tactical call signs for VHF radio communication. Aircraft radio frequencies are all preset and limited to selected air-to-air and ground channels, such as the regiment command post, a GCI handler, and departure and destination controllers for cross-country flights. Each quarter, pilots are assigned a different three-digit personal call sign prefixed by a two-digit regiment number, which is normally never used. Air-to-air missions may have opposing fighters talking to separate GCI controllers sitting side by side at a common radar console but assigned individual frequencies.[49]

Pilots are taught to maintain radio discipline by keeping voice communications to a minimum. For example, an element or flight leader's signal on the runway for engine runup before brake release is to pull the control stick fully aft to cause nose-up deflection of the horizontal stabilizer. Formation takeoffs maintain loose spacing within elements, with the wingman positioned on the runway 45 feet to the right or left of his leader, depending on wind, and 75 feet aft, making almost for individual single-ship takeoffs in close proximity to one another. The runway itself at most airfields is made of large, precast concrete blocks laid side by side with tar joints. Former VVS Captain Alexander Zuyev reported that during rainy weather, the concrete blocks would shift position and swamp water would come squirting up through the joint lines. Scattered debris that could cause engine foreign-object damage (FOD) if sucked down an air intake is not systematically cleaned up but typically is ignored by VVS supervisors, in sharp contrast to the no-nonsense attitude toward FOD that is characteristic of most Western air forces.

As for tactics applications, Zuyev reported one KFA practice that featured the wingman positioned in echelon formation 150 feet or less from his leader entering a fight, making the wingman not only useless as a covering element but potentially dangerous to the leader because of the risk of a midair collision. Zuyev also alluded to what Western fighter aircrews call "resolution-cell" tactics in noting that two MiG-29s might approach an intercept in such close proximity to one another that they would appear to the opposing GCI or air intercept radar as a single target. He noted the use of odd and even altitudes by opposing flights to maintain a safe vertical separation of the converging aircraft and thereby minimize the chance of a midair collision during head-on training engagements. And he indicated a minimum altitude (or "hard deck") of 1,800 feet for maneuvering during intercept training.[50]

There were other reported VVS operating practices that would be considered by Western commanders as not only tactically unsound but downright unsafe. For example, in air-to-air setups, MiG-29 pilots were instructed to enter a fight with the master arm switch on and the missile launch button depressed, so that any live missile would automatically fire once its infrared seeker head locked up a target within lethal parameters.[51] Relatedly, Zuyev reported that he always flew MiG-29 air-to-air training sorties with a full load of 30-mm cannon rounds.[52] Either practice would be deemed by any Western flight supervisor to be a recipe for eventual disaster.

On the other hand, the impressive maneuvers performed by Russian test pilots on the international air show circuit since the MiG-29's Western debut at the Farnborough Air Show in Great Britain in 1988, notably the tail slide and "cobra," remain prohibited for line VVS pilots because of the danger of putting the airplane into a departure-prone flight condition. On this point, an article by a senior test pilot and two Mikoyan Design Bureau engineers described the controlled nature of the dramatic cobra maneuver and its susceptibility to producing a departure from controlled flight if not properly executed. They also dispatched the common misconception that the cobra constituted an effective last-ditch guns-defense maneuver, rightly noting that any fighter executing such a maneuver at only 200–250 knots (the proper entry airspeed) would "reduce its speed in relation to an attacker insignificantly, while sharply increasing the area to aim at"—in effect rendering itself an airborne strafe target. They added that the maneuver would also reduce the aircraft's energy to the point that the fighter would "lose any subsequent opportunity to perform even limited maneuvers."[53]

The collapse of funding for fuel and other consumables has ended indefinitely most of the daily operating routines described above. This shortage, which has had the VVS on its knees since the early 1990s, can be traced as far back as the late 1980s, when the faltering Soviet economy first began to undermine the training regime of line VVS units.[54] Even in 1989, squadrons were reportedly standing down for two-week intervals at a time because of a lack of fuel, with some aircrews flying only two or three times a month.[55] In some instances such interruptions were attributed not to a lack of fuel per se but rather to a unit's mismanagement of its fuel allocation.

In the Soviet VVS, jet fuel was apportioned quarterly against a regiment's projected flying hours. Often weather or other unforeseen constraints, such as lapses in aircrew currency, would cause units to fly fewer than their planned hours during a given training period. If aircrews needed to fly more during the subsequent cycle to make up for lost training, commanders would often feel bound, by a literal interpretation of rules, to not use fuel over and beyond that quarter's allocation. The problem was not a shortage of fuel but poor resource management due to blind and unimaginative adherence to standard procedures.

Even at the height of the cold war's intensity, only around 65 percent of the flight activity in VPVO fighter units was dedicated to mission-related events. The remainder was taken up by such ancillary functions as upgrading new pilots, conducting daily weather reconnaissance, and providing targets for other interceptors. A typical MiG-31 intercept sortie lasted two hours, with the intercept portion itself taking slightly less than an hour. As an economy measure, the VVS and VPVO have both started using older fighters like the MiG-23UB, or even the L-39, for operational support flying not directly related to mission readiness. A single fuel load for a MiG-31 can generate 10–12 sorties of equal duration in an L-39.

In both the VVS and VPVO, upgrading pilots are now caught in a situation in which they cannot qualify for a First-Class rating even in six years because of the ever-increasing shortage of fuel.[56] Worse yet, given the low number of available flying hours pilots are unable to retain even their *existing* ratings. As a result, Russia's most experienced pilots now face the near certainty of losing their currency certification within a year or two of attaining First-Class status and being forced to requalify in order to retain that rating. When this problem first manifested itself, before the USSR's demise, one pilot lamented: "The prospects are unenviable— to go once again through all the wickets and retake examinations to qualify for ratings they previously held. This is simply an erosion of combat training."[57]

Flight Simulator Use

Maintenance and planning days were also used to give pilots needed simulator practice if the regiment had a simulator that was functioning properly. Full-mission simulators, if they existed at all, were rare in the VVS even during the best of days, however, with most units being limited to rudimentary procedures trainers. Simulator training at the unit level was underutilized to the point that pilots were said in at least one instance to have reacted with near panic when informed by an inspection team that they would be tested for partial-panel instrument proficiency with the attitude director indicator (ADI) disabled. New pilots routinely made mistakes, often basic ones, in instrument flying technique. The VVS monthly magazine reported the example of one upgrader who, given a partial-panel situation with several instruments disabled during a simulator check, rolled onto the final approach too far out and on the wrong heading.

In fairness to that situation, Russian pilots voiced legitimate gripes about their simulators, the reliability and design of which were said to "leave a great deal to be desired."[58] One experienced pilot noted that the simulators provided by industry to the VVS not only were not helpful but indeed imparted *negative* training because of their design imperfections. Another common complaint focused on the regimental supervisors' frequent failure to fully harmonize and integrate simulator training with the unit's flight training program.

Indeed a shortage of up-to-date simulators was long a bane of VVS training, especially for units converting to new equipment. Aircrews would frequently check out in a new aircraft type without the benefit of a simulator because of the excessively slow construction of simulator buildings and the lengthy start-up times and delayed adjustment work caused by indifferent technical support from the manufacturer. Underutilization of simulators in line units (often as little as three hours a day) was not uncommon. Commanders often encouraged inflated reporting of simulator use, logging as actual "flying time" the entire operating time of their simulators, from morning start-up to evening shutdown.

Weapons Training and Range Use

The VVS during its best days operated scorable ranges for gunnery, rocketry, and bombing practice, as well as tactical ranges with more complex target arrays. According to Zuyev, those local *poligony,* as they are called in Russian, were situated close enough to most bases that aircrews could fly as many as three or four day range missions and two at night during mission-employment training.[59]

Soviet range facilities were not up to Western standards by any means. Technical backwardness and a shortage of funds required almost all installations to be built locally by hand. In one reported case a night bombing target was illuminated by being surrounded by flat dishes of burning diesel fuel, which required constant refilling and relighting. Aggressive scrounging of copper cable and the private purchase of light fixtures and bulbs enabled the installation of jury-rigged electrical lighting at one range.

Scoring systems were also primitive and typically involved a range officer calling out eyeball assessments. The fudging of scores was common, with figures padded more or less "depending on the rank of those who did the shooting." Critics of such practices often spoke out forcefully against "His Majesty the average rating, which ignores the obvious fact that the target is either destroyed or it isn't."[60] Critics noted that automated scoring systems could easily eliminate such abuses. However, a search for an enterprise in the defense industry that might develop such systems eventually fizzled out because of a lack of funds.

General Shaposhnikov was a frequent critic of the VVS's failure to make the most of its range facilities. "Year in and year out," he once observed, "pilots attack one and the same target, from sector to sector, on the same unchanging heading." Up to a point, he conceded, such repetition was an unavoidable consequence of airspace restrictions or of the geographic setting of the range. Yet more often than not, it reflected "conservatism and a lack of desire among some commanders to think and to alter their routine."[61]

In addition to day-to-day training at local ranges, VVS regiments during happier days periodically took part in surge exercises and weapons deployments. Fighter units flew one or two regiment-level tactical air exercises and five or six squadron-level exercises per year. During the early 1980s the Soviet VVS conducted periodic day and night airfield-attack exercises involving squadron- and regiment-sized forces operating out of forward deployment locations. The number of such exercises in 1983 reportedly exceeded the combined total for the preceding three years.

One 1983 exercise featured multievent air-to-air and ground-attack operations, including fighter escort, low-altitude airfield attack, and independent search. Another featured operations against a high-value target, including the extensive use of electronic countermeasures. By one informed account, it showed "a capability for coordinated attack not previously demonstrated by the Soviets."[62] Nevertheless, such mission-employment scenarios remained highly simplistic compared with what the USAF was doing at Red Flag and what the U.S. Navy was concurrently doing in its fleet-deployment workup training at Naval Air Station Fallon. Dissimilar air-combat training that pitted fighters of different types and performance characteristics against one another was typically limited to radar intercepts against nonmaneuvering targets.

In another exercise involving a Su-24 regiment tasked with simulating a maritime attack out of a forward operating location, last-minute changes were introduced into the strike scenario, necessitating mission preparations under tight time constraints. A squadron commander authorized his aircrews to brief and fly a low-level attack profile—notwithstanding the fact that they "had not mastered this bombing technique before"—because he had read about its successful application by Soviet airmen in World War II! The predictably poor outcome prompted a recommendation that each squadron maintain dedicated aircrews expressly trained for "out-of-the-ordinary" tasking. A similar recommendation for a building-block approach suggested, "After outstanding results are achieved in one mission category, effort should be shifted to assimilating the next tactical application." As matters stood, the author wrote: "The conveyor-belt method of training, in which aircrews go through the KBP with their afterburners on, so to speak, cannot . . . produce convincing evidence of improved proficiency."[63]

Before the disintegration of the USSR, the VVS's master operational air-to-air evaluation center was the Mary range complex adjacent to the Caspian Sea in the Kara Kum desert of Turkmenistan. Units would deploy there periodically for large-force employment operations and live weapons firing. The complex featured two airfields, one of which—Mary Two—was a full-time KFA fighter base. Mary One was more developed and diversified, with weapons and other depots to service a variety of combat aircraft types.

During such unit evaluations an entire regiment, from the commander through all aircrews and maintenance personnel to clerks, cooks, and drivers—and even the civilian waitresses in the officers' dining hall—would deploy to Mary. The intent was to simulate a unit rotation to the Warsaw Pact forward area during a prelude to war. Deployments began with a formal briefing of all regiment aircrews by the evaluation center staff. During the deployment, a unit could expect to receive a no-notice instruction to perform one or another of its most critical wartime tasks. Acceptable scores for a regimental evaluation at Mary were 5/5 ("excellent") and 4/5 ("good").[64]

Toward the end of a two-week deployment, the unit would fly a regiment-sized operation against an equally large assemblage of aircraft simulating an enemy force. There was no incorporation, however, of resultant operational "lessons learned" into the unit's subsequent training after its return home from Mary. There also was little or no tactical interaction or other cross-communication between the various units deployed to Mary for weapons delivery evaluation.[65]

During his short tenure as commander in chief of the Soviet VVS, Shaposhnikov indicated that because of budget cuts and Moscow's shift toward a defensive doctrine, the number of such annual exercises by the VVS was being reduced. As a result, he said, a new role was being assigned to these exercises as an "innovation laboratory." Shaposhnikov explained that he wanted to separate these tactics-development exercises from the ORI process and make them pure learning opportunities, seemingly along the lines of Red Flag and comparable exercises conducted by U.S. fighter forces.[66]

A shortage of available weapons ranges had begun to develop even during the late Soviet period, when the number operated by the VVS (including those in Eastern Europe) dropped by one-third after the withdrawal of the WGF from the Warsaw Pact forward area. Further exacerbating the problem, the gradual liberalization of Soviet life under Gorbachev opened the gates for a profusion of citizen noise complaints and charges that the VVS weapons ranges were public nuisances that ought to be shut down. The resulting "range starvation," in the expression of one lieutenant colonel, meant that opportunities to practice weapons delivery were becoming "more and more a rare holiday for pilots."[67]

Today, weapons training in the VVS has fallen almost wholly into remission because of the collapse of state funding to all the services for operations and support. According to the commander of KFA, Colonel General Nikolai Antoshkin, the Soviet VVS at its peak operated 80 weapons ranges, most of which were approved for live munitions drops. The majority of those—including the Polessky range in Belarus, the Mary complex in Turkmenistan, and a missile test range in Kazakhstan—were lost to the other newly independent states when the USSR collapsed. By 1995, Antoshkin said, the VVS maintained only 36 ranges, 20 of which had been set up solely to support rudimentary ground-attack training by the VVAULs.[68]

One measure of the VVS's determination to show that it remained operationally robust in the face of its mounting economic crisis was the Voskhod '93 exercise conducted on May 18–19, 1993, under General Deinekin's personal direction. That exercise was portrayed as an attempt to "simulate problems associated with the intratheater maneuvering of men, equipment, and weapons and with interaction between various air components during operations."[69] The stated intent was to fuse the actions of staffs, command posts, and airfields and to monitor activities spread over a great distance with no major failures.

The main deployment consisted of 6 Tu-95 bombers, 10 Su-24s, and 4 Su-27 escorts. These were supported by 12 Il-78 tankers, 1 A-50 AWACS, and 2 airborne command posts for General Deinekin and his battle staff. The aircraft took off from three airfields in European Russia at 1:00 A.M. local time on May 18 and proceeded toward the Far East. The Su-24s conducted two in-flight refuelings during a 12.5-hour flight, with the Su-27s landing and refueling at intermediate airfields.[70]

That deployment and the subsequent mission events performed at the Amur region test ranges were later described as something that had "no counterpart in the past decade" in Soviet or Russian practice in terms of complexity.[71] General Deinekin remained aboard an Il-62 airborne command and control center throughout the exercise to monitor its progress, with his headquarters staff chief, Colonel General Anatoly Malyukov, handling ground coordination from the VVS central command post in Moscow.

The deployment covered a distance of some 5,000 miles and reportedly demonstrated good coordination, plus the ability of VVS aircrews to shift into a combat mode immediately after a long flight. The weather at the test ranges was bad enough to keep the Su-24s on the ground for a time. Their aircrews later performed low-level attacks against simulated targets. The two-day exercise ended with all aircraft returning to their home bases at 5:00 P.M. local time on May 19.

In all likelihood, several motivations underlay the Voskhod '93 exercise. First, it showed a VVS commitment to make good on the emerging Russian military doctrine emphasizing rapid deployment of combat power to remote spots along Russia's periphery. Second, it demonstrated, both to demoralized VVS officers and to others, that the VVS had not lost its operational will despite its severe funding predicament. Finally, the exercise may have been seen by the VVS as a chance to exercise a new type of training so as to broaden its repertoire and identify hidden problems and weaknesses. What the exercise lacked was an appreciation that the VVS's asset of greatest note for post-Soviet Russia's security needs was not high-performance strike aviation of the sort exercised in that deployment but rather the less glamorous projection and sustainment of a ground presence through military airlift, as was painfully attested by Moscow's involvement in Chechnya two years later.

Tactics Development

VVS fighter tactics, like all other Soviet force-employment plans, were considered state secrets throughout the long years of the cold war. Even today they are not deemed appropriate for discussion in the more relaxed Russian military literature. Nevertheless, since the collapse of many former security barriers with the disintegration of the Soviet state, former Soviet pilots have provided some interesting insights into the way in which the VVS pursued tactics development and application.

The home of VVS tactics development is the Center for Combat Readiness at Lipetsk. There the KBP is written and periodically updated by a permanent staff of instructors. Advanced tactics are also developed there for promulgation to line units.[72] Tactics documents developed at Lipetsk are endorsed by the Combat Training Directorate at VVS headquarters. The "new" tactics thus passed along were typically ignored down the line throughout the cold war, however, with little change over time in the actual pattern of a unit's training cycle.

Soviet air-to-air tactics were formalized in a VVS document titled "Tactical Devices for Air Combat." Among other things, it described named offensive and defensive fighter maneuvers such as the "knot," "fork," and "mussel."[73] The document also prescribed a comprehensive set of moves and countermoves, for single aircraft and larger formations, aimed at exploiting the full range of a weapon system's capability. Its directed repertoire included countering or negating anticipated enemy tactics through the use of maneuver, fire, jamming, and other measures.

Air-to-air tactics were divided into four categories:

- *Offensive,* for achieving a firing solution against an enemy from a tactically advantageous position
- *Defensive,* to negate an attack
- *Defensive-offensive* (or counteroffensive), to defeat an attack and regain the initiative
- *Neutral,* to create a situation in which other friendly fighters might bring offensive tactics to bear

Soviet fighter-tactics development was described as a four-step process:

- First, assessing operational threat
- Second, diagramming an enemy's likely force employment, followed by determining a means of achieving surprise in breaking up the enemy's plans
- Third, scoping out the area in which initial moves will take place, with due allowances for one's own and the enemy's SAM dispositions and command, control, and communication and intelligence (C3I) nodes, as well as tactically significant weather, sun position, topographical features, and so on
- Fourth, deciding on appropriate formations and spreads, attack tactics, desired weapon configurations, use of electronic warfare support, and a disengagement plan that anticipates possible enemy counters[74]

Western analysts long suspected that there was a pronounced difference between what the Soviets preached in their tactics manuals and what they actually practiced in day-to-day training. That suspicion has since been borne out by revelations from Russian pilots and commanders. Lieutenant General A. Bobrovsky and Colonel V. Shubin, for example, noted in 1990 that tactics development had "not undergone any significant change, even with the arrival of the latest aircraft into operational service." They also revealed that too many commanders concerned themselves "only sporadically" with tactical matters. Finally, they cited an absence of close and regular interaction between operators and the VVS research and educational institutions—a deficiency that necessarily limited "possibilities for integrating new tactical insights into combat training."[75]

Although each Soviet fighter unit had a tactics officer who attended a four-month qualifying course at Lipetsk, he got little direct guidance from above, since of the many documents that poured into VVS units daily, virtually none addressed "the development of new tactical techniques." To fill the gap, Bobrovsky and Shubin said, squadron pilots would develop their own tactical concepts, sometimes borrowing from squadrons with different aircraft types and amending the concepts to reflect the capabilities and limitations of their own equipment. There evidently was no mechanism, however, for disseminating these "unofficial" tactics beyond the unit and integrating them into an overall VVS mission-employment repertoire, since generally pilots in other regiments did "not know of them."[76]

In a regiment that was among the first to convert to the MiG-29, tactics development was done in a "tactical theory class" in which pilots were given several situations and then directed to come up with the optimal solution. The most promising results were incorporated into the flight operations schedule and were validated in the air. Then the most effective of these would be distilled and disseminated to all pilots. Squadron and regiment instructors encouraged line pilots to decide for themselves what to do in "nonstandard situations."[77]

Fighter tactics developments during the Soviet period were spread largely via word of mouth. Little information on Western tactics was made available to line aircrews. What was accessible was usually passed on to pilots during their conversion to new aircraft. There were no dedicated advanced training programs like the USAF Weapons School at Nellis Air Force Base in Nevada, the U.S. Navy Fighter Weapons School and Strike Leader Attack Training Syllabus (SLATS) at Naval Air Station Fallon in Nevada, and the U.S. Marine Aviation Weapons and Tactics Instructor's course at Marine Corps Air Station Yuma in Arizona. Tactics conferences for line aircrews were almost unheard of.

Bobrovsky and Shubin complained of a common situation: mission plans looked elaborate on paper, yet actual training sorties were flown "according to a time-worn scheme, without active opposition by an 'adversary.' And if there *was* opposition, the opposing force as a rule flew the same type of aircraft, and all moves were known beforehand right down to the slightest details."[78] Zuyev later confirmed the absence of dissimilar air-combat training as "one of the weakest points in Soviet training."[79]

The best VVS instructors had long recognized that effective fighter employment was a matter not just of good flying skills but also of clever tactics and anticipatory thinking aimed at defeating an enemy through guile. They had also long appreciated that tactics manuals could never provide "specific recommendations for every sudden twist of combat."[80] Even when breakthroughs were achieved in getting restrictions waived or regulations made less onerous, all too often there was no fuel or live ordnance available to permit the testing of ideas. As a result, VVS critics said, much of the innovative thinking that led to new concepts remained "on paper."[81]

The ten-year war experience in Afghanistan was a realism laboratory par excellence for Soviet fighter aviation. Inculcation of an operational mindset among VVS pilots began soon after a unit was informed that it would be deploying for combat. During initial workups of a squadron in Zuyev's MiG-23 regiment before deploying to Afghanistan, the aggressive commander declared frankly to his pilots: "Safety will always get in the way of combat training. We're going to turn things around, and to hell with the safety inspector." The unit pressed ahead with its training as needed, often exceeding its weather minimums. But the commander reassured his pilots that there were no safety inspectors at the forward operating bases in Afghanistan.[82]

During their training workups before deploying, unit pilots flew multiple twenty-minute range sorties every day. In Afghanistan they averaged 300 combat missions during their year-long tour, often flying as many as four combat sorties in a single day.[83] Pilots on strip alert would often be assigned a target and be airborne within ten minutes, routinely carrying out their mission despite the often tightly compressed time window within which to plan and prepare. Such success, one returned pilot said, was a natural outgrowth of the predominance of the mission over form and procedure.

Those who returned were different—seasoned by war, operationally mature, and no longer disposed to honor many of the canned procedures they had been taught in peacetime. An abiding attribute brought home by these combat-hardened pilots was a cultivated disdain for the bureaucratic routines that had previously dominated their professional lives. These pilots were beyond illusion, having experienced firsthand the virtues of flexibility in operations and tactics. They were indifferent to the old peacetime rules and harbored a case-hardened attitude toward their profession and its real-world imperatives.

One deputy squadron commander who flew 300 combat missions during his thirteen months in theater said that he had observed fewer mistakes, mishaps, and situations conducive to accidents while in Afghanistan than he had during peacetime. Why? "I later understood that they trusted us, didn't harass us for trifles, and didn't foist office instructions upon us." By contrast, the peacetime VVS thought "more about honoring guidelines than about the job at hand." He added, "Here [back in the USSR], I'm completely at the mercy of restrictions." He proposed establishing an experimental regiment stripped of unnecessary rules and paperwork, just to prove what professionals could accomplish if left alone to focus on the mission. "It was tough in Afghanistan. But I felt myself a pilot there. There I was flying, whereas here I'm just meeting arbitrary requirements."[84]

Such battle-hardened cynicism and disdain for headquarters types (referred to dismissively by Zuyev as "staff rats") naturally unnerved many VVS leaders, who were concerned that the jaded outlook and disrespect for authority harbored by these seasoned war veterans might infect the remainder of the VVS.[85] Accordingly, rather than being used to pass along valuable combat experience to line squadrons, fighter units returning from the war were disbanded and their pilots spread randomly throughout the VVS to prevent the formation of clusters of rebelliousness.[86] For much the same reason, there was never any systematic effort by the VVS to identify and assimilate successful operational tactics learned in the war experience.[87]

6. The Operating Milieu

Until the last days of the Soviet VVS, paperwork dominated daily life at the unit level. The regiment commander was constantly bombarded with documents containing instructions seemingly for every conceivable circumstance of life. The resultant profusion of red tape and the accompanying petty micromanagement (called *kantselyarshchina,* in colloquial Russian) reflected an innate disregard on the part of VVS leaders for the professionalism and competence of their subordinates. The result was a stifling work environment fostered by the encrusted command-administrative system of governance that for years dominated all Soviet military life.

We now know, from firsthand testimony by Russian pilots, that the many rules and reporting requirements imposed on regiment commanders by higher headquarters were such that if a commander followed each restriction to the letter, his unit would be unable to generate a single sortie and remain legal. Thus regiment commanders were forced to observe a double standard and, in effect, to live a lie on a daily basis. They would assiduously pay lip service to the rules when reporting to higher headquarters yet would implement those rules only as they saw appropriate to support their training needs. The shameless cynicism and dishonesty of this practice reconfirmed the enduring relevance of the well-known saying of Mikhail Soltykov-Shchedrin, the nineteenth-century Russian satirist, to the effect that the severity of Russian laws is softened by the nonnecessity of their enforcement.

A VVS flying unit provided an inhospitable environment for officer career development. For those pilots who truly loved flying, a fighter squadron offered the most appealing job in the country and the worst possible bureaucratic environment in which to perform it. Arbitrariness on the part of commanders was common, with little concern for people and their needs. A narrow focus on numbers and "looking good" forced constant compromises of integrity. Individual initiative was suppressed lest it result in a black mark on the unit. Cronyism was rampant, as was an emphasis on the wrong priorities. Typically, mission readiness took a backseat to these considerations. Yet after the collapse of the USSR, and with the lifting of many of the former Soviet restraints on free expression, thoughtful officers began owning up to these skewed values and acknowledging a serious need to fix the system.

A Tyranny of Bureaucratism

The Soviet pilot was always under a microscope, constantly taking written examinations, being subjected to monitoring on the ground and in the air, and having his mistakes broadcast openly by his squadron and regimental supervisors in a humiliating way for all to hear during group *samokritika* (self-criticism) sessions.[1] He was incessantly beseeched by multiple bosses to "show initiative." Yet he knew that behind all this seeming encouragement was the unspoken cardinal rule: "Don't screw up!" Particularly concerning the possibility of losing or damaging airplanes, the Soviet VVS was a zero-mistake air force.

One instructor bemoaned the "patent absurdity" of the way in which tactical training was conducted in line units. The Combat Training Course (*Kurs boyevoi podgotovki,* or KBP), which he called the "fundamental document" for training, was smothered by a bureaucratic approach that fostered "an absence of normal thinking and initiative" and a system that saw to "the welfare of careerists, the ungifted, and the play-it-safe crowd," who together obstructed the realization of the performance goals laid out in the KBP. Constantly hovering over the squadron commander was such a "knot of directives" levying upon him so many requirements from higher headquarters that he ended up being "tied hand and foot just reading them." On top of that, a squadron commander would frequently work late into the night with his deputies building a sensible flying schedule for the next day, only to have the phone ring from higher headquarters with some supervisor announcing: "I'll be flying with you tomorrow, so plan this many flights." The predictable result was to send everyone back to square one, "with cursing and nervous strain."[2]

VTA was no less afflicted by bureaucratism than were the fighter and bomber communities. A thirty-year VTA veteran railed against the proliferation of documents and forms that, he said, "swamped everyone from pilots to maintenance technicians, and especially commanders." He added: "Ask any of them what hamstrings them the most. Without hesitation, they will single out the paperwork. It corrupts the operational sense of pilots, dulls their memory, and breeds lethargy. Wags even joke about it—'the scratching of pens drowns out the whine of turbines.'"[3]

This critic, a retired lieutenant colonel, went on to complain that all preparation for flying was "pervaded with formalism" and was reduced essentially to "filling out forms in the interest of management oversight" that, at best, had "little bearing on the performance of the mission." Such VTA directives, he grumbled, were "more suited to a robot than an intelligent human." He further faulted the prevalence of cronyism, which meant that people whose qualifications lay "well below those of their subordinates" were nevertheless sometimes picked to fill supervisory positions. They were not selected on their merits, "but rather as a result of patronage from above."[4]

Career prospects were not bright for senior captains and majors hoping to gain positions of command and higher leadership. For one thing, advancement in rank, even for lieutenants, required an available billet appropriate to the next level, which explains why there were so many forty-year-old captains and majors in line regiments. Promotion required not just satisfactory performance of one's duties but patronage.

Also, unlike U.S. military pilots, who are typically rotated from one assignment to another every three years, Soviet pilots often remained at the same base, and even with the same unit, for most of their careers unless they expressly requested a transfer. This allowed, at least in principle, for the development of a closely knit unit. Yet because the influx of new blood was typically limited to new RTU graduates coming in to replace older pilots retiring from flight status, units easily tended toward complacency and stagnation.

During the 1980s it was not uncommon for VVS headquarters to force experienced pilots into early retirement to make room for new flight school graduates. One officer who flew in Afghanistan and later retired as a major general sharply criticized the practice of summarily declaring that pilots with eight to ten years of cockpit time were "old" and lacked a future when, in fact, they represented the core of the VVS's talent pool. The officer charged that it was senseless to invest a million rubles in producing an experienced military pilot only to turn him out at the prime of his proficiency so that the same amount of money might be reinvested in training a new pilot.[5]

Cronyism was a major factor in selection for command. It was widely known that at the VVS working level, the fates of all commanders were "decided in the nether reaches of the personnel world." One officer complained: "And it is no secret that family ties or the backing of influential people, sometimes with no connection whatever to aviation, can have a determining significance. The secrecy associated with the selection of regiment commanders is one of the main reasons for the encroachment of mediocrity up the service hierarchy."[6]

By almost unanimous testimony of both defectors and those who stayed to criticize the system from within, arbitrariness was the rule governing peacetime VVS training. Typically it took years for a pilot to attain First-Class status, often due to nothing more than the needlessly lethargic pace of a commander's training program. Alexander Zuyev pointed out how a VVS ruling that all new pilots would henceforth be expected to achieve Third-Class status within a year forced his regiment commander to work harder than he would have otherwise. That underscored the near-total absence of homogeneity in the way VVS fighter units were run.[7] Zuyev further cited the case of a regiment commander who would routinely cancel flying during "dangerous" weather, arbitrarily determining what constituted "dangerous." That commander was unabashed in acknowledging that his only interest was avoiding the loss of any aircraft, even if that meant ignoring the needs of readiness altogether. Indeed he went so far as to proclaim: "The less you fly, the longer you keep on flying."[8]

Safety almost invariably took precedence over realism in mission-employment training. Zuyev told a story about his RTU commander who tried to set an example during workups to a division weapons meet. As the commander was leading his pilots in trying out a new maneuver to defeat the U.S.-made Stinger shoulder-fired infrared missile at the weapons range, the safety supervisor came on the radio, shouting: "Stop this gross violation! Stop this hooliganism immediately!" The squadron commander was reprimanded afterward but was not seriously disciplined. Zuyev remarked that the innovative maneuver might have saved lives in Afghanistan but that it was never added to the combat training syllabus.[9]

There was likewise a pervasive emphasis on "looking good," even if that too impeded readiness. Pilots were repeatedly forced to perform "vitally important housekeeping duties" at the expense of their primary responsibility: staying mission-ready. As one pilot complained, it was no wonder that aircrews were fed up with being upbraided more often for a fence that needed fixing around the regiment's headquarters than for a near midair collision in air-combat training. Such distortions of legitimate priorities were a major reason so many pilots were electing to resign their commissions and leave the service for civilian life. Commanders at all levels, this pilot said, were paid to see to their unit's readiness, not to paint fences. Yet all too often, they defaulted on that responsibility by "cooking the books" to look good while squandering their remaining time on marginalia. "Reports above all!" was the main measure of a commander's merit, he charged, leading to the dominance of "formalism and efforts by commanders to meet their assigned goals at any cost, whatever the consequences."[10]

Self-Deception as a Way of Life

A triumph of form over substance characterized VVS self-assessment throughout the many years of Soviet rule. In a case in point, one general admitted that the flying establishment had come to judge a pilot's skills "mainly by the number of badges on his chest—namely, on the basis of his class rating"—when what truly mattered was his ability to hit targets accurately in various weather and tactical conditions. This general commented on the existing rating system: "Everything is turned upside down. We make weather conditions the dominant criteria, while the ability to employ one's weapons, which reflects the true level of proficiency, is buried away in obscure columns on a mission evaluation form."[11]

In parts of the USSR, notably in Central Asia, a pilot could *never* earn the top aeronautical rating, since the adverse weather conditions required for such a rating never occurred there. That circumstance prompted a lapse of integrity in which commanders would simply lie about the weather on the certification forms in order to allow a pilot to attain a First-Class rating. In lieu of that misplaced focus on weather minimums, the VVS general complained, "the key measure of a military pilot's skill should be his ability to fly a combat mission. Airfield weather conditions . . . should be of only secondary importance."[12]

Worse yet, the recurrent practice of dishonest reporting made for a guaranteed safety hazard, since pilots could be cleared for flight in meteorological conditions for which they had never actually qualified. At the root of that problem was a rampant "percentomania" that impelled regiment commanders to accelerate the advancement of their pilots to First-Class status so that their units might look good on the books, regardless of whether the pilots in question had actually accomplished the events and undergone the proficiency checks required for that aeronautical rating.[13]

Another example of dishonesty cited during the early revelations of glasnost was a willful falsification of a mission write-up in the wake of an over-G incident in which the aircraft exceeded its normal stress limit during a requalification mission flown by an experienced pilot with an instructor in a two-seat fighter-trainer. The requalifying pilot had not performed advanced handling maneuvers in more than two years. The scheduler knew that fact yet raised no objections when the requalifying officer was approved to fly a sortie and perform events for which even the accompanying instructor was not qualified. After landing, the instructor failed to report the over-G incident. The whistle was nevertheless blown by the chief of the squadron's flight recorder section. The issue eventually percolated up to higher headquarters, prompting a ruling that faulted the requalifying pilot for having introduced a control input that the instructor had been unable to countermand in time to prevent the over-G—rather than leading to a ruling that reprimanded the instructor for allowing an unqualified pilot to exceed his limitations and then failing to report the event.[14]

Lieutenant Viktor Belenko, the VPVO pilot who defected with his MiG-25 to Japan in 1976, described from personal experience a related instance of "cooking the books" years earlier, indicating that such self-deception had a long tradition in Soviet military aviation. During unit workups before a scheduled headquarters inspection, he was slated to fly a one-hour intercept mission against an upgrading student in a MiG-17. On the morning of the scheduled event, local area thunderstorms threatened to cancel the mission. Belenko was nevertheless ordered by his deputy regiment commander to fly the mission, with the following assurance: "Listen to me. Just tell your student to climb up to 500 meters. You make a quick intercept, and both of you come right back down. It won't take five minutes. I'll show you how to fix it when you get back." For the next three days, Belenko and his deputy commander juggled gun-camera film and flight-recorder tapes to concoct a record of an elaborate and successful mission. To mask the discrepancy between the sixty minutes of reported flying time and the six minutes of actual flying time, they dumped the unconsumed fuel—thousands of pounds—onto the ground.[15]

Even before his appointment as commander in chief, Colonel General Yevgeny Shaposhnikov freely acknowledged the overbureaucratization of the Soviet VVS that occasioned such unconscionable lapses in integrity. At one point he stated, "Our entire service life is thoroughly regimented and regulated by the requirements of multiple orders, directives, and regulations."[16] One of his favorite targets was rampant micromanagement and the arrogation of all wisdom and decision-making power to the highest levels of command. Representative of that attitude was a remark he made while still air commander in the Group of Soviet Forces in Germany (GSFG): "Excessive supervision brings nothing but harm to training."[17]

Similar concerns were later expressed by the commander of VPVO fighter aviation, Colonel General Vladimir Andreyev. With remarkable understatement, he described how he had been fired by General Ivan Tretyak, VPVO commander in chief, during the final year of Soviet rule because, after drawing attention to rampant corruption and abuses, he had become "inconvenient." In a seminal comment on the importance of integrity, he stressed: "If you begin practicing deceit in aviation, the consequences will be tragic." Andreyev said that it had been his practice to highlight problems for the VPVO commander in chief as he saw them, drawing freely on the related experience of the VVS, naval aviation, and other air forces around the world. Nevertheless, he confessed, the views of the professionals in his fighter directorate were given no respect, with Tretyak routinely issuing contrary decisions: "He would hand down orders that caused line pilots to pull their hair out." Repeatedly, Andreyev was forced to protect his people from unjustified attacks by their out-of-touch commander in chief. Looking ahead, he concluded: "I don't want to discuss him any more. What matters is that there will be fewer such military leaders in the future."[18]

The Beginnings of Soviet Awakening

The absence of realism in fighter training, long a repressed concern throughout the flying community, came under increasing attack from within the Soviet VVS ranks once glasnost lifted the lid on open criticism of established practice. Although the Soviet fighter pilot was expected to be fully ready in case of war, "the sad thing," two officers complained in 1988, was that this was not likely: "We talk a lot but are doing far from everything possible to attend to this."[19] The two officers added: "You would think we were doing anything but sitting on our hands, since the airfields know no silence day or night. Yet take a closer look. Little gain is being achieved. You will notice that here they played it safe, there they made things easy, and over there they overlooked things. As a result, we aren't getting the payoff that we should."[20]

These critics stopped short of a blanket indictment of Soviet VVS practice. Yet they were frank when they insisted, "Some of the provisions [of the rules] are out of date, are geared toward training pilots under simplistic conditions, and fail to reflect current needs." They complained, "Flights are standardized by official documents literally from takeoff to landing." As a result, they said, "the slightest deviation or initiative by a pilot" was penalized as "aerial hooliganism" (the Soviet term for wanton disregard for air discipline), even though it was common knowledge among pilots that "one can't do the job properly in combat training without intelligent and measured risk."[21]

Toward the end of the Soviet era, senior flight supervisors at the unit level were openly demanding that demonstrated competence in basic and advanced aircraft maneuvering should be a prerequisite for more complex mission-employment training. As one remarked: "The minimum [requirement] stipulated by the training plan must not be confused with adequacy. The minimum is *only* a minimum, and meeting it even 100 percent hardly constitutes grounds for rejoicing." Citing the well-known fact that an aviator skilled in air-combat maneuvering should also be adept at less-demanding mission events, he noted that he had "never encountered an outstanding aerobatic pilot who had difficulty with other forms of flying," whereas "situations involving the reverse are not uncommon." VVS aircrews voiced similar complaints over the culture of dishonesty that senior echelons had allowed to predominate in VVS practice for years. A February 1988 article lambasted the absence of integrity within units and the commanders' pervasive resort to the "whitewashing of shortcomings" and even to outright cheating in order to score well in operational readiness inspections.[22]

The ultimate indictment of the VVS's shortcomings in training was the acid reply of a Soviet pilot who was asked whether he felt that the 1991 Persian Gulf War would have ended differently had Iraq's aircraft been flown by Soviet pilots. That officer replied: "Hardly, because Iraq's pilots were trained by our pilots."

When the interviewer responded that "surely" Soviet pilots were "not that bad," the officer countered: "Any thinking [Soviet] pilot today knows that in case of war, he is assigned the role of cannon fodder. He also knows that this bothers very few people at the top."[23]

In a headquarters response to these outcries of discontent, the Soviet VVS deputy commander for combat training, Colonel General Anatoly Borsuk, kicked the ball back to subordinate commanders, stating that in so complaining, they were failing to exercise their vested command prerogatives. Rejecting the charge that all restrictions "flow from the central VVS staff and nowhere else," Borsuk maintained that although "some time ago such prohibitions did exist," under perestroika the responsibility for the most important prerogatives connected with aircrew training had "been delegated directly to regiments and squadrons." Suggesting that unit commanders should look to themselves rather than point the finger of blame at higher echelons, he insisted: "Today, all the guidance documents are oriented toward giving commanders the greatest possible independence." Borsuk acknowledged the errors of the past, "when initiative could only flow from the top down." Yet he stressed: "Under [current VVS] guidance, regiment commanders have been given every opportunity to decide independently how to conduct the training of their units' pilots."[24]

With the gauntlet thus thrown down for operators to show their ability to exercise the new latitude that had been granted them from above, it was only a matter of time before bolder voices from the flying community would sound off in reply. One of the first came not from the VVS but from the Mikoyan Design Bureau. In a hard-hitting critique of the stolid conservatism that continued to afflict VVS training and tactics application, Valery Menitsky, the respected chief test pilot, cited from his own experience cases of pilots whose air-combat prowess had been all but nonexistent from their first day of graduation from flight school because of the "ban that existed at that time on advanced aerobatics." The root cause, he added, was not the pilots or their commanders but "the system itself. . . . The problem was that none of the top leaders were willing to face up to this during those 'stagnant' times."[25] Menitsky noted with dismay how seasoned test pilots on his staff would routinely visit line regiments to see how the users were doing with their new equipment, only to discover all too often "units where they downplay[ed] the role of flying skills and approach[ed] tactics in a cookbook manner."[26]

Menitsky chided the VVS for its reluctance to run legitimate risks in the interest of increased air-combat proficiency: "True enough, safety can be achieved through bans. But such safety is illusory, producing unhappy results in the end. The bitter experience of bans has more than once put military pilots in a bad situation." He added: "Almost all pilots understand this, but unfortunately, not all commanders share their view. They command regiments and squadrons as prisoners of old concepts. Such commanders oversimplify tasks in all sorts of ways, instruct subordinates to fly over the same routes and execute attacks using simple types of maneuvers, thereby seeking to reduce the number of accident-prone situations in the air. In so doing, they train pilots not to be creative."[27]

Menitsky's complaint was echoed by a retired colonel who, with thirty years of fighter experience, revealingly noted that once attention had become focused on air-to-air missile employment, "the training of pilots in close maneuvering air combat was halted. Such exercises were removed from the KBP. What did that lopsided arrangement lead to? The well-known Israeli-Egyptian military conflict revealed the unsoundness of the idea of arming the VVS only with long-range and short-range missiles." He added that this was not merely a point of quaint historical interest: "*At the present time, supporters of the elimination of close maneuver air combat from the arsenal of tactical methods of pilots are appearing once again.* There is a need for serious study of tactics today."[28]

Although much had improved since the earlier days of stereotyped conduct, in 1990 two officers stated that the combat training system remained "unfortunately to this day grounded on the old foundation." They added, "Its essentials have remained unchanged." The coauthors of this complaint charged that existing VVS approaches to tactical training continued to "lag far behind the sophistication of contemporary aviation equipment," in considerable part because of the "voluminous instructions fall[ing] plentifully on decrepit regiments 'from above.'" They further warned that it would be no mean feat to change the existing state of affairs for the better, since the long-established VVS approach to aircrew training had occasioned "a dearth of initiative, creativity, and capacity to assume responsibility." Finally, in summation, they added that the prospects for any real revolution in combat training would "depend on how soon we begin ridding ourselves of our serf mentality."[29]

In an indication of how far the Soviet VVS had yet to go in converting promise to reality, one squadron commander, whose pilots were actually trying to apply the new license granted by higher headquarters to experiment with exercising greater initiative, concluded that things were not working out. "[For years] we were forced into a situation in which combat training . . . amounted to a one-way road to mediocrity, which is, judging from all the evidence, where we've ended up." Following that confirmation of a truth about Soviet training that had long been widely suspected in the West, the squadron commander added: "We learned to suppress any initiative during our many years of living under the thumb of the command-administrative system. We still are fearful of legalizing it altogether—what if everything that goes around today comes around again tomorrow?" The commander recalled in frustration how he and his deputies had struggled unsuccessfully to escape the old mold by examining individual records and seeking to determine the actual proficiency of each pilot all over again: "Most notable about this was how it showed that we'd succumbed to the illusion that we knew each other. Fat chance! We didn't even know ourselves well, since that had not been particularly important before. The abstract image of some statistically average First-, Second-, and Third-Class pilot had been formulated automatically. The entire process of combat training had been geared toward statistically average mediocrity." This conscientious leader spoke enviously of having recently read an interview with an RAF fighter squadron commander who had revealed a standard of excellence to which Soviet professionalism could still only aspire.[30]

The Road to Recovery

During his brief incumbency as commander in chief, Shaposhnikov laid the groundwork for a top-to-bottom revamping of VVS approaches to fighter operations and training. He clearly recognized the Soviet VVS's long-unrequited need for greater training realism, and he advocated innovations, alluded to in the preceding chapter, that sounded more than passingly analogous to accepted Western practices. Examples included his suggestion that exercises should be geared more toward training and tactics development than toward readiness certification, his insistence on strict standards for allocating sortie events among aircrews in squadron training, and his call for a yardstick by which Soviet pilot proficiency might be measured using an approach that sounded, in concept if not in form, roughly comparable to the USAF's Graduated Combat Capability (GCC) evaluation system.

Finally, and most important, Shaposhnikov recognized the weakness emanating from the VVS's suppression of pilot initiative, as well as from its overreliance on scripted sortie profiles under close GCI control. Soviet pilots had routinely grumbled about this limitation for years.[31] This was the first time, however, that a VVS commander had openly agreed and announced a determination to bring about needed changes. In earlier times of East-West tension, the rise of such an innovator to be commander in chief of the VVS would have been grounds for serious concern among NATO planners. Yet with the USSR well on its way toward self-destruction in December 1991, the most pressing question was whether Shaposhnikov would be able to overcome the bureaucratic drag, long-standing habits, and deep political uncertainty that together threatened to obstruct the realization of his sought-after reforms.

Today, with the Soviet system repudiated and an uncertain horizon looming ahead, the Russian VVS stands on the threshold of *potentially* the most radical departure from its familiar ways since the earliest days of the Soviet state. As the chief of VVS education and training commented before the USSR's final collapse: "The events of August 1991 have accelerated the process of radical change in the country's armed forces. It is gratifying to note that common sense is returning to us, albeit slowly."[32]

That reflection helps to underscore the important point that throughout the VVS's history, the main problem was the Soviet system, not the individual pilot or his equipment. The Soviet pilot was selected by exacting criteria, and he represented the best pilot talent that Soviet society had to offer. Soviet aircraft and air-to-air missiles were always respectable from a technical standpoint. Properly employed, the latest-generation MiG-29 and Su-27, with their AA-10 Alamo and AA-11 Archer missiles (as they are known by their NATO designators), are without question a match for any comparable systems the West currently operates. In some respects these Russian aircraft and missiles command a decided performance edge. The improved MiG-29M, the Su-35, and a new Russian active radar homing missile comparable to the U.S. AIM-120 AMRAAM (advanced medium-range air-to-air missile) promise further advantages yet. The reason the VVS has long had such trouble getting the most out of these assets is that the Soviet pilot was inevitably a product of his training environment. Naturally, his techniques and skills were heavily conditioned and circumscribed by the inhibiting influence of the VVS's uniquely "Soviet" operational culture.

Considering the many restrictions that hampered VVS pilot initiative and tactical prowess throughout the cold war, it was all but inevitable that the Soviet MiG-21 pilots who were lured into battle by the Israeli Air Force over Suez in July 1970 would be so completely outmatched. According to firsthand accounts by the Israeli pilots, the Soviets were aggressive and flew textbook formations going into the fight. Once the engagement was joined, however, their mutual support quickly fell apart, and they began making elementary mistakes, including indiscriminately firing their early-generation infrared missiles outside of effective parameters, seemingly out of panic and to no apparent tactical purpose. By the end of the five-minute melee, five MiG-21s were downed, with no Israeli losses.

The difference was not in the quality of the individuals who were pitted against one another in that engagement but rather in their diametrically opposed approaches to training and force employment. With their heavy dependence on GCI and their unfamiliarity with anything beyond the broadest essentials of free air-combat maneuvering, the Soviet pilots lacked the situation awareness and the implicit knowledge of appropriate moves and countermoves that are crucial for surviving and winning in a dynamic, multiparticipant air battle. That said, it is a safe bet that a Russian fighter pilot today could be picked virtually at random from squadron service, detrained of his most counterproductive habits acquired through long exposure to Soviet influence, enrolled in a USAF F-15 qualification course or its U.S. Navy F-14 equivalent, and emerge with creditable air-to-air skills.

Since the USSR's collapse, the VVS has been freed of the organizational chokehold that limited its capacity to innovate under Soviet rule. In principle it is now at liberty to cast aside its old ways and develop a new repertoire aimed at extracting the fullest leverage from its capable equipment. Yet with a shoestring operations and support budget that forces commanders to bend every effort simply to maintain their pilots' basic aircraft handling proficiency and instrument and landing currency, it is hard to imagine how they might conduct the sort of training that would be required, at a minimum, to bring Russia's pilots up to accepted Western standards.

General Borsuk's successor as deputy commander in chief for combat training, Colonel General Yevgeny Zarudnev, conceded in late 1992 that the state of training at the regiment, division, and air army levels had become "catastrophic."[33] In contrast to the former Soviet ideal norm of 140 to 160 flying hours a year for fighter pilots, he reported that the Russian VVS was registering only one-fourth to one-fifth of that number because of inadequate funding. Zarudnev added that maintenance manning was down to 50–70 percent of normal levels in most units. He confirmed that VVS leadership had given "little thought" to the requirements for realistic training throughout the Soviet period and that the Russian VVS now faced the hard choice of whether, in the face of its pilot surplus, to let its youngest pilots go and thus sacrifice the next generation or to retire its more experienced pilots early, thus leaving the VVS with no significant combat capability. The extent of the VVS's troubles in that respect was graphically shown two years later by the deficient performance of its ground-attack pilots in the war in Chechnya, thanks in large part to chronically underfunded training (see Chapter 8).

To repeat a point made earlier, some of the afflictions noted by Russian airmen since the onset of glasnost are endemic to air forces the world over. The one tendency that remains unique to the Russian VVS is the top-down rigidity in both operations and thought, an inflexibility that the communist system for years imposed on pilots and commanders who knew better but who were obliged to pretend otherwise. Because old habits die hard, elements of the Soviet rigidity persist to this day, even though flight activity has been reduced to a near-halt because of the budget crisis. It is this legacy of the now-discredited Soviet approach to operations and training that Russian airmen will have to work the hardest to overcome.

7.

How Might They Have Done If . . .

With the end of the cold war and the collapse of the Soviet Union, it is instructive to revisit the Western debate about Soviet air-combat prowess in the 1980s. As a result, we may gain better insights into the once-deadlocked question of how the Soviet VVS might have acquitted itself in an aerial showdown over Central Europe. Such an inquiry, drawing on the evidence presented in the preceding chapters, can help inform a retrospective look at where observers of Soviet and Russian air power were right, where they were wrong, and what lessons might be derived regarding mistakes to avoid in future efforts to come to grips with force-employment practices that diverge sharply from our own.

Early in the nuclear age, when the USSR remained all but opaque to outside scrutiny, Raymond Garthoff wrote: "In order to understand an alien military culture, it is first necessary to escape the confines of one's own implicit and unconscious strategic concept. The ideas of others, when these are interpreted in terms of the military or political analyst's own strategic preconceptions, will appear distorted or, often, obsolete. And the comfort derived from a superficial assessment of differing views, in such a manner that these views seem to represent a simple 'cultural lag' on the part of our opponent, may obscure the recognition of these views as manifestations of a different underlying doctrine and strategic concept."[1] At the time these words were written, such inquiry was severely hampered by Soviet secrecy and societal closure. Today, with the Soviet past more accessible, there is considerable value to be had from revisiting that past and drawing appropriate conclusions for future reflection.

A Level-of-Analysis Problem

Between the contrasting Western images from the mid-1970s through the mid-1980s—portraying the Soviet air threat as ten feet tall or three feet short—many protagonists on both sides of the debate failed to see that they were grappling with the wrong issue. Each of these opposing images, outlined at the beginning of Chapter 5, contained some elements of truth. Yet each dealt with only a part of the problem. The first view gave the Soviet VVS too much credit for such non-quantifiable factors as training, tactics, leadership quality, operational prowess, and all the other intangibles that were excluded from the analysis and that, for better or worse, make up the critical link between equipment capability and combat outcomes. The second view looked only at the Soviet pilot, in isolation, and ignored the fact that wars are not decided by individual dogfights but rather by the interaction of all countervailing air, land, and naval forces. The cardinal error made by *both* sides was to work one level of aggregation too low by failing to ask how an air force's hardware might combine with its proficiency and style to make its influence felt in a campaign context.

Looking at the issue today, with the benefit of hindsight and better evidence, we can confidently say that the edge in that debate belonged to those who took the second view—that is, those who saw the Soviet pilot as rigorously trained and technically literate yet also highly regimented and bound to scripted scenarios heavily dependent on close GCI control, with little room for exercising initiative and with virtually no opportunity to develop the proficiency at free air-combat maneuvering that Western fighter pilots routinely practiced. Complicating the drawing of easy conclusions from that revealed pilot deficiency, however, was the ongoing improvement in Soviet equipment, as attested by the introduction of the MiG-29 and the Su-27 into front-line fighter regiments. As improvements in VVS training and tactics proceeded, in contrast, at a snail's pace, by the late 1980s the VVS was in a genuine intellectual turmoil, with its brightest lights both at senior leadership levels and at the grass roots recognizing and admitting their shortcomings.

Despite those signs of ferment, inertia and continuity for the most part predominated. Soviet fighter aviation remained heavily tied to ground-based direction and reflected ingrained habits that were intrinsic to Soviet culture—not just to VVS culture but to that of the armed forces and society in general. It was a culture that emphasized the primacy of the collective over the individual. What it produced, and what Russian military professionals now recognize to have been a potentially fatal liability, was expensively trained pilots with leading-edge equipment who were given little leeway to use that equipment and training to their fullest capability.

Ambiguities in the Changing Threat Picture

Does this mean that had an air-combat showdown taken place over the Fulda Gap, the skies of Germany would quickly have been swept clean of Soviet and Warsaw Pact fighters by U.S. and NATO airmen? Probably. But the question that really matters is, What would have been the ultimate effect? For one thing, the Soviet air threat would not have been quite the pushover that the Iraqi Air Force proved to be against the allied coalition in Operation Desert Storm. Like the poor Egyptian and Syrian performances against Israel during the succession of Middle East air battles since 1967, the Soviet-trained Iraqi Air Force bore the heavy imprint of the Soviet VVS's air-to-air style. But it also represented a highly misleading baseline from which to project how the Soviet VVS would have performed in an air war against NATO.

Several years after the USSR's collapse, a thoughtful VVS general rightly admonished me not to equate Russian pilots with Arab pilots. Had the Israelis encountered Soviet fighter pilots rather than Syrians in the aerial engagements over Lebanon's Bekáa Valley in 1982, there would almost surely have been perceptible differences both in the chemistry and in the outcome of the ensuing combat. To begin with, simply by virtue of their professionalism and upbringing, Soviet pilots would have shown greater air discipline, as well as a purposeful aggressiveness that would have led them to stay and fight rather than turn and run when engaged. They most likely would have operated more consistently within recognizable tactical principles. They would have been more knowledgeable about the performance parameters and limitations of their weapons and therefore would have been better positioned to take full advantage of passing opportunities to get off a killing air-to-air missile shot against the opposing side. In the end, however, the outcome would still have been heavily weighted in favor of the Israelis. It would not have been an 85–0 shutout by any means, as the Israeli Air Force accomplished over the Syrians, but the Soviet pilots almost surely would have ended up on the losing side simply because they were not trained for the sort of free-form, multiparticipant air combat that ensued once the fights began.

Had such engagements continued for any length of time, measured in months rather than days, Soviet pilots would not have remained hapless losers. Notwithstanding their rigidities, the Soviets were (and the Russians remain) capable of purposeful change under stress. Necessity being the mother of invention, they would have licked their wounds and come up with smarter ways, just as they did slowly over the four-year evolution of World War II. The reason such a recovery was never given much credence in the NATO–Warsaw Pact context was that there was little chance that a war would last long enough (or remain conventional long enough) to allow such a learning curve to develop and register its effects.

Even this more circumspect assessment of the VVS's shortcomings offers little ground for complacency, however. Although NATO air-to-air pilots could be assured of going into a fight with a pronounced edge in tactical proficiency over their Soviet opposites, NATO planners and commanders did not enjoy that luxury because they had to worry about a bigger picture. Whatever one might say in hindsight about the individual Soviet pilot and his training inadequacies by

Western standards, the VVS fighter force in the aggregate demanded respect. First, it had a definite, if not overwhelming, edge in numbers, which translated into an ability to concentrate force and sustain an air operation despite high attrition. The VVS further operated within a doctrinal framework that was supremely offensive in orientation. That gave the Soviet side the power of the initiative, plus an advantage in preserving the offensive momentum that naturally accrues to the side with the prerogative of striking first. Finally, the Soviet military leadership's attitude toward attrition was not much concerned about the prospect of high loss rates so long as Warsaw Pact ground forces advanced on schedule at the operational and strategic levels.

The Fallacy of Mirror-Imaging

This all suggests that analysts erred whenever they sized up the Soviet air threat using Western measures of effectiveness rather than asking how Soviet planners might assess their own capability. What was needed was an appraisal of the Soviets by their own standards and an explicit recognition that their training activities necessarily took place in a uniquely Soviet context. Soviet commanders may have operated in accordance with a seemingly inflexible operational philosophy, but they were not stupid, and it is highly doubtful that they ever believed that what they were doing was inappropriate to their needs. They knew perfectly well how USAF and NATO aircrews trained, for they could read Western defense establishments almost like an open book. They also were quite adept at borrowing selectively from Western technical practice whenever it suited their needs, as best exemplified by the design features of the MiG-29 and the Su-27. Nevertheless, they remained wedded to their own concepts of operations. That they did not elect to emulate Western employment practices with their fourth-generation fighters did not indicate a "slowness to converge." Rather, it revealed a fundamentally different concept of warfare and of the role of air power in it.

Soviet commanders almost surely did not see the VVS training gap that many in the U.S. fighter community saw. The greater likelihood is that they viewed their approach to training as *better,* given the way they planned to fight. As one knowledgeable USAF officer remarked, what might have appeared to an American observer as "an unimaginative tactic" might have appeared to the Soviet commander "as sophisticated and advanced as his doctrines, force structure, and mission would dictate. And who is to say that fluid attack and independent maneuvering would work better than regimental control in their battle schemes?"[2]

Simply put, the idea of allowing flight leaders to make autonomous force-commitment decisions was anathema to mainstream Soviet military thought. The General Staff was not only content but also determined to treat its fighter pilots as pawns and to elevate tactical decision-making authority to a higher level—

where, in their view, it properly belonged. U.S. threat assessors would have waited forever for the Soviets to adopt Western operational concepts as refined at Red Flag and at similar large-force training exercises around the world. That expectation was a classic case of the fallacy of mirror-imaging in its easy assumption that Soviet development of equipment similar to that of the West would inevitably drive the VVS to adopt similar tactics and concepts of force employment. What the West needed, and was all too slow to gain, was a recognition that the Soviets were marching to their own drummer. Soviet air-campaign philosophy, with its heavy combined-arms influence, derived from a unique Soviet military tradition. It yielded an image of tactical air power, and of the role of that air power in combined-arms warfare, that was dramatically different from the parallel philosophy that had evolved in the West.

Often to the detriment of a clear understanding of the dynamics of warfare, U.S. analysts characteristically carved war up into neatly defined categories, such as air-to-air combat, surface attack, electronic combat, and land operations, and then treated these categories as though they were hermetically sealed domains of activity with few significant interrelationships or interdependencies. The Soviets, by contrast, saw war as a seamless web. To them, what happened in one category affected activity in all others. In conventional land warfare, air power was regarded as a supporting combat element in a combined-arms approach to force employment. *Everything* the VVS did in air-to-air training had to be viewed within that context to be properly understood. Bluntly stated, Soviet air-to-air pilots performed their assigned function only if, by keeping NATO's ground-attack aircraft from slowing up the advancing Warsaw Pact tanks and infantry, they helped the Soviet front commander accomplish *his* mission of putting a wall of armor on the Rhine River by D-plus-whatever. How the pilots fared in aerial combat itself was a side issue. In this regard Soviet and Warsaw Pact air-to-air pilots were worlds apart from their NATO opposites in mission tasking and expected performance.

With the introduction of longer-range aircraft like the Tu-22M Backfire and the Su-24 Fencer, the VVS acquired a range-payload capability that promised to yield something like an independent strategic air-offensive option for use in a possible theater war in Europe. Nevertheless, there was never an autonomous role for tactical air power in Soviet military thought. "Frontal aviation," the generic Soviet term for tactical air power, meant exactly what it implied— namely, air power tasked by the front commander to support his operational needs. At the General Staff level, Soviet planners were simply not interested in air-to-air kill ratios as ends in themselves. As Barry Watts observed, they would have been quite content "to ensure that Pact ground forces [attained] their objectives on the desired time lines, even if most of the American F-15 drivers [became] multiple aces." The Soviet image of the proper use of air power was a carefully crafted offensive air operation, not the putative leverage of "a handful of pilots trained to a razor's edge."[3] That fact was well captured in the famous cartoon showing two Soviet marshals in Brussels sitting over a bottle of liberated Napoleon brandy and celebrating their victory over NATO, at which point one looks at the other and asks: "By the way, comrade, did we win the air war also?"

Even had the VVS lost 80 percent or more of its air-to-air and ground-attack assets during a war against NATO, the Soviet High Command might have considered that figure to be an acceptable buy-in cost if it helped pave the way for a theater victory. This approach to war also posed a nontrivial air-discipline problem for defending NATO air-to-air pilots. It was not at all uncommon at the height of the cold war during the early 1980s for Western fighter pilots to claim, with quiet confidence, that should war come, they would make ace during the first thirty minutes because of their superior training and air-combat prowess. Yet if the price of their making ace on Day One was abandoning their defensive combat air-patrol duties and thus enabling VVS strikers to reach targets deep inside NATO lines, they would have made ace for nothing. By contrast, the VVS was never in the business of producing fighter aces as a desired end in itself. That point is crucially important for a correct understanding of how air-to-air combat related to the larger Soviet scheme of war.

The Limits of Informed Hindsight

Had the cold war continued, the USSR would eventually have lost some of its former quantitative advantages as an inevitable result of technological advance. For one thing, the VVS's new fourth-generation fighters represented more complex and costly equipment than it had ever acquired before, portending a slower production rate and reduced total force size. Although NATO faced a similar problem, the overall trend was nevertheless a narrowing of the former numerical asymmetry that had long favored the Warsaw Pact. A Soviet-U.S. standoff in Europe circa 1995–2000 would not have seen the deployed combat aircraft imbalance that NATO suffered in earlier years.

Furthermore, with the increased complexity of their latest fighters, the Soviets themselves bought into many of the same problems of maintenance and sustainability that the USAF experienced for a time with the F-15 because of the F-15's leading-edge engine technology and more sophisticated avionics. To cite but one illustration, as was pointed out in Chapter 2, it was not uncommon for VVS maintenance officers in the late 1980s to complain openly about seemingly intractable problems of radar fault isolation.

Finally, the heightened unit costs and the reduced numbers of the new Soviet fighters would have made it much more difficult for Soviet planners to continue thinking of their air-to-air assets almost entirely as attrition fillers. A Soviet air commander in 1995–2000 would most definitely not have enjoyed the luxury of contemplating burning off MiG-29s at the same rate he could have acceptably lost MiG-21s or MiG-23s a decade earlier.

Offsetting those adverse trends, the VVS fighter community by the cold war's end was on the verge of acquiring new capabilities that would have noticeably stressed NATO air defenders, particularly in air-to-air missile range and lethality. It has long been a rule of thumb among fighter pilots that whichever side can get off the first missile shot can control the ensuing engagement. With its new look-down/shoot-down capability, the VVS by 1989 had reached a point where it could deny an F-111 or Tornado crew a confident low-altitude sanctuary against air threats. Finally, with improved infrared missiles offering expanded forward-hemisphere launch envelopes, coupled with a point-and-shoot helmet-mounted sight, even a weak Soviet pilot would have been a threat to respect, since he would have possessed a weapon offering greater shot opportunities than ever before. The fact that he had little in the way of basic fighter maneuvering skills would have been of only marginal significance for such a scenario.

In all, this juxtaposition of changing strengths and weaknesses leaves us with something of a wash on the question of whether the Soviet VVS had vulnerabilities that could have been decisively exploited by NATO. There is little doubt that the USAF would have maintained a commanding edge in air-combat maneuvering prowess. On the other hand, the Soviets had compensating advantages in superior numbers, the power of the initiative, an offensive doctrine, a greater insensitivity to attrition, and the beginnings of an equipment qualitative parity that would have undermined that NATO edge, at least at the margins. They might also have had more permissive rules of engagement regarding target identification in beyond-visual-range air-to-air missile employment.

Even today, then, we cannot reach a conclusive answer to the question of how Soviet conventional forces might have fared against NATO had they been put to the test of combat. Now that the former leaders of the Soviet VVS, both active and retired, are freer to discuss such matters openly, and now that this is a legitimate question for cold war history rather than one with intelligence-collection overtones, it might be interesting to ask the VVS fighter community how *they* saw the issue at the height of the cold war. Such an exchange could make for an enlightening dialogue between U.S. and Russian fighter pilots and defense analysts. After the Soviet Union's demise, an intelligent and reflective VVS general calmly assured me: "We were never afraid of you." If he meant that, it would be instructive to understand why.

8.

Russia's Air War in Chechnya

The Russian VVS experienced its first trial by fire during Russia's 1994–96 embroilment in Chechnya.[1] The only previous combat exposure of comparable note by Soviet forces occurred in Moscow's unsuccessful war in Afghanistan nearly a decade earlier. Although the Chechen operation was largely a failed attempt by Russian infantry and armored forces to use military overkill to suppress a local rebellion, air power played a notable part in providing recurrent, if ineffective, support to Russia's beleaguered and hapless ground contingent.

Being forced into a needless war at a time of financial stress created a substantial drain on scarce resources, which was inopportune, to say the least, for the VVS leadership. Nevertheless, the war offered a telling test of the VVS's declared primary role in the post-Soviet era—namely, the projection of air power to conflicted areas along the periphery of the former Soviet Union. Ever since the allied coalition's resounding success in Operation Desert Storm more than three years earlier, Russia's military leaders, notably including those in the VVS, had spoken respectfully of the coalition's achievement in the air campaign and had repeatedly invoked that achievement as the role model to be followed. They had also claimed, rather optimistically, that despite its manifold problems, the VVS had the needed know-how to deliver an analogous performance.

Because of the topography and weather, in addition to the operational challenge, Chechnya was scarcely the clear-cut venue for an air war like the one the allies had enjoyed against Iraq. Rather the VVS's mission entailed backstopping Russian ground troops in putting down an uprising of irregulars more than it did frontally engaging organized formations and attaining well-defined objectives on a battlefield. There were few fixed targets of military significance in Chechnya, and there were no front lines whatsoever, rendering the situation more like what NATO had faced in Bosnia between 1992 and 1995 than what the allied coalition had been forced to contend with in Desert Storm. Nevertheless, Chechnya provided a low-risk laboratory for testing the new Russian strategy, as well as the VVS's capabilities under live-fire conditions. The returns were highly mixed at best.

The VVS's airlift arm carried its share of the burden in Chechnya remarkably well, despite severe serviceability problems and its substantial loss of assets to Ukraine and Kazakhstan (almost half of the Soviet VVS's 500 Il-76 jet transports) following the USSR's breakup. VVS combat aircraft also performed well in unopposed ground attacks against unsheltered Chechen aircraft during the war's preliminaries. However, as the initial ground war unfolded and problems mounted due to weather complications and the demand for high-accuracy bombing in the face of effective low-altitude Chechen air defenses, repeated degradations in VVS performance clearly attested to the deprivation that the VVS continued to suffer in curtailed training due to a lack of adequate funding.

This was Russia's first military venture to be conducted under the full glare of international press attention. Never before had outsiders been able to monitor Russian military operations as closely as in Chechnya. Not surprisingly, the increased openness of post-Soviet Russia made for a recurring approach-avoidance conflict among military authorities. On the one hand, the badly underfunded Ministry of Defense, clearly intent on making the best of this opportunity to "show its stuff," sought to use the war as an occasion to cast its strengths in the most favorable light, as well as to win sympathy for the privations it had been forced to suffer since the collapse of Soviet communism. On the other hand, by long-standing force of habit, the Russian High Command continued to carry an appreciable amount of Soviet baggage in its day-to-day routines. It was plainly discomfited at having its every action observed and criticized by the media. Military leaders repeatedly fell back on secrecy and security arguments to evade pointed questions. They also sought, sometimes aggressively, to hinder the work of reporters.

For the most part, Colonel General Pyotr Deinekin, VVS commander in chief, spoke candidly about the VVS's performance and problems in Chechnya. Not surprisingly, he remained mute on such important matters as the tempo and level of intensity of air operations, the total number and types of aircraft employed, detailed numbers of combat and combat-support sorties flown, and weapons delivery modes used in ground-attack operations. Moreover, he provided little in the way of an accounting of weapons effectiveness and operational results. Nevertheless, he disclosed enough to allow Western observers to see at least the big picture through Russian eyes, something that would have been out of the question during the years of Soviet rule. Along with statements by other Russian military leaders, not limited to those wearing blue uniforms, his remarks were revealing of the role played by Russian air power in the Chechen war, as well as of what the VVS's performance—and that of Russia's forces more generally—indicated about Russia's emerging strategy and near-term potential for regional conflict management.[2]

Highlights of the Air Campaign

The region of Chechnya, a mountainous enclave in Transcaucasia, is approximately the size of the U.S. state of Connecticut, with a population of 1.3 million people, including a multitude of truculent and feuding ethnic clans. It is legally a part of the Russian Federation, having been annexed by Russia during tsarist times. For manifold reasons not pertinent to the issues at hand here, Chechnya was a time bomb that was bound to go off in Moscow's face in the wake of the USSR's demise.

To summarize the origins of the conflict, separatists in the Chechen-Ingush region recognized a ripe opportunity for secession as the USSR careered toward collapse in 1991. On August 21, the third and last day of the failed Soviet coup attempt, Chechnya began its disengagement; it declared independence from the Russian Federation on September 6. Two months after the abortive coup, Major General Dzhokar Dudayev, a former Soviet VVS bomber pilot and air division commander, was elected president of Chechnya.[3] He reaffirmed Chechnya's independence and promptly established an iron rule over what Pavel Felgengauer, a Moscow defense correspondent, later described as a "strange buccaneer republic."[4]

Moscow first ignored the problem, then tried twice to topple Dudayev through clandestine operations. The initial attempt, which bore heavy marks of involvement by the Federal Counterintelligence Service, strove to exploit opposition to Dudayev among the Chechen population. That ill-fated effort unraveled in late 1994 when Chechen rebels successfully countered the mission. The second attempt, on November 26–27, failed catastrophically, with Dudayev claiming that sixty-seven Russian tanks had been destroyed. A Russian airborne spokesman later admitted that the attack was doomed from the outset because "without infantry cover, it was really senseless to bring tanks into the city."[5] After the embarrassment of that second failed attempt, President Boris Yeltsin decided to move directly by committing Russian forces to a massive intervention on the ground.[6]

Without question, Chechnya presented Russia with a nettlesome difficulty. Indeed Moscow's Chechen problem had roots running well back to pre-Soviet times. Neither the tsars nor the communists had fully succeeded in subjugating the fiercely independent Muslims who populated Chechnya and who had sustained a burning hatred for Russians ever since their forced assimilation. During World War II, Joseph Stalin had deported the Chechens wholesale to Kazakhstan out of fear that they would collaborate with the Nazis. Nikita Khrushchev finally permitted them to return home in the mid-1950s, whereupon they discovered that everything they had left behind had been taken over by Russians. This situation

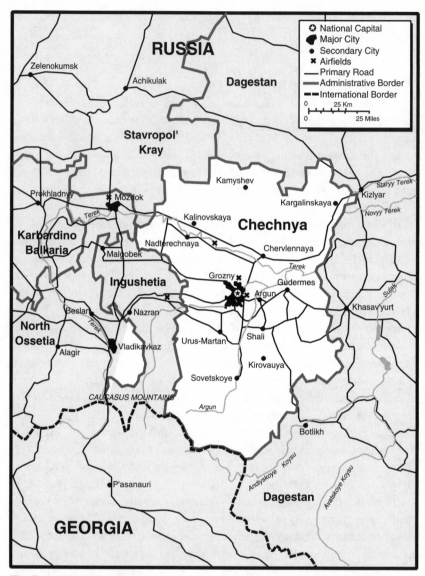

The Republic of Chechnya

triggered a vicious underground ethnic campaign against the despised Russians, who were routinely victims of indiscriminate knife killings at the hands of embittered Chechens. Russian vigilante groups soon formed to return the violence in kind, with the result that Soviet troops had to be called in by 1959 to restore order.

Nevertheless, local discontentment continued to simmer, and Chechnya remained an unwelcoming place for Russians. Lieutenant Viktor Belenko, the

MiG-25 pilot who defected with his aircraft to Japan in 1976, received basic flight instruction at the Armavir flight school, which maintained an auxiliary training field just outside the Chechen capital of Grozny. Belenko recalled that at a local-area orientation after his class had first reported to Grozny, the KGB officer had warned: "Most of all, you must guard yourself against the Chechens. The Chechens use knives wantonly, and under stress they will butcher you."[7] Belenko further remarked that many Chechens had been reared from birth to believe that one could never attain full manhood without first killing at least one Russian.

Dudayev's government was illegitimate and irresponsible in equal measure. It offered safe haven to a motley assortment of Russia's criminal underworld, and it was no more accountable than the Yeltsin government in failing to negotiate a peace settlement, or at least a modus vivendi, throughout the three years before Russia's armed intervention. In the spring of 1993 Dudayev dissolved Chechnya's parliament and proceeded to rule as a warlord. Shortly thereafter dissenters clashed with Dudayev's presidential guard, with nearly fifty dissenters killed in the process. Dudayev repeatedly went out of his way to irritate Moscow. Chechen bandits seized hostages for ransom in several cities in southern Russia, and the capital city of Grozny earned a deserved reputation as a hotbed of criminal gangs. Grozny was also, according to one account, "the destination of choice for anyone hijacking a Russian airliner."[8] Moscow's tolerance of such behavior was bound to wear thin. By November 1994 the forbearance of the Yeltsin government finally broke.

The Operational Setting

Chechnya's force structure, such as it was, consisted of arms and equipment left behind by the departing Soviet military after the breakup of the USSR. Spoils accruing to the Chechen ground forces included 42 Soviet tanks (a mix of T-62Ms and T-72s), 66 armored combat vehicles, 18 Grad multiple-rocket launchers, 30 122-mm towed howitzers, and 523 RPG-7 antitank grenade launchers. Chechnya's air defenses included 4 mobile ZSU-23/4 radar and optically tracked antiaircraft guns, 6 ZU-23 and DShK optically sighted machine guns, portable grenade launchers, and small arms mounted on trucks and passenger cars. General Deinekin said that the Chechen irregulars also possessed "several thousand" shoulder-fired infrared SAMs.[9] The SAMs included the SA-7/14 Strela and possibly also the SA-16 Igla. Neighboring Azerbaijan was said to have provided Dudayev with additional infrared SAMs.[10]

Chechnya had only a limited air capability, consisting of 152 Czech-built L-39 jet trainers, 94 older L-29s, and several MiG-15 and MiG-17 first-generation Soviet jet fighters inherited from the Armavir flight school.[11] Some Chechen pilots reportedly received training in Azerbaijan after the USSR's collapse. Chechnya was said to have "several dozen" fully trained military pilots, along with some mercenary pilots hired from the former Soviet republics. Since Chechen L-39s were believed to have taken part in the Georgian-Abkhazian war by bombing Georgian positions, their combat potential was more than hypothetical.

Russian air operations in the Chechen war played themselves out in three phases: (1) preparatory moves, (2) the gaining of air control, and (3) sustained air support to ground operations. According to one Russian media account, only "several dozen" combat aircraft took part in those operations.[12] Considering another report that as many as 26 Russian VVS aircraft sustained battle damage during the course of the war, however, the former estimate was probably low by a considerable margin.

Preparatory Moves

Russian air operations were conducted by units from the VVS's VTA, KFA, and LRA, as well as by assets from the separate Russian VPVO and army rotary-wing aviation. The last group included both attack and transport helicopters. Russian naval aviation did not participate in the war.

There were early reports of undeclared VVS participation in air strikes against Chechnya both before and during the second incursion on November 26, including alleged attacks on a tank unit at Shali and other missions against Braginsky, Tersky, Katayama, and the Grozny North airfield.[13] The first formal air involvement occurred later that month in response to intelligence reports claiming that a peaceful settlement was unattainable.

VVS combat aircraft used in the war were drawn mainly from units reconstituted from disbanded Soviet ground-attack regiments formerly based in Eastern Europe. After the Warsaw Pact's dissolution, those reformed units had relocated to bare bases in the North Caucasus Military District, which offered little infrastructure and only half the needed fuel, rations, ammunition, and spare parts.

Su-24MR reconnaissance jets conducted detailed photography of the three Chechen airfields of Kalinovskaya, Khankala, and Grozny North. They also collected target information on potential military objectives in Grozny and its suburbs and in other areas. According to VVS accounts, they produced "conclusive evidence" that Dudayev was gearing up for combat. Fortified areas were being erected, and L-29 and L-39 jet trainers were being fueled for possible use.[14] VPVO had detected Dudayev's forces preparing highways and road segments as alternate runways to accommodate flight operations. At least some of the L-39s were configured with wing stations for carrying 250-pound bombs and rocket pods.[15] Those aircraft could have been used against Russian troops, as well as against such lucrative targets as nuclear reactors, chemical plants, and weapons storage dumps. By the VVS's admission, however, they lacked sufficient range to reach Moscow, particularly if loaded with munitions.[16]

The invasion by Russian ground units was preceded by a VTA airlift into Mozdok, just to the northwest of the secessionist republic, on November 30. Poor weather hampered the airlift. Nevertheless, VTA played a key role in the buildup, which totaled some 40,000 troops at the height of Russia's involvement in the fighting. It was reported on December 1 that 38 VTA An-12 transports with troops and equipment had flown into Vladikavkaz airport in adjacent North Ossetia. A report the following day noted that airborne troops from the Tula airborne division had been delivered to Mozdok. Equipment airlifted into the war zone included tanks, multiple-rocket launchers, self-propelled howitzers, bridge-laying components, and support vehicles. That hardware came from stocks of the North Caucasus Military District. The troops were a mix of officers and conscripts from the Ministry of Internal Affairs (*Ministerstvo vnutrennykh del,* or MVD), mobile-force light infantry brigades, and airborne assault forces. Two squadrons each of Mi-24 Hind attack helicopters and Mi-8/17 Hip/Hip-H medium-transport helicopters were also deployed to the theater to support the impending combat operations. They were supplemented by Mi-26 Halo heavy-lift helicopters and an Mi-9-equipped command and control center.

VPVO played an active role by maintaining round-the-clock A-50 Mainstay AWACS tracks on all sides of Chechnya to monitor air traffic coming in or out. On November 30 the VPVO's commander in chief, Colonel General Viktor Prudnikov, indicated that his command had been under orders since the preceding August to "close" Chechen airspace to prevent the influx of military assets of any kind to Dudayev. Since then, he said, no aircraft had landed in Chechnya or departed without his personal authorization. VPVO also kept 2 to 6 MiG-31s or Su-27s on constant combat air patrol to intercept any aircraft that might resupply Chechnya or threaten Russian troops on the ground. These were the only fighters used in the war. Since there was no air-to-air threat, the MiG-29 was not a player.

By the end of January VPVO interceptors had logged some 1,500 hours on combat air patrol to blockade Chechnya's borders from external resupply. The chief of the VPVO headquarters staff, Colonel General Viktor Sinitsyn, reported that the A-50 AWACS covered "virtually the entire region," supplemented by low-level gap-filler coverage provided by individual VPVO radar platoons and companies.[17]

A serious bottleneck during that initial phase was the overburdened Mozdok airfield, where most Russian military aircraft were concentrated. By one account, air traffic control personnel suffered a "colossal load," and aircrews recovering from combat missions "were literally forced to maneuver around to land their aircraft safely on the runway."[18] VTA delivered most military personnel first into the Mozdok and Vladikavkaz airfields and later directly into Grozny North after it was secured by Russian ground units in January.

The Gaining of Air Control
The second phase of the air war overlapped the first and entailed taking out Dudayev's limited air force in a three-day airfield attack operation on November

28–30. This was not an imposing task, since the Chechen aircraft were unrevetted and Dudayev posed no counterair challenge to speak of. By one account, only 6 Su-25s out of VVS bases in the North Caucasus Military District were used in bombing and rocket attacks on the three Chechen airfields of Khankala, Kalinovskaya, and Grozny North.[19] However many Su-25s actually participated in the operation, those attacks destroyed or neutralized all 266 Chechen aircraft, including 1 Tu-154, 6 Tu-134s, and 3 helicopters in addition to the L-29s and L-39s. According to Russian press accounts, little collateral damage was caused to runways and taxiways, airport installations, and radio and lighting equipment. Immediately after the destruction of his L-29s and L-39s by the VVS, Dudayev wired a defiant note to his former commander, General Deinekin: "I congratulate you and the Russian VVS on another victory in achieving air superiority over the Chechen Republic. Will see you on the ground."[20]

Sustained Air Support to Ground Operations

The third phase of the air war began with the advance of Russian ground troops toward Grozny on December 11. Concurrently, the weather took a turn for the worse, confronting VVS aircrews with ground fog, blowing snow, severe icing, and a heavy cloud buildup with a low ceiling and tops above 15,000 feet. This weather made both high- and low-angle manual bombing impossible and also precluded any resort to electro-optical or laser-guided weapons. Instead the VVS was forced to employ Su-24s in day and night level bomb releases from medium altitude (15,000–20,000 feet) against radar offset aim points, or in inertial bombing against geographic coordinates, through heavy cloud cover. The gross inaccuracy of those weapons deliveries resulted in the loss of many Russian troops to friendly fire.

Russian Defense Minister Pavel Grachev, who organized and commanded the operation, made slow and indecisive use of his air assets, just as he did with his forces on the ground. There was a report on December 14 that 5 Su-25s had carried out a late-afternoon rocket and strafing attack against targets in the center of Grozny.[21] Not until December 19, however, was the Grozny television tower brought down. News reports on December 22 confirmed that the VVS was bombing Grozny with Su-24s and Su-25s operating out of the military airfields at Yeisk and Budennovsk. By Christmas Day 80 percent of Chechnya lacked electricity, and gas supplies to half the country had been severed as a result of the air attacks.

Early in the war, reported bombing inaccuracies underscored the pilot proficiency shortfall that the VVS had been forced to endure as a consequence of four years of underfunded aircrew training. Most VVS aircrews who participated in the initial attacks had not flown more than 30 hours in the preceding year. Few were night-current or maintained any precision weapons delivery proficiency, if indeed they ever had any. As a result, General Deinekin was forced to assemble a "tiger team" from among his most experienced weapons instructors and test pilots to send to the war zone. Only then did battlefield air-interdiction operations begin to show positive results. For a time Deinekin experimented with a "blue-gold" aircrew arrangement, whereby the crew ratio in the theater would be doubled and aircraft could be turned more quickly with fresh pilots.[22]

On December 22 the VVS used 4 Su-24s—with FAB-500 1,000-pound general-purpose bombs—to attack the highway between Staraya Sunzha and Verkat-Yurt northeast of Grozny to preclude rebel gunmen from moving into the city. Once the weather broke on December 29–30 VVS pilots used electro-optical and laser-guided weapons to attack Chechen command posts and to drop bridges over the Argun River, 10 kilometers east of the city, to prevent Dudayev from bringing reserves into Grozny. The destruction of the bridges was later confirmed by reconnaissance overflights providing battle damage assessment.

General Deinekin admitted that the VVS had "regrettably" used cluster bombs against rebel force concentrations, but he denied that the VVS had employed flechette weapons, which were banned by international convention.[23] The VVS used parachute-retarded flares during night operations to provide illumination for visual bombing whenever the weather permitted. Deinekin also noted that in some cases the VVS flew intentional low supersonic passes over Grozny, laying down sonic booms to simulate bomb explosions in an effort to intimidate the resistance.

Later, on January 17–18, the VVS used 7 Su-25s, carrying rockets and concrete-penetrating BetAB 3,000-pound unguided bombs, to conduct a high-accuracy attack against the presidential palace. Two of those bombs penetrated the palace from top to bottom. Another five took out an underground tunnel and a command post buried deep beneath an adjacent building.[24] Also, an arms dump on the northern outskirts of Arshty was reportedly destroyed by Su-25s. The attack on the presidential palace was said to have been led by an experienced pilot, possibly detached from the VVS weapons center at Lipetsk.

The first VTA transport deployed into Grozny North on January 18, after which construction personnel from army aviation radiotechnical support battalions installed a control tower, radio and landing aids, a navigation beacon, and runway and taxiway lights. They also brought in fire trucks and washdown vehicles. After that, the airfield operated at full capacity for the remainder of the hostilities.

On January 25 the VVS employed 8 Su-25s to attack Chechen underground ammunition dumps located in four former Soviet intercontinental ballistic missile (ICBM) silos. Those were destroyed, along with an underground battalion command post, ventilation intakes and vents, mobile antennas, an installation and testing building, and adjacent trailers piled high with ammunition.

Mobile air defenses operated by the Chechen resistance were close-controlled by radio. They shifted position constantly, further impeding their detection and destruction by Russian forces. Dudayev shamelessly positioned ZSU-23/4 anti-aircraft artillery and infrared SAM defenses in the midst of densely populated residential areas. Their effect, according to General Deinekin, was "pretty fierce."[25] Portable SAMs did not see high use, although several were fired against both fixed-wing aircraft and attack helicopters. VVS attack aircraft released flares on occasion to counter infrared SAMs. The first VVS aircraft downed was a Su-25 on February 4. During an attack on a rebel strong point 2 kilometers south of Chechen-Aul, a two-ship element of Su-25s was working a bridge on the Argun River when a ZSU-23/4 opened up on both, bringing one down and killing its pilot, Major Nikolai Bairov.[26]

Russia's rotary-wing aviation likewise received a renewed baptism of fire in Chechnya. It had experienced only limited combat exposure previously, in Abkhazia, South Ossetia, Transdniestria, and Tadzhikistan, all related hot spots that had sprung up in the wake of the USSR's collapse. The Afghan experience offered a solid foundation from which to improvise helicopter operations and tactics. Mi-24 Hinds used target approaches roughly comparable to those battle-tested in Afghanistan. Techniques used in Chechnya included conducting nap-of-the-earth (NOE) operations, approaching an objective from alternating directions, randomly maneuvering before a final attack run, executing a hard-maneuvering NOE egress, and relying heavily on mutual fire support, electronic countermeasures, and flares. One expert said: "Life forced constant corrections to our operating tactics."[27] More often than not, Russian intelligence on Dudayev's limited air-defense dispositions was poor to nonexistent, forcing helicopter crews to operate outside the lethal envelopes of rebel air-defense weapons for extra insurance.

In a related problem, the high density of enemy defenses in certain areas made it impossible for helicopters to use antitank guided missiles (ATGMs) against hardened structures. Instead attack helicopter crews were forced to resort to S-24 high-velocity unguided rockets. The effective slant range of those rockets was only 3,000–5,000 feet, which put the helicopter inside the engagement parameters of enemy defenses and dictated a never-before-tested tactic of launching rockets out of a radical maneuver in which the pilot would pull up hard to gain altitude, then push over hard to fire rockets at the target, and then quickly descend back to the relative safety of treetop level. One concern was that the helicopter's engine might fail during the maneuver as a result of air starvation due to the ingestion of rocket exhaust fumes.

Ground forces aviation commanders were not ready to risk taking hits from rooftop snipers. Their commander in chief, Colonel General Vitaly Pavlov, stated that it was the formal doctrine of his command that "urban combat is not suited to helicopters." Helicopters, he said, were most effective against open-country targets, using unguided rockets and the AT-6 Shturm guided missile.[28] (According to Pavlov, Russian attack helicopters did not drop gravity bombs.)

The Chechen rebels made widespread and effective use of ambush tactics, concealing their presence and starting to shoot from multiple directions once a helicopter entered their zone of fire. Typically a helicopter returning to base after sustaining battle damage would indicate hits from multiple directions and multiple weapons. An experienced pilot graphically recalled one such ambush involving a two-ship element of Mi-24s in three successive combat sorties on a mission near Gudermes. In each case the helicopters made preliminary landings en route to update their target information. The third time that the now predictable element entered the combat zone, it took intensive fire from three directions. One Mi-24 was downed, although the crew was safely extracted, and the other sustained damage. The pilot noted afterward: "This is how stereotype is punished in war."[29]

Dudayev's tactical intelligence elicited grudging Russian respect. Russian attack aircraft and helicopter radio call signs were changed daily. Nevertheless, one Russian participant stated, "One had a feeling that they [the Chechen irregulars] knew a great deal."[30] Rebel forces made a special effort to hunt down VVS FACS (forward air controllers, or *avianavodchiki*), of which some forty had been attached to the ground forces. In one example cited, no sooner had a FAC gone on the air near Chechen-Aul than massive shelling commenced on his position. The rebels did good work triangulating his location until a Russian motorized infantry unit finally pinpointed and seized the offending direction-finding equipment. FACs in Chechnya were said to have performed better than in Afghanistan, although they were hampered by obsolete communications and navigation equipment.[31]

After Dudayev's forces escaped Grozny, the VVS unleashed daily air attacks over a two-month period against the outlying road net and associated villages harboring enemy units. The VVS hoped thus to deplete resistance assets and secure Russia's position on the ground. From early March through June the weather stayed generally cooperative, making possible round-the-clock battlefield air interdiction, as well as photo reconnaissance, battle damage assessment, and attacks with precision munitions, including the AS-12/14 missiles and the KAB 1,000-pound laser-guided bombs.

In a little-reported combat evaluation, the VVS took advantage of the fighting in Chechnya to test the ability of its new Pchela-1 unmanned aerial vehicle (UAV) to provide battlefield intelligence and real-time targeting support to air and ground operations. That vehicle, powered by a 32-horsepower piston engine, had a launch weight of 138 kilograms, carried a gyrostabilized optical camera, and was ramp-launched and parachute-recovered. Operated from the Khankala air base, it was often used to conduct reconnaissance and battlefield surveillance, to provide target coordinates for multiple-launch rocket systems, and to gather tactical information for Russian infantry units. Although a major limitation was its endurance of only two hours, operations with the vehicle were said to have been so successful that Chechen rebels launched repeated raids against its ground stations. The head of VVS procurement for UAVs during the Chechen conflict, Colonel Valery Barkovsky, later disclosed at an international UAV conference in Paris that the Pchela-1 was found to require an automatic target detection and recognition system because "often the operator had not enough time to interpret all incoming information." Only one vehicle, however, was lost during combat operations against the Chechen resistance.[32]

President Yeltsin tried to put the best face on a bleak situation in mid-January by peremptorily declaring the war won and turning occupation duties over to the troops of the MVD while at the same time firing the war's most vocal critics in the senior military ranks.[33] In a transparent bid to invoke the image of the Red Army's triumphant hoisting of the Soviet flag over the Reichstag in Berlin in 1945, the Yeltsin government ostentatiously announced the raising of the Russian Federation flag over the gutted presidential palace in Grozny on January 19. That, in turn, prompted an effort by nationalist elements in the Russian parliament to propose awarding the commander of the 276th Motorized Infantry Regiment the title of Hero of Russia.[34] The proposition was voted down.

A fleeting truce from May 1 to 12 gave way to renewed fighting and a resurgence of VVS air attacks. By that time Dudayev's forces had taken refuge in the mountains, and the Yeltsin government found itself with a situation comparable to Britain's predicament with Northern Ireland. General Deinekin correctly predicted that rebel operations on the ground would resume in midautumn 1995, since inclement weather would again work to restrict air operations.[35] He further predicted that in the spring, when the trees were dense with foliage, aerial reconnaissance would be less effective against rebel strongholds in the mountains. More somberly, Grachev conceded that the situation could devolve into a partisan war, with rebel hit teams operating clandestinely at night all over Chechnya to penetrate Russian positions. He said that such a slow-motion, bleeding war of attrition could continue "for a lengthy period of time. For months, if not years."[36]

A turning point in the war came on June 14, 1995, when a Chechen guerrilla team led by Shamil Basayev carried out a successful out-of-area raid in the Russian town of Budennovsk. That terrorist operation, which held more than 1,000 civilians hostage in a city hospital for six days, left at least 123 others dead and triggered two abortive counterattacks by Russian security forces. The event thoroughly swung Russian public opinion against the war and prompted an eventual cease-fire once Prime Minister Viktor Chernomyrdin secured a bloodless end to the hostage crisis by promising negotiations in return for a release of the captives and safe passage for the Chechen guerrillas.

After that, the heaviest fighting in Chechnya drew to an end, and a Russian-appointed administrator was installed in Grozny. There still remained no conclusion in sight, however, to Russian military involvement in Chechnya. In a renewed outbreak of mass violence, Russian forces sealed off Gudermes, Chechnya's second-largest city, on December 14, 1995, and shelled it indiscriminately for eleven days, killing an estimated 600 people (half noncombatant civilians) after Chechen rebels seized the city commandant's headquarters and held 130 MVD troops captive.[37] Although the battle resulted in a Chechen retreat, it signaled an end to the shaky truce that had been in effect since July and left Moscow, as before, with no more than a Carthaginian peace in Chechnya. This action was followed in early January 1996 by the siege of Pervomaiskoye by Russian ground and air units; the siege ended in an ignominious escape by most of the Chechen rebels, who had sought to stage a replay of Budennovsk after several weeks of confrontation. Commenting on the general haplessness of the Yeltsin government's strategy toward Chechnya, one Russian reporter concluded presciently after the failure of the initial assault on Grozny in December 1994: "Foreign Minister [Andrei] Kozyrev has a powerful new argument he can easily use for opposing admission of the former socialist countries into NATO. . . . There is no need to be afraid of us. We cannot do anything anyway. And Chechnya is the best confirmation of this."[38]

Results and Costs

By the end of January 1995, Russia's reported ground-force equipment losses to enemy fire numbered more than 100 tanks and twice as many infantry fighting vehicles and armored personnel carriers.[39] The Russians lost as many men during the first month of the Chechnya operation as the Soviets had during the first six months of the far larger Afghan war. During the first three months of combat operations after the attainment of air control, Russian aircrews destroyed 3 Chechen helicopters, 20 tanks, 25 armored personnel carriers, 130 cars, 7 bridges, 6 self-propelled antiaircraft weapons (including SA-9s and SA-13s), and an artillery battery.[40] After the dust had settled and a truce between the Yeltsin government and the Chechen resistance was close at hand, General Deinekin reported that the VVS had flown a total of 14,000 combat and combat-support sorties since the beginning of hostilities.[41]

The price of Moscow's miscalculation of what it was getting itself into in Chechnya was substantial. In the harsh judgment of the deputy executive director of the Russian Council on Foreign and Defense Policy, the debacle "exposed to the whole world (including not only Russia's friends) that the Russian leadership and Russian armed forces cannot resolve militarily even a limited conflict."[42] By the official count of the MVD, 1,867 Russian troops were killed in action and 6,481 wounded, with 36 still being held prisoner by the Chechen rebels as of midsummer 1995. Contesting those figures, the Chechen government head, Salambek Khadzhiyev, claimed over 4,000 Russian fatalities, adding that 6,000 Chechen civilians died in the fighting. He went on to say that the war had produced more than 400,000 civilian refugees.[43] Since truth is the first casualty in war, there is no telling where the correct numbers lay among those conflicting claims. But there is also no denying that Moscow's sacking of Grozny produced a human tragedy by any measure. Western reporting at the end of 1995 indicated that the Chechen war had taken at least 20,000 lives.[44] Later that number was placed more than three times higher by former Army Lieutenant General Aleksandr Lebed, who successfully negotiated a cease-fire in August 1996 while serving as Yeltsin's security adviser.[45]

The war was extremely unpopular within the military. A report in April 1995 by the head of the Defense Ministry's Main Personnel Directorate indicated that 557 officers who had refused to fight had been dismissed from service and that some had been served with criminal charges.[46] In a further aggravation of the general discontent within the ranks, the heavy tapping of Russian war reserves required to support the Chechnya operation forced many military districts to reach into their emergency rations to feed their personnel.

The war claimed the lives of four VVS airmen through the downing of two Su-25s and a Su-24 by Dudayev's forces. At least 26 VVS aircraft sustained battle damage. Ten Russian helicopters were shot down, and two crews were summarily executed by Chechen rebels. Chechen air defenses, which General Deinekin credited as "very effective," produced these results without the support of a single surveillance radar. There were reports as well that U.S. Stinger shoulder-fired infrared SAMs had fallen into Chechen hands. This seems unlikely, however, considering the Stinger's proven effectiveness against Soviet forces in the last days of the war in Afghanistan. Had the Chechens possessed Stingers, aircraft losses by the VVS and by army aviation almost certainly would have been considerably higher.[47]

As the stalemate continued before the eventual cease-fire in August 1996, Chechen agents aggressively sought to gather the names of Russian pilots who had flown combat missions against Grozny; the agents were operating in support of what appears to have been an assassination plan for revenge. General Deinekin indicated that bands of Chechen operatives had been observed reconnoitering VVS bases but that Russia's security services were taking "appropriate countermeasures."[48] No doubt this assurance offered cold comfort to those Russian airmen affected by the assassination threat. Later Deinekin revealed that such efforts by Chechen hit squads had continued into early 1997 and that one squad had been detected and caught in time due to "unorthodox measures"—which, he said, would remain unspecified.[49]

By unofficial reckoning the war cost the Russian treasury upward of $5 billion in direct operating expenses, not counting the additional cost of aircraft and vehicles lost or damaged.[50] VVS activities in conjunction with the war diverted fuel purchased by appropriations originally intended to support VVS-wide continuation training. The war cut deeply into the VVS's fuel and munitions reserves, with no hope of near-term replacement. The head of the Defense Ministry's budget department acknowledged that the war's combined costs had not been anticipated and that, as one result, every second servicemen was forced to forgo a paycheck in July 1995. The effect was to exacerbate an already dire funding crisis. Ministry of Defense arrears in wages and debts to suppliers by that point totaled over $2 billion, forcing the ministry to take the extraordinary step, "impossible in any other state," of seeking bridge loans from commercial banks.[51]

The chief of the General Staff, Army General Mikhail Kolesnikov, candidly admitted that whereas the cost of such an operation in days past would scarcely have been felt by the High Command, "the conflict in Chechnya . . . required the concentration of our entire financial potential there." He added: "So far, we have not managed to get full reimbursement from the federal budget for the expenses we have incurred."[52] In the end, to no one's surprise, such reimbursement proved unforthcoming.

Grachev confirmed that in going into Chechnya, the Russian military had been forced to rob Peter to pay Paul: "For the most part, funds appropriated for defense are being spent in Chechnya for munitions, food and clothing for servicemen, and fuel and lubricants. Many assets are being siphoned off there, creating a negative impact on the status of units not fighting in Chechnya."[53] The war further aggravated an already low state of military morale. One Western reporter noted the deep bitterness of Russian soldiers in Chechnya and their "almost universal willingness to express that anger to foreigners with notebooks in their hands." A twenty-year-old tank gunner, who had asked an interviewer to take a souvenir snapshot of him, said: "This way I can prove that I was part of the stupidest campaign of our time. If I live, I can show this picture to my grandchildren and tell them how the Russian army was destroyed."[54] Not surprisingly, corruption and cynicism spread rapidly as a result of the breakdown of morale and discipline. On numerous occasions Chechen fighters boasted that they had been able to buy weapons from disgruntled Russian officers and conscripts.

Morale and motivation among Russia's aircrews were reportedly better. General Deinekin said that the Chechen situation was "not easy for the pilots there" but that they were "fulfilling their duties" and that the VVS had "not had a single desertion among the soldiers or officers in the force."[55] One Western report, however, indicated that some unit commanders had flatly refused to allow their regiments to participate in the bombing of Grozny.[56] On reflection, such recalcitrance on the part of Russian aircrews was understandable. Unlike the army, which had been called on repeatedly to deal with domestic political and civil unrest, Russian airmen had not previously been directed to commit violence against a designated foe on Russian soil. By all indications, most followed their orders with dispatch. It would not be surprising, however, if many did so with the greatest reluctance. Only time will tell how the professionalism and self-respect of Russia's aviators will be affected by the Chechen experience, particularly by the high incidence both of noncombatant fatalities and of losses to friendly fire stemming from VVS actions.

Finally, the war further embarrassed an officer corps already humiliated and deeply riven at all levels. In the apt words of one U.S. analyst, "Nearly every aspect of military activity—from training, supply, coordination among services, strategy, tactics [to] morale and fighting spirit—failed the test of battle, feeding a growing resentment among the military leaders toward defense minister Pavel Grachev and, more serious still, increasing the potential for a breakup of the armed forces into feuding factions."[57] Among the problems and fault lines aggravated by the war, this analyst noted, were the emergence of rivalries between elite and regular components of the armed forces; the rise of parallel services, such as the Federal Counterintelligence Service and MVD troops, in direct competition with the Ministry of Defense for funds and missions; a degeneration of regional military districts into de facto warlord enclaves; a dramatic decline in overall readiness; and the politicization of the military, as reflected by the participation of serving officers in organized factions—and by the fact that more than 120 officers actively campaigned for seats in the State Duma during the run-up to the 1995 parliamentary election.

Key Accomplishments

The war in Chechnya offered a tailor-made test of Russia's new regional security doctrine. By almost every indicator, the armed forces fell far short of a respectable showing. Nevertheless, the experience—even as a negative one—bore out the essential correctness of the Russian military's power-projection emphasis, for Chechnya proved a convincing prototype of the sort of security challenges that Russia is likely to confront along the former Soviet periphery for at least the next decade. It further reaffirmed what the VVS had already come to recognize— namely, that its greatest acquisition need was not new combat aircraft but more airlift.

On balance the Russian VVS handled itself better in Chechnya than did the Russian ground forces by a perceptible margin. Informed U.S. government analysts gave the VVS "a passing grade for a credible performance, even though saddled with a poor military plan."[58] In particular the VVS ran an airlift operation that, by all signs, handily met the needs of ground commanders. It also did better, albeit with some egregious exceptions, than either the ground forces or the higher military leadership in owning up to its deficiencies and failings.

A Validation of Airlift

Although badly truncated in the wake of the USSR's disintegration, VTA performed effectively in Chechnya and deserves high marks for having done as well as it did under conditions of great adversity, including a need to pull together assets from widely dispersed locations throughout Russia. Despite frequent foul weather, a severe shortage of spares, and reduced aircrew proficiency owing to curtailed annual flying, it maintained a high sortie rate throughout the initial buildup without losing a single aircraft. In all, VTA reportedly moved over 20,000 troops and 1,000 units of Russian hardware into the theater. With a reported total of 40,000 troops committed at the height of Russia's involvement, that added up to about half of all Russian ground forces deployed.[59] From the end of November 1994 through February 1995, VTA transports flew a total of 492 reported sorties for 4,020 flying hours, during which 22,000 men, 1,140 vehicles, and 3,057 metric tons of cargo were delivered.[60]

As noted in Chapter 3, an analysis by the VVS Central Research Institute had predicted that with its reduced assets, VTA would have to commit virtually all its serviceable transport aircraft to move just a single airborne division in two sorties.[61] Indeed VTA's funding had been cut back so severely that it had been driven into the commercial airlift business in pursuit of nonbudgetary income to sustain its operations. Yet despite that acknowledged handicap, the Central Research Institute's assessment proved overly pessimistic. VTA ran an efficient operation into Mozdok and Vladikavkaz by handling its problem piecemeal, using a mixed fleet of Il-76, An-12, and An-22 transports. Early on, the An-124 was used as well to transport 1,000 commandos and their armored personnel carriers from the 104th Guards Airborne Division in the course of a twenty-four-hour period.

The Beginnings of Candor in Self-Assessment

The war in Chechnya also revealed at least parts of the Russian military to be refreshingly honest in owning up to their shortcomings as well as in congratulating themselves on their meager successes. That characteristic stood in sharp contrast to the Soviet High Command's unseemly reaction following the lopsided fighting between Israel and Syria over Lebanon's Bekáa Valley in 1982, when the Soviets proved incapable of comprehending the main implications of the failings displayed by their Syrian clients.[62] It also contrasted with the Soviet military's reluctance to face up to its own combat failings in Afghanistan. In both cases the Soviets chose a selective view of the losses for much the same reason: To have done otherwise would have required the Soviets to concede their fallibility.

The Russian military still has a way to go, however, before it can be said to have completely unburdened itself of its former Soviet bad habits. Once the chrome was knocked off the halo of Soviet communism by 1991, Russian defense professionals were freed to do an objective job of assessing combat operations on both sides in the Persian Gulf War. This they did with, by and large, remarkable insight and intellectual acuity.[63] Those same professionals, however, showed a less uniformly impressive performance in making sense of their own subsequent combat experience. Because of the humiliation caused by Russia's debacle in Chechnya, at least some military spokesmen had, once again, a hard time facing up to combat facts.

Typical of the post hoc rationalization and excuse-making apparent in some quarters was the contorted reaction of Major General Yevgeny Nikitenko, the deputy head of the General Staff's Military Science Directorate. Explaining why things seemed to be going so wrong in Chechnya, he said: "Under no circumstances should events in the Chechen Republic be considered combat operations in the classic sense." In near-flawless Orwellian doublespeak, he added that Russia's forces were "not conducting a military operation as such," adding that the sort of incursion being carried out in Chechnya did "not figure in basic military texts." Accordingly, he wrote: "No one ever formulated for the military the procedure, methods, and means of conducting such an operation." Admitting that a "miscalculation" had been made in anticipating the scale and intensity of rebel resistance, General Nikitenko suggested that the hurried decision to send tanks into Grozny without infantry cover had been based on "a glimmer of hope" that the rebels had only a limited number of ATGMs, a hope that "regrettably did not prove to be the case." He implied that had the Russian High Command had its way, a fundamentally different force would have been sent in, organized along the lines of allied ground formations in Desert Storm. Chechen civilians would have been asked to leave the zone of impending operations, and Russian troops would have entered Grozny only after "massive bombardment" by Su-24Ms and Su-25s to "completely destroy the mini-army that Dudayev had set up." Using "all the might available to the Russian armed forces," he added, there would not have been "even a shadow of Dudayev's cutthroats left on the face of the earth. At the same time, they could not have done any palpable damage to our troops." This was not learning; it was nonrecognition and denial.[64]

Indeed Russia's military leadership went so far as to forgo including any putative teachings of the Chechen war in the studies curriculum at the General Staff Academy and at other senior service schools, on the dubious ground that the conflict was "atypical" in having been conducted on Russian soil.[65] In February 1995 Grachev chaired a narrowly focused "lessons learned" session among technical specialists conducting a postmortem on the combat employment of armor. He concluded that Russian tanks showed "excellent battlefield characteristics," notwithstanding their gross misuse in being committed in ones and twos without protective cover.[66]

With greater insight, the Russian airborne commander, Colonel General Yevgeny Podkolzin, remarked that the first mistake was the government's failure to prepare public opinion, closely followed by the decision to begin the operation at a time of year when second-year servicemen were being discharged and new conscripts inducted. Yet a third needless complication was the prohibitive weather known to afflict the North Caucasus region in November through January. "In these conditions," he conceded, "it is impossible to send your aviation up. Or if it does get airborne, it has to stay at high altitude, which naturally makes it hard to fulfill its missions." He added that the U.S. leadership wisely spent a solid six months getting its citizens ready for Desert Storm.[67]

General Kolesnikov admitted that the Chechen experience "graphically illustrated a large number of problems that [had] built up in the military." He said the war provided "food for thought and a basis for making certain changes in operational tactics, especially with respect to urban combat, the organization of communications, psychological training, and tactical interplay between units." He added that most of the difficulties spotlighted were simply a consequence of the dire funding situation and that the problem could not be resolved "without a substantial economic upsurge in Russia."[68]

With conspicuous exceptions dictated by the Yeltsin government's determination to cover up its worst excesses in Chechnya, the Russian VVS was generally candid about the problems its air campaign revealed. By the admission of its own airmen, the performance of the VVS in Chechnya "exposed shortcomings in the combat training of Frontal Aviation [KFA] pilots," many of whom had to "regain lost skills in the midst of military operations." That deficiency was described by one serving officer as partly the natural result of a long-standing fixation on flight safety at any cost, an emphasis that dated back to the introduction of the MiG-21 into service during the mid-1960s: "Where that led to can be seen from the present state of tactical air training. Pilots complain of numerous restrictions in practicing difficult aspects of training sorties." According to this officer, the unstated but binding watchwords of the VVS leaders remained: "Take no risks, do not complicate, and avoid innovation."[69]

To his credit General Deinekin more than once stressed: "Honesty in aviation is an absolute must."[70] Partly as a result of that outlook, his commentary on air operations in Chechnya was factual and generally frank, in marked contrast with previous Soviet practice. He was forced onto the defensive early on, however, by a barrage of media allegations that the VVS was indiscriminately bombing Chechen hospitals, schools, and residential areas. One press account characterized his aircraft as "almost haphazardly bombing a nearly defenseless city."[71] A Moscow television station reported a still-burning flare that had come down by parachute as a Russian bomb that had gone off in a Grozny housing project.

In the worst cases the VVS was accused, sometimes justifiably, of outright falsification about its activities. For example, the VVS initially denied that it was involved in air operations in Chechnya at all. Only on December 5 did Grachev admit that Russian combat aircraft had bombed the airfield in Grozny. On December 23 the respected human rights envoy Sergei Kovalev charged that government representatives the previous night had "claimed that the night bombing raids on Grozny had stopped and that the explosions in the town were initiated by Dudayev himself." Kovalev added, "That is a blatant lie."[72] There was also a question a week and a half later as to whether the VVS's bombing of Grozny had been halted in accordance with President Yeltsin's January 4 edict to that effect. Pointedly upbraiding Grachev on that score, Yeltsin openly admonished him at a Security Council meeting: "And I want to hear absolutely precise information from the defense minister."[73]

The VVS was also evasive about the participation of LRA in the war. General Deinekin insisted that only KFA ground-attack aircraft and army helicopters had taken part in actual combat operations. Senior VVS officials denied that LRA bombers were used to bomb cities.[74] Official statements claimed that the Tu-22M3 Backfire was used only for dropping night flares and propaganda leaflets over Grozny.[75] Foreign reporters alleged, however, that the Backfire was also used on several occasions to bomb Chechen forces directly.

General Deinekin appeared distressed at allegations that his pilots had inten- tionally bombed noncombatant civilians, calling such accusations "an evil fabri- cation." In the face of such charges, he launched a postattack reconnaissance mission on December 29, the results of which reportedly "confirmed" that VVS strikes had been directed solely against military targets. Those targets were said to have included a Chechen tank-repair facility, troop-marshaling areas, and the presidential palace. Deinekin later complained that because of such alleged slan- ders, the public was "set against the Russian armed forces and their aviation." He added: "Absolutely no attention is paid to the pilots' arguments, and they are blamed for virtually all the misfortunes of the war. . . . They had to operate against what was virtually a full-scale army, armed to the teeth. . . . Quite often tanks and guns were set up not in an empty field but near schools and kinder- gartens and in the yards of apartment compounds. . . . If the air force had not ful- filled its missions, the number of dead Russian soldiers would have been far greater. We have every ground for taking pride in our fliers' courage."[76]

Because of complex front lines and the inaccuracy of radar bombing through clouds (with an average miss distance of 450 feet or more), Russian officials did not deny that some VVS bombs landed on Russian troops. General Deinekin was uncomfortable with charges to that effect, and he repeatedly defended the pro- fessionalism and discipline of his pilots. However, on one occasion in early Janu- ary 1995 he conceded that he could not rule out inadvertent fatalities, as well as the destruction of civilian apartment compounds, as a result of accidental stray bombs.[77]

Deinekin also acknowledged the "many conflicting assessments" of his air force's performance in Chechnya. Yet he insisted that notwithstanding objective difficulties, Russia's pilots "fully coped with their missions, demonstrating the high effectiveness and reliability of Russian weapons and aviation equipment and their own high skills." Giving credit where it was due, he also conceded that the Chechen rebels were as effective as they were because they had received the same training and used the same equipment as Russian forces.[78]

Indeed Deinekin was so concerned to correct the bad press that the VVS had received after its initial poor showing in Chechnya that he staged a firepower demonstration at a weapons range not far from the war zone for the air attachés from forty foreign nations. He was unambiguous about his motives: "A powerful propaganda ploy was recently organized in the press in connection with events in Chechnya. Its intent was to prove that our aviation is not capable of using precision weapons, that our bombs hit hospitals, markets, and children's homes. Of course, it was hard for us to endure this, so we decided to show the military intelligence people and attachés representing other countries in Russia what our Russian aviation is capable of."[79]

To provide a suitably appropriate venue, Deinekin picked the VVS test range in Kabardino-Balkaria, situated at an elevation of 9,000 feet above sea level in the Elbrus Mountains. The demonstration, most likely performed by the VVS's most proficient aircrews from Lipetsk, included a simultaneous launch of two precision-guided air-to-ground missiles.[80] Afterward Deinekin said: "I'm very satisfied. The pilots have shown flying skills of the highest class. Despite the marginal weather, all landed safely."[81] He later reiterated that the demonstration had been held to counter negative comments about Russia's armaments, comments that were intended, he felt, to "shatter their glory." He added, "Today we showed the best our aviation industry has."[82]

Problems and Lessons Indicated

There were few profound lessons to be drawn by the Russian VVS from its experience in Chechnya, since so many of the problems dramatized by its uneven performance reflected nothing more complex than the severe funding shortage that had afflicted it since the USSR's collapse. If anything, the main lessons amounted simply to worst-fears-confirmed about the VVS's eroded capabilities. What the war did, in the final tally, was to bathe the VVS's problems in the cold light of reality and to identify beyond question the hurdles that remain ahead on the road to recovery.

The following discussion will not try to account for VVS "lessons learned," for two reasons. First, such lessons are rarely self-evident to the outside observer. Second, and more important, such an approach all too often assumes— wrongly—that the adduced "lessons" have in fact been understood and assimilated. A more useful approach is to think less definitively in terms of "lessons indicated." Four such sources of reflection, in particular, no doubt captured the attention of the VVS leaders in the wake of their combat trial in Chechnya.

The Burdens of Bad Planning

The VVS found itself pitted against needlessly high odds from the outset in Chechnya. To begin with, the weather deteriorated at precisely the time the initial ground invasion began. Defense Minister Grachev, moreover, underestimated the fighting capacity of the resistance. Finally, Russian ground forces failed to encircle the capital city of Grozny before entering, thereby allowing enemy reinforcements to enter and later enabling many irregulars to escape and continue fighting from the surrounding hills. There is nothing that air power could have done to compensate for those flat-footed miscalculations.

By all accounts, the decision to commit Russian troops to the invasion was made within Yeltsin's inner circle, without any consultation of the senior military leadership. Grachev willingly, even reflexively, acceded to that decision yet failed to carry out any prior assessment of the situation or to prepare his forces for what was to come. There was no apparent concept of operations behind the incursion beyond a vaguely defined injunction to "disarm illegal formations" and to lend fire support to MVD troops. Grachev had assured his superiors that his army would "cleanse the city of rebels" by the week's end.[83] Indeed on November 29—before the botched invasion two weeks later—he boasted that a single airborne regiment could take Grozny in two hours.[84] The plan was for a quick Russian advance into Grozny, after which resistance from Dudayev and his forces was expected to collapse.[85]

The VVS can hardly be blamed for the uncooperative weather, which during the opening phase of the invasion all but precluded effective air-to-ground operations. Even the following February General Pavlov stated that 95 percent of the month was nonflyable by normal peacetime training rules because of meteorological conditions below First-Class pilot minimums. Any air force would have been similarly constrained in such circumstances. Indeed adverse weather repeatedly hampered allied air operations during the Persian Gulf War, often nullifying the capabilities of the coalition's precision-guided munitions (PGMs). And weather had a similar complicating effect on later NATO air activities over Bosnia.[86]

The invasion of Chechnya was sharply scored by some of Grachev's most senior subordinates, including his deputy minister, General Boris Gromov, and Lieutenant General Lebed.[87] Gromov complained that the operation had been planned in "profound secrecy" and that no one on the military collegium had been consulted.[88] Another critic flatly charged that in acceding to such a hastily contrived operation, Grachev was following "principles of political expediency rather than military science."[89] According to that same account, the Defense Ministry's intelligence reporting on the state of Dudayev's forces was badly in error. Russian troops were accordingly unprepared, their ingress routes had not been properly secured, and timely measures to neutralize Dudayev's forces had not been undertaken. One anonymous army officer pointed out that many of his superiors regarded Grachev as a "weak, incompetent minister with the mentality of a commander of a troop division rather than of a minister." That critic faulted Grachev for "surrounding himself with an entourage of dull but loyal hacks" and disparaged him as one who "manages to hang on because of his loyalty to his patron."[90]

Those in Yeltsin's kitchen cabinet who elected to initiate the war could not have picked a worse time of year from a weather perspective, as noted. But an even bigger mistake was to drive into the center of Grozny with tanks and armored personnel carriers exposed to sappers hidden inside and atop buildings. Having failed first to encircle the city, clear an ingress route, and secure a safe escape option, Grachev sent in some 250 unprotected tanks and armored personnel carriers, which were quickly bottled up and decimated by Dudayev's irregulars. The Russian tank crews had received little prior training worthy of the name and no exposure whatsoever to the most elementary principles of urban warfare. Nor did they show any significant degree of coordination, since they had been cobbled together only days earlier from often widely dispersed units. Russia's poor performance further reflected the fact that most conscripts had less than a year's service time, according to the ground forces commander at the time, Colonel General Vladimir Semenov.[91]

Because of poor planning, the invading tanks became separated from supporting infantry almost immediately. That made the tanks easy prey for Chechen snipers armed with ATGMs and rocket-propelled grenades (RPGs). The invasion repeated almost to the letter the same errors that had been committed during the earlier November 26–27 incursion, except this time with a significantly higher cost in Russian casualties. Only after this debacle did Grachev call in elite detachments from Yekaterinburg and from the Tula airborne division.

Regarding the army's sorry showing in Grozny, General Lebed remarked that amazingly enough, "all the mistakes" the Soviet troops had made in Afghanistan were repeated in Chechnya. He noted: "The army totally ignored local conditions, religion, and customs. No one planned the operation. It was started 'Russian style' on the off-chance that it would work."[92] For its part, the VVS played the hand it was dealt by Defense Minister Grachev. Even had the ground campaign been conducted with greater forethought, effective air preparation would have been difficult to achieve because of the built-up urban setting of the fighting.

The Price of Financial Starvation

The VVS also felt the effects of the curtailed funding for operations and training, a shortage it had been forced to endure since the collapse of the Soviet Union. In Operation Desert Storm the United States and its coalition allies saw the payoff of fifteen years of prior intensive training and experience at mission planning, force integration, and combat employment. In Chechnya the VVS saw the painful results of the absence of those crucial equities. Both examples, in their way, strongly reaffirmed the long-standing axiom that, for better or for worse, you fight like you train. The war in Chechnya came close on the heels of Grachev's plaintive lament in parliament about the Russian Army: "Not a single army in the world is in such a catastrophic state." Grachev warned the legislators what would happen without supplemental funding: "The irreversible process of losing our capability will occur, and the armed forces will simply collapse."[93]

Low proficiency as a result of reduced flying hours and curtailed training opportunities was a serious problem for the VVS. General Deinekin frequently conceded the impaired readiness of his aircrews owing to training cutbacks caused by a lack of fuel. He stated that some of his "pilots" (he intentionally set the word in quotation marks for effect) were averaging only 15 flight hours a year, in bleak contrast to the Western norm of 180–240 hours annually. He also disclosed that VVS pilots with night currency were "few and far between" and admitted that the toughest challenge was often simply to find pilots who would not collide with each other in midair. Because of curtailed training, the VVS found itself steadily losing its cadre of First-Class pilots due to their inability to meet annual currency minimums in both flying hours and mission events. As a result, weapons instructors from the VVS combat training center at Lipetsk and test pilots from the military's flight-test center were the only pilots proficient enough to use PGMs in combat. They were accordingly pressed into service for most PGM attacks in Chechnya. That fact was not openly emphasized by the VVS, for understandable reasons. But it was alluded to on at least one occasion.[94]

Ground forces aviation experienced similar consequences from the preceding four years of curtailed funding for operations and support. Its commander, General Pavlov, stated that 59 percent of his helicopter aircrews were Afghan war veterans and that all his aircraft commanders flying in Chechnya were First-Class pilots. Few, however, were current in night and adverse weather operations or in weapons delivery. First-Class pilots were cleared to fly to minimums of a 300-foot ceiling and a half-mile visibility. Most, however, had flown only 40–50 hours during the preceding year, barely one-third their peacetime training norm. They also complained about operating old equipment. The average service time on the Mi-24 airframes used in Chechnya was more than fifteen years. Most aircraft had previously seen hard use in Afghanistan. To add insult to injury, virtually everything needed to support rotary-wing operations in the war was in short supply. General Pavlov said his staff had to scour the entire country to scrounge enough flak jackets and flight helmets for his helicopter crews. General Pavlov also said that the limited annual flying hours allotted to his pilots had approached a "danger threshold," adding: "With this amount we will only be able to maintain a set level of combat readiness for one or two years. But after the departure of those fliers with 10 to 15 years of flight experience on their shoulders, these '48-hour kids' will never be fully ready for combat."[95]

Disjunctions in Joint Force Integration

Attack helicopters were often used in conjunction with ground-attack aircraft. In addition, combined-arms operations pit Russian artillery, multiple-launch rockets, attack helicopters, and fixed-wing jets against rebel targets. Coordinating attack helicopter operations with infantry and armor proved more than once to be a problem. Lessons learned the hard way in Afghanistan were frequently forgotten, making it necessary, according to one account, for Russian forces "to step on the same rake again."[96]

General Lebed, who did not participate in the fighting but was well positioned to know what was happening, afterward remarked on the operations in Chechnya: "Planes fly on their own, guns fire on their own, without coordination, and no one can come to any agreement with anyone even theoretically, because each has his own boss."[97] His comment suggested that there was no on-scene commander in chief with clearly subordinated joint force component commands—nothing like the arrangement from which the allied coalition took its tasking in Desert Storm. More likely, the component commanders, in classic Soviet fashion, reported separately to, and took directions from, the Russian High Command in Moscow—in this case General Grachev.[98]

Russian attack helicopter operations, in particular, showed the effects of a less-than-seamless integration with the ground forces. Rotary-wing aviation, previously assigned to the Soviet VVS, had been transferred back to Soviet Army ownership in 1990. The VVS commander in chief at that time, Colonel General Yevgeny Shaposhnikov, noted that there were no real alternatives to this transfer, considering that attack helicopters, as a prime antitank asset, would immediately be remanded to combined-arms commanders in case of war. That prompted concerns among members of the helicopter community that they might find themselves forgotten stepchildren of the ground forces, commanded by dilettantes untutored in flight operations and stuck last in line for such amenities as food, housing, and uniforms.

As it turned out, all the Russian combat arms suffered the deprivations of post-Soviet budget cuts. But the helicopter community proved prescient with respect to the first concern. Commenting on the possibility of incompetent directives from unschooled ground-force commanders, Shaposhnikov insisted that although ground commanders would assign the mission, "the process of carrying it out" would be "developed by the aviation staff."[99] Things did not always work out so smoothly in Chechnya, however.

A particular difficulty, in the words of one helicopter pilot, was that many combined-arms commanders had only a "vague idea" of the combat capabilities of helicopters and of the restrictions on their use with respect to weather, aircraft and weapons limitations, weapons range, airspeeds, and aircraft load-carrying capacity. "What [the commanders] are *not* short of," he added wryly, "is resolve. And if aircraft are subordinated to such a commander, it is tough to predict the consequences." Typically, an infantry unit commander would assign his helicopter pilots the mission of destroying a rebel tank in the streets of Grozny. "His logic was simple: 'You have ATGMs, and that means you can destroy it.' But suppose the tank's location was unknown? 'Fly along the street, then, and as soon as it appears . . .' Actual combat, however, is not an American film hit. Sending a helicopter in on such an assignment means losing both the crew and the helicopter. Misunderstandings often arose because of a lack of coordinated operations."[100]

The Limits of Air Power in Irregular War

The VVS had a golden opportunity in Chechnya to learn that air power cannot invariably work its well-reputed magic in circumstances where the target set is elusive, problems predominate in target location and identification, and the possibility of unintended harm to noncombatants is ever-present. In the analogous case of Bosnia, retired USAF General Charles Boyd, the former deputy commander in chief of the U.S. European Command, wrote soon after the successful use of NATO air power in Operation Deliberate Force: "Despite its appeal to the amateur strategist, a reliance on air power alone—the strike option—in this type of terrain with these kinds of targets has never held any real promise of conflict resolution." Although a robust and effective use of air power, he suggested, might alter enemy behavior in the short term, as it evidently did in Bosnia in producing the 1995 Dayton Accords, it would never vitiate the larger reality that an intervention strategy "cannot produce an enduring solution with military force—air or ground—only one that will last until it departs."[101] Among all possible lessons from the war, it is perhaps this one that Russian defense planners might most usefully ponder as they continue to reflect on their grim experience in Chechnya.

Implications

In one considered assessment, Russia's sacking of Chechnya may yet "come to be seen as one of the greatest disasters in Russian military history," not because of Russia's losses, which turned out to be limited, but because of what the abortive effort "revealed about the humiliating depths of contemporary Russian military decline."[102] At a minimum, the experience in Chechnya was emblematic of the security challenges that the VVS is most likely to face in the decade ahead. The war was regional yet remote from the center of Russia. It featured a technologically unsophisticated yet almost fanatically determined ethnic opponent. It presented no air-to-air threat and offered a congenial operating environment for air power, except at low altitude, where widely dispersed antiaircraft guns and shoulder-fired infrared SAMs posed a constant danger. Finally, it entailed no air opposition and few target arrays and, accordingly, did not place great demands on the VVS for high-technology performance. All in all, despite the occasional effective use of PGMs against key targets, quantity prevailed over quality in VVS operations in Chechnya.

A year and a half earlier, the VVS had conducted a rehearsal of sorts for its new role in Russian strategy in a two-day deployment of Su-24s, Tu-95s, and Tu-160s in a long-range strike exercise called Voskhod '93, as described in Chapter 5. As successful as that exercise proved to be, however, the war in Chechnya was more typical of the real-world demands that the VVS is likely to face in its future tasking. The fighting in Chechnya placed a greater premium on airlift and sustainability for prolonged air support to ground operations than on rapid response, complex force packaging, and high-technology weapons employment.

At least one unspoken motive behind the VVS's involvement in Chechnya may have been an urge to show that it could do anything the USAF is capable of doing. General Deinekin spoke with measured respect for the "much-vaunted Americans," noting of the Russians: "We always try to compare ourselves with them."[103] Since the end of the cold war, Russians have repeatedly chafed at not being unquestioningly accepted by Western leaders as an equal power. They also have been sensitive about the allied coalition's bravura performance in the 1991 Gulf War, in considerable part conducted against Soviet weapons and Soviet operating doctrine. In Chechnya those same sensitive Russians may have seen an opportunity to emulate, at the least, the largely painless U.S. intervention in Haiti.[104]

Any such hopes, however, fell short of being realized by the VVS's performance. General Deinekin characterized Chechnya as a "serious test of the Russian Air Force's combat capability."[105] He made a special point to portray VVS operations there as proof that the VVS was capable of a performance comparable to that of the allied air campaign in Desert Storm. Yet the Chechen war and the tasks that befell the VVS in conducting that war did not mirror the magnitude, the complexity, or the character of the far more intensive and demanding Persian Gulf War. More important, Russia's combat experience in Chechnya did not at all prove that air power has emerged as the dominant force element in Russian defense planning. General Deinekin more than once insisted, probably correctly, that the VVS contains the intellectual cream of the Russian military. He also showed an abiding determination to make the VVS the central force element in the armed forces.[106] Nevertheless, there was a predominant ground emphasis in the Chechen campaign, and the war was planned and led by ground forces officers throughout.

That said, the VVS did passably well, considering the many problems that have afflicted it since the USSR's demise. General Deinekin has freely admitted that the troubles he inherited when the Russian VVS was first established in May 1992 were mighty enough to "make his head spin." In the ensuing years of the post-Soviet era, those troubles showed little sign of abating. By all indications VVS operations in Chechnya were not constrained by a lack of fuel, munitions, or other consumables. Deinekin conceded, however, that assets expended during the fighting "were replaced, to a considerable extent, not by deliveries from industry but by removal from the stocks of other air formations."[107] Those material demands of the war in Chechnya set back an already strained VVS recovery effort by placing burdens on limited fuel and war reserve stocks that could not be replenished.

Two years later the VVS was the apparent instrument of choice that finally succeeded in taking out the Chechen leader, Dzhokar Dudayev, in a precision air attack on April 24, 1996. In an operation that probably reflected a blend of proficiency and good luck, Russian intelligence reportedly zeroed in on Dudayev's position and transmitted coordinates to VVS ground-attack aircraft, which then fired radio-frequency homing missiles that targeted Dudayev while he was talking on a satellite field telephone.[108] According to press accounts, two missiles were electronically guided by signals bouncing between the portable phone's antenna and a relay satellite. Although the Defense Ministry refused to confirm or deny that account of the events, Dudayev's death was conceded by his key deputies shortly thereafter, making him possibly the first victim of Russian "information warfare."

That single event notwithstanding, the extent to which the VVS was hindered in fulfilling its tasking in the relatively low-intensity war in Chechnya indicated that as long as it remains financially deprived, the VVS will constitute, at best, only a regional air arm with little sustainability and little capacity for high-technology combat. Considering that it faces no challenge that would justify a force structure more capable than a reconstituted variant of what it already possesses, some of the VVS's declared ambitions, notably a fifth-generation air-combat fighter (discussed in detail in the next chapter), will continue to exceed its grasp. The VVS needs to set more modest and tailored acquisition goals, for the near term at least, if it is to recover and flourish as a viable institution.

9.   Waning Prospects for a New Fighter

One of the most intriguing questions about the Russian VVS's fitful adjustment to the post–cold war era has concerned the near-term likelihood of its fielding a new air-combat fighter to replace its current fourth-generation MiG-29s and Su-27s.[1] In early 1988 the U.S. government predicted that two follow-on aircraft to the MiG-29 and the Su-27 would enter production by the mid-1990s. These aircraft were then generically labeled the Air Superiority Fighter (ASF) and the Defensive Counterair Fighter (CAF).[2] Following the 1988 Farnborough Air Show in Great Britain, however, Soviet aerospace officials led Westerners to believe that the only fighter prototypes they were working on were developmental variants of the MiG-29 and Su-27. That belief was later underscored by the Soviet VVS commander in chief, Colonel General Yevgeny Shaposhnikov, when he suggested that two new fighter types planned for deployment in the late 1990s would be step-upgrades of the MiG-29 and the Su-27.[3] By 1990 the U.S. Defense Department's annual *Soviet Military Power* report had scaled back earlier projections of a fifth-generation replacement for the MiG-29 and Su-27, noting merely that the possibility a new Soviet fighter would appear sometime after the turn of the century remained "a concern."[4]

In 1994, however, the USAF declared its expectation that a new Russian air-combat fighter would be test-flown by 1997 and would enter line service one to three years after the scheduled deployment of the USAF fifth-generation F-22, which at the time was slated to attain initial operational capability (IOC) in 2004.[5] The USAF further projected that Russia would field four wing-equivalents of that new fighter by 2020 and would produce additional numbers for sale abroad.[6] Since then, mounting evidence suggests that any plans the VVS may once have had to field an F-22-class fighter have been set back indefinitely by the financial crisis that has beset all the Russian services. Accordingly, it now seems likely that the VVS may be forced to skip the deployment of a fifth-generation fighter altogether as a necessary price for attending to its more immediate priorities.

Russia's Interest in a Follow-on Fighter

If Soviet communism and the USSR had not disintegrated, the advent of the USAF's F-22 would undoubtedly have prompted the deployment of a counterpart Soviet fighter in due course. It is now widely known that both the formal issuance of military requirements for new Soviet combat aircraft and the key design features of those aircraft were directly responsive to development initiatives in the West. On the first count, Russian engineers frankly indicated, after the walls of Soviet secrecy began crumbling, that Soviet fighters were developed in emulative reaction to U.S. aircraft. One engineer flatly stated that the Su-24, Su-25, Su-27, and MiG-29 were conceived as Soviet "answers" to the U.S. F-111, A-10, F-15, and F-16. "Without the F-15," he said, "there would never have been a Su-27. Without the F-16, there would never have been a MiG-29."[7]

Moscow's tendency to emulate what had already been successfully prooftested elsewhere inevitably occasioned a systemic lag in the appearance of new Soviet aircraft intended to offset their Western counterparts. In 1985 a former Soviet engineer with more than eighteen years of helicopter design experience revealed that in the USSR new aircraft developments were "usually authorized, financed, and supported only after they [had] actually been realized in the West." The military, he said, would first receive "all new information on Western developments" and would then be spurred into "swift and energetic action" by its fear of dropping behind. Only then, he added, would new system proposals be funded by the Soviet government.[8]

Even with the Soviet Union gone and Russia now facing a largely regional threat environment, strong incentives remain among Moscow's military-industrial elites to develop and produce a next-generation fighter. That interest is partly due to Russia's natural competitive urge. Shortly before the USSR collapsed, the Soviet view was that, notwithstanding changes for the better in Soviet-U.S. *political* relations, U.S. combat aircraft would remain the principal rivals of Soviet aircraft worldwide, requiring that the Soviets' efforts to improve their aviation technology "should be comparable to corresponding steps by the Americans."[9] That view has endured throughout the post-Soviet era among Russia's aviation professionals.

The incentive in Russia's aerospace sector to pursue the development of a new fighter is also due partly to that sector's sense that it lags behind the West in technology application and that it has an obligation to catch up. In 1989 the Mikoyan Design Bureau's chief, Rostislav Belyakov, admitted that Soviet avionics were inferior to those of the West in weight, size, and power consumption and that improved efficiency was a goal toward which redoubled efforts were required.[10] Belyakov added that his biggest problem was avionics integration. In 1992 Viktor Pugachev, a test pilot for the Sukhoi Design Bureau, likewise reported an avionics fraction of total Russian aircraft weight higher than that of U.S. combat aircraft, conceding that in this category, if not in overall performance, Russian electronics remained inferior to their Western counterparts and that resolving this deficiency would "take time."[11] Following his appointment as Soviet defense minister in the wake of the abortive 1991 coup, Shaposhnikov concurred that the USSR was "behind."[12] He also stressed, several times, that Moscow could not accept settling for a "second best" position in relation to its new U.S. "partner."[13]

Partly too, the continued appeal of a new air-combat fighter has concerned the unrelenting determination of Russia's defense principals to ensure that Russia emerges from the collapse of communism with more than just a hollow claim to great-power status. Belyakov left little doubt about his own thoughts on that score when he declared at the 1991 Paris Air Show: "We know how the F-22 will perform. Therefore, we must also have a new fighter."[14] In 1993 Valery Menitsky, Mikoyan's chief test pilot, likewise stated emphatically, even passionately, that if the United States needed the F-22, Russia had every need for a fighter of comparable sophistication and performance.[15]

Finally, continued interest in developing a follow-on to the MiG-29 and the Su-27 relates to the opportunity that such an aircraft might offer Russia for remaining a credible competitor in global aerospace technology and thus attracting much-needed hard currency through foreign sales. Throughout the Soviet period, new fighters would not typically find their way into the hands of Soviet allies until well after they had been integrated into the VVS and VPVO. Today, however, with the greater independence of Russia's aircraft industry and its demonstrated willingness to sell virtually anything to foreign buyers ready to pay the price, such an aircraft could be aggressively marketed in the international arms forum.

Russian air power specialists have had enough to say about stealth applications over a long enough period of time for us to know that their interest in acquiring a "low-observable" fighter has been more than academic. They have followed U.S. fighter development closely and have given extensive thought to the role and value of stealth in air warfare. In one telling example, a VVS expert on fighter technology, Colonel A. Krasnov, noted in 1991 that with the advent of low-observable fighters, search and detection effectiveness would become the dominant factor in shaping the contours of an air battle.[16] He went on to predict that stealthy fighters armed with launch-and-leave missiles would put conventional fighters at a pronounced disadvantage in detection range, especially if the stealthy attackers entered the fight with their radars not emitting and with their threat awareness drawn passively via data link from such offboard sensors as an AWACS.

Because of the asymmetrical weapons engagement ranges resulting from such an unequal standoff (Colonel Krasnov suggested 70 kilometers for a stealthy attacker versus 15 kilometers for a conventional defender), no nonstealthy defender would dare press an attack to the point where visual contact with a stealthy opponent was established, since destruction by enemy missiles fired from beyond visual range would occur long before the defender could establish a firing solution of his own. As for a scenario in which *both* sides possessed stealthy fighters, Krasnov suggested that aerial combat might revert to the within-visual-range tactics of the 1950s and 1960s, with front-quarter attacks being effectively ruled out because of short detection ranges and with engagements devolving once again into classic dogfights.[17] Colonel Krasnov acknowledged that there remained "no complete answer" to the question of how a conventional defender might cope with a stealthy air-to-air threat. He proposed that one avenue might include such options as jamming the enemy's missile radar and cleverly using deceptive tactics to degrade a technically superior attacker's situation awareness. He concluded, however, that a stealthy fighter with a predicted radar cross-section as low as 1 percent of that of the F-15 or F-16 meant that working out effective techniques of aerial combat would be "a task for tomorrow."

Signs of Advanced Prototype Development

Throughout the 1990s diverse Russians in a position to know gave numerous indications that Russia's aircraft industry had advanced quite far toward developing a fifth-generation fighter prototype. In one of the first references to possible Russian activity in the realm of a next-generation fighter, Mikoyan's Belyakov stated to a reporter in 1991 that his design bureau was hard at work on two new aircraft: a counterpart to the U.S. YF-22 and YF-23 stealth prototypes that had just flown the year before and an analogue of the less advanced French Rafale.[18] Belyakov added that he was not sure that Mikoyan's fifth-generation prototype would ultimately be the basis of the next Soviet air-combat fighter to be fielded in unit strength. He did say, however, that his effort had been given a project number, suggesting a formal development start sometime earlier.[19] During his short tenure as the Soviet VVS commander in chief, Shaposhnikov likewise asserted that the Soviet aircraft industry was working on two new "stealth-optimized" fighters in response to VVS requirements, as well as on new technologies for countering stealthy weapons. He added that any deployment of those systems would depend on whether the United States continued with its stealthy B-2 bomber and F-22 fighter, both of which he characterized as offensive weapons that had no place in the post–cold war era.[20]

A false rumor, evidently triggered by a comment made by the president of the Russian Aviation Union, Vladimir Laptev, circulated in early 1992 claiming that both the Mikoyan and the Sukhoi Design Bureaus had prototypes "under flight test" for a Russian answer to the U.S. advanced tactical fighter (ATF). That report further claimed that despite a 50 percent reduction in Russia's military R&D budget since 1991, Sukhoi and Mikoyan had been directed to focus on core military programs, including new fighters.[21] A year later Belyakov volunteered that a fifth-generation Mikoyan fighter prototype was indeed in hand but that it had not yet been test-flown because of continuing delays in engine development. Belyakov said: "A completely new aircraft has been assembled. We had been planning its first flight in 1991, but we could not have done it. There is no money to continue the development of its engine. The airframe and the engine pioneer new technologies."[22] Belyakov did not identify the aircraft, but informed conjecture at the time held that he was referring to "Article 1.42," the reported company designator for the project. That conjecture called the aircraft a Rafale look-alike and characterized it as the Multirole Frontal Fighter (*Mnogofunktsionalny frontovoi istrebitel,* or MFI) that had reportedly been developed in fulfillment of a VVS requirement.[23]

Because of problems with the new Al-41 engine being developed by Lyulka/Saturn, rumor had it that the first of two Article 1.42 prototypes believed to have been completed would fly with interim Al-35 engines, which were being used in the Su-35, a developmental improvement of the Su-27. Later reports indicated that the new engines had been installed on the fighter and that they were full-scale development items mounting three-dimensional thrust-vectoring nozzles. According to Lyulka/Saturn's president, Viktor Chepkin, the Al-41 was said to operate at a turbine-inlet temperature 250 degrees higher than that attainable by the Al-35. Chepkin added that his company's product was "in no way inferior to the Pratt and Whitney F-119 engine powering the F-22."[24]

The Article 1.42 airframe itself was variously described as having a blended body design similar to that of the F-22 and as having a delta planform with forward-mounted canard vanes more like the Eurofighter, in either case featuring twin engines, twin vertical stabilizers, and the use of shaping and radar-absorptive material to enhance its low observability. Mikoyan's deputy general designer, Anatoly Belosvet, said that the airplane was in the 30-metric-ton class (about 66,000 pounds), which would put it above the normal gross weight of an F-15C.[25] A French journal speculated that the aircraft was designed to carry the R-77, R-73, and R-37 air-to-air missiles internally, much in the manner of the F-22.[26]

Reportedly Belyakov personally lobbied President Boris Yeltsin for the Article 1.42 project on several occasions and conceded that the Defense Ministry had not come through with the needed funds to underwrite the aircraft's final preparation for flight testing. Despite the mounting federal budget crisis, which threatened to derail most, if not all, R&D activities, Belyakov pressed hard for at least concept validation testing to maintain the design bureau's potential for developing a more promising follow-on fighter sometime during the first quarter of the twenty-first century.[27] Later Belyakov claimed that the development of Article 1.42 was continuing to make progress and that the first flight would occur before the end of September 1994.[28] At press conferences during the Farnborough Air Show earlier that month, both he and Colonel General Pyotr Deinekin had reiterated that the first flight of Mikoyan's MFI prototype was "imminent."

The chief of the VVS headquarters staff, Colonel General Anatoly Malyukov, underscored in early 1993 the VVS's interest in continuing with Article 1.42. Seemingly contradicting Belyakov's complaint that the VVS was not supporting the new fighter's development, Malyukov said: "We're not going to kill the program. We will try by all means to support this work, and we have some more freedom in the form of nonbudgetary funding, which has not been available up to now."[29]

Constraints on Russia's Fighter Ambitions

There is little question that the Russian defense industry has the wherewithal in principle to produce a fifth-generation air-combat fighter. There also by 1994 seemed to be every possibility that the Mikoyan Design Bureau, which a year later was absorbed by the Moscow Aviation Industry Organization (MAPO, in its Russian acronym), had indeed been true to its word in having built an Article 1.42 prototype and having readied it to the point that it might be rolled out any day. Lending further strength to that possibility, the VVS in 1996 appeared to assign that putative aircraft the designator MiG-37, in a departure from its long-standing practice of not issuing new Mikoyan aircraft types a "MiG" number until the aircraft had been formally accepted by the VVS.[30] Yet because of its deepening economic troubles, the Russian defense establishment today faces constraints that militate strongly against the series production and the deployment of a next-generation fighter anytime soon.

As far back as 1992, well before Russia's financial situation had descended to its current dire circumstances, General Deinekin said that his first priority was to eliminate many of the "several dozen" different types of equipment in the existing VVS inventory and concentrate on creating a leaner force based on the most current bomber, fighter, and transport types then in service. As for new acquisitions, Deinekin conceded that the Ministry of Finance's meager cash outlays for procurement were insufficient to refurbish the VVS and that, for the moment, he was looking to buy new hardware only "in the minimum amounts that [might] assure the survival and profitability of aircraft plants."[31] First Deputy Defense Minister Andrei Kokoshin likewise confirmed in 1992 that the defense budget authorized by the Ministry of Finance would permit little more than providing the armed forces with "at least a minimal amount of new equipment."[32] A year later Deinekin reported that Russia's economic crisis had forced the VVS to abandon the development and production of a number of new equipment types.[33]

Competing Air Force Investment Priorities

Confirming a VVS requirement for a follow-on to the MiG-29 and Su-27, the first deputy commander in chief, Colonel General Viktor Kot, reported in January 1994 that VVS acquisition planners were focusing on, among other things, the "top-priority development of fifth-generation aviation complexes."[34] Yet even then, acquiring a new fighter was anything but the VVS's most urgent concern. Before the collapse of the USSR, General Malyukov acknowledged that the VVS would face an uphill struggle in attempting to secure the funds needed to replace the MiG-29 and the Su-27 with a new aircraft type. As for stealth applications in general, he said: "We are working on it, as are all nations that develop their own aircraft." However, he declared that the USSR was not developing any aircraft like the USAF's F-117, in which all other performance attributes would be subordinated to stealth. More ominously for the near-term prospects of Article 1.42, he added: "We find ourselves in a difficult position in funding research and development." In light of that he suggested: "It might be better to cut back on procurement and leave funding for R&D, even though [that] may mean stopping production factories and putting thousands of people out of work."[35]

An earlier press article noted that although Russia's existing fighters had limited growth potential and that any cutback in the development of follow-on systems would cause a lag in one of the areas in which Russia still held "world-class positions," serious financial difficulties required that preference be given "to the radical upgrading of existing aircraft rather than the creation of fundamentally new designs."[36] Even General Deinekin repeatedly declared that the main goal of VVS force modernization up to the year 2000 was the creation of a mobility capability to support Russia's peacekeeping needs around its conflicted periphery, notably in Transcaucasia and Central Asia, and that the acquisition of new transport aircraft was the VVS's top procurement need.[37] As for future fighter acquisition options, he said that the VVS would definitely continue striving to develop and deploy a next-generation aircraft, but only "as Russia's economic situation stabilizes."[38]

The VVS leadership's seeming lack of total commitment to Mikoyan's putative MiG-37 project in the face of more pressing needs was reflected in what came across as, at best, a lukewarm endorsement of the program by General Malyukov in 1993. Regarding Mikoyan's financial needs to keep the program alive, he said: "We can help them with cash injections, but it is hard to look ahead." He frankly added that the VVS was torn between continuing with the follow-on fighter and concentrating its meager resources on more immediate priorities: "We might save this program through a big investment, but we are in a complicated position, because the Su-27 is in production and because proposed modifications are wide-ranging and *in principle will satisfy our requirements.*"[39]

Malyukov further stated that because of cash shortages, the VVS's first fighter priority would be Su-27 modifications, including the Su-35 ASF and the Su-32 two-seat all-weather strike aircraft, as well as a reconnaissance variant and a much-needed electronic warfare version.[40] He also conceded that the VVS's most pressing acquisition need was in the transport area, considering Russia's new power-projection emphasis and the fact that more than half of the VVS's Il-76s had been lost to Ukraine as a result of the USSR's breakup. A senior aviation industry official, Viktor Laptev, concurred that the principal emphasis in Russian weapons development policy was on upgrading existing platforms, casting yet another shadow on any near-term prospects for the would-be MiG-37.[41]

Competing Defense Ministry Priorities

In yet another indication of the waning near-term prospects for a new Russian air-combat fighter, First Deputy Defense Minister Kokoshin declared in 1992 that the Defense Ministry's intended strategy for stemming further dissipation of industry resources was to concentrate on tried and proven equipment and to forgo investment in programs that would not attain their projected specifications for years to come. Although he acknowledged that the ministry wanted to accelerate initiatives toward seeking new technological breakthroughs as a hedge against mortgaging Russia's defense future, he said nothing about going from concept development to production.[42]

Whatever may have been in the development pipeline at the time, Kokoshin stated that the Defense Ministry had already settled on its acquisition plans up to the year 2000.[43] He later indicated that decisions had been reached regarding incremental growth in expenditures for weapons procurement, with two principal areas targeted in the near term: first, modernizing systems that had shown the greatest performance, value, and growth potential; and second, methodically laying down an R&D base that would enable "a certain qualitative leap and expanded series production of the most modern equipment *at a time when we are a little richer.*"[44] That statement suggested that although the Defense Ministry would try its best to keep a modicum of sustainer funding channeled into the MiG-37 program, any full-scale engineering development of the airplane would be subordinated to the task of improving the Su-27 and other fighters already in service.

Kokoshin admitted that Mikoyan was developing a follow-on fighter and that the Defense Ministry would like to order "more promising machines" rather than waste further outlays on more MiG-29s, which already existed in adequate numbers. However, he noted that upgrading the existing MiG-31 would be eight times less expensive than developing and producing a new long-range interceptor and that an improved MiG-31M would have "almost the same tactical-technical specifications" as a replacement aircraft. He added that Russia's defense industry was past the brink of falling behind and called the financial crisis "one of the most dramatic moments in all the many centuries of Russian history," with the pendulum having swung "from surpluses directly to the other extreme."[45]

One telling effect of the crisis was that the VVS and VPVO together acquired only 17 new combat aircraft in 1993.[46] That number continued to go downhill in later years, to the point that the 1996 budget provided for the purchase of *no* new combat aircraft. Only a few weeks before General Kot stated in 1993 that a next-generation fighter was a VVS "top priority," Kokoshin declared that upcoming R&D and procurement for all services would focus mainly on reconnaissance, command and control, supply to mobile forces, and precision munitions.[47] That alone seemed enough to suggest that any follow-on Russian fighter fielded in enough numbers to make a difference would remain a VVS pipe dream until well into the twenty-first century.

The Absolute Funding Shortage

As far back as 1989 Belyakov, Mikoyan's general designer, anticipated that a combination of declining defense resources and the recently declared Soviet defensive military doctrine could lead to pressures to curtail, or even forgo altogether, the deployment of successor-generation Soviet combat aircraft of all types for the indefinite future.[48] Despite those constraints, Belyakov said, Russia needed to continue aggressively pursuing new aircraft designs, since design and proof-of-concept development are the ultimate source for technological progress. Belyakov added, however, that because of the mounting cost of new weapons, it would become increasingly difficult to proceed from technology demonstrators to series production without an ironclad military justification.

This was *before* the collapse of the USSR. The subsequent trend toward a predominantly social-welfare orientation in the defense budget was confirmed by the chief of the Central Finance Directorate of the CIS armed forces, Lieutenant General Vasily Vorobyev, in February 1992. Vorobyev reported that about 70 percent of the total defense expenditure approved by the Russian Federation Supreme Soviet in the first quarter of 1992 would go to the welfare needs of servicemen and their families.[49] In a similar vein, the general director of the aviation industry department of the Ministry of Industry, Anatoly Bratukhin, told reporters that the volume of military production orders in 1992 was down by a factor of five from 1991.[50] According to Prime Minister Yegor Gaidar, half the procurement funds spent in 1992 went directly to compensate producers for canceled orders and to keep them temporarily out of bankruptcy.[51]

Those cuts in allocations for procurement were so severe that the Sukhoi Design Bureau was reported to be in danger of losing both the naval and the all-weather ground-attack variants of its Su-27. A Sukhoi official reported that production of the Su-27K carrier version had been halted as a result of insufficient funds. The Su-27IB development (since redesignated the Su-32) was also said to be operating on a shoestring budget, with only two prototypes built and with a decision on series production deferred for the indefinite future.[52]

In a grudging eleventh-hour acknowledgment that defense was being underfunded, the Ministry of Finance, under duress, granted the Defense Ministry a 10 percent increase in its 1993 procurement allocation.[53] That scarcely eased the hard times at Sukhoi's fighter production facility in Komsomolsk-na-Amure. The factory director complained that from a steady production rate, he had been suddenly informed in February 1992 that all state orders had been canceled and that his products "were not needed by anyone." This meant that his only source of income was a percentage of the hard-currency proceeds from a small Chinese order and that the latter would cover his expected costs only through the following October.[54] The factory director further reported that aside from a handful of carrier variants, not a single new Su-27 had been delivered to line units in 1993. He said that a number of previously ordered Su-27s stood unpaid for and unclaimed on his flight line and that his plant had been notified by the Defense Ministry that there was no money allocated for any Su-27 modification.[55]

In response to a question about how the VVS intended to deal with a situation in which its R&D funding had been essentially frozen, General Deinekin in 1993 confirmed that he had been forced to abandon a series of projects that would have ensured a competitive position for Russia. He said: "There are no resources for basic research, development, or even the maintenance of a distinctive experimental base." He added that without such investment, there would be "no future for the country's aviation—either military or civil" and warned that "only the adoption of urgent measures at the very highest level" would enable Russia "to remain an independent aviation state."[56] No doubt some of that dire language was intended for lobbying purposes, which would have rendered it an overstatement of a bad-enough situation. There was no question, however, about the VVS's sense of beleaguerment as a result of its continuing funding crisis. Asked about Mikoyan's new fighter project during an interview in May 1994, General Deinekin admitted: "We are doing our best." But he added that the lack of adequate financing was a major hindrance. For that reason, he concluded, the most demanding new projects would not come to fruition anytime soon.[57] Later that prognosis was only reinforced by the steady diversion of scarce funds from more needy defense accounts to Russia's subsequent misadventure in Chechnya.

During the final weeks that preceded the August 1995 Moscow Air Show, expectations were high that Mikoyan's putative Article 1.42 fighter would at long last be rolled out and put on static display. Those expectations, repeatedly stoked by hints dropped by Mikoyan's leadership, were dashed at the eleventh hour by

Defense Minister Pavel Grachev's reported decree that it was "too early" to unveil the new product. By the end of the year there were reports that the fighter would make its maiden flight early in 1996.[58] The persistence of such rumors about the aircraft's existence and imminent flight was enough to prompt unnamed U.S. officials to state, in January 1996, that the new fighter would have sixteen control surfaces driven by a fly-by-wire system and would embody limited stealth characteristics, although without any capacity for internal missile carriage.[59]

The longer the rumored new fighter remained masked behind this "any day now" posturing, however, the more likely it seemed that the program's financial troubles were grave enough to cast doubt on whether Russia might ever produce a fifth-generation successor to the MiG-29 in squadron strength, at least through the first decade of the twenty-first century.[60] Even during less troubled times, Belyakov conceded that because of the aircraft's size and cost, it would constitute no more than 20–30 percent of the VVS's fighter force. More recently Belosvet, Belyakov's principal deputy at the time, was said to have urged a major review of current Russian combat aircraft programs, an action that seemed certain to force the Article 1.42 program to die on the vine, with the VVS settling on an upgraded Su-35 to replace the Su-27 as a fifth-generation fighter substitute.[61] Belosvet admitted that the VVS could not afford to buy the MiG-37 in enough numbers to be operationally useful and that the program would most likely become a departure point for a more affordable next-generation fighter.[62] At the 1996 Berlin Air Show he gamely insisted that the Article 1.42 prototype could still fly "in a few months" if the needed funding came through.[63] He conceded elsewhere, however, that the MiG-29M and the MiG-31M might well be his company's last new fighter designs to fly in the twentieth century.

Finally, on January 12, 1999, MiG-MAPO showed its hand by unveiling at Zhukovsky what it described as the long-awaited fifth-generation Russian fighter intended to match and surpass the USAF's F-22.[64] At first glance, this highly advertised event seemed to signify a resounding end to the long-cultivated mystery about the existence of Article 1.42 by making good, once and for all, on Mikoyan's repeated "any day now" promises of years past. Within days, however, both Western and Russian fighter experts were openly questioning the new aircraft's putative stealth characteristics, with some going so far as to suggest that the rollout had been intended wholly for show and that the new airframe did not even appear to be flightworthy (see Chapter 10 for more details). Whatever the case, the Defense Ministry had announced nearly two years earlier, in March 1997, that it had decided to cancel any production plans for Article 1.42 for lack of funds, while leaving open the possibility that any existing prototype might be eventually flown as a technology demonstrator.[65] On the occasion of the new prototype's rollout in January 1999, MiG-MAPO leaders confidently insisted that the aircraft would make its maiden flight no later than the following March. However, in the wake of the unveiling, no one in authority in the Russian government gave any indication that the earlier cancellation decision was even remotely likely to be rescinded.

10. From Hard Times to Crisis

As Russia entered the second half-decade of its post-Soviet experience, the well-being of the VVS sank even further, thanks to a faltering economy that by July 1998 had driven the country to the brink of financial ruin, with interest rates on short-term treasury bills up to 120 percent a year and the Central Bank losing several hundred million dollars of hard currency reserves each day.[1]

With no relief in sight for the continuing cash shortage, discretionary funds for force modernization were all but zeroed out after 1995. Aircraft maintenance grew ever more erratic, due to a pervasive shortage of spare parts. With the lack of fuel, the annual flying time allotted to those few pilots still on flight status was reduced to below the minimum required for them even to be safe, let alone remain proficient. As a result, meaningful training all but ceased, denying the VVS even the pretense of having a serious combat capability. Summing up the situation in early 1997 Colonel General Pyotr Deinekin, VVS commander in chief, said: "In a word, it is critical."[2] Deinekin refused to concede that Russia's air power had fallen into such difficulty that it was now operating in a survival mode. He clearly insisted, however, that the VVS was in a deepening crisis, with little hope of improvement in the foreseeable future.

Echoing Deinekin's lament, a report issued at roughly the same time by the prestigious Council on Foreign and Defense Policy concluded that the condition of Russia's armed forces could be described only as a "catastrophe," which would become "a national catastrophe in the near future" if society and the state did not move to stave off the impending threat.[3] President Boris Yeltsin's adviser for aerospace, retired Marshal of Aviation Yevgeny Shaposhnikov, likewise echoed Deinekin. He remarked that Russian air power had so many "disgraceful" problems that if those in a position to change things continued to "waste time and do nothing to solve them," the "negative processes" that he saw eating away at

Russian air power would become irreversible. Shaposhnikov punctuated that declaration with a grim judgment that the country was "not prepared for anything—not for winter, not for spring, and not for war."[4] But perhaps the most arresting characterization of the decay that had come to afflict the Russian defense establishment since the USSR's collapse was that offered by the deputy chairman of the State Duma's Committee on Defense, Aleksei Arbatov. In one of the most balanced expositions on defense issues yet to have emanated from post-Soviet Russia, Arbatov charged: "Not since June 1941 has the Russian military stood as perilously close to ruin as it does now."[5]

On the plus side, in early 1997 the Ministry of Defense, in the face of its deepening crisis, finally undertook the first of a series of long-overdue measures aimed at rationalizing the Russian armed forces and bringing them more into line with Russia's real security needs. Some of those measures were well advised. One of them, a long-awaited merger of the VVS with VPVO, was announced in May 1997 after years of speculation over whether such a union would eventually come to pass. The merger was expected to result in a substantial reduction in the size of both services and in an integration of their many overlapping and duplicative functions.

Along with such sensible initiatives, however, were other announced changes that seemed less certain to work to the best interests of Russian air power. Notable among these was a decision by the Ministry of Defense in early 1997 to disband the VVS's recently constituted KFA, which had put all VVS fighters under the control of the VVS commander in chief for the first time, and to subordinate those aircraft once again to the ground commanders of Russia's eight military districts. This had the effect of fragmenting Russian air power at precisely the time when it needed closer integration. The change also created visible friction between the VVS leadership and the Defense Ministry.

Indeed, in considerable part because General Deinekin continued to disagree with his superiors in the Yeltsin government over the advisability of that move and of other proposed reform measures that affected the VVS, the government decided in December 1997 to retire Deinekin at the normal retirement age of sixty, after he had served as VVS commander in chief for six years. Aside from the natural uncertainties that attended a change at the top in such troubled times, this decision raised some basic questions about what lay behind Deinekin's directed retirement, on the eve of the VVS-VPVO merger over which he had been expected to preside, and about what the resultant leadership change implied for the near-term outlook for Russian air power.

Impact of the Continuing Budget Crisis

Russia's gross domestic product (GDP) shrank by 6 percent in 1996 and another 2 percent in 1997.[6] At around $400 billion by the end of 1997, it was little more than one-quarter of the Soviet Union's GDP at the latter's height. The mounting effects that this near-economic collapse was having on disposable state funds finally led First Vice Premier Anatoly Chubais to declare that the country was "in the midst of a monstrous budget crisis, the scope of which challenge[d] the capacity of the state to perform its functions."[7]

The precipitous decline in federal income had a deeply deleterious effect on the armed forces. Russia's third minister of defense since the USSR's collapse, retired Army General Igor Rodionov, stated in early 1997 that the Russian defense budget for that year amounted to roughly $25–30 billion in U.S purchasing power, barely one-tenth of the U.S. defense budget.[8] In the end, Rodionov's ministry received only 30 percent of its budget request for 1997. A sequester of state funds reduced Russia's actual defense allotment to $14 billion, only one-twentieth of the USSR's annual defense appropriation at the latter's height. The percentage of Russia's defense budget devoted to VVS procurement dropped to 10 percent in 1997, compared with 15–20 percent in 1992.[9] In all, Russian defense industry production in 1997 was down 90 percent from that of 1991.

In the face of its funding crisis, the VVS sought to make ends meet by earning nonbudgetary income through the approved use of its transport aircraft to move civilian cargo for hire. The revenue generated by that activity helped to keep Russia's airlifter inventory at least marginally serviceable pending a hoped-for increase in funding for operations and support. General Deinekin complained, however, that the VVS was receiving no windfall benefit whatever from the "billions of foreign currency" that Rosvooruzheniye, the Russian arms-export agency, earned annually from military sales abroad.[10]

Suspended Force Development

Owing largely to the funding crisis, the procurement plans of the VVS lay "in tatters," according to one Western observer writing in 1997.[11] In a reflection on the extent to which that crisis had stalled equipment purchases by all services, the VVS chief of acquisition, Lieutenant General Yury Klishin, reported that the Ministry of Defense had bought merely one aircraft in 1996 and none in 1997.[12] These numbers were down from 32 in 1992 and some 400 or more a year at the height of the Soviet era.

As for airlift assets, Colonel General Vyacheslav Yefanov, the commander in chief of VTA, said that his roster of serviceable aircraft had effectively been halved because of reduced funds for maintenance and repair. Production of the An-12, VTA's main intratheater workhorse, ended in 1972, with no procurement of the larger Il-76 or any other aircraft by VTA since 1991. In light of that situation Colonel General Mikhail Soroka, the VVS deputy commander in chief, said in early 1997 that VTA would begin atrophying before the year 2000 with the planned retirement of the An-12, the An-22, and early-series Il-76s from line service.[13]

To fill the gap, according to VVS spokesmen, VTA needed to acquire a minimum of 8–10 new transport aircraft per year starting in 1997 and upward of 20–30 per year after 2003. Numerous replacement options remain available. Tupolev's Tu-330VT is a contender to replace the An-12, as is the swept-wing An-70 with four turboprop engines, which is in flight test and could enter service by 2000.[14] The Ministry of Defense has invested considerable development funds in the An-70, but support for the longer-range Il-106 has reportedly been frozen. As an interim measure, VTA announced plans to offset the impending retirement of its An-22s and older-model Il-76s by buying the stretched Il-76MF, which meets all requirements and is ready for series production.[15] The establishment of the Ilyushin Transnational Financial-Industrial Group in March 1997 signaled that Ilyushin's main production facility in Tashkent, Uzbekistan, would retain its ability to manufacture Il-76MFs into the twenty-first century. Ilyushin also was positioning itself to develop the Il-106, although it had not, as of mid-1998, received any military backing. Available procurement funds in 1997 allowed only for the purchase of new engines for 25–30 percent of VTA's existing transports.

In the bomber realm, General Deinekin confirmed renewed Ukrainian heel-dragging regarding the negotiated return of LRA's Tu-95s and Tu-160s inherited by Ukraine when the USSR collapsed. (Of 25 production variants of the Tu-160 manufactured out of an original VVS plan to procure 100, 19 remain in Ukraine.)[16] Deinekin reported that despite Russian negotiation in good faith, the VVS was "still unable to arrive at a mutually acceptable decision regarding the return of [these] aircraft to Russian territory."[17] After much fruitless dickering, he finally decided in June 1997 that the VVS would forgo further attempts to buy back 10 Tu-160s and 15 Tu-95s, since the aircraft had fallen into such disrepair that they were no longer worth the effort. Given the unlikelihood that Russia would recover any additional aircraft from Ukraine, the Defense Ministry's chief of acquisition, Colonel General Anatoly Sitnov, declared that the VVS might be forced to withdraw its few remaining Tu-160s from service. Plans also were announced to reduce the number of existing Tu-95s in the VVS inventory, consolidating them at the air base at Engels.[18]

For the more distant future, the Sukhoi Design Bureau was said to be continuing work on the T-60 to replace the Tu-22M medium bomber. This prospective new aircraft, with a design weight of more than 160,000 pounds, reportedly dated back to the 1970s, when Sukhoi began looking at a Su-24 derivative with much greater takeoff weight. The T-60 was revealed in 1993 through leaked hints from Sukhoi staffers, although its existence continues to be denied by the Russian defense establishment.[19] That new bomber option, said to incorporate some degree of Russian stealth technology, could yet be canceled. Already, some reports suggest that the VVS has shifted funds from the T-60 to a Tu-22M3 upgrade.[20] In perhaps the most extreme view aired to date on the long-term outlook for LRA, Yeltsin's aerospace adviser, retired Marshal of Aviation Shaposhnikov, went so far as to assert that Russia had no more need for intercontinental-range combat aircraft, since it now relies on nuclear missiles for deterrence. Shaposhnikov proposed that the VVS get out of the heavy bomber business altogether rather than continue spending "colossal amounts of money." Instead, he suggested, the VVS should concentrate its main energy on acquiring a new tactical bomber to replace the Su-24.[21]

In the potentially lucrative area of new jet trainer aircraft, the Ministry of Defense ordered 10 MiG-ATs and 10 Yak-130s in January 1997 for eventual use in the VVS's UPT program. General Deinekin noted that the digital flight control systems of those new trainer prototypes could be programmed to replicate the handling features of any fighter now in service. In tacit proof of the extent to which the VVS finds itself short of operations and support funds, he suggested that to save money, the VVS might use those aircraft not only for UPT but also for upgrade and continuation training "so as not to use a heavy aircraft every time for this." Deinekin suggested gamely, if unpersuasively, that to do otherwise would be "like using a Mercedes 600 to teach people to drive a car."[22]

The VVS continues to negotiate with Mikoyan and Sukhoi over their competing trainer candidates because it would like to provide work to both firms. It cannot afford both types, however, and eventually will have to settle on one or the other. The original VVS requirement was for 800–1,000 new trainers to replace the aging L-39. That requirement was later reduced to 500 aircraft. One source reported in late 1997 that 100 new trainers would be ordered before 2009 and that another 100 would be procured after that.[23] However, the first deputy commander in chief of the VVS, Colonel General Viktor Kot, indicated that acquisition of a new trainer would not occur before 2007 at the earliest. The Moscow Aviation Industry Organization (MAPO) reportedly sees a market for 600 of its $11-million-a-copy MiG-AT trainer candidates with the VVS.[24] In the meantime, the Myasishchev Design Bureau has received a VVS contract to restore several hundred L-39s that have been grounded by a lack of spare parts and the expiration of the warranty from the Czech manufacturer. The refurbishment plan involves installing new Russian avionics and other subsystems.

In the critical area of fighter modernization, the most optimistic estimates held that the Defense Ministry would be able to marshal the required funds to procure at most only 5–10 new fighters a year until 2005.[25] Senior ministry officials reportedly advocated terminating most new combat aircraft development programs, including helicopter programs, so that a few of the most essential ones might be protected. General Sitnov told a special government meeting on aerospace in 1997 that the defense establishment could finance only two next-generation combat aircraft programs at a time. Sitnov stressed the overriding importance of the

Su-27IB strike fighter to replace the Su-24 and sharply criticized the VVS's continuing effort to acquire a fifth-generation air-combat fighter. "What's the use," he asked, "of developing, for instance, the Sukhoi fifth-generation fighter if the aircraft's cockpit dates back to a second- or third-generation design?"[26]

During the late 1990s General Deinekin began backpedaling on his earlier remarks about the likely near-term appearance of a Russian fifth-generation fighter, almost as if to concede a growing realization on his part that any such appearance was not to be. At the 1994 Farnborough Air Show, as noted in the preceding chapter, Deinekin spoke of an imminent maiden flight by such an aircraft. In more recent years he has merely conceded that Russian designers are at work "creating a super-new aircraft which is not to be discussed at news conferences."[27] When queried about Mikoyan's presumed Article 1.42 project, he replied that he had "no idea what was meant by the question."[28] He did, however, suggest that a new Russian stealth attack aircraft would enter service after the year 2000.[29]

In early 1998 the newly appointed general designer for MiG-MAPO, Mikhail Korzhuyev, disclosed that the Defense Ministry had allocated $2.5 million to prepare the Article 1.42 aircraft, said to be hangared at Zhukovsky, for a first flight in August 1998.[30] By and large, however, rather than continue promising the imminent flight and eventual deployment of a fifth-generation fighter in the class of the USAF's F-22, VVS spokesmen settled on advocating what they began to call "4.5 generation" fighters, with the main emphasis directed toward improving *existing* platforms so as to keep the aircraft industry at least minimally employed. One example of such a "4.5 generation" aircraft was the MiG-29-917, which was first flown at Zhukovsky in November 1997. That latest modification of the basic MiG-29 incorporated a larger wing, a new cockpit layout featuring liquid crystal multifunction displays, a ground-mapping radar, and an extra internal fuel tank adding some 300 much-needed miles to the aircraft's range.[31]

Affirming the VVS's retrenchment from earlier claims of having an F-22 counterpart waiting in the wings, General Klishin noted that development work on fifth-generation aircraft was "still being carried on at a slow pace" but that in a number of cases, it had been "practically suspended because of the sharp reduction in RDT&E [research, development, test, and evaluation] funding in the aircraft construction area." He warned that if the funding reduction was not soon reversed, design and development entities would "no longer be able to carry out advanced development, and the VVS would cease being augmented with new models of weapons even with a restoration of full funding." Klishin did not rule out that the VVS might acquire a fifth-generation aircraft "tomorrow, [or] maybe the day after," but he cautioned that much would depend on financing.[32] He further declared that the Su-32FN and the Su-37 (an improved Su-35 incorporating thrust vectoring) would be in production by 2003–5. Pending that, the Su-27IB remained the best near-term prospect for continued VVS support, since the operational need for it was far greater than the need for any other new aircraft type in contention for funding. It was one of the few Russian combat aircraft types still receiving state financing in 1998, with five preproduction variants having been delivered to the VVS by the Sukhoi Design Bureau's production facility in Novosibirsk.[33]

Despite that apparent retrenchment, Sukhoi in late 1997 flew the "S-37," an advanced twin-engine fighter testbed with forward-swept wings. Mikhail Simonov, the general designer, said that the aircraft was being flown as a technology demonstrator and that it was wholly "of an experimental nature."[34] Previously known in the West as the S-32, the aircraft was conceived during the second half of the 1980s, most likely in response to the forward-swept Grumman X-29 concept demonstrator built and test-flown by the United States. The aircraft, in the size and weight class of the Su-27, was said to have received no funding from the VVS and evidently was supported through revenue acquired by Sukhoi as a result of foreign sales of the Su-27. It is doubtful that the aircraft is the basis of a future multirole fighter for the VVS or the Russian Navy.

Thus the Defense Ministry, with reluctant VVS concurrence, seemed to have postponed any earlier plans it may have had for procuring additional combat aircraft before the year 2005. By one account, an expanded session of the VVS Military Council reached a collective decision in February 1996 to "forgo substantial purchases of existing aircraft in the near to midterm future in favor of supporting the scientific-technical base and new aircraft development."[35] Apparently confirming such a decision, General Deinekin conceded that the time had come for the VVS to "give up the procurement of series-produced aircraft, using its funds to maintain in good working order the pool of aircraft already in service." Deinekin frankly admitted that the VVS was "not in any position to tell aviation plants, design bureaus, and aviation science" what they were "waiting to hear, namely, will there be any funding and, if so, what sort of funding and when?"[36] In a similar vein, Shaposhnikov conceded that although the country needed to reinvigorate its defense industrial base, Russia's defense industry clearly could not be "strong everywhere and in everything."[37]

As if to dispel the gloom hovering over Russia's near-term fighter prospects with a single coup de main, MiG-MAPO, as noted in Chapter 9, finally broke the many years of suspense by unmasking its long-awaited Article 1.42 prototype fifth-generation fighter in a formal rollout ceremony at Zhukovsky on January 12, 1999. MiG-MAPO spokesmen had indicated several days earlier that the unveiling would take place soon in an official presentation to the Russian government, and pre-rollout photos of the aircraft were prominently featured in at least one Western aviation trade magazine the month before the rollout.[38] When the event finally occurred, the aircraft was taxied onto the hardstand at Zhukovsky with great fanfare to an invited audience that included the Russian defense minister, a bevy of foreign military attachés, and a large gathering of reporters.

Confirming many of the rumors that had abounded about the aircraft since the early 1990s, the Article 1.42 prototype was a heavy, twin-engine, single-seat fighter with a clipped delta wing and an all-moving forward canard stabilizer loosely analogous in configuration to the French Rafale and the British Typhoon "4.5-generation" fighters. The aircraft was said to incorporate thrust vectoring by means of movable exhaust nozzles for agile maneuvering at high angles of attack and to have a thrust-to-weight ratio of 1.3-to-1 at combat weight. One press account reported that the Soviet Communist Party's Central Committee had given the Mikoyan Design Bureau a green light in principle to commence work on the next-generation fighter in 1986, with the program initially conducted under the supervision of the bureau's acclaimed former chief test pilot, Grigory Sedov. That account added that leadership of the Article 1.42 program was later transferred to Yury Vorotnikov and that assembly of the aircraft was completed in 1994, at which time the prototype was handed over to Mikoyan's chief test pilot, Roman Taskayev, at Zhukovsky for initial taxi tests.[39]

At the rollout the director general of MiG-MAPO, Mikhail Korzhuyev, announced that only taxi tests had been conducted to date but that the aircraft was slated to make its initial flight by the end of February. He added that the Article 1.42 prototype was equipped with the long-promised Saturn/Lyulka Al-41F jet engines, that it was designed to supercruise at Mach 1.3–1.6 without the use of afterburners, and that it was capable of reaching a top augmented speed of Mach 2.6. The design was said to be statically unstable (a first for a Russian fighter), with the aircraft equipped with a digital flight-control system to compensate for that instability. Air-to-air missiles were reportedly carried in internal weapons bays, although the prototype displayed at Zhukovsky was fitted with wing-mounted pylons for external weapons carriage. The aircraft that was unveiled appeared to be equipped at best with a range-only radar, as attested by its small radome, although Korzhuyev declared that the production version would have a pulse-doppler radar with a phased-array antenna offering a beyond-visual-range engagement capability and an ability to track twenty targets simultaneously.[40] The aircraft was said to feature composite materials in 16 percent of its structure, and the production variant was expected to increase that figure to 30 percent. The prototype displayed at Zhukovsky was equipped with an internal 30-mm cannon and had no evident provision for in-flight refueling.

In his remarks at the rollout, Korzhuyev claimed that the capabilities of the Article 1.42 would match or exceed those of the USAF's F-22, adding: "If this plane [had been] used to beat off the British-American air raids on Iraq, 90 percent of all the launched guided weapons, including cruise missiles, would [have been] shot down before they reached targets on the territory of Iraq."[41] Within days, however, senior West European officials and industry observers were openly questioning not only the aircraft's stealth properties but also its flight-worthiness.[42] There were further intimations that the aircraft was not even the vaunted Article 1.42 at all but was rather an Article 1.44 developmental variant intended solely to provide a flying testbed for the new Al-41F engines. One Russian aviation writer declared that when the aircraft was finally unmasked, he was "taken aback. . . . It was not the long-rumored stealth interceptor. It was something else."[43]

Although this remains to be seen, the aircraft that MiG-MAPO rolled out seemed to have dubious stealth characteristics even to the untutored eye. The leading edges of the wings and canards did seem to be closely aligned with each other, one known low-observable design feature. However, numerous other aspects of the aircraft (including the rough surface finish, exposed pitot tubes, and canopy configuration, to say nothing of the wing pylons for external weapons carriage) did not appear to be designed to minimize the aircraft's radar cross-section (RCS). Asked why the aircraft was not covered with radar-absorptive material (RAM), Korzhuyev replied: "It's senseless to start with [RAM] coating on the very first plane. It's not of major importance."[44] Korzhuyev stated, however, that the inlets were treated with RAM and that their air ducts were snaked to prevent the Al-41F engine faces from being visible to enemy air-to-air search radars. He further insisted that the aircraft's stealth properties would be comparable to those of the F-22.

That latter claim scarcely comported with the announced fact that the Article 1.42's RCS was a full 0.1 square meter, admittedly 10 times less than that of the MiG-29SMT but more than 100 times greater than that of the USAF's currently deployed stealth combat aircraft, let alone the F-22. As a baseline reference in this respect, the forward-aspect RCS of the tri-service Joint Strike Fighter now in development by the United States will reportedly be only 0.001 square meter, barely the equivalent of a metallic sphere the size of a golf ball. That would be on a par with the RCS of the USAF's stealthy F-117 and B-2 ground-attack aircraft and slightly more than that of its fifth-generation F-22 air-combat fighter.[45] In light of that seeming discrepancy, perhaps the fairest interim conclusion that can be made about the Article 1.42 prototype is that ascribed to some French aeronautical experts, who portrayed the aircraft as unquestionably fast and maneuverable but "certainly not representative of the combat characteristics typically associated with the fifth-generation."[46]

What might MiG-MAPO have expected to gain from the rollout if the Article 1.42 prototype was indeed that much less than met the eye? One Western expert flatly dismissed the event as "industry hype."[47] Certainly the rollout could have been intended, among other things, as an eleventh-hour gambit for seeking enough government funds to finance at least initial flight testing, if not further development of the aircraft. Given the announced price tag of roughly $70 million per aircraft, it is scarcely surprising that the VVS was said to be "noncommittal" about the Article 1.42 prototype as a procurement option.[48] Beyond that, the event could have been, at least in part, a desperate attempt by MiG-MAPO to stave off its directed merger with the more solvent Sukhoi Design Bureau, a development that the Mikoyan contingent had long opposed as a matter of fierce institutional pride. If so, the attempt failed, since barely a month later Sukhoi's deputy director general, Nikolai Nikitin, was announced as taking over as the new leader of MiG-MAPO in the first step toward the integration of the two enterprises in the interest of consolidating Russia's faltering defense industry, which at the time was running at only 5 percent of capacity.[49]

As for the fate of the Article 1.42 prototype itself, in the early aftermath of the rollout Western experts generally assumed that the aircraft might well get into the air in due course, assuming the provision of enough funds to support at least a modest flight-test program, but that it would, in the best of circumstances, be used only as a technology demonstrator from which a recovered Russian aviation industry might eventually develop a smaller and cheaper fighter possessing fifth-generation characteristics. On that count, however, one senior Russian official remarked that Russia had "overslept the fifth-generation fighter" and that "it would be more appropriate to launch the development of a sixth-generation machine."[50] On the heels of the unveiling of the Article 1.42 prototype there was no hint of any change in the Defense Ministry's long-standing position that Russia should upgrade its existing fighters before advancing to the next generation.[51] Indeed a ministry official flatly declared that the aircraft remained unaffordable by Russia and that it was "clear to everyone" that the state would be unable to provide even a fraction of the $43 million estimated by MiG-MAPO to be the cost of a seven-year flight-test and development program. That led a Russian reporter to suggest that the vaunted fighter "may yet be destined for nothing more glorious than being displayed at the Air Force museum at Monino."[52]

For the near term, the Defense Ministry in 1997 announced as its main priorities the development of improved ISR (intelligence, surveillance, and reconnaissance), enhanced command and control, better navigation equipment, and better precision munitions, along with the preservation of Russia's nuclear deterrent. First Deputy Minister of Defense Andrei Kokoshin admitted that although many new types of conventional weapons, presumably including MiG-MAPO's Article 1.42, were almost ready for production and needed only to complete their testing, there were no funds in the state coffers to pay for them. Only after the Russian military had shrunk to a sensible size, organized itself more rationally, and fixed its existing equipment and readiness shortcomings, said Kokoshin, would it be in a position to start acquiring new hardware. That would not occur, he added, until after 2005 at the earliest and would be contingent on the broader prospects for economic recovery.

Deprived Operations and Support

The funding crisis also curtailed the delivery of fuel and spare parts to VVS flying units, with inevitable downside consequences for aircrew proficiency and mission readiness. As a rule, the VVS received only about one-third of its declared minimum fuel requirement each year after the early 1990s. In 1996 it was allotted only 38 percent of its petroleum, oil, and lubricants (POL) request, and only 30 percent of that allotment was actually delivered. The same year, only 17–22 percent of the planned fuel allocation was delivered to LRA's three air armies. The commander in chief of VPVO, Colonel General Viktor Prudnikov, reported that his flying units were provided funding for only a quarter of their minimal POL needs in 1997. Lieutenant General Leonid Bokov, the deputy commander of VPVO fighter aviation, reported that the average annual flying time for VPVO pilots had fallen by a factor of three to five over the past five to seven years, reaching a low of only 17–20 hours a year.[53]

In addition to the paucity of available fuel, a shortage of funds for maintenance also undermined aircraft operability. General Klishin reported that 62 percent of a flying regiment's annual budget typically went to pay for operations expenses, with maintenance and salaries accounting for the second and third priorities. Thanks to chronic underfunding of the second category, he said, the aircraft in-commission rate had fallen to 60 percent in LRA, to 40 percent in VTA, and to a "record low" in KFA.[54]

More specifically, General Soroka reported that only half of LRA's aircraft were serviceable at the beginning of 1997 and that 20 percent were in need of major overhaul.[55] Another account stated that of LRA's 134 Tu-22M3 bombers, only 49 were serviceable, and that only 2 of LRA's 6 Tu-160s were flyable. Of VTA's 248 Il-76 transports, only 110 were said to be serviceable, with only 3 of its 26 An-124 C-5 equivalents still flyable. Worst of all, according to that account, only 35–40 percent of KFA's combat aircraft were reported in working order, with half of all fourth-generation fighters grounded due to engine and spares shortages. The prognosis, said General Soroka, was that all VVS aircraft would be down by the beginning of the twenty-first century unless the situation improved dramatically in the meantime.

VVS infrastructure in 1996 also continued to suffer from the budget crisis. Half of the VVS's airfields were said to be in need of refurbishment, a percentage expected to increase to two-thirds over the ensuing four years.[56] Base security was described as minimal, and regimental facilities, including command and control spaces, were inadequate; the supply system all but ground to a halt. Line maintenance units typically worked at only 30 percent of their capacity, with the rest of the maintenance workload going to regional depots. In 1996 the 4th Air Army received only 1.6 percent of its required automobile tires and 4.2 percent of its needed batteries.[57] General Klishin noted that poor storage conditions were threatening to reduce the shelf life of VVS precision munitions by one-half to two-thirds.[58] The VVS director of operations, Lieutenant General Aleksandr Ionov, reported that since the termination of new aircraft deliveries in the early 1990s, all discretionary funds had been channeled into keeping as much as possible of the VVS's existing equipment serviceable. Ionov warned that unless the funding situation improved, the declining level of aircraft readiness would "snowball."[59]

In combination, the fuel and spares shortages occasioned a monumental reduction in available flying time for Russian pilots, to the point that the situation was worse in 1996 than at any other time since the disintegration of the USSR. General Soroka said that only 35 percent of the flight-hour plan for KFA and 45 percent for the VVS as a whole was fulfilled during that year. The average number of hours flown by pilots still on flight orders was 45–50 in VTA, 42 in LRA, and 19 or less in KFA. The only reason VTA topped the list was because it was hauling commercial cargo in pursuit of nonbudget revenue. That additional "business activity" caused VTA to exceed its allotted flight hour ceiling by 150 percent, an overrun that came at the direct expense of needed training in other commands. Even at their peak operating tempo, VTA airlifters flew only 5 or 6 hours in a 24-hour period, barely half the norm.

In one air division, to cite a typical example, only 10 percent of the needed fuel was delivered during the first quarter of 1996. That left assigned aircrews only 5 percent of the flying hours allotted to them in the annual plan and made it impossible for them to maintain their "professional fitness" *(profprigodnost).*[60] Prompted by this state of affairs, the chairman of the State Duma's Defense Committee, retired Army Lieutenant General Lev Rokhlin, angrily noted that the VVS in 1997 flew only 35 percent of what it had planned, for a total of 190,000 hours, including 44,000 at night.[61] In contrast, the total number flown by the USAF the previous year was more than two *million* hours.[62] The projected Russian flight-hour total for 1998 was down by 45,000 from 1997, leading General Ionov to warn that if the trend continued for two or three years more, the VVS's critical condition could become irreversible.[63]

Immobilized Training

The shortage of fuel and spares also forced VVS leaders to impose draconian restrictions on operational training in line units. They ordered a selective allocation of flight hours and reduced training standards across the board. VVS commanders were obliged to focus on keeping only their most experienced pilots proficient by allotting most of the available fuel to a regiment's first and most seasoned squadron, leaving those less-experienced pilots in the second squadron and those in the third squadron who were directly out of conversion training largely to languish in frustration on the ground. Maintenance of at least a semblance of mission readiness was reserved for those pilots "of the leadership echelon, deputy regiment commanders and squadron commanders," who were described as "the ones who must be kept in shape above all, like the queen in a beehive, to 'multiply' and pull the entire chain of combat training up to a decent level."[64]

Toward that end, the commander of KFA's 4th Air Army in the North Caucasus, Lieutenant General Vladimir Mikhailov, reported that he had decided not to dilute his command's fighting strength by attempting to train all flying personnel assigned to it. Instead he elected to give priority to each regiment's first squadron, thus ensuring at least one passably proficient pilot for each serviceable aircraft. Mikhailov noted that he had managed to sequester enough additional fuel to put his younger pilots into the air on occasion but that only his most experienced pilots were allotted enough time to maintain any real proficiency.[65] Similarly, VPVO's General Bokov commented that in order to maintain a minimally acceptable level of proficiency for a few, regiment commanders had been forced to divide their pilots into "those who fly and those for whom there is neither fuel nor a machine." Bokov added that because of their lack of anything remotely approaching minimal mission currency, VPVO pilots no longer felt confident in the cockpit.[66] To any Western air commander, that would have raised a valid question as to why they were being permitted to fly at all.

The fuel shortage also caused a pronounced decline in VVS continuation training standards, with a new overlay of restrictions and simplifications in the interest of flight safety. In fighter and ground-attack units, the diluted training regime that was thus imposed featured a low volume of operations, a sharply reduced number of pilots with the requisite proficiency to fly, and a decline in mission-qualification sorties flown in instrument weather and at night. There was no air opposition or coordination with other air components or service branches, and there was no training that involved advanced maneuvering. There also was no effort to incorporate lessons from Afghanistan or Chechnya into what remained of mission-employment training, and no live weapons drops were conducted. General Mikhailov reported that reduced fuel allocations had forced him to allow his pilots to perform only one mission event per sortie, rather than the usual two or three incorporating various maneuvers and weapons delivery modes. He noted that in those circumstances, one could meet minimal training standards but could not achieve high proficiency.[67]

Another example of watered-down training was LRA's continued use of transport aircraft as bomber surrogates because of their lower operating costs. Colonel General Igor Kalugin, the commander in chief of LRA, noted that in 1996 his aircrews participated in an exercise called Redut ("Redoubt"), which involved in-flight refueling and live missile launches from Tu-95MS aircraft. The aircrews reportedly earned a rating of "excellent."[68] This was clearly the exception to the rule, however. As noted above, the average flying time for LRA aircrews in 1996 was only 42 hours, much of which was conducted on Tu-134 and An-24 transports.

Still other instances of reduced proficiency standards included allowing senior pilots with only Second-Class ratings to become squadron commanders because of an insufficiency of hours needed to allow them to meet the annual requirements for maintaining a First-Class rating. Another proposal suggested giving recent UPT graduates their Third- and Second-Class upgrades on the L-39 rather than on their assigned operational aircraft, allowing them from 46 to 75 hours of time toward that end depending on their proficiency. In addition the VVS capitalized on air shows as windfall opportunities for pilots to log flight time, with line pilots competing intensely for such flights so that they might remain proficient at least at basic aircraft handling. Finally, the erosion of standards saw an increased reliance on flight simulators in lieu of actual flying. In 1996 simulator use in LRA increased by more than 15 percent from the year before.

All of these changes exacted a significant price in training realism. As one article warned: "We must note the hidden danger in simplifications. If they exceed permissible limits, an entire generation of air commanders may end up being threatened. They themselves will not only lose skills in organizing tactical air training, but also will determine for many years the attitude toward it on the part of their successors, in whom a sense of caution and inability stemming from a lack of understanding will escalate into fear."[69]

The fuel shortage also afflicted UPT and conversion training. In 1989, as discussed in Chapter 4, VVS flight schools terminated their initial checkout program in combat aircraft and substituted an increase—from 130 to 220—in the number of hours flown in the L-39. The transition to combat aircraft was instead conducted at RTUs after UPT graduation. As a result, newly minted pilots reported to their assigned units with more than 300 hours of basic flight experience.

Beginning in 1994, however, according to the VVS chief of education and training, Lieutenant General Yakim Yanakov, the number of flight hours in the UPT syllabus fell from 220 to only 90–110. That resulted in a pronounced undertraining of UPT cadets and a consequent shift of the UPT top-off burden to the RTUs. In 1996 some two hundred lieutenants fresh out of UPT were reportedly undergoing conversion training on the MiG-29 at Borisoglebsk. They were said to be spending most of their time in simulators, logging actual flights only as "a great rarity." The RTU deputy commander complained that his MiG-29s could "only nominally be considered aircraft" in any case, since they lacked needed spare parts. He added that even if by some miracle additional fuel did become available, the aircraft still could not be flown because their condition had deteriorated so badly from nonuse.[70]

Those who graduated from Borisoglebsk and went on to line units also flew mainly simulators, rather than their assigned aircraft. Not surprisingly in light of such limited flight opportunities, many UPT graduates did not convert to operational status at all. Of 234 UPT graduates who went on to KFA in 1992–94, more than half were never checked out on their assigned combat aircraft.[71] As Yanakov put it: "Many graduates have not gotten into a combat aircraft at all. They have clogged up operational units for more than four years, and there as well they do not fly." In yet another stopgap measure that would have made no sense to a Western air commander, Yanakov noted that the "underfulfillment of flying hours" in the L-39 was forcing the basic training program to be completed instead in combat aircraft, with the result that the final training of a MiG-29 pilot increased expenditures "many times." Yanakov added that the reduced number of instructor regiments and RTUs had brought the VVS to a new low, from which it would soon be "unable to ensure their quality training." He further noted that prospects for near-term improvement were few and that as a result, the VVS was "essentially standing on the brink of the total destruction of the existing system of fighter pilot training." He added: "Graduates [now] go to line units with the nominal status of aircraft commander, yet their low professional qualifications are threatening the combat readiness of air regiments."[72]

As an indication of how strapped continuation training in VVS units had become, General Yanakov noted that UPT training in 1993–96 accounted for 32 percent of the total hours flown by the VVS, even though it represented only 7 percent of the fuel consumed. That contrast reflected the wide disparity between the fuel consumption rate of the L-39 and that of the more voracious fighters and bombers. Yanakov rued the fact that units were being supplied with "untrained pilots." As an attempted corrective, he noted that an experiment had been conducted in 1997 with a group of cadets from the Kacha UPT school; selected to make early conversion to the MiG-29 and the Su-27, each cadet chosen for this experiment would be provided 30 hours of fighter time. As for the UPT syllabus itself, Yanakov said that the total flight time allotted for students in 1997 would not exceed 95–100 hours and that advanced flying, to include night, formation, and mission-employment training, would not be provided.[73]

General Ionov admitted that the situation for young pilots—"the future of aviation," as he called them—had become a full-fledged "calamity" for the VVS. Yet he conceded that all that could be done at the moment was to implore them to remain patient, since the VVS had no choice but to focus on its most experienced aircrews to ensure the highest proficiency for the best pilots. Ionov said that over the longer haul, the VVS might "gradually bring the rest up to that level," but that for the time being, more than 75 percent of the most recent UPT graduates would have to leave the service. Of the remainder, he said, only some 15 percent, "the most capable and determined," could count on finishing their promised operational conversion training. The others would have to be retrained within the air force or move to other services and acquire different skills.[74] The clear implication of all this was a looming aircrew and leadership replacement problem for the VVS at all levels. As just one indicator, the test pilot school at the Gromov Flight Research Institute at Zhukovsky produced only three graduates in 1997, down from an average annual class output of eleven to thirteen new test pilots during less challenging times.[75]

Characteristically, General Deinekin tried to put the best face on this bleak situation. In a masterpiece of understatement, he allowed that the VVS was "not experiencing the best time in its history just now." As for its watered-down training and growing use of simulators in lieu of flying, he drew on his experience as an amateur boxer to warn candidly: "No matter how much shadowboxing you do, you will lose the sense of distance and the sense of a real opponent, and you will not be able to fight." Deinekin noted that the combat capability of the VVS was not only falling but had already fallen, and "very markedly at that."[76] He further acknowledged that the VVS was not capable of performing all its assigned missions and was having "great difficulty in maintaining combat readiness at even a third its potential level."[77] However, he disagreed with the suggestion that the VVS should assemble a single crack unit from its many weakened assets so that it might have at least one able to acquit itself commendably against any challenge. Deinekin rightly countered that merely a single such unit, however capable, could never command enough firepower to make a winning difference in modern war.

Mounting Safety Problems

The apparent determination of VVS and VPVO leaders to sustain at least the appearance of a "business-as-usual" flying program despite the eroded proficiency of their pilots left a definite mark on the accident rate, which had been on the rise since the USSR's collapse even as the number of flying hours had drastically fallen. Throughout the 1970s the number of VVS accidents attributable to pilot error did not exceed 70 percent. But the number reached 72 percent in 1992, 74 percent in 1993, and 80 percent in 1994 and has been growing ever since.[78] At the same time, the number of major mishaps increased three years in a row following a respite from the peak of 19 in 1990. There were 12 accidents in 1996, up from 7 in 1995 and 5 in 1994.[79]

That increased accident rate was a natural outgrowth of the Russian military's chronically underfunded training accounts. To note some examples, in March 1996 a midair collision occurred between two MiG-29s flying in formation near Chita. Both pilots ejected successfully, but the total flying time between them in the previous year was only 15 hours.[80] Such a recipe for disaster would never have been allowed in any properly disciplined Western air force. Later in 1996

VPVO experienced two MiG-31 takeoff and landing accidents within a single week. It lost another MiG-31 in September 1997 after an engine caught fire. Both crew members ejected safely. The following month a VPVO Su-27 two-seater crashed, killing both pilots. VPVO's commander in chief, General Prudnikov, admitted afterward that VPVO pilot proficiency was suffering badly, with his interceptor pilots averaging less than 20 hours of flight time a year.[81] According to one knowledgeable account, only 32 percent of the most recent VVS and VPVO aircraft losses were the result of equipment malfunction. The remainder were attributable to pilot error (26 percent) and violation of published flight rules and safety regulations (more than 40 percent).[82]

Even the putative cream of the crop were adversely affected by the flight-hours crisis. To note a particularly unfortunate case, the VVS's premier flight-demonstration team, the Russian Knights *(Russkiye vityazi),* experienced two fatal Su-27 crashes in 1996 when the aircraft were dragged into a ridge while flying in close formation with an Il-76 transport that was leading them through instrument weather en route home from an air show in Vietnam. To add insult to injury, on arrival at the Bratislava airport in Slovakia in June 1997 to participate in an air show, the number-three Russian Knights pilot failed to lower his landing gear and inadvertently landed gear up. Fortunately the accident resulted in only slight damage to the aircraft's nose, underfuselage weapons pylons, and ventral fins, though it caused considerable embarrassment for the pilot.[83]

Earlier a Moscow press report noted that the VVS's Su-25 flight-demonstration team, the Heavenly Hussars *(Nebesniye gusary),* had been disbanded because of a shortage of funds and fuel. The writer asked whether it made sense to retain the Su-27 and MiG-29 teams when the latter were suffering comparable fuel and spares shortages. The pilots assigned to those teams were allotted only one-tenth the annual flying hours budgeted for the USAF Thunderbirds and the U.S. Navy Blue Angels teams. And unlike their U.S. counterparts, they also lacked access to the consistently good flying conditions needed for year-round practice. The article noted that if the Knights and Swifts *(Strizhy)* wanted to deploy southward from their base at Kubinka to find such better weather, the fuel required merely to get them there would exhaust the unit's allocation for a whole month. The article rightly foresaw that this would eventually lead to a safety issue.[84]

Retired Marshal of Aviation Shaposhnikov admitted that VVS and VPVO aircrews were being allowed to fly even though their commanders were fully aware that the aircrews lacked the requisite skills. Partly as a result, he said, Russia had become "almost the world's leader" in the annual number of aircraft accidents.[85] As for the fighter community, one report noted that fewer and fewer pilots were capable of operating "under any conditions, day or night, resulting in a consequent rise in the likelihood of accidents." Yet, continued that report, pilots simply shrugged it off with a cynical refrain: "If there are flights, there can be situations conducive to an accident. If there are no flights, then there will be no problems. We will reduce the accident rate to zero!"[86]

Flagging Morale

Finally, the continued underfunding of the VVS for all but the barest essentials was matched by extended delays in the disbursement of state outlays. As a result VVS headquarters ended up in arrears for officer salaries that had been paid as much as two years late or even not at all. This situation forced the VVS into a game of pick-up ball with respect to meeting the social needs of its personnel. In 1996 direct payments to personnel accounted for 40 percent of all military expenditures, with another 10–15 percent going for food, clothing, and housing. Thus the Ministry of Defense looked, to all intents and purposes, like a welfare agency. By 1997 more than 70 percent of the ministry's expenditures were spent on social welfare. Yet even so, disbursements were inadequate to support more than a bare subsistence level for most recipients.

As a result of their substandard living conditions, many experienced pilots simply left the VVS, which had no one at hand to replace them. On an optimistic note General Deinekin observed that in contrast to the early 1990s, when the number of applicants for pilot training had fallen from eight to two per available slot, in recent years the situation had begun to improve.[87] In mid-1997 Deinekin reported that the pool of airmen was "being replenished with the amount that drains away" and that VVS boarding school students were approaching their education "with fire in their eyes, with a straight back, [and] with a splendid attitude."[88] On the downside, however, the Defense Ministry's failure to pay officers' salaries for ten months straight in 1997 prompted two junior officers to declare a hunger strike for the first time in the history of the post-Soviet VVS, with the wives of unit officers blocking the runway at the base and demonstrating at a rally at the regiment commander's headquarters.[89] Bitter complaints also began to be heard about how Russia's well-heeled nouveaux riches in the cities were allegedly hiring "slaves in uniform" to perform their menial temporary jobs. Those complaints noted that such "latter-day exploiters," knowing full well that Russia's military professionals were reliable, ruthlessly took advantage of them for the most miniscule pay.[90] These were not good signs for the VVS's prospects for attracting a successor generation capable of surmounting the challenges that had come to confront its leadership.

The Merger of the Russian Air Force (VVS) and Air Defense Force (VPVO)

In May 1997 President Yeltsin relieved Defense Minister Rodionov for willful heel-dragging on the implementation of military reform. Rodionov had repeatedly fought with Yeltsin's security adviser, Yury Baturin, over the details of reform, insisting that he supported cuts and improved troop quality but could not abide being constantly told that reform could be "implemented without financing, without money."[91] In fact Rodionov was a throwback who, at one point, reportedly advocated increased defense spending to support Russian preparations for a possible conflict with NATO. That stance brought him into conflict not only with Baturin but also with Yeltsin.[92] In the end, Yeltsin replaced Rodionov with General Igor Sergeyev, commander in chief of the Strategic Rocket Forces (SRF), whom he ordered to step out briskly on military reform.[93]

Sergeyev promptly announced six reform priorities, which were endorsed by Yeltsin on June 9, 1997: (1) reductions of force structure and manpower to an "optimal" level; (2) improvement in the quality and education of military personnel; (3) improvement in training and discipline; (4) improvement in equipment quality; (5) development of less-expensive manning and infrastructure; and (6) ensuring of the social rights of active and retired military personnel.[94] Sergeyev further announced that the defense budget ceiling would be 3.5 percent of Russia's GDP, and he confirmed the goal of shifting from a conscription to an all-volunteer force. As he pithily summed up his intent: "The moment of truth has come. We now have to become . . . real pragmatists and make efficiency, cost, and feasibility our decisive criteria."[95]

Sergeyev's plan was to reduce overall military manning to below one million, as well as to attack the inefficient five-service structure with a view toward reducing the number of services to four and, later, three. Under the announced terms, the ground forces would disappear altogether as a separate service, with their units resubordinated directly to the General Staff. The fighter and the command and control assets of VPVO would go to the VVS, with VPVO's SAMs going to the military districts and with the missile attack warning system and the Moscow antiballistic missile (ABM) system going to a planned Strategic Deterrent Force. In moving to implement these plans, Sergeyev showed a clear determination to streamline the military rather than just make hollow promises. "To draw up a budget like Mozambique but demand armed forces like the United States," he said bluntly, "is not entirely logical."[96] One account noted that in his first thirty days in office, he had managed to achieve more toward that end than had all his predecessors combined over the five-year history of the Russian military.[97]

Even before the USSR's breakup, various reform-minded advisers in Moscow had argued that maintaining separate air and air defense forces was a costly indulgence entailing needless duplication of effort. With good reason, those defense critics argued that the two services should be combined, in the interest of savings and greater efficiency. The tendency throughout Pavel Grachev's tenure as defense minister was to defer any such move to the later years of reform rather than fight the bureaucratic battles that almost surely would attend an earlier implementation. Common sense, however, suggested that it was only a matter of time before such a measure would be forced on the Russian leadership in the course of any serious effort at downsizing Russia's military.

On July 16, 1997, Yeltsin signed an order backed by Sergeyev and the chief of the General Staff, Army General Anatoly Kvashnin, to merge the VVS and VPVO and to integrate the SRF, Space Forces, and ABMs into a new Strategic Deterrent Force. Yeltsin's order mandated that at least the formalities of the VVS-VPVO merger would be completed by January 1, 1999. In commenting on the announcement afterward, Baturin stated that the mergers were being implemented to make better use of resources and to eliminate duplication and waste. Baturin reassured those in VPVO that Russia's air defense forces were "here to stay," even though they would be subsumed into a new and broadened VVS. He also noted that the acronym VPVO-VVS had been considered for a time as a possible name for the expanded organization, along with VVO (*Voenno-vozdushnaya oborona,* or Military Air Defense Forces), which was ultimately rejected because it would have in effect eliminated the air force with the stroke of a pen.[98]

Once the word was officially out on the VVS-VPVO merger, Deinekin declared that he was "very satisfied" with the decision. He called the merger "long overdue," agreeing that all of a country's air assets should be "subordinated to a single will" in order to extract the greatest leverage from the air weapon. Even more, said Deinekin, a merger reflected the principle that the "master of the sky is that branch of the armed forces that has the deciding role in winning and maintaining air supremacy." He added, "And there is no question that the VVS has been, is, and will be such."[99] He noted also that the merger was a pragmatic acknowledgment of Russia's limited economic and human resources.

Deinekin stressed that the announced merger, developed under the overall direction of First Deputy Minister of Defense Kokoshin, would enhance the efficiency of Russia's air arm by providing for a single system of procurement, training, airfields, and maintenance.[100] He added that Russia needed to integrate all its military flying training under one roof and that he had never understood the sense of creating separate flying schools for the Border Guards and other "forces agencies." Deinekin said that the pilot candidates of those agencies could just as well learn to fly in the VVS schools, which had been in existence for many decades and which the VVS was being "forced to close." He added that the merger of the VVS and VPVO would allow for the integration and standardization of the hundreds of Su-27s in the two services, as well as for the incorporation of hundreds of VPVO MiG-31s into "a most powerful aviation group," which could be transferred from east to west or in any strategic direction "literally within hours."[101]

Deinekin argued that taken together, the assets of the new VVS would be able not only to "execute an intertheater maneuver according to the pendulum principle and close breaches in the air defense system of Russia and the CIS, but also inflict harm on an air opponent." He added that the "deciding role" in modern military operations belonged to a nation's air force rather than to its air defense forces. Deinekin remarked that as commander in chief, he could see "no disadvantages in amalgamating the forces of the VPVO and VVS; quite the contrary." He stated: "Our combat capability is multiplied, and we eliminate everything superfluous, the redundant structures, and countless military officials." He repeatedly stressed that maintaining a separate service for homeland air defense made no operational sense, noting that no other country in the world had such an unnatural arrangement. Even the prominent Soviet military theorist Aleksandr Lapchinsky had written in vain as early as 1939, Deinekin noted, that the consolidation of VVS and VPVO forces would be crucial for ensuring the fullest versatility for Soviet air power.[102]

As might have been expected, VPVO partisans waged a strenuous rear-guard action to head off the merger. No sooner had Deinekin begun defending the decision than he encountered "unexpectedly stubborn resistance to hasty reforms" from VPVO veterans, who took their case both to the public and to Yeltsin directly. In particular a bevy of former VPVO leaders—including General Ivan Tretyak, who had been forced out in disgrace six years earlier, after the failed 1991 coup, for supporting the anti-Gorbachev plotters—argued that the district-front command element into which Russia's air defenses would be subsumed under the new arrangement was "incapable of exercising command and control of air defense on an operational-strategic scale." (They could have said the same, however, for all of Russia's air power.) The former leaders pointed out that the existing VPVO system had been improved steadily over more than a decade, and they warned: "Resubordinating and fragmenting it will mean the destruction of what has been created and the end of its future development." What was needed instead, they maintained, was a "Strategic Aerospace Defense Command," which might "permit the safeguarding of the air defense forces against being broken up and washed away to various structures."[103] Less persuasively, these VPVO "gray eagles" also argued that VPVO was "more science-intensive and technologically complex than the air force."[104]

The commander in chief of VPVO, General Prudnikov, had consistently opposed the merger ever since it first arose as a reform issue during the Grachev era. However, he was removed from command of VPVO at the end of June 1997, just two weeks before the merger announcement, and was reassigned as chief of staff for military cooperation in the CIS. As was most likely intended, that action took him out of the fight before the announcement became a fait accompli. Like the good professional that he was, Prudnikov embraced the merger decision with resigned acceptance. "If all goes according to promise," he said dutifully, "there will be no problems with the merger." He added that the decision had been made by Russia's president and that the affected commanders were accordingly obliged to comply within the specified time frame. He stressed, however, that the full potential of both services must be preserved and that hundreds of thousands of personnel must not be cast loose without a safety net.[105] Prudnikov suggested that it would take nine months to set up the appropriate command arrangements and more than two years to iron out the wrinkles and retire old and unneeded equipment.[106] In a similar vein, the commander of VPVO fighter aviation, Colonel General Vladimir Andreyev, said he was confident that because of their importance to the nation's security, Russia's air defenses would not be forsaken. However, he acknowledged that they would lose their independent status and would be merged, hopefully "harmonically," with the VVS, "as is the case in other countries."[107]

For his part, the chief of the VPVO headquarters staff, Colonel General Viktor Sinitsyn, recalled an earlier VPVO reorganization in 1978–80, when the Soviet air defense system was split up between those sectors nearest the USSR's borders and more interior areas equipped with different command and control systems. That, he pointed out, had led to "elements of formalism" in VPVO procedures and training and to a resultant decline in overall mission readiness. It also, he added, was partly at fault for the downing of Korean Airlines Flight 007 in 1983 and for the later unopposed landing in Red Square by a Cessna 172 flown by a West German teenager, Matthias Rust. Together, he said, those embarrassing incidents "demonstrated the thoughtlessness and subjectivity of such reorganizations." Sinitsyn indicated that VPVO's leaders had sought to convince the Yeltsin government that in the absence of adequate funds, any major reorganization of the nation's air defense system should be postponed until at least the year 2000.[108]

In contrast to VPVO's efforts to maintain the status quo, those of a more integrationist bent stressed: "Any state's airspace is unified and should have one boss who organizes various kinds of military operations . . . and exercises command and control over them." One such observer, a retired VVS general, noted that air defense forces alone could not "engage troops, ships, air defense assets, installations in the deep rear, or other enemy installations on land and sea" and could not "provide air support to ground forces on either the defensive or the offensive." He stressed that the attack assets of KFA and LRA remained "the only means of inflicting decisive damage upon enemy reserves in the immediate operational depth," considering that the depth of ground force fires, including army aviation, did "not exceed 50–70 kilometers and a maximum of 100 kilometers from the line of contact." He added, "Beyond those lines is the undivided dominance of air power in the engagement of enemy targets." That by itself, the retired general said, offered compelling enough reason for making the unification of Russia's air force and air defense forces "one of the most important tasks of military reform." He added that the merger did not "degrade the role of air defense forces nor elevate the role of the air force," but rather aimed "to improve the effectiveness of performing a mission of vital importance to Russia and its people."[109]

On completion of the merger, the new VVS was expected to inherit some 300 Su-27s and 400 MiG-31s from the former VPVO's fighter aviation branch, as well as to take over from VPVO approximately 20 Ilyushin A-50 airborne early-warning aircraft.[110] By some accounts, the MiG-31 acquisition was thought to be an uncertain prospect, since senior VPVO leaders had threatened to ground the aircraft because limited flying hours made operating it too dangerous for aircrews who had lost their proficiency. However, on the books at least, Deinekin said the merger would give the expanded VVS more than 1,200 MiG-29, Su-27, and MiG-31 fighters. In conjunction with the VVS's other assets, those fourth-generation aircraft promised a capability to deploy to wherever was needed within a matter of hours, at least in theory. Such a capability, Deinekin said, was essential in light of the fact that the weakened Russia of 1997, with its vast expanses, could not be "equally strong everywhere."[111] In addition, there were intimations that Russia and Belarus might seek to mount a joint air defense system aimed at being up and running, at least in its essentials, by the year 2000. Lieutenant General Valery Kostenko, the commander of VPVO for Belarus, told a conference on the air defense problems facing the CIS that the hope was to establish a single command and control center, probably located in Minsk and perhaps modeled on the Canadian-U.S. North American Air Defense Command (NORAD) system, with details to be finalized before the end of 1998.[112]

Finally, the announced merger of the VVS and VPVO envisaged a downsizing of each service by at least 120,000 personnel from their combined level of around 400,000. General Deinekin said that the existing VVS might even be forced to release as many as 140,000 personnel over the next few years to reach that goal.[113] Such a cutback would entail considerable social dislocation, since more than one-third of all current VVS and VPVO personnel would be discharged. The intent, Deinekin said, was to conduct the drawdown without causing harm to anyone, although it was unclear what protections the Yeltsin government might be able to provide those unfortunates who found themselves suddenly on the outside looking in.[114] Other measures said to be planned in connection with the downsizing included amalgamating the research institutes, academies, and flight schools of the two services and considering, at least for the near term, the procurement of light aircraft in lieu of jet trainers to provide operating units with 150–200 new pilots a year. Additional planned moves, according to the chief of the VVS Financial and Economic Directorate, included getting rid of all depots configured for servicing only a single aircraft type, combining VVS and VPVO maintenance centers, and looking for more sources of extra-budgetary financing through the leasing of POL and hangar space, along with setting up airfields for joint use and getting foreign students to pay for their training in hard currency.[115]

The End of the Deinekin Era

The fear among VPVO supporters was that VPVO would end up the loser in the merger of the two services. It later appeared, however, that the air defenders came out on top in at least one important respect. On December 14, 1997, the Yeltsin government announced that General Deinekin would not be retained as commander in chief of the new VVS. A little more than a month later, on January 20, 1998, the government declared that Colonel General Anatoly Kornukov, of VPVO, would be the new VVS leader.

Earlier, Defense Minister Sergeyev, who evidently backed Deinekin as head of the new VVS, had formally requested that Deinekin be extended on active duty beyond the mandatory retirement age of sixty. On December 11, three days short of Deinekin's sixtieth birthday, Yeltsin turned down Sergeyev's request without reason, simply reiterating the mandatory retirement rule. Two days later, however, a Moscow news report spoke of Deinekin's "probable dismissal," noting that it had been discussed repeatedly within leadership circles over the preceding year, beginning with Rodionov's appointment as defense minister in 1996 and ending with a series of catastrophic air accidents in late 1997.[116]

There was a surface plausibility to the air accident connection. Less than a week earlier, on December 6, in the Siberian city of Irkutsk, a VTA An-124 jet transport had crashed into an apartment building immediately after takeoff, killing sixty-seven people, including all twenty-three aboard the An-124. That accident followed by only six days a midair collision involving another VTA aircraft, an An-12 transport, which had clipped a health services Mi-8 helicopter while on final approach to landing in marginal weather, killing eight people aboard the helicopter.[117] The An-124 had been airlifting two export-model Su-27UB fighters from the Irkutsk Aircraft Production Plant to Vietnam on a VTA business run. Accordingly, its crash prompted an independent investigation of commercial air operations by the VVS.[118]

Afterward Deinekin ordered all VVS aircraft other than those on alert grounded for a week while investigators sought to determine the causes of the accident.[119] Initial speculation was that three of the four engines had failed because of a mix of "summer" and "winter" fuels that had allowed the fuel lines to become clogged with ice particles. Although that clearly would have suggested an oversight failure had it been shown to be a contributing factor, Deinekin told reporters that the fuel had in fact been up to standards and that the reason for the failure of the three engines lay elsewhere.[120] Shortly thereafter Deinekin offered to resign in the face of Duma representatives' stinging criticism for the Irkutsk tragedy, as well as for other alleged failings said to have contributed to military aviation safety deficiencies. Rokhlin, the reactionary head of the Duma's Defense Committee, particularly savaged Deinekin, under whose leadership, he charged, "the VVS [had] been robbed, torn apart, and broken up, and [was] effectively coming to the end of its miserable existence."[121]

One comment suggested that Yeltsin's decision to retire Deinekin had no connection with the Siberian air crash, since both Rodionov and the former navy chief, Admiral Feliks Gromov, had also been retired on reaching age sixty.[122] That suggestion was too ingenuous by half, however, considering that Rodionov had plainly been relieved because of his opposition to military reform and that the law allowed the president to waive mandatory retirement. A contrary report stated it was "clear" that Yeltsin's decision had been influenced by the two air accidents in close succession. However, the report added: "Clouds had begun to gather around Pyotr Deinekin earlier, and the fact that the leading media gave him virtually no space [after the An-124 accident] was only one symptom of the general's impending dismissal." More tellingly, that report proposed: "The number of conflicts the VVS commander in chief was simultaneously involved in had passed the critical mark."[123]

It was not as though Deinekin was obviously on the outs with the Yeltsin administration. Earlier Sergeyev had singled out both Deinekin and Prudnikov, along with First Deputy Defense Minister Kokoshin and Chief of the General Staff Kvashnin, as being among his most trusted associates on military reform.[124] Yeltsin had even recently awarded Deinekin the honorific title of Hero of Russia. Until the Irkutsk tragedy, it seemed that Deinekin was maintaining the inside track to command the expanded VVS. He had briefed both Sergeyev and Kvashnin on his thoughts regarding the merger, and the press was reporting "no signs" that he was in any danger of being replaced.[125] Indeed, one account suggested that *only* Deinekin had any chance of heading up the new force. Reporters called him a survivor who had outlasted three successive ministers of defense—Shaposhnikov, Grachev, and Rodionov. One remarked that he could confidently inscribe on the door to his office at VVS headquarters the motto from the Paris coat of arms: *Fluctuat nec mergitur,* "rocking but not sinking."[126] Another observed that Deinekin commanded "absolute authority" not just among airmen but among military men in general. Especially after Prudnikov was moved over to his CIS assignment shortly before the merger announcement, it appeared that Deinekin was all but certain to take over the new VVS. What, then, accounted for his abrupt retirement?

As one Moscow commentator rightly noted, Deinekin found himself "fighting a battle on two fronts" with respect to military reform.[127] Not only was he a strong backer of the VVS-VPVO merger, but he no less strongly opposed other announced or suggested measures that, in his opinion, threatened to work against the best interests of Russian air power. Some had to do with massive proposed deactivations of VVS flying units and an impending mothballing of even current-generation fighters for which there was no prospect of sustainment funding for the foreseeable future. Others, no doubt, entailed proposed organizational changes that, in Deinekin's view, threatened to undermine even further the already weakened combat capability of Russia's air power. To note a particularly egregious example of the latter, the new KFA that had been set up just four years previously by Deinekin was ordered disbanded in early 1997 by a decree from the Ministry of Defense. That same decree also disestablished the VVS's new Reserve and Training Command, which had been activated at the same time. The aircraft assigned to KFA were resubordinated, for the time being, to VVS headquarters—to be later assigned, as in years past, to the military district commanders. The VVS's four pilot-training schools in the Reserve and Training Command were transferred to a new headquarters called the Volga Military District Air Force.[128]

By the spring of 1997 rumors abounded about impending reorganization plans for Russian air power. On the premise that "everything that flies should be within the structure of the air force," one such rumor speculated that the attack helicopters assigned to the ground forces would be resubordinated to the VVS, a prospect about which the VVS was said to be less than enthusiastic.[129] There also were reports that the Defense Ministry was dabbling with the idea of forming a "Strategic Air Command" that would merge LRA and VTA, on the dubious premise that both organizations operated aircraft with heavy takeoff weights and used airfields with long runways. Former commanders of both service branches were rightly skeptical of that idea because the missions of the two commands were so radically dissimilar.[130] It was suggested as well that LRA might then be folded into the Strategic Deterrent Force by 2002, a notion that overlooked what had become the predominantly conventional role of LRA's bombers since the USSR's collapse.

Whatever the validity of those rumors, clear differences began to emerge between Deinekin and the chief of the General Staff, General Kvashnin, over the organization and roles of the new VVS. Deinekin opposed reassigning military aviation to the jurisdiction of the "Strategic Operations Command" that was reportedly being created to supplant the military district commanders. For his part, by all signs, Kvashnin felt that this contemplated change in the ownership and control of Russian air power was more important even than the merger of the VVS and VPVO, since such a change would allow "almost all levers of operational command and control of the general purpose forces, irrespective of which branch of the air force they belonged to, to be concentrated in the General Staff."[131] In this new arrangement, the main purpose of the VVS would be reduced to organizing, training, and equipping Russia's air forces rather than employing them operationally.

Deinekin voiced concern over these and other proposed reorganization moves that threatened to undermine the VVS's unity of command. He said he was "particularly worried by the views held by some military leaders who [were] planning to cut the air force into separate fragments, like a pie, and then assign them to other military structures; for example, assigning fighter aviation to air defense forces, dispersing Frontal Aviation among the Military Districts, and organizing independent air armies out of LRA and VTA." Deinekin said that such "fatal mistakes" could be prevented only by "collegial discussions at each step of military reform." Even under existing arrangements, he complained, the VVS was incapable of maintaining an effective concentration of force on all fronts. The decentralization of Russian air power to the operational control of the military district commanders, he warned, would only make matters worse: "As some experts suggest, if aggression is initiated against Russia, we may repeat our country's tragic experience of the initial period of the Great Patriotic War."[132]

Likewise arguing in favor of unity of command for Russian air power, Deinekin's director of operations, General Ionov, noted: "A number of prominent air force specialists, citing foreign experience as grounds, consider this decentralization of the air force command to be a mistake." Ionov invoked the now-casebook example of the 1991 Persian Gulf War, in which centralized control of air power was critical to the success of the allied air campaign against Iraq. He added that the Soviet military's acceptance of decentralized control of air power on the eve of World War II had ignored the lessons of both history and common sense. As a result, he said, the VVS entered the war with 186 combat units under the control of various dispersed ground force commanders. That arrangement did not "meet the requirements of a dynamic battle environment" and led to a situation in which each ground commander thought his attached air assets were his alone to use as he saw fit, rather than viewing them as part of a larger theater-level force to support the front effort as a whole.[133]

That mistake, said Ionov, was further compounded in 1980, when KFA's air armies were transferred to the military district air forces over the opposition of VVS headquarters. Ionov noted that the result was the "totally unfounded return" of the VVS structure to the old approach, which had "completely failed to justify itself." Indeed, he recalled, the situation had reached such absurd heights at one point that the VVS leadership had to request approval from the military district commander to inspect the training of VVS units in the military district air forces! A related downside result was that the training of military district forces to swing from one strategic sector to another "declined dramatically." In sharp contrast, Ionov noted, the direct subordination of air operating units to theater-wide air commanders was long a well-founded rule of Western command and control practice.[134]

For his part, General Deinekin stressed that the main concern was "not to lose Russia's combat aviation as an independent branch of the armed forces." He added that it was bad enough that KFA and the Reserve and Training Command had been disbanded, and he declared categorically: "Aviation must not be dispersed among the districts. It must not be handed over to military leaders who are not professionally trained to make the fullest use of this VVS component."[135] From a perspective of classical air power theory, Deinekin was on target in that assertion. Nevertheless, his insistence on it played at least a contributing part, in all likelihood, in eroding his chance of becoming the first commander of the combined VVS and VPVO.

No replacement to head up the new VVS was immediately announced, although speculation named the following as among the candidates: General Andreyev, commander of VPVO fighter aviation; Colonel General Nikolai Antoshkin, commander of KFA until its disestablishment in early 1997; General Kornukov, commander of the Moscow Air Defense District; and General Sinitsyn, chief of the VPVO headquarters staff.[136] Three of those four rumored candidates were VPVO officers, and VPVO campaigned hard for its contenders. By one account, the VPVO generals "launched a surprise bureaucratic counteroffensive," even going so far as to insist to Sergeyev that VPVO headquarters should become the command center of the new VVS.[137] Deinekin, on the other hand, was reportedly so confident of his prospects of taking over the new VVS that he saw no need to groom a successor. Clearly, he wanted to command the new service. After all, he was one of the most vocal proponents of merging VPVO with the VVS once such open support became politic. In the end, however, he accepted his retirement stoically and in keeping with the professionalism that had marked his stewardship of the VVS ever since he first took command in August 1991. Earlier in 1997, when asked how he might handle disagreements with his superiors on the subject of reorganization, Deinekin displayed that professionalism in his reply: "If you find yourself in opposition and cannot carry out orders, fill out your request and leave the armed forces."[138]

Many factors may have been at work against Deinekin, including "an old friendship with Pavel Grachev, the potential surfacing of a dacha [country home] compromise, chronic nonpayment of wages to pilots, [and] an increase in crashes."[139] Darker allegations by Rokhlin and other right-wing detractors further accused Deinekin of shady financial dealings, though they gave no specifics, let alone substantiation. Whatever the case, once it had become clear that Deinekin would not be retained as VVS commander, Sergeyev proposed Kornukov as a compromise candidate.[140] Yet another coup for VPVO was the report that the new VVS headquarters would indeed be established in the spaces of the old

VPVO's headquarters in the Balashinsky region outside Moscow. That announcement came as a major blow to VVS officers, who for years had commuted in relative comfort to the VVS headquarters on Pirogovskaya Street in downtown Moscow. In the view of one assessment, that literal and symbolic change, along with Deinekin's involuntary retirement, confirmed that the VVS had lost "a decisive battle."[141]

11. Toward Uncharted Horizons

The retirement of Colonel General Pyotr Deinekin in December 1997 and the concurrent onset of the associated VVS reorganization moves marked, both for better and for worse, the end of one era in Russian air power and the beginning of another. A bomber pilot by upbringing and an officer with a predominantly nuclear orientation before his appointment as commander in chief in 1991, Deinekin had tried, with determination and against extremely difficult odds, to bring a new look to the post-Soviet VVS. He understood the lessons of the allied air campaign against Iraq in Operation Desert Storm and what they suggested regarding the promise of conventional air power if properly equipped, trained, and used.[1] He also knew implicitly the failings of the Soviet approach to air power application and recognized what needed to be done, at least by way of first steps, to correct them. Arguably, it was time for Deinekin to go, since he had been commander in chief of the VVS for more than six years, a long time by Western standards if not by those of the Soviet VVS in which he had been brought up. It is unlikely, however, that the stalled rebirth of post-Soviet Russian air power would have fared any better had Deinekin been replaced by a new leader any sooner.

The ultimate results of Deinekin's successor, Colonel General Anatoly Kornukov, in seeking to rescue Russia's air power from its deepening plight remain to be seen. At the time of his selection at age fifty-six, he was commander of the Moscow Air Defense District. Although he had served as a VPVO officer for most of his career, Kornukov assumed command with prior VVS experience as well, having received his basic flight training at the VVS's former UPT school at Chernigov. He also flew VVS MiG-23s with the Group of Soviet Forces in Germany (GSFG) during the darker cold war years.[2] On the plus side, Kornukov noted that Deinekin had congratulated him on his appointment and that he would seek out Deinekin's advice. He also took over the helm, as had Deinekin before him, as a guarded optimist concerning the VVS's situation and near-term prospects. As he told one reporter immediately following his appointment as commander in chief, he acknowledged that he faced a "headache" in reforming the VVS and merging it with VPVO, yet he was confident that Russian air power was not yet in a "catastrophic" state, "only somewhere on the way to that."[3]

Among other things, Kornukov entered office determined to clean house. "I am quite convinced," he declared sternly, "that both in the Air Force and in the High Command of the Air Defense Forces, there are some people whom I shall have to thank and say goodbye to. . . . I have been in the service a long time and I know a great deal about a lot of people, and I will have to part with those who have shown themselves to be other than hard workers."[4] He admitted that he faced challenging times and that getting on top of the funding crisis would be his "task of tasks." He also promised to crack down on corruption in the VVS. The issue of the use of military aircraft for commercial purposes, he said, was "a slippery question" that he had not yet considered seriously. He conceded that such activity was providing an important source of revenue for the VVS, but he recognized the need to control attempts by aircrews and others to personally profit from the activity.[5] Kornukov further confirmed that the VVS-VPVO merger would be complete by January 1999 and that 125,000 personnel in each service would lose their jobs along the way.[6]

Interestingly enough, Kornukov previously served as the commander of the VPVO air division that intercepted and shot down Korean Airlines Flight 007 over the Sea of Japan in September 1983, and it was he who gave the final authorizing order for that notorious act.[7] That he was given command of the VVS in the first place carrying such baggage—at least partly complicit in what President Boris Yeltsin had earlier called one of the greatest tragedies of the cold war—seemed cause enough for raised eyebrows. Yet on being selected to head the new VVS, Kornukov was almost truculently unrepentant about his involvement in the tragedy, stating: "I am absolutely certain now that this action was planned and with quite definite goals." Kornukov said that he would "always be sure that the order was given correctly" and added, "If something like that were to happen now, I would act in the same way." He hewed, without qualification, to the hard line articulated by Marshal Nikolai Ogarkov, the chief of the Soviet General Staff at the time, who insisted that the downed Boeing 747 jetliner had been on an espionage mission. Kornukov admitted that his authorization of the downing had left him with "unpleasant feelings," but he insisted that such was the price of vigilance. Indeed, he all but boasted that his decision was proof positive that he had the wherewithal to make tough calls, claiming that someone needed "to take responsibility." He noted that sometimes at the front, "they sacrificed battalions to save an army."[8]

Kornukov's stance was a far cry from the genuine concern shown almost a decade earlier, in July 1989, by Colonel General Yevgeny Shaposhnikov when, as the newly installed commander in chief of the Soviet VVS (and the last one, it turned out), he had spoken publicly following a tragic MiG-23 accident. Shortly after takeoff from a VVS base in Poland, the aircraft's pilot had been forced to eject because of an unclearable compressor stall at low altitude, and the aircraft had flown on by itself, eventually crashing into a house in Belgium and killing a teenage boy. Shaposhnikov was plainly discomfited by the poor performance of the air defense component of the Northern Group of Forces, whose controllers had monitored the flight of the pilotless MiG and had reported, without further checking, that the aircraft had flown harmlessly into the sea. Shaposhnikov was a model of contrition at a press conference convened at the Soviet Foreign Ministry the day after the incident, apologizing and offering to compensate the Belgian family for its losses.[9] Yet Kornukov, when offered a similar opportunity to show such remorse in front of interested onlookers both in Russia and abroad, chose instead to repeat the righteous claims of Marshal Ogarkov in defending the latter's version of the Korean airliner shootdown, a version that even most Russian military professionals now reject as contrived.

More important than Kornukov's views on the propriety of his actions connected with a reprehensible but now largely forgotten cold war episode, however, were his thoughts on the proper direction for Russia's air power as the VVS prepared to embark on the next stage of its post-Soviet quest for resurrection. During his first months in office, he had little to say in public on that score. Yet he had his work cut out for him. Beyond the continued challenge of grappling with a funding crisis that had left the VVS not only immobilized but unsure of its future livelihood, he faced the added challenge of a General Staff–directed reorganization that risked undoing much of what his predecessor had sought to accomplish by way of leveraging Russian air power to its fullest potential.

Indeed the contretemps between Generals Deinekin and Anatoly Kvashnin over the ownership and control of Russia's fighter assets resembled the controversy that took place in the spring of 1998 in Washington between the USAF and the other three services, particularly the U.S. Army and U.S. Marine Corps, over which force component commander should control fires in a future theater of operations. Much like General Deinekin, the USAF chief of staff proved less than successful in convincing his ground-force counterparts that airmen should work for airmen in any joint-force operation, with only the overall air component commander reporting to the theater commander, in the interest of achieving the greatest theater-wide efficiencies in the use of air power.[10] The similarity of the two debates, at least in broad outline, and the setbacks that air power sustained in both cases served to underscore that the relative weight to be assigned to air and land forces in joint warfare remained a hot-button issue in Russia no less than in the United States.[11]

Not long after assuming command, Kornukov moved to remold the leadership of the new VVS into a composition more to his liking, with reports that he planned to retire such prominent VVS and VPVO generals as Viktor Kot, Nikolai Antoshkin, Anatoly Malyukov, and Vladimir Andreyev. Kornukov was further said to be planning to reduce the number of generals at VVS headquarters by twenty-four, to forty.[12] Finally, there were hints that he intended as well to stock the VVS's uppermost echelons disproportionately with his own chosen VPVO loyalists. According to one high-ranking Russian aerospace official at the time, "The most qualified Air Force generals are being practically dismissed from their duties, and the Air Defense generals are taking the lead."[13]

As things turned out, however, this charge seemed to be misplaced in at least one respect, for Kornukov reportedly tapped Colonel General Vladimir Mikhailov, the commander of the VVS Fourth Air Army in the North Caucasus Military District, to be his first deputy commander in chief, occupying the slot that General Kot had long filled under Deinekin's leadership. (This reported appointment, however, suggested a patron-protégé relationship of another sort, since Mikhailov had previously served under General Anatoly Kvashnin during the latter's tenure as commander of the North Caucasus Military District. In his later capacity as chief of the General Staff, Kvashnin had figured prominently in the decision to retire Deinekin.)[14]

It soon became apparent that Kornukov intended to march to his own drummer as the new VVS commander. He flatly declared: "I disagree with many aspects [of Deinekin's planned approach]."[15] Among other things, he was said to have opted to allow former VPVO interceptor regiments to retain their existing status, with some of those units absorbing elements of former VVS fighter units. Such a move would almost surely never have been allowed had Deinekin remained in charge.

The new VVS-VPVO joint command was formally declared in place and operating as of March 1, 1998. Kornukov stressed that the merger had been a true amalgamation leading to the genuine establishment of a new service, with no talk that VPVO had "joined" the VVS or vice versa.[16] Along the way, some duplicative structures were eliminated immediately. For example, it was decided to close down 20 percent of the military educational institutions in the two former services and to return to a four-year pilot-training program in those UPT schools that survived. Also, VTA and LRA were disbanded (much as KFA had been during the last year of Deinekin's tenure), with their aircraft resubordinated under newly established air armies. The VTA air army consisted of 10 regiments of An-124, An-22, and Il-76 transports. In all, the goal of the plan was 12 air armies comprising 15 divisions and 81 regiments in the newly merged VVS and VPVO.

As for personnel reductions, Kornukov indicated his determination to retire immediately 45 generals in the former service, with 77 total to be retired by the end of 1998. During the first six months of 1998, some 90,000 personnel in both former services were summarily released into the civilian ranks. Kornukov further anticipated transferring all young Second- and Third-Class pilots in the former services into the inactive reserve and retaining only those who had attained First-Class status, so as to maintain as high an experience level as possible.[17] In early 1998, only 1,500 of some 4,800 recent graduates from VVS and VPVO commissioning schools had assignments, leading Kornukov to propose that the remainder should simply be given their diplomas and directed to resign, with the service's apologies.[18]

Before long, Kornukov announced that the combined VVS and VPVO organizations would be nearly halved in size, with planned cuts of 45 percent in personnel and 40 percent in the combined service's aircraft inventory.[19] By mid-1998, 496 former VVS and VPVO units had been declared disbanded.[20] The VVS air base at Mozdok in North Ossetia, from which many operations against Chechnya were conducted, was deactivated, and all flyable Tu-95s were relocated to the former LRA base at Engels.[21] The intent was to exploit as many retired current-generation aircraft as possible to serve as "donors" for spare parts, since the delivery of spares to line units had long since been reduced to a trickle at best. The announced goal was to get 75–80 percent of the aircraft remaining in the active inventory restored to flyable condition.[22] (As of March 1998 only half of the VVS's assigned aircraft were said to be serviceable.)[23] At the end of the drawdown, strike aviation (consisting of bomber and ground-attack aircraft) was expected to compose roughly one-third of the new VVS force structure, with the remainder being air-to-air fighters, home-defense interceptors, and transports.[24] These reductions promised to reduce the new VVS from more than 5,000 aircraft at the time of the USSR's collapse to only some 1,500 aircraft by the end of the century, resulting in a literally decimated Russian air force barely more than one-tenth the size of the former Soviet VVS at its cold war height.

Kornukov, as evidenced by his early remarks concerning the magnitude of the challenges involved in keeping Russia's air power alive in the face of the continuing financial crisis, is under no illusions about the grim prospects for VVS force modernization in the near term. He did note the decision, made by Yeltsin's Security Council, that preliminary design work for a successor to the Tu-95 long-range bomber would begin in 1999, with initial deliveries to the VVS envisaged sometime after 2010.[25] However, he was conspicuously absent from the official delegation that attended the unveiling of MiG-MAPO's Article 1.42 fighter at Zhukovsky in January 1999. With all of his energy focused simply on managing the dire consequences of the continuing VVS drawdown, he is most likely thinking of *anything* but acquiring new hardware. In 1998 the Defense Ministry was budgeted for only one-third of what it had received in 1997, and it reportedly actually received only half of what it was formally authorized. Because of the devaluation of the ruble in the wake of the August 1998 financial collapse, the $4 billion budgeted for defense in 1999 was likely to mean only half that amount in actual discretionary funds. As a result, Russia would spend on its military less than 1 percent of what the United States would spend in 1999.[26] That, perhaps more than any other factor, defined the stark reality that General Kornukov inherited when he took over the reins from Deinekin as VVS commander at the start of 1998.

For Russian airmen, one of the most welcome by-products of the USSR's demise was the concurrent disappearance of all the Soviet doctrinal and organizational impedimenta that, for decades, had kept VVS commanders from making the most of the resources at their disposal. For a time, before Russian-U.S. relations took a downturn from their early post–cold war euphoria and before the state funding crisis attained such cataclysmic proportions, it appeared as though the leaders of the VVS might take a page from their reading of Desert Storm and selectively emulate those proven elements of Western force development, operations, and training that made the most sense for Russia's security needs. Yet the subsequent move to resubordinate Russia's air assets to ground commanders at the military district level seemed almost a step backward, toward reembracing the old Soviet conception of air power as a supporting element in a combined-arms approach to war dominated by surface forces.

Those behind that move in Moscow may well have had in mind refashioning their military district commanders (or the "Strategic Operations Command" commanders said to be slated to supplant them) into something like Russian analogues of the U.S. joint-force theater commanders in chief around the world, with attached air assets of the sort exercised in the U.S. case by the Joint Force Air Component Commander (JFACC). If so, the change would entail something quite different from a reversion to the old Soviet approach. Until this becomes clearer, however, General Kornukov would appear to have been presented with a General Staff–mandated change in the command and control of Russian air power—a change that left the VVS as far away as ever from making the most of its assets. If that indeed was an issue behind General Deinekin's forced retirement, the first turnover of VVS leadership in the post-Soviet era may also have been the first that occurred, at least in part, over a point of doctrinal principle.

In summing up this account of decline and repeatedly thwarted efforts at renewal, we have every reason to wonder whether the sun is rising or setting on Russian air power. Although the best of the post-Soviet VVS leaders have freely acknowledged their past failings under Soviet rule and have articulated a vision of what needs to be done to correct those failings, the hard truth is that the main factors that will determine the course and outcome of the VVS's struggle for recovery to good health lie largely beyond its leadership's control. At bottom, the fate of Russia's air power, like that of the Russian armed forces as a whole, is inseparably tied up with the fate of Russia itself.

As far back as 1993 the chief of the VVS headquarters staff, Colonel General Malyukov, stated his belief that the worst of the crisis had passed and that the VVS had successfully weathered the initial maelstrom of post-Soviet change. Outmoded or counterproductive practices, he declared, were being done away with, and new relationships were forming within the VVS and between the VVS and other sectors of the defense community. That turbulent passage was no mean accomplishment, in General Malyukov's view, considering the union's collapse and the loss of many VVS equities to the breakaway republics. "It was very difficult," he said, "for us to keep the rest of the pieces of our air force operating. Now we know, more or less, on what we can depend; which factories, which supply bases, which units. Basically the work in these areas is already done, and our thoughts are turned to building a powerful air force." Most of the problems still confronting the VVS, added Malyukov, were "long term, relating to combat readiness and air-combat capability."[27]

Despite that optimistic view, the VVS's funding predicament has remained acute. Force modernization has all but ground to a halt. Even R&D for the improvement of existing systems seems to be dead in the water. The VVS is barely managing even to meet the payroll needs of its officers. Fuel supplies are adequate only to enable a small percentage of line pilots to remain on operational flight status. Even those, at 25–30 hours a year, are at best able to maintain proficiency at basic aircraft handling in clear weather. Operationally meaningful air-combat training has become a thing of the past. At the end of 1994 General Deinekin noted that VTA pilots were still getting a passable amount of annual flight time because of the diverse mobility demands placed on them, notably by the festering situation in Chechnya. "As for fighter pilots," he said, "they do not do much flying."[28] The situation has steadily worsened in the years since and has become an increasing threat to flight safety, with a rising VVS accident rate as proof.

On the brighter side, the Russian VVS's withdrawal from Eastern Europe and from the other former Soviet republics was completed by 1995. That phased withdrawal placed a heavy burden on the VVS's annual budget and came at the expense of needed operational support. Its conclusion opened up the possibility, at least in principle, for a gradual resumption of funding support for aircrew training and readiness. Even in the best case, however, as Colonel General Mikhail Soroka, a deputy commander on the headquarters staff, indicated in 1995, the VVS had no realistic chance of offsetting its recent losses in strength by "a growth in quality of armament and equipment within the next few years." More than half its inventory in 1997 consisted of second- and third-generation aircraft slated to be retired by the years 2000–2005. When that happens, only 20 percent of the current force will remain operational. The VVS's stated annual need is for 250–300 new aircraft to meet the demands of the Defense Ministry's declared power projection and mobility doctrine. The 1994 defense budget provided, however, for 32 for all services. For the first time in the history of Soviet and Russian military aviation, the 1995 budget provided for *no* new aircraft purchases. Seventy percent of the VVS's airfields were reported to be incapable of handling night or adverse weather flights. Of a total of 209 airfields, 133 were in need of major repair and modernization, for which there was—and remains—no money. With the termination of production of the workhorse Il-76 jet transport, VTA's numerical strength began a sharp decline in 1997 as the first of those aircraft were retired.[29]

According to Pavel Felgengauer, a Moscow defense correspondent, the war in Chechnya proved that Russia's weapons were "outdated and ill-suited even for a local war with a second-rate enemy" and that the Russian military needed "up-to-date communications facilities, combat helicopters, and airplanes capable of operating at night, in bad weather, and so forth."[30] That statement was true enough as far as it went, but it did not capture the main priorities, which had more to do with first making the VVS's *existing* hardware work.

It remains hard to tell, beyond the broadest of generalizations, what the future holds. Regarding force modernization, the VVS leaders have openly stated their near-term plans and goals through the year 2000. Those goals are not unreasonable for the sort of air force that would seem appropriate for post-Soviet Russia, given its limited operational challenges and requirements in the immediate years ahead. Yet the VVS may be unable to take more than the first steps in that direction at a time when, because of the continuing budget crisis, its procurement power has vanished and it is having trouble merely providing its pilots with enough flying time to keep them free from accidents.

As for doctrine and concepts, the VVS has long since discarded its canonical "Warsaw Pact Air Operation Plan," if indeed it ever paid more than lip service to that plan in its routine training, and now confronts a need to develop new strategies consistent with the emerging mission requirements of post-Soviet Russia. Russia, however, has yet to develop a coherent and fully articulated foreign policy—or even, for that matter, a considered set of national interests upon which such a policy might be based. Accordingly, its much-vaunted "new military doctrine," published in late 1993, remains little more than a statement of broad principles for an ideal world. In the absence of a clear threat or a readily definable operational challenge, any attempt to produce a more detailed repertoire for Russian air power would be putting the cart before the horse.

There is no clearer testament to the acuteness of the many problems the VVS faces today than its continued inability to do much beyond intellectualize over the implications of the 1991 Persian Gulf War. As the fall of Soviet communism neared, the VVS had a ringside seat from which to observe the allied coalition's successful air campaign against Iraq. That campaign opened the eyes of Soviet airmen not just to what Western aviation could accomplish but to what air power in general (including Russian air power) could do if properly equipped, configured, and applied. Unfortunately for the VVS, however, that realization dawned precisely as its own operational and institutional moorings had become loosened by the winds of international and domestic change.

Not long after the Gulf War ended, the head of the Soviet VVS Combat Training Directorate, Lieutenant General Anatoly Borsuk, suggested that the Desert Storm experience was forcing the VVS "to consider opportunities for elevating the role of air forces in contemporary warfare, operational employment, and training, and to make appropriate corrections in all those areas."[31] The deputy chief of the Operational Art Department at the General Staff Academy similarly pointed out, "The lessons of Desert Storm are of practical interest to us." He added, "It would simply be shortsighted to ignore them in creating the Russian armed forces." He stressed the pivotal role played by coalition air power in demonstrating, for the first time, that strategic as well as tactical goals can be attained directly through the use of precision firepower. He further noted how the VVS's recently concluded Voskhod '93 exercise had indicated Russia's potential for conducting standoff attacks at great distances from home base.[32] So far, however, even as the new millennium approaches, the VVS has been unable to go much beyond lip service in assimilating the most important teachings of the Desert Storm experience.

Nevertheless, the powerful role model provided for Russian air tacticians by the allied coalition's performance in Desert Storm, coupled with the subsequent lifting of many of the former inhibitions that blocked any serious effort at tactical reform in the VVS, leads to the reasonable speculation that at least some of the impending changes in Russian operational practice, once they take root, will show a heightened Western orientation. The air-to-air arena warrants special attention in this regard. Because improvement in air-combat prowess is essentially cost-free in that it turns largely on changed procedures rather than new equipment, the VVS is now positioned to begin applying its best tacticians' long-ignored recommendations for new directions in air-to-air training.

One constraint here, almost certainly a preclusive one for the near term, concerns the extent to which even seemingly "low-cost" changes in operational training may be preempted by a diversion of already scarce operations and maintenance funds toward providing housing and other needed quality-of-life improvements for officers and their families. Another constraint concerns where the VVS Combat Training Directorate will find suitable homegrown, experienced instructors to develop and pass along to Russian pilots a fundamentally new air-combat repertoire. As amply proven by the USAF's hard-earned experience over the two decades since its first days of realistic training following the Vietnam

War, developing and acquiring such a repertoire takes far more than merely reading the right books.

Exactly how the new VVS will respond to what remains of its opportunity for self-improvement remains hard to say. Much will depend, in the near term at least, on the extent to which the Russian defense sector's continuing near-insolvency will permit the channeling of enough funds into VVS operations and maintenance accounts to underwrite a training program commensurate with the VVS's much-broadened latitude for improvisation. Farther down the road, much will also hinge on the extent to which the dismantling of the old Soviet order has yielded a permanent change in the daily pattern of organizational life for Russian pilots and commanders.

Despite the many difficulties outlined above, the VVS's predicament is far from completely hopeless. For all its compound troubles, it has been granted an end to political controls, an increased freedom of expression, genuine encouragement from higher headquarters for the exercise of initiative and independent judgment from below, and an easing or elimination of the most odious former Soviet operating rules and restrictions. All of that has been geared toward enhancing opportunities for talented pilots and commanders to achieve their fullest potential. The system remains slow to change, and old habits linger on. But at least the door to reform is now open. Toward that end, General Deinekin as early as 1993 acknowledged the value of learning lessons from the West's experience: "There is something to adopt from abroad. We must train our pilots to world standards."[33] He further noted that his many trips to visit foreign air forces had offered him useful food for thought: "Much of what I got to see and learn, I feel, would be expedient and possible to adopt into the combat training and everyday activity of the Russian Air Forces even today."[34]

Lean years lie ahead for military aviation in Russia. Much will hinge on the still-uncertain prospects for economic stabilization and reform throughout the country as a whole. General Deinekin frequently noted that the VVS, to its credit, retained a positive and solutions-oriented attitude even during the darkest years of stagnation under the rule of Communist Party General Secretary Leonid Brezhnev. In acknowledging that, he highlighted what may well be the VVS's greatest strength. Its core dilemma is that just as the VVS has come within reach of an opportunity to institute sweeping changes in its repertoire, it has been denied the financial means to take anything more than the first halting steps. Yet whatever path is ultimately adopted for instituting selective belt-tightening and otherwise making the most of a grim situation, the Russian VVS is well into its post-Soviet restructuring and has made visible progress in adjusting to its new realities. More to the point, its leaders have candidly admitted their problems and have indicated what they believe needs to be done to start fixing those problems, removing at least one obstacle from any road to recovery that may yet lie ahead.

Notes

1. Introduction

1. Von Hardesty, *Red Phoenix: The Rise of Soviet Air Power, 1941–1945* (Washington, D.C., Smithsonian Institution Press, 1991), 8.
2. That event and its background are chronicled in Georgy Baidukov, *Russian Lindbergh: The Life of Valery Chkalov* (Washington, D.C., Smithsonian Institution Press, 1991).
3. For a particularly engrossing memoir, see Marshal of Aviation Ye. I. Savitsky, *Polveka s nebom* (A half-century with the sky) (Moscow: Voyenizdat, 1988).
4. After the war, the USAF test-flew a MiG-15 provided by a North Korean defector. Although the aircraft showed numerous undesirable handling characteristics compared with the F-86, it was found to be equally good, or better, in the critical parameters of maximum speed, service ceiling, and turn performance. The 10-1 kill ratio achieved by the F-86 over the MiG-15 in Korea reflected solely the superior training and proficiency of U.S. pilots compared with that of their North Korean and Chinese opponents.
5. Air Vice Marshal R. A. Mason, RAF, and John W. R. Taylor, *Aircraft, Strategy, and Operations of the Soviet Air Force* (London: Jane's Publishing Company, 1986), 9–10.
6. Interview with General Pavel Grachev by V. Starkov, "General Grachev on the Military and on the Soldier," *Argumenty i fakty,* no. 5 (February 1993): 1–2.
7. For more on this, see Benjamin S. Lambeth, "Russia's Wounded Military," *Foreign Affairs,* March/April 1995, 86–98. See also Pavel K. Baev, *The Russian Army in a Time of Troubles* (London: Sage Publications, 1996).
8. For a thorough treatment of this astonishing decline in so short a period of time, see William E. Odom, *The Collapse of the Soviet Military* (New Haven, Conn.: Yale University Press, 1998).
9. Interview with Colonel General Pyotr S. Deinekin by Yelena Agapova, "A Russia without Wings Is Not Russia: It Does and Will Have Them," *Krasnaya zvezda,* August 15, 1992.

2. The Soviet Legacy

1. Colonel (Res.) V. Dudin, "Through a Mass of Stereotypes," *Aviatsia i kosmonavtika,* no. 1 (January 1992): 4–6.
2. "Senior Air Force Appointments Confirmed," *Jane's Defense Weekly,* April 9, 1988, 705.
3. Zuyev said this notwithstanding the fact that as first deputy VVS commander, Shaposhnikov headed the inquiry into Zuyev's theft of the MiG-29. See Alexander Zuyev, with Malcolm McConnell, *Fulcrum* (New York: Warner Books, 1992), 354.
4. Later, Shaposhnikov claimed his readiness to attack the Kremlin if the putschists had sought to take the White House by force. See Michael Evans, "Marshal Was Ready to Bomb Kremlin," *London Times,* September 13, 1991.

5. Shaposhnikov presented a remarkably honest reflection on his experiences during the coup and the subsequent collapse of Soviet communism in his book *Vybor: Zapiski glavnokomanduyushchevo* (A choice: Notes of a commander in chief) (Moscow: Nezavisimoye Izdatelstvo PIK, 1993).

6. See Eurasia report (Foreign Broadcast Information Service, Washington, D.C., September 3, 1991), 54.

7. Interview with General Deinekin by N. Belan, "Gaining Altitude," *Sovetskaya Rossia,* September 6, 1991.

8. "Revive the Prestige of the Army: Minister of Defense Marshal of Aviation Ye. I. Shaposhnikov Replies to Questions from a *Krasnaya zvezda* Correspondent," *Krasnaya zvezda,* August 31, 1991.

9. "USSR Defense Minister's Appeal," *Krasnaya zvezda,* September 3, 1991.

10. Belan, "Gaining Altitude."

11. Interview with Ye. Shaposhnikov by V. Izgarshev and A. Chernak, "I Follow My Conscience and the Law," *Pravda,* September 25, 1991.

12. "Revive the Prestige of the Army."

13. For background, see Stephen Foye, "Evgenii Shaposhnikov: A New Defense Minister for a New Era," *Report on the USSR,* Radio Liberty Research, September 31, 1991, 8–11.

14. Belan, "Gaining Altitude." General Deinekin recalled how in earlier days the VVS, wanting to advance a promising young officer, would often hit a brick wall in the party's Central Committee, where "some young man in a gray suit and blue shirt would pick up a special telephone and say that this candidacy did not suit them."

15. Quoted in Alexander Velovich, "Soviet Forces Face Restructure," *Flight International,* September 25–October 1, 1991. Later Deinekin added with pride, "The spirit of democracy is inherent in aviators." Interview by Yelena Agapova, "The Skies Are the Same—the Concerns Different," *Krasnaya zvezda,* October 26, 1991. He also affirmed, during a press interview in Germany, that the leadership in Moscow had broken with communism once and for all. Rudiger Moniac, "All Commitments Regarding Germany Will Be Precisely Honored," *Die Welt,* December 12, 1991.

16. Marshal Yevgeny Shaposhnikov, "National and Collective Security in the CIS," *Krasnaya zvezda,* September 30, 1992.

17. General Prudnikov, former commander of the Moscow Air Defense District and a respected fighter pilot, was chosen to replace Army General Ivan Tretyak as commander in chief of VPVO after the latter was fired for having backed the coup attempt.

18. Interview with Colonel General V. Prudnikov, "A View of the Problem: What Should Aerospace Defense Be Like?" *Krasnaya zvezda,* November 30, 1991. In 1987 some prominent Soviet civilian analysts, notably Aleksei Arbatov, had proposed merging VPVO aviation with the VVS. See Arbatov's "How Much Defense Is Enough?" *Mezhdunarodnaya zhizn,* no. 3 (1989): 41–43, and his later "Toward the Question of Sufficiency in Air Defense," *Voennaya mysl,* no. 12 (1989): 41–45. That suggestion was roundly rejected by the High Command.

19. "Lobov Assesses Military Reforms, Ramifications," *Krasnaya zvezda,* September 10, 1991.

20. For background discussion, see John W. R. Lepingwell, "Gorbachev's Strategic Forces Initiative: Dissolving the Air Defense Forces," *Report on the USSR,* Radio Liberty Research, December 6, 1991, 4–9.

21. Interview with Colonel General V. Sinitsyn, "How Many Duplicates for the Keys to Heaven Are There?" *Krasnaya zvezda,* December 24, 1991.

22. Interview with Colonel General Viktor Prudnikov, "Rely On Our Own Forces," *Armia,* no. 24 (December 1991): 7–11.

23. Interview with Colonel Viktor Demediuk, "It May Not Be Just Rust Who Will Fly In," *Pravda,* January 11, 1992.

24. Comment by Shaposhnikov in an interview with Colonel V. Litovkin, "A New Chance," *Priorities and Prospects,* no. 3 (September 1992): 15–19.

25. Aleksandr Stukachin, "The CIS Air Defense System Is Disintegrating: Shaposhnikov Is Trying to Save the Air Shield," *Kommersant,* October 16, 1992.

26. Moscow television First Program, July 20, 1992.

27. Interview with Colonel General A. Kornukov, "The Eyes and Ears of the 'Zone of Continuous Operations,'" *Moskovskaya pravda,* July 11, 1992. General Kornukov took special pains, however, to stress that he saw no designated threat. As for who the likely enemy might be, he stressed that labels like "aggressive U.S. imperialists," "German revanchists," and the "cynical British" all came "from the realm of political hypocrisy." He noted, "This is unprofessional. . . . 'Violator' is an expansive enough term to define my attitude toward a stranger."

28. Interview with Colonel General V. Prudnikov, "Will the Likes of Rust Get through Again?" *Rossiiskiye vesti,* December 12, 1992.

29. Interview with Prudnikov, "A View of the Problem."

30. V. Litovkin, "The Army Is Ready to Obey the Presidents: The Presidents Are Trying to Agree among Themselves," *Izvestia,* December 31, 1991.

31. See "The New Russian Air Force: Interview with the Commander in Chief of the Russian Air Force," *NATO's Sixteen Nations,* no. 3 (March 1993): 39.

32. Kornukov reported that half his interceptor regiments and all his SAM regiments were tested on the range in 1993, with an overall "firing efficiency" of 95–96 percent. That claim strained credulity, considering the multiple constraints that by then had come to afflict VPVO and VVS units of all types. Nikolai Poroskov, "The Air Defenses of Russia's Central Region Have Been Checked: The Results Are Reassuring," *Krasnaya zvezda,* November 30, 1993.

33. TASS report on a comment by General Deinekin, March 27, 1992.

34. Quoted in an interview with Colonel General Anatoly Malyukov by Piotr Butowski, "Flying in the Face of Adversity," *Jane's Defense Weekly,* April 17, 1993, 19.

35. Quoted in N. Belan, "When We See Clearly It Will Horrify Us: Notes from Marshal of Aviation Ye. Shaposhnikov's News Conference," *Sovetskaya Rossia,* January 7, 1992.

36. Moscow television First Program, January 15, 1992.

37. Ibid., January 17, 1992.

38. Interview with Lieutenant General Stanislav Ivanov, "The Rear Is Becoming the Front As Well," *Aviatsia i kosmonavtika,* no. 9 (September 1991): 2–3.

39. Pavel Felgengauer, "The Army Is Under Fire from the Politicians," *Nezavisimaya gazeta,* January 11, 1992.

40. See the interview with Ye. Shaposhnikov in *TASS-Skript,* no. 62 (March 23, 1992).

41. Moscow television newscast, January 17, 1992. On the eve of the failed attempt in Minsk to reach agreement on a unified CIS defense arrangement, he remarked: "Ultimately I dream of a military that does not have to think about where its next meal is coming from." Moscow television newscast, February 13, 1992.

42. Interview with Ye. Shaposhnikov, "The Russian Army's History Did Not Start Today," *Izvestia,* May 8, 1992. In one sense, doing away with the political officers amounted to throwing out the baby with the bathwater. Many were pilots, occasionally even respected ones. They fulfilled important roles that went beyond political indoctrination, such as counseling junior officers and performing other duties that might be provided by a chaplain or social worker in Western military establishments. Accordingly, the plan was not to force those officers out entirely but rather to redefine their functions and put them under the purview of a depoliticized education and training administration.

43. Holos Ukrainy report, March 27, 1993. The comment came in response to an interview with General Deinekin, "The Russian Air Force Will Have Only the Most Up-to-Date Aircraft," *Izvestia,* March 24, 1993.

44. A. Krainy, "A Chronicle of Mutinous Bombers: What Politicians Had Long Been Seeking Has Happened—the Military Has Split," *Komsomolskaya pravda,* March 27, 1992.

45. Aleksandr Anin and Vladimir Svartsevich, "Conversion Commerce and Combat Training: The Division Commander Did Not Wish to Speak to Your Air Force Commander," *Nezavisimaya gazeta,* March 27, 1992.

46. Lieutenant Colonel A. Aleksandrov, "Russia Will Not Abandon Its Sons in Their Hour of Need," *Krasnaya zvezda,* July 2, 1992.

47. Major S. Prokopenko, "Whose Side Are You On, Guys, Who Will Lead You into Battle?" *Krasnaya zvezda,* May 20, 1992.

48. Douglas Jehl, "Ukraine: A Nuclear Power, But Untested Loyalties," *New York Times,* December 2, 1993.

49. Formerly commander of the Soviet VVS's Vinnitsa Air Army, General Vasilyev voiced his intent to model Ukraine's air force along the lines of the Vinnitsa Air Army, with headquarters in Vinnitsa. In effect, that amounted to little more than a name change from the Vinnitsa Air Army to the Ukrainian VVS. See Nikolai Baras, "Air Forces Organized in Vinnitsa," *Pravda Ukrainy,* May 6, 1992.

50. Interview with Lieutenant General Valery Vasilyev, "Aviators Have Chosen to Serve the People of Ukraine," *Narodna armia* (Kiev), June 2, 1992.

51. Captain Vasily Verbitsky, "'Idle' Aircraft," *Narodna armia* (Kiev), June 24, 1992.

52. Lieutenant Colonel Nikolai Gorenko, "Responsible for the Sky: Today the Ukrainian VVS and VPVO Are Equally Responsible; However, Service Commanders Have Different Views on the Organization of Air Defense," *Narodna armia* (Kiev), July 31, 1992.

53. Vladimir Kaushansky, "Soon There Will Be No Military Districts in Ukraine; Instead There Will Be Air Defense Forces," *Krasnaya zvezda,* September 5, 1992.

54. That mirrored similar mergers of air and air defense forces in several other former Warsaw Pact countries, notably Poland, Hungary, and the Czech Republic. For a good account of the formation of the Ukrainian VVS and the development of its doctrine, roles, and missions, see Ustina Markus, "Ukraine Restructures Its Air Forces: New Role, New Problems," *RFE/RL Research Report,* October 22, 1993, 48–53.

55. Interview with Lieutenant General Sergei Sedov by Colonel Valery Kovalev, "What Kind of an Air Force Will Belarus Have?" *Krasnaya zvezda,* November 17, 1992. The idea that 70–80 hours, low by Western standards, was an acceptable norm for maintaining operational proficiency was not wildly out of keeping with known Soviet practice. One Russian pilot told me that even in the best of times, a Soviet fighter pilot would not fly much more than 100–110 hours a year. Soviet pilots flew greater numbers of shorter-duration sorties, and they logged actual flight time only from takeoff to touchdown, with no increment for taxi time. Nevertheless, 100–110 hours a year was low compared with accepted Western practice.

56. See Sonni Efron, "Pro-Communist Elected Head of State in Belarus," *Los Angeles Times,* January 29, 1994.

57. See Michael Specter, "Belarus and Russia Form Union, Reuniting Two Former Soviet Lands," *New York Times,* March 24, 1996.

58. Radio Moscow domestic service, November 30, 1991.

59. Lieutenant Colonel V. Rudenko, "Russia Scrambles the Tu-160," *Krasnaya zvezda,* August 4, 1992.

60. Interview with Lieutenant General V. Vorobyev, Radio Moscow domestic service, February 14, 1992. Vorobyev frankly added that the sale of military hardware in the commercial market was "an uncharacteristic function" for the military, even though the need for self-financing had made the practice increasingly unavoidable.

61. John Lloyd, "Sharp Cut in Soviet Defense Orders," *London Financial Times,* October 28, 1991.

62. Interview with Colonel General Anatoly Malyukov by Dmitry Grinyuk and Piotr Butowski, "An Unusual Conversation at the Main Staff," *Krylya rodiny,* no. 11 (November 1991).

63. Nikolai Poroskov, "The Time for Stating Problems Is Past; Initiatives and Quests for Reserves Are What Is Needed," *Krasnaya zvezda,* December 9, 1993.

64. Interview with Colonel General Vasily Vorobyev, "Simple Solutions Don't Exist in the Financial Sphere," *Krasnaya zvezda,* December 17, 1993.

65. "The Air Force and Commerce," *Rossiiskaya gazeta,* March 26, 1992.

66. Moscow television report, May 2, 1992.

67. Account of a speech by General Grachev at the Seventh Congress of Russian People's Deputies, *Krasnaya zvezda,* December 8, 1992.

68. Moscow television service, December 12, 1992.

69. Interview with Colonel General Pyotr S. Deinekin, "A Country without Wings? No," *Trud,* March 10, 1992.

70. Lieutenant Colonel A. Vetakh, "Waiting for an Aircraft: Combat Pilots Await Their Turn," *Krasnaya zvezda,* May 15, 1992.

71. Interview with Lieutenant General Aleksandr N. Osipenko, "We Will Have Enough People Who Desire and Are Trained to Fly," *Krasnaya zvezda,* December 18, 1992.

72. More than one hundred new cadets were enrolled at the flight school at Tambov in 1992. Among its graduates the same year, forty were immediately released into the reserve.
73. Quoted in Vetakh, "Waiting for an Aircraft."
74. *Aviation Week and Space Technology,* January 11, 1993.
75. Interview with Major General Vasily Kuznetsov, "Inflation Devours the Military Budget Before It Can Be Approved," *Krasnaya zvezda,* October 15, 1992.
76. Colonel Yu. Timchenko, Colonel S. Shumilo, and Lieutenant Colonel S. Bolotin, "Is the General Always Right?" *Aviatsia i kosmonavtika,* no. 2 (February 1992): 10–11.
77. Guards Major A. Gornov, "Prohibition Mania," *Aviatsia i kosmonavtika,* no. 5 (May 1991): 30.
78. General Deinekin once stated that in the best of times, when he was a line pilot in LRA, he used to fly 500 hours a year. That would be a dream for any LRA pilot today.
79. Report by ITAR-TASS correspondent Vadim Byrkin, February 16, 1993.
80. Interview with Lieutenant General A. Tarasenko, "In a Holding Pattern: Comments on Problems of the 16th Air Army," *Krasnaya zvezda,* March 27, 1992.
81. Ibid.
82. Jeffrey M. Lenorovitz, "Reduced Russian Operations in Germany Eroding Pilot Proficiency, Readiness," *Aviation Week and Space Technology,* June 1, 1992.
83. Interview with General Kalugin, "In the First Strategic," *Aviatsia i kosmonavtika,* no. 10 (October 1991): 2–3.
84. Interview with Colonel General Anatoly Borsuk, "A Regiment Commanded from Three Countries At Once—On Top of This, the Commander Is Threatened with Court Action," *Krasnaya zvezda,* April 18, 1992.
85. Quoted in Aleksandr Manushkin, "Things Are Never Boring for the Duty General," *Krasnaya zvezda,* October 23, 1993.
86. Weather may have been an extenuating factor here, considering that the sortie number provided by General Slukhai was recorded in October, whereas that given by General Deinekin was recorded in August, when flying conditions in Russia are best. Nevertheless, the difference spoke for itself. Deinekin further noted that on that same flying day in August 1992, 980 sorties were reported by VPVO, 409 by the Strategic Rocket Forces, and 432 by the navy. Interview with Colonel General Deinekin by Yelena Agapova, "A Russia without Wings Is Not Russia: It Does and Will Have Them," *Krasnaya zvezda,* August 15, 1992.
87. For a background treatment of VVS maintenance practices during an earlier period of the cold war, see Andris Trapans, *Organizational Maintenance in the Soviet Air Force,* RM-4382-PR (Santa Monica, Calif.: RAND, 1965).
88. Colonel General Yevgeny I. Shaposhnikov, "Results and Prospects," *Aviatsia i kosmonavtika,* no. 1 (January 1991): 2.
89. Interview with General Vitaly M. Shabanov, "Military Parity Is Not a Game of Give-Away," *Kommunist vooruzhenykh sil,* no. 13 (June 1991): 12.
90. Guards Major V. Fomin, "Seconds Equal to Years," *Aviatsia i kosmonavtika,* no. 3 (March 1991): 6–7.
91. Interview in *Izvestia,* June 2, 1992.
92. Interview with Colonel General Prudnikov by Colonel A. Belousov and Major A. Ivanov, "A Unified System Is Needed," *Krasnaya zvezda,* April 11, 1992.
93. Operational units in all services in 1992 were reportedly manned on average at only around 60 percent of their assigned strength. Statement by the chief of the General Staff, Colonel General Mikhail Kolesnikov, cited in Viktor Litovkin, "The Army Pins Hopes on the Help of Legislators . . . and Women," *Izvestia,* October 17, 1992. During the first half of 1992, nearly 70 percent of Russian youths who were eligible for service dodged the draft. Sergei Ostanin, ITAR-TASS, October 15, 1992.
94. Major N. Barabanov, "Flying Safety Suffers," *Krasnaya zvezda,* June 20, 1991.
95. Lieutenant General G. Shinkarenko, "I Don't Want to Be an Instructor," *Krasnaya zvezda,* March 12, 1988.
96. Zuyev, *Fulcrum,* 136.
97. Not surprisingly, pilots routinely complain about maintenance. One commented sarcastically, "We have two probable enemies, NATO and ORATO." (The latter is the Russian acronym for

the VVS auxiliary airfield technical support unit.) Major N. Chebotarev, "For the Planes to Fly," *Aviatsia i kosmonavtika*, no. 1 (January 1993): 14.

98. Ibid.

99. Lieutenant Colonel A. Vetakh, "'Donor' Aircraft," *Krasnaya zvezda*, April 15, 1992. Colonel General Kalugin singled out the Tu-160 as a maintenance nightmare because of its unusual complexity. The aircraft requires a dedicated air base equipped with special ground-support equipment, high-pressure hydraulics, and an extensive supply train. Kalugin complained that its design was still being debugged and that a more user-friendly and less expensive bomber was needed.

100. Captain Vladimir Pasternak, quoted by Colonel Viktor Baranets, "Word to Rally," *Pravda*, January 17, 1992.

101. Shaposhnikov, "Results and Prospects," 2.

102. Interview with Major General Aleksei I. Alekseyev, "The Formula for Reliability: Man—Aircraft—Environment," *Krasnaya zvezda*, January 13, 1993.

103. Comment on a letter to the editor from a Zhukovsky Air Force Engineering Academy student by Colonel A. Andryushkov, "We Are Flying Less and Less, We Are Crashing More Often: Will Russia Become Wingless?" *Krasnaya zvezda*, June 19, 1992.

104. Interview with Colonel General Deinekin by Yelena Agapova, "The Skies Are the Same—the Concerns Different," *Krasnaya zvezda*, October 26, 1991.

105. Interview with Colonel General Pyotr S. Deinekin by I. Chernyak, "The Man Sitting in Moscow Is Going into a Spin Again," *Komsomolskaya pravda*, March 17, 1993.

106. Marshal of Aviation P. Kirsanov, "There Are No Minor Details on This Question," *Krasnaya zvezda*, April 22, 1988. Confirming that the VVS has had its share of avoidable accidents, Marshal Kirsanov gave as examples a pilot who flew too slow and spun his aircraft during an intercept; pilots who flew through their own bomb fragmentation patterns during live weapons drops on tactical ranges; maintenance personnel who forgot to properly fuel an aircraft before takeoff; and controllers who cleared aircraft for takeoff with another aircraft obstructing the runway.

107. These included twenty-four-hour watch duties, such as supervising conscripts, inspecting barracks and mess halls, and generally enforcing discipline. John Barron, *MiG Pilot: The Final Escape of Lieutenant Belenko* (New York: McGraw-Hill Book Company, 1980), 96.

108. Kirsanov, "There Are No Minor Details on This Question." Similar criticism was offered by a retired major general: "In investigating an accident, efforts must be aimed not at looking for a culprit or at what was done wrong by those who got into trouble, but at what is wrong with the management system, with organization, with the technological process, and with production activity." That officer charged, "The command-pressure method of leadership continues to shake loose the foundations of air unit flight safety and combat training." He attributed that to "inertia in thinking, adherence to stereotypes, and, most important, the fear of 'what if something happens?'" Major General of Aviation (Ret.) A. Bystrov, "The Concept of Preventing Mishaps: Theory and Practice," *Aviatsia i kosmonavtika*, no. 8 (August 1990): 16–18.

109. Interview with Lieutenant General Vladimir I. Andreyev by Colonel A. Andryushkov, "We Need to Know the Threat by Sight," *Krasnaya zvezda*, November 22, 1991. By "threat," General Andreyev had in mind not the United States or NATO but situations that lead to flying accidents: "The word 'safety' [in Russian, *bezopasnost*, or 'absence of danger'], both in its derivation and in life, has as its root 'danger.' In order not to end up at risk, you need to know risk well, by sight, as they say, and to know how to act not to end up in danger and to know how to deal with it. . . . Efforts to introduce this approach into the training of pilots have not gone very smoothly. Rumors have circulated that VPVO pilots are being made to 'study some sort of dangers.' Our critics have not understood that in imparting knowledge of danger, we are saying what matters most, namely, that a pilot can recognize and emerge successfully from an encounter with a nonstandard situation."

110. Colonel V. Dudin, "A Pilot Can Encounter an Emergency: Is He Ready to Master It?" *Krasnaya zvezda*, September 7, 1991.

111. Colonel N. Ryabnikov, Lieutenant Colonel M. Subbotin, and Lieutenant Colonel S. Bolotin, "So Just What Did Happen?" *Aviatsia i kosmonavtika*, no. 7 (July 1992): 13.

112. Colonel Yu. Timchenko, "Thirty Seconds during a Takeoff," *Aviatsia i kosmonavtika*, no. 5

(May 1993): 10. A good review of early post-Soviet debate over accident investigation and flight safety management in the VVS is provided in Dennis Marshall-Hasdell, *The Reform of Flight Safety in the Soviet Air Force* (Camberley, England: Soviet Studies Research Center, Royal Military Academy Sandhurst, 1993).

113. Lieutenant Colonel V. Skurikhin, "Cleared for Departure," *Aviatsia i kosmonavtika*, nos. 3–4 (March-April 1992): 5–6.

114. Characteristically, graft was a common lubricant of the Soviet system. The head of the Interdepartmental Commission of the unified ATC (air traffic control) system, Major General Boris Kushneruk, complained how one VTA crew on a scheduled military mission was delivering refugees from hot spots and, on arrival, was shaken down for "a tidy sum for landing support." Kushneruk asked: "Where is the crew supposed to get the money?" Interview by Vitaly Moroz, "Can the Skies Be Privatized? Military Aviators Are Convinced They Cannot," *Krasnaya zvezda*, December 22, 1992.

115. Interview with Lieutenant General Grigory K. Dubrov, "Who Will Be a Pilot in the CIS's Sky?" *Krasnaya zvezda*, March 24, 1992.

116. Colonel A. Tsalko, "We Do Not Value Thrift," *Krasnaya zvezda*, January 24, 1989.

117. Interview with Colonel General Ye. Shaposhnikov, "So When Will Pilots Get Apartments?" *Krasnaya zvezda*, March 3, 1991.

118. Interview with Lieutenant General Gennady Benov on the program "I Serve the Soviet Union," Moscow television, August 18, 1991.

119. Colonel V. Sobolev, "Stop Teaching in a Retrograde Way," *Aviatsia i kosmonavtika*, no. 3 (March 1991): 4–6.

120. Lieutenant Colonel Nikolai Pechen, "With What Do We Fill the Void?" *Vestnik protivovozdushnoi oborony*, no. 9 (September 1993): 30.

121. Interview with Lieutenant General Ivanov, "The Rear Is Becoming the Front As Well," 2–3.

122. Daniel Schneider, "Russian Fighter Pilots Wax Nostalgic for Days of Top Gun Status," *Christian Science Monitor*, August 5, 1992.

123. Interview in *Krylya rodiny*, no. 3 (March 1993).

124. Interview with General Kalugin, "In the First Strategic," 2–3.

125. Lieutenant Colonel V. Vysotsky, "A Stumbling Block; or, Problems of Combat Training," *Aviatsia i kosmonavtika*, no. 11 (November 1991): 4–7. On this point, two VVS flight surgeons reported in 1992 that 80–90 percent of VVS pilots, including fighter pilots, were sedentary, more than half smoked, and roughly 45 percent were overweight. Colonels of Medical Service A. Ivanchikov and V. Chuntul, "Risk Factors and Flight Longevity," *Aviatsia i kosmonavtika*, no. 1 (January 1992): 10.

126. Interview with Colonel V. Shevtsov, "Pilots Who Never Developed: Can We Halt the Outflow of Cadets from Military Schools?" *Krasnaya zvezda*, March 12, 1991.

127. Ibid. At the end of 1991, the VPVO situation was a little better. According to its chief of fighter aviation, Lieutenant General Vladimir Andreyev, there was a maximum of 1.5 applicants competing for each position. But that was not much of an improvement over the VVS's situation. General Andreyev said that in 1966, when he entered the VPVO flight school at Armavir, he had already flown 40 hours on light aircraft in the Lugansk paramilitary aero club operated by DOSAAF (*Dobrovolnoye obshchestvo sodeistvia armii, aviatsii, i flot*, or AllUnion Voluntary Society for Cooperation with the Army, Air Force, and Navy) and that Armavir had accepted only applicants with prior paramilitary flight training. He also noted that the competition then was seven applicants per slot. Andryushkov, "We Need to Know the Threat By Sight."

128. Conversation with a former Soviet fighter pilot.

129. "Military Pilots Are Reluctant to Serve," *Izvestia*, July 4, 1992.

130. Major General Ya. Yanakov, "From Retrograde to Modern," *Aviatsia i kosmonavtika*, no. 1 (January 1992): 2–3.

3. Evolving Organization, Doctrine, and Forces

1. "Russian Air Strategy and Combat Aircraft Production: A Russian Air Force View," in Randall Forsberg, ed., *The Arms Production Dilemma: Contraction and Restraint in the World Combat Aircraft Industry* (Cambridge: MIT Press, 1994), 17–60.

2. ITAR-TASS, October 12, 1992.

3. Interview by Marina Churnukha, Interfax, November 20, 1992.

4. General Vladimir N. Lobov, "The Sacred Right of Russia," *Sovetsky patriot,* no. 8 (February 1992): 4.

5. Pavel Felgengauer, "The Army Is Under Fire from the Politicians," *Nezavisimaya gazeta,* January 11, 1992.

6. A more comprehensive review of this background is presented in Roy Allison, *Military Forces in the Soviet Successor States,* Adelphi Paper no. 280 (London: International Institute for Strategic Studies, 1993), especially 3–35. On broader strategy and foreign policy developments, see also Renee de Nevers, *Russia's Strategic Renovation,* Adelphi Paper no. 189 (London: International Institute for Strategic Studies, 1994).

7. Quoted in *Rossiiskiye vesti,* January 4, 1993.

8. "Russian Federation Defense Ministry Press Center Reports New Appointments," *Krasnaya zvezda,* August 22, 1992.

9. ITAR-TASS report, October 6, 1992.

10. Michael Parks, "Soviet Army Will Be Cut, Says New Defense Minister," *Philadelphia Inquirer,* September 21, 1991.

11. Lieutenant Colonel A. Dokuchayev, "The Russian Armed Forces: Phases of Formation," *Krasnaya zvezda,* June 23, 1992.

12. Interview with Grachev, "A Strong Army Heightens the Self-Respect of the People," *Armia,* nos. 11–12 (November-December 1992): 3–8. Grachev also reaffirmed Russia's commitment to a nuclear no-first-use pledge, a commitment later retracted in the new Russian military doctrine.

13. Colonel O. Falichev, "Building the Russian Military Is a Task for All the People," *Krasnaya zvezda,* May 26, 1992.

14. See "Army General Pavel Grachev: Clear Calculation and Common Sense Are Needed in Forming the Russian Military," *Krasnaya zvezda,* July 21, 1992.

15. For a balanced analysis, see Charles J. Dick, "The Military Doctrine of the Russian Federation," *Journal of Slavic Military Studies,* no. 3 (September 1994): 481–506.

16. Interview on Radio Rossia, November 21, 1993.

17. Interview with General Pavel Grachev by Sergei Ovsiyenko, "The Army: Overcoming Arrhythmia," *Rossiiskiye vesti,* May 29, 1992.

18. Moscow First Program television interview, May 31, 1992. For a more detailed treatment of post-Soviet military reform plans and their prospects, see Richard F. Staar, *The New Military in Russia: Ten Myths That Shape the Image* (Annapolis, Md.: Naval Institute Press, 1996).

19. Interview by Yelena Agapova, "Before You Form an Army, You Should Know What It Is For, Expert Andrei Kokoshin Believes," *Krasnaya zvezda,* March 17, 1992. No first use of nuclear weapons was always a Soviet propaganda ploy. One of the many skeletons let out of the former Soviet strategic closet was a disclosure by Germany's defense minister, Gerhard Stoltenberg, citing former East German archives, of a Warsaw Pact contingency plan to carry out a preemptive strike with 840 nuclear warheads to smash NATO opposition and break through NATO's defenses in case of war in Central Europe. See Mikhail Shchipanov, "Will There Be Secrets from Our Ally?" *Kuranty,* February 7, 1992.

20. Interview with Colonel General Anatoly Malyukov by Piotr Butowski, "Flying in the Face of Adversity," *Jane's Defense Weekly,* April 17, 1993, 15.

21. The VVS was by no means the only service so afflicted. In a speech to the Congress of People's Deputies in December 1992, Grachev starkly characterized the dregs that Russia found itself left with following the disintegration of the former Soviet armed forces: "Ruins and debris, basically. Communications, command and control, intelligence, missile attack warning, air defense, and logistical support systems were wrecked. We inherited forces from the second strategic echelons. The most combat-capable units, equipped with the latest armaments, were left outside the Russian Federation. Thousands upon thousands of Russian servicemen and their families ended up outside." *Krasnaya zvezda,* December 8, 1992.

22. Interfax, November 28, 1992.

23. "News Breaks," *Aviation Week and Space Technology,* August 2, 1993. That could only have come as good news to the VVS pilots stationed there. The regiment at Iturup was the only one from which Russian pilots flew single-engine fighters over water. As a press comment

somberly noted: "The first failure of a MiG-23's engine automatically becomes the last failure in the pilot's life. A ship or submarine will arrive at the accident site three days later at best." Burevestnik was described as a bare-base facility, with no hangars and with aircraft "rusting year-round under the open sky." I. Kots, "Islands in Shoulderboards: Whom Is the Military Deterring in the Southern Kurils?" *Komsomolskaya pravda*, July 28, 1992.

24. Interview with Colonel General Pyotr S. Deinekin, "Russia Will Not Remain without Wings," *Krasnaya zvezda*, November 5, 1994.

25. The figure for VPVO includes personnel assigned to SAM and radar units in addition to fighter aviation, as reported in the successive annual editions of *The Military Balance* (London: International Institute for Strategic Studies, 1989–97).

26. That view has not, however, been universal by any means. As one might expect, the chief of the ground forces headquarters staff conceded that although aircraft in Desert Storm "showed themselves to be a maneuverable, effective weapon" and played the leading role in that particular war, this in no way belittled "the significance of ground forces' military actions in the attainment of the ultimate goal." Indeed, he said, the war "confirmed the philosophical tenet of their determining role." Interview with Lieutenant General Yury D. Bukreyev, "I Favor the Ground Forces," *Krasnaya zvezda*, November 28, 1991.

27. See his "Editor's Comment: Military Reform and the Air Force," in Forsberg, *The Arms Production Dilemma*, 51–60.

28. The seeds of such a scenario certainly exist among those secessionist leaders of potential breakaway Muslim republics in southern Russia who would seek aid and comfort from their Muslim brethren in Turkey. Dzhokar Dudayev, the former Soviet VVS major general who led the rebellion in Chechnya, appealed to a Turkish reporter in late December 1994 for Ankara to supply him with combat aircraft that he could use to bomb Moscow. See Sonni Efron, "Yeltsin Defends Continuation of Chechnya War," *Los Angeles Times*, December 28, 1994.

29. For an independent Western view on the plausibility of this scenario, see S. Enders Wimbush, "When China Absorbs the Russian Far East," *Wall Street Journal*, April 25, 1996.

30. Colonel General Deinekin, "Former Soviet Strategic Bombers May Turn into Scrap Metal," reprinted in R. W. Dellow, *Organization and Equipment: Priorities for the Russian Air Force* (Camberley, England: Conflict Studies Research Center, Royal Military Academy Sandhurst, 1993), 8.

31. Colonel General Pyotr S. Deinekin, "Always Ready for Action," *Krasny voin*, August 7, 1993, 3.

32. Interview with Colonel General Pyotr S. Deinekin, "The New Russian Air Force: Interview with the Commander in Chief of the Russian Air Force," *NATO's Sixteen Nations*, no. 3 (March 1993): 39.

33. Interview with Colonel General Pyotr S. Deinekin, "Russia Will Not Remain without Wings."

34. Ibid.; Aleksandr Ivanov, "VPVO Forces Retained as a Branch of the Armed Forces," *Krasnaya zvezda*, April 12, 1994.

35. Colonel V. Kistanov, "Composite Air Wings: A New Element in the USAF's Structure," *Zarubezhnoye voyennoye obozreniye*, no. 6 (1992): 48–51.

36. That concept involved putting multiple combat and combat-support aircraft types such as F-15s, F-16s, B-1s, and tankers into a single wing that could deploy on short notice and operate effectively as a single unit. It was later replaced by a similarly intentioned but more flexible and economical "air expeditionary force" concept. See, respectively, General Merrill A. McPeak, "For the Composite Wing," *Airpower Journal*, fall 1990, 4–12, and Brigadier General William R. Looney III, "The Air Expeditionary Force: Taking the Air Force into the 21st Century," *Airpower Journal*, winter 1996, 4–9.

37. Interview with Colonel General Anatoly Malyukov by Dmitry Grinyuk and Piotr Butowski, "An Unusual Conversation at the Main Staff," *Krylya rodiny*, no. 11 (November 1991). The CFE (Conventional Forces in Europe) Treaty was a major factor in the breakdown of some former Soviet secrecy rules. General Malyukov said it was now permissible to identify bases, units, and force levels. Also, the commander of VPVO, Colonel General Viktor Prudnikov, summarily declassified the locations of his fighter bases and the names of VPVO unit commanders in 1992. See Irina Pankova, "The Missile Troops Take a Hit—on Their Secrets," *Nezavisimaya gazeta*, August 3–10, 1992.

38. "Russia to Scrap 2,000 Aircraft," *Flight International,* March 31–April 6, 1993, 5.
39. Interfax, April 13, 1994.
40. Butowski, "Flying in the Face of Adversity," 15.
41. Agapova, "Before You Form an Army."
42. As reported in the successive annual editions of *The Military Balance.*
43. "The Follow-On to the Su-27 Fighter" (paper delivered at the First International Air Power Conference, London, February 11–12, 1993).
44. *The Military Balance, 1994–95* (London: International Institute for Strategic Studies, 1994), 112–13.
45. "Strategic Bombers Leave Kazakhstan," *Washington Times,* March 1, 1994.
46. One of those conducted a live cruise missile launch in late 1992. See Sergei Prokopenko, "A Russian Tu-160 on the Combat Line," *Krasnaya zvezda,* October 23, 1992, and Viktor Beltsov, "Russian Air Force Aircraft Inventory Augmented," *Krasnaya zvezda,* February 13, 1993. General Deinekin later indicated that this launch occurred during delivery of the aircraft from the factory to its base.
47. Moscow television report, April 30, 1994.
48. ITAR-TASS report, March 23, 1993.
49. The VVS also was to get 15 Tu-95MS bombers returned. In an offset arrangement, Russia agreed to transfer 8 MiG-29UB two-seaters, 4 Su-27s, and several transport aircraft to Ukraine. See "Ukrainian Bombers for Russia," *ConCISe,* April 23, 1996, 461.
50. As a testament to the Tu-160's problems, the report added that the first aircraft was accepted at Priluki from the factory in April 1987 and that since then, only 19 Tu-160s had been delivered. The report added that ground servicing of this modern aircraft was "prehistoric," requiring ten fuel trucks to transfer its full complement of 180 tons of fuel. One aircraft was lost to an engine fire due to an electrical system problem. All four crew members ejected successfully. See Leonid Kostrov, "The Blackjack: Not a Game for Politicians," *Vechernyaya Moskva,* March 3, 1992.
51. TASS report on a statement by General Deinekin, March 27, 1992. Defense Minister Grachev later painted an even starker picture: "We have been left with less than one-half of [the former Soviet] Military Transport Aviation. . . . Two of its five divisions have remained on Ukrainian territory, one regiment has remained in Belarus, and one in Uzbekistan. To all intents and purposes, Russia actually has only two military transport regiments." Interview by Nikolai Burbyga and Albert Plutnik, "Pavel Grachev: 'In Essence the Russian Military Must Be Recreated from Scratch,'" *Izvestia,* June 2, 1992.
52. *The Military Balance, 1995–96* (London: International Institute for Strategic Studies, 1995), 115.
53. Igor Andreyev, "Aircraft Competition: MiG or Yak?" *Izvestia,* February 22, 1994.
54. Major V. Malev, "A Problem Requiring a Decision," *Krasnaya zvezda,* September 21, 1991.
55. See Alexander Velovich, "Russian Trainer Decision Close," *Flight International,* February 22–27, 1994, 22. See also "MiG-AT Trainer Completes First Flight," *Aviation Week and Space Technology,* April 11, 1996, 21, and "First Flight for Yak-130 Trainer," *Aviation Week and Space Technology,* May 6, 1996, 17.
56. As reported in the successive annual editions of *The Military Balance* (1991–94).
57. *The Military Balance, 1994–95,* 113.
58. See Captain Brian J. Collins, USAF, "Soviet Military Reform: Structuring Aerospace Forces," *International Defense Review,* no. 6 (June 1991): 562.
59. Interview with Major General Nikolai A. Rogov, "Russia's Naval Aviation: What Kind Should It Be?" *Morskoi sbornik,* nos. 8–9 (August-September 1992): 3–5.
60. Admiral F. Gromov, "The Russian Navy: Yesterday, Today, and Tomorrow," *Morskoi sbornik,* no. 1 (January 1993): 7.
61. Colonel General V. Potapov, "Naval Aviation: Problems and Solutions," *Morskoi sbornik,* no. 6 (June 1993): 29.
62. Vladimir Shirokov, Valery Gromak, Aleksandr Pilipchuk, and Valery Polikarpov, "The Deck-Based Pilots Are Losing Their Deck but Believe Their Problems Can Be Solved," *Krasnaya zvezda,* June 30, 1993.
63. Captain First Rank V. Kuzin, "Aircraft-Carrying Cruisers," *Morskoi sbornik,* no. 7 (July 1991): 64.

64. Cited in "Does the Soviet Navy Need Aircraft Carriers?" Novosti press agency report, in English, September 6, 1991.
65. "Sukhoi Beats Mikoyan in Navy Contest," *Flight International,* September 8–14, 1993, 11.
66. Pavel Maslov and Valentin Rudenko, "The Su-33 Attacks from the Sea," *Krasnaya zvezda,* March 11, 1994.
67. Conversation with Sukhoi Design Bureau test pilots at the Zhukovsky Flight Test Center, August 31, 1993.
68. The Yak-38 experienced an unacceptably high attrition rate due to reliability problems with its stability augmentation system. A Soviet press account noted that pilots on one carrier hung a sign on a Yak-38 declaring that the airplane was "unfit for human use." See Norman Friedman, "World Naval Developments," *U.S. Naval Institute Proceedings,* September 1990, 139.

   The Yak-141, originally intended to replace the Yak-38, was also canceled as a result of development problems, budget constraints, and a questionable post–cold war requirement for the aircraft. See also "Russia Ditches Forgers and Carriers," *Flight International,* March 1, 1994.

4. Undergraduate Pilot Training

1. VPVO and VVS fighter pilots, however, operated in markedly dissimilar ways, with the former much more heavily tied to GCI close control throughout intercepts. Zuyev implied that KFA pilots looked on their VPVO brethren with condescension, saying of one VVS MiG-29 squadron commander whose upbringing had been in VPVO on the clumsy Yak-28: "He might well have flown thousands of 'elevator ride' sorties as a VPVO interceptor pilot, but that fact had little to do with his true ability as a fighter pilot." Alexander Zuyev, with Malcolm McConnell, *Fulcrum* (New York: Warner Books, 1992), 210.
2. John Barron, *MiG Pilot: The Final Escape of Lieutenant Belenko* (New York: McGraw-Hill Book Company, 1980), 59.
3. For a classic example, see Lieutenant Colonel V. Smirnov, *Vybirayu aviatsiyu: Dlia tekh, kto khochet stat' ofitserom VVS* (I choose aviation: For those who want to become an air force officer) (Moscow: Voyenizdat, 1989).
4. Lieutenant Colonel V. Smirnov, "For Those Who Choose the Sky," *Aviatsia i kosmonavtika,* no. 3 (March 1990): 40–41.
5. One notable example was Tokhtar Aubakirov, who in 1989, while serving as deputy chief test pilot of the Mikoyan Design Bureau, made the first arrested landing of a MiG-29 aboard the Soviet carrier *Admiral Kuznetsov* and who later went on to fly in space as a pilot-cosmonaut. Others included the late Major General Sulambek Oskanov, the respected commander of the VVS fighter weapons training center at Lipetsk, who was killed in a MiG-29 accident caused by an uncommanded roll during approach to landing in 1992.
6. Indeed the Soviet approach to pilot selection showed many similarities to that used by the heavily fighter-oriented Israeli Air Force. For early details on the latter, see Edward W. Youngling et al., *Feasibility Study to Predict Combat Effectiveness for Selected Military Roles: Fighter Pilot Effectiveness,* MDC E1634 (St. Louis: McDonnell Douglas Astronautics Company, 1977), 3.79–3.83.
7. Zuyev, *Fulcrum,* 123.
8. Ibid.
9. Ibid., 125.
10. Ibid., 85.
11. Barron, *MiG Pilot,* 66. In fact, the USAF used no such tests, at least through the mid-1980s. By one informed account, Soviet competition for pilot-training slots was more competitive than that of the USAF, which did "very little preselection testing of personnel prior to their entering pilot training," relied on "a relatively antiquated system of undergraduate academic grades, officer qualification test scores, and 20/20 vision," and did not "differentiate between skills necessary for fighter pilots and other pilots such as airlift or bomber pilots." In one weakness the USAF shared with the Soviet VVAUL system, such a distinction was made much later in the training cycle, restricting the system to selecting only from among those who had already been admitted into the program. Colonel Mike Press, "The Human Factor: The United States versus the Soviet Fighter Pilot," *Air University Review,* November-December 1986, 74.

12. Colonel of Medical Service (Ret.) I. Chernyakov and Lieutenant Colonel A. Shishov, "Diagnosing Hypoxia in Flight," *Aviatsia i kosmonavtika*, no. 11 (November 1991): 10–11.
13. Conversation with a former Soviet fighter pilot.
14. Major General Ya. Yanakov, "From Retrograde to Modern," *Aviatsia i kosmonavtika*, no. 1 (January 1992): 2–3.
15. Zuyev, *Fulcrum*, 140.
16. Zuyev made it in only two years and three months, indicating the radical differences in pacing depending on units. Zuyev, *Fulcrum*, 154.
17. Ibid., 112.
18. Interview with Colonel Leonid N. Pakhnin, "For Those Who Choose to Fly," *Krasnaya zvezda*, February 27, 1993.
19. Interview by Major S. Prokopenko, "A New Four-Stage Training Program for VVS Pilots," *Krasnaya zvezda*, October 6, 1990.
20. Straight-in approaches or long final approaches from an extended downwind leg are standard practice in Russian fighter operations, as was uniformly confirmed by my own flight experiences in the MiG-29, Su-27, MiG-23, and MiG-21.
21. Colonel V. Sobolev (deputy commander of the Chernigov VVAUL), "Stop Teaching in a Retrograde Way," *Aviatsia i kosmonavtika*, no. 3 (March 1991): 4–6.
22. Interview with Colonel General Viktor S. Kot, "We Train the Pilot, We Educate the Person," *Krasnaya zvezda*, March 18, 1993.
23. Colonel General A. Goryainov, "How to Breed the Next Generation of Fliers," *Krasnaya zvezda*, August 3, 1988.
24. Major S. Goroshkin, "Disquieting Symptoms," *Aviatsia i kosmonavtika*, no. 1 (January 1990): 10–11.
25. See A. Gorokhov, "On the Modern Ones," *Krylya rodiny*, no. 8 (August 1987): 1–2.
26. According to the VVS deputy chief for education and training, only two of eight planned boarding schools had opened by early 1992, with one reported to be on the verge of forced closure because local authorities had failed to uphold their promise to help finance it. Yanakov, "From Retrograde to Modern," 2–3.
27. "Moscow's Air Defense Commander," *Air Forces Monthly*, January 1993, 21.
28. Lieutenant Colonel V. Smirnov, "Special Flight Boarding Schools," *Aviatsia i kosmonavtika*, no. 1 (January 1991): 18. DOSAAF was disbanded in 1991 and replaced by the Russian Defense Sport-Technical Organization. Its chairman noted the difficulty of sustaining flight activities in the face of the funding crisis but said that its forty-eight aero clubs nevertheless were training fifteen hundred candidates a year for entry into VVAULs. Major General Aleksei Anokhin, "Our Main Task Is to Educate Patriots," *Military News Bulletin* (Moscow), no. 7 (July 1993).
29. Similarly, VPVO in 1998 was down to two pilot training schools, the Armavir VVAUL, named for Marshal of Aviation P. S. Kutakhov, and the Stavropol VVAUL, named for Marshal of Aviation V. A. Sudets. The latter also trained MiG-31 backseaters.
30. For a full list, see "Air Force Military Educational Institutions Invite You," *Krasnaya zvezda*, February 27, 1993.
31. Lieutenant Colonel V. Beltsov, "In the Skies of Altai," *Vestnik vozdushnovo flota*, no. 2 (1995): 44–47.
32. Conversation with a former Soviet fighter pilot.
33. Barron, *MiG Pilot*, 75.
34. Interview with Colonel V. Shevtsov, "Pilots Who Never Developed: Can We Halt the Outflow of Cadets from Military Schools?" *Krasnaya zvezda*, March 12, 1991.
35. Goryainov, "How to Breed the Next Generation."
36. Lieutenant Colonel N. Gorchakov, "Put in a Word for the Poor Instructor," *Aviatsia i kosmonavtika*, no. 10 (October 1991): 10–11.
37. Barron, *MiG Pilot*, 79.
38. Gorchakov, "Put in a Word."
39. Ibid.
40. He added that pilots with stall and spin familiarization were more likely to teach these techniques to their students, whereas those lacking such experience tended to emphasize training in departure region avoidance. He said it was time to force an "unambiguous answer" to the

question of whether the more aggressive, "know your airplane" approach or the more conservative, safety-oriented approach was preferable in combat training. Colonel G. Rayevsky, "Should the Spin Be Taught?" *Aviatsia i kosmonavtika,* no. 3 (March 1990): 6–7.

41. Hero of the Soviet Union and Honored Test Pilot A. Shcherbakov, with A. Klimov and A. Gorlov, "Teach the Spin," *Aviatsia i kosmonavtika,* no. 1 (January 1991): 10–11.

42. Retired U.S. Navy Captain Jerry O'Rourke well summarized such thinking: "A fighter pilot must use his airplane right up to its limits in his routine flying, be it in combat or training for combat. These fine edges between what the plane can do and what it cannot are his ballpark. The mark of the true professional is his ability to get into that ballpark and to drive his enemy out. So he must *use* his airplane and his weaponry right up to these limits. If he doesn't—if he reserves a little cushion for safety, or for the wife and kids, or for any lack of personal confidence—he's not really a fighter pilot, and, when combat comes, he'll soon be beaten by one who is." Quoted in "Fighters That Never Got to the Fight: Part II," *U.S. Naval Institute Proceedings,* April 1982, 76–77.

43. Colonel (Ret.) Nikolai Lysenko, "How Can Maximum Flight Modes Be Mastered?" *Aviatsia i kosmonavtika,* no. 7 (July 1992): 6–7.

44. Ibid.

5. Combat Training in Front-Line Units

1. Lieutenant Colonel Mike Press, "Aggressor Reflections," *USAF Fighter Weapons Review,* summer 1981, 4.

2. In the words of one of the Israeli F-4 pilots who scored a kill in that encounter, the Soviets showed "a very low skill level" and committed "all imaginable errors" once the engagement was joined. See Colonel Aviam Sela, "A Trap for the Russians," in Merav Halperin and Aharon Lapidot, *Chalifat Lachatz* (G-Suit) (Tel Aviv: Israeli Ministry of Defense, 1987), 69–72.

3. Michael Skinner, *USAFE: A Primer of Modern Air Combat in Europe* (Novato, Calif.: Presidio Press, 1983), 122.

4. Captain Rana J. Pennington, "Closing the Tactics Gap," *Air Force Magazine,* March 1984, 83. A year later, Captain Pennington similarly wrote: "Rather than painting the Soviet pilot as ten feet tall, we have consistently depicted him as a midget—a dwarf at best. It has long been a matter of reassurance to the Air Force that no matter how many aircraft the Soviets had, the poor skills of their pilots would significantly hamper their ability to use those aircraft effectively." Captain Rana J. Pennington, "Another Look at the Soviet Fighter Pilot, *Air Force Magazine,* April 1985, 83.

5. *Soviet Military Power* (Washington, D.C.: U.S. Government Printing Office, 1983), 43.

6. See "U.S. Intercepts Soviet Fighter Transmissions," *Aviation Week and Space Technology,* September 12, 1983.

7. Robert L. Shaw, *Fighter Combat: Tactics and Maneuvering* (Annapolis, Md.: U.S. Naval Institute Press, 1985), x.

8. Bill Gunston, *Mikoyan MiG-21* (London: Osprey Publishing, 1986), 36, 47, 64, 88–92.

9. The Finnish Air Force, which also acquired and continues to operate the MiG-21, reported a similar experience. According to its former commander, retired Lieutenant General Heikki Nikunen, introductory training on the aircraft for the initial Finnish cadre at Lugovaya included no tactical flying and proceeded so slowly that the Finnish team leader finally called a halt to the training and brought the group home to complete the process on its own. The MiG-21 was evaluated at the Finnish Air Force flight-test center, and optimum tactics were then developed based on those results. Letter to the author from General Nikunen, April 16, 1993.

10. Air Vice Marshal Tony Mason, RAF (Ret.), *Air Power: A Centennial Appraisal* (London: Brassey's, 1994), 211.

11. Conversation with a former Soviet fighter pilot.

12. Ibid.

13. Major S. Goroshkin, "Disquieting Symptoms," *Aviatsia i kosmonavtika,* no. 1 (January 1990): 10–11.

14. Lieutenant Colonel A. Zhukov, "Is There a Way out of the Impasse?" *Aviatsia i kosmonavtika,* no. 6 (June 1990): 12.

15. Ibid.

16. Interview with Colonel General Ye. Shaposhnikov, "The Air Force Today and Tomorrow," *Aviatsia i kosmonavtika,* no. 8 (August 1990): 2–3.

17. Ibid.

18. That autocratic style of command and its associated diminution of the role of the individual had roots running back at least to World War II days. For some fascinating insights into its early manifestations as far down as the flight-leader level, see Generalleutnant Walter Schwabedissen, *The Russian Air Force in the Eyes of German Commanders,* USAF Historical Studies no. 175 (Maxwell Air Force Base, Ala.: USAF Historical Division, Air University, 1960).

19. Interview with Shaposhnikov, "The Air Force Today."

20. Senior Lieutenant of Medical Services O. Rybnikov, "What Was Said over the Radio," *Aviatsia i kosmonavtika,* no. 10 (October 1989): 8–9.

21. Telephone conversation with Air Vice Marshal R. A. Mason, RAF (Ret.), citing "authoritative RAF sources."

22. Colonel V. Dudin, "Both Strength and Precision," *Aviatsia i kosmonavtika,* no. 10 (October 1991): 6–7.

23. Quoted in Michael Smith, "East Meets West as MiGs 'Fall' to Soesterberg F-15s," *Air Force Times,* October 14, 1991, 25.

24. Quoted in Pavel Felgengauer, "We Fly Only on Aircraft: The Air Force Commander in Chief Meets the Luftwaffe Commander in Chief," *Nezavisimaya gazeta,* July 16, 1992.

25. Lieutenant Colonel Ye. Shaposhnikov, "Responsible for the Flight," *Krasnaya zvezda,* September 10, 1975.

26. Lieutenant General Ye. Shaposhnikov, "Devalued by Time," *Aviatsia i kosmonavtika,* no. 3 (March 1988): 4–5.

27. Ibid.

28. Lieutenant General (Res.) Nikolai Kryukov and Colonel Nikolai Litvinchuk, "What Is on the Horizon for the Ukrainian Air Force?" *Narodna armia* (Kiev), July 3, 1993.

29. See Colonel V. Skrynnik, "Each Has His Own Minimum," *Aviatsia i kosmonavtika,* no. 10 (October 1991): 28–29.

30. Shaposhnikov, "Devalued by Time."

31. Lieutenant General Ye. Shaposhnikov, "Toward a High Level of Combat Readiness—through Concern for Others," *Aviatsia i kosmonavtika,* no. 7 (June 1989): 1–3.

32. Ibid.

33. Ibid.

34. Interview with Lieutenant General A. Tarasenko, "In a Holding Pattern: Comments on Problems of the 16th Air Army," *Krasnaya zvezda,* March 27, 1992.

35. John Barron, *MiG Pilot: The Final Escape of Lieutenant Belenko* (New York: McGraw-Hill Book Company, 1980), 1.

36. Guards Major V. Bazhenov, "Navigation Support of Flight Operations," *Aviatsia i kosmonavtika,* no. 10 (October 1988): 20–21.

37. One instructor voiced contempt for this ever-present "Notebook for Immediate Flight Preparations," with its detailed schematics of maneuvers, tiresome explanations of the proper way of executing them, safety rules, techniques for correcting deviations, and so on. He groused that such "orthography lessons" were oppressive enough to deny even an experienced pilot any freedom of action during a sortie.

38. Conversation with a former Soviet fighter pilot.

39. Alexander Zuyev, with Malcolm McConnell, *Fulcrum* (New York: Warner Books, 1992), 124.

40. Conversation with a former Soviet fighter pilot.

41. Russian aircraft cooling and braking systems use pure grain alcohol, which is readily available to pilots, from commanders on down. Pilots call it "white gold." The MiG-25 carried 1,000 pounds of it, leading pilots to refer to the aircraft jokingly as "the flying restaurant." Barron, *MiG Pilot,* 81, 97.

42. At one point in his memoirs Zuyev insisted that alcohol abuse was rare among Soviet fighter pilots. He also expressed surprise to learn that U.S. and RAF pilots "almost ritually frequented their officers' club bars every evening after flying" and that they evidently considered

drinking to be "a sign of masculinity." Yet elsewhere, he spoke of a lethal indulgence among Soviet pilots. In this game, called "polar bear," the pilots would sit around a table with tumblers of alcohol in front of them, bet money on each shot, and wait for someone to shout "polar bear." The pilots would then down the shots and dive under the table to hide from the imaginary bear. This would typically continue for hours, with the winner being the sole survivor who could pick himself up from underneath the table and walk away. *Fulcrum,* 123, 175.

43. Ibid., 14.
44. The MiG-29, for example, carries less than 7,000 pounds of internal fuel, as opposed to 11,000 for the F-15. In my MiG-21 and MiG-23 flights at Zhukovsky, we flew in clean configuration with full internal fuel. With normal afterburner use for an advanced handling demonstration no more than 25 nautical miles south of the field, we landed with minimum fuel within a half-hour. (The Su-27 is a conspicuous exception to this rule, with an internal fuel capacity of 22,000 pounds.)
45. Zuyev, *Fulcrum,* 23.
46. Rene Van Woezik and Tieme Festner, "Bear Tracks in Germany: The Soviet Air Force in the Former German Democratic Republic," *Air International,* October 1992, 210. A former Soviet pilot told me that a maintenance supervisor who truly wanted to discipline an errant subordinate would assign him to a two-seater because of its higher utilization rate.
47. Conversation with a former Soviet fighter pilot.
48. Colonel Yu. Kuzmin, "Worth Its Weight in Gold," *Aviatsia i kosmonavtika,* no. 12 (December 1992): 10.
49. Zuyev, *Fulcrum,* 23.
50. Ibid., 24–26.
51. Ibid., 22. This may explain how one Iraqi MiG-29 pilot apparently shot down his own wingman during the 1991 Persian Gulf War.
52. Ibid., 19.
53. A. Shcherbakov, A. Klimov, and A. Gorlov, "On the Road to Supermaneuverability," *Aviatsia i kosmonavtika,* no. 9 (September 1991): 12–13. The "cobra" maneuver, first popularized by Viktor Pugachev, a Sukhoi test pilot, at the 1989 Paris Air Show and since performed routinely at air shows by both the Su-27 and the MiG-29, is mainly a demonstration of aircraft stability and aerodynamic efficiency at high angles of attack. The maneuver has been extolled by some Russian publicists not just as a last-ditch guns-defense technique but also as a means for executing a snap-up missile attack (see, for example, Colonel A. Andryushkov, "The Pugachev Cobra," *Krasnaya zvezda,* June 13, 1989). Mikoyan's former chief test pilot, Valery Menitsky, has dismissed it as a "circus event."
54. Even during the Soviet military's best days, fighter pilots did not routinely fly as many hours per year as did their Western counterparts. For example, it took Lieutenant Colonel Timur Apakidze, one of the first Russian Navy pilots to carrier-qualify in the Su-27K aboard the *Admiral Kuznetsov,* twenty-three years of service to accumulate 2,500 hours of total time. See Captain Second Rank V. Pasyakin, "Salamander Clears a Landing: Naval Pilots Have Landed on the Deck of the Carrier *Kuznetzov* for the First Time," *Krasnaya zvezda,* October 19, 1991.
55. Senior Lieutenant V. Shurygin, "A Reader Poses a Question: Excess Fuel," *Krasnaya zvezda,* September 13, 1989.
56. Under normal circumstances, one regimental commander reported, it was possible to advance from basic to First-Class pilot in as little as two years. See Colonel V. Kudryavtsev, "With Whom Are We to Fly into Combat?" *Krasnaya zvezda,* March 3, 1987.
57. Lieutenant Colonel V. Usoltsev, "Victory in the Air and Problems on the Ground," *Krasnaya zvezda,* January 28, 1990.
58. Colonel N. Gostev, "Perestroika in Training: What Is It to Be Like?" *Aviatsia i kosmonavtika,* no. 1 (January 1988): 28–30.
59. Zuyev, *Fulcrum,* 114.
60. Lieutenant Colonel I. Kovalenko, "It Doesn't Seem Possible to Close the Ranges," *Aviatsia i kosmonavtika,* no. 5 (May 1991): 28–30.
61. Shaposhnikov, "Devalued by Time."
62. Captain Rana J. Pennington, USAF, "The Soviet Ability to Execute an Air Operation" (pre-

sentation to a conference organized by the German Strategy Forum, Bonn, West Germany, 1984), 4. For a well-informed discussion of the concept of operations underlying such exercises, see Philip A. Petersen and Major John R. Clark, "Soviet Air and Antiair Operations," *Air University Review*, no. 3 (March-April 1985): 36–54.

63. Colonel A. Tareyev, "An Operational Evaluation over the Sea," *Aviatsia i kosmonavtika*, no. 11 (November 1987): 10–11.

64. Zuyev, *Fulcrum*, 190–203.

65. Conversation with a former Soviet fighter pilot.

66. Shaposhnikov, "Toward a High Level of Combat Readiness."

67. Kovalenko, "It Doesn't Seem Possible to Close the Ranges." In contradiction to this, a knowledgeable Russian told me in 1993 that the loss of the Mary range complex to Turkmenistan following the USSR's breakup would not significantly hurt KFA mission-employment training, since there were enough range facilities in Russia to provide adequate weapons training opportunities for the considerably smaller Russian VVS.

68. Interview with Colonel General N. Antoshkin, "Was There No Way the Missile Could Have Hit a Nuclear Power Station?" *Trud*, April 5, 1995.

69. Report by Aleksandr Manushkin, "A Large-Scale Exercise Begins in the Russian Air Force," *Krasnaya zvezda*, May 18, 1993.

70. Colonel Aleksandr Manushkin and Major Viktor Beltsov, "A Dash across the Ural Mountains: The First Part of a Tactical Exercise Is Completed Successfully," *Krasnaya zvezda*, May 20, 1993.

71. Colonel Aleksandr Novikov (senior navigator at the VVS Central Command Post) and Colonel Aleksandr Andryushkov, "*Voskhod* '93: The Command Post Is the Nerve Center of the Exercise," *Krasnaya zvezda*, May 21, 1993. During the early 1980s the Soviet VVS conducted squadron and regimental surges and demonstrated the ability of a fighter regiment to mount three separate regiment-sized attacks within a six-hour period. Those activities did not, however, involve anything like the extended-range deployment featured in Voskhod '93. See Pennington, "The Soviet Ability to Execute an Air Operation."

72. Lipetsk is the VVS's closest approximation to the USAF Weapons Center at Nellis Air Force Base. It has long been a weapons training complex aimed at tactics development and validation for new equipment, syllabus development and manual writing, and upgrade training on new equipment for aircrews. For a snapshot overview of its mission and its tribulations caused by the funding crisis, see the interview with its commander, Major General Nikolai Chaga, "On a Wing and a Promise," *Pravda*, January 25, 1995. See also Alexander Velovich, "Preparing for Combat," *Flight International*, February 14–18, 1995, 26–27.

73. Colonel Ye. Kulikovsky, "If Approached Creatively," *Aviatsia i kosmonavtika*, no. 7 (July 1992): 4–5.

74. Colonel Kulikovsky's article that provided this outline suggested that tactics should be gamed out on the ground, using computer simulations and a full rehearsal of anticipated air combat, before being employed in the air. Unless he was referring to new tactics development and validation, this indicated that even post-Soviet VVS tactical approaches remain highly scripted in comparison with Western practice.

75. Lieutenant General A. Bobrovsky and Colonel V. Shubin, "Tactics in Air Combat Training," *Aviatsia i kosmonavtika*, no. 1 (January 1990): 1–3.

76. Ibid.

77. Colonel I. Vokhubov, "A Direct Relationship," *Aviatsia i kosmonavtika*, no. 10 (October 1988): 16–17.

78. Bobrovsky and Shubin, "Tactics in Air Combat Training,"

79. Zuyev, *Fulcrum*, 24.

80. Lieutenant Colonel V. Drugovenko, "On Stratagem," *Aviatsia i kosmonavtika*, no. 12 (December 1987): 12–13.

81. Lieutenant Colonel V. Korotovsky and Captain S. Frolov, "A Hobbled Initiative," *Krasnaya zvezda*, March 20, 1988.

82. Zuyev reported that at one point the VVS sent, to Afghanistan, groups of replacement pilots who were only six months out of flight school, with barely more than a brand-new Third-

Class rating. One unit commander said: "Putting young boys like that into the cockpit of a Su-25 and sending them against Stingers is like sending sheep to the slaughterhouse." Zuyev, *Fulcrum,* 121, 172.

83. Many returning pilots vividly remembered the spartan living conditions at their bare bases. Asked of his most lasting recollection, one young captain said: "Plain *kasha* [buckwheat porridge]! I ate enough to last me the rest of my life! That's all we had for months." See Galina Marchenko, "Encounters at Airfields," *Aviatsia i kosmonavtika,* no. 3 (March 1990): 28–30.

84. Quoted in ibid.

85. Zuyev, *Fulcrum,* 120.

86. Conversation with a former Soviet fighter pilot.

87. For more on this, see Dennis Marshall-Hasdell, *Soviet Military Reform and the Afghan Experience: Military Lessons* (Camberley, England: Conflict Studies Research Center, Royal Military Academy Sandhurst, 1993), 37–40.

6. The Operating Milieu

1. Captain Yu. Zhukovsky, "The Price of Carelessness," *Aviatsia i kosmonavtika,* no. 11 (November 1987): 28–29.

2. Ibid.

3. Lieutenant Colonel (Res.) V. Shishkin, "A Hope Undimmed By Years," *Aviatsia i kosmonavtika,* no. 12 (December 1991): 6–7.

4. Ibid. In an interesting side comment, he further noted that even with digital computers now installed in most current-generation aircraft, aircrews remain forced to do their mission planning using the venerable NL-10M wooden calculator. He granted that headquarters recognized the problem but typically countered with the lame excuse that there was "no funding for the *Luch*-84 computer." To that, the colonel wryly commented: "One can, of course, also drive nails with an electric iron and crack nuts with a crystal vase. But wouldn't it make more sense to use these items, and the system, for their intended purposes?"

5. Colonel A. Tsalko, "We Do Not Value Thrift," *Krasnaya zvezda,* January 24, 1989.

6. Shishkin, "A Hope Undimmed."

7. Alexander Zuyev, with Malcolm McConnell, *Fulcrum* (New York: Warner Books, 1992), 114.

8. Ibid., 111.

9. Ibid., 129. The introduction of the Stinger in Afghanistan in October 1986 had such an impact on the VVS's loss rate that Soviet strike aircraft pilots were forced to deliver their ordnance from higher altitudes, seriously eroding their bombing accuracy. For a time, Mujaheddin rebels were claiming at least one Soviet combat aircraft downed each day, with a reported 65–70 percent kill rate per missile launch. See John Gunston, "Stingers Used by Afghan Rebels Stymie Soviet Air Force Tactics," *Aviation Week and Space Technology,* April 4, 1988, 46–48.

10. Captain S. Prokopenko, "Both Pilot and . . . Trackman," *Krasnaya zvezda,* April 8, 1989.

11. Major General N. Posrednikov, "The Class and Proficiency Rating," *Krasnaya zvezda,* January 11, 1990.

12. Ibid. General Posrednikov argued against eliminating proficiency rating pay, which served as a stimulus for improving one's proficiency. He maintained, however, that the effectiveness of that stimulus could be enhanced "by rejecting leveling practices." He added: "The amount of the reward should depend directly on the number of hits and misses on range missions and on the complexity of training sorties and the skill with which they are carried out. Then no pilot will take off on a range mission with a defective sight."

13. Colonel T. Sheshenya, "The Combat Nucleus of a Regiment," *Krasnaya zvezda,* June 15, 1988.

14. Colonel V. Yudin, "Deformation," *Krasnaya zvezda,* May 5, 1988.

15. John Barron, *MiG Pilot: The Final Escape of Lieutenant Belenko* (New York: McGraw-Hill Book Company, 1980), 82–83.

16. Lieutenant General Ye. Shaposhnikov, "Toward a High Level of Combat Readiness—through Concern for Others," *Aviatsia i kosmonavtika,* no. 7 (June 1989): 1–3.

17. Lieutenant General Ye. Shaposhnikov, "The Degree of Readiness," *Krasnaya zvezda*, June 8, 1988.
18. Interview with Lieutenant General Vladimir I. Andreyev by Colonel A. Andryushkov, "We Need to Know the Threat by Sight," *Krasnaya zvezda*, November 22, 1991. Andreyev was quickly reinstated following the abortive 1991 coup after General Tretyak was fired for backing the putschists.
19. Lieutenant Colonel V. Korotovsky and Captain S. Frolov, "A Hobbled Initiative," *Krasnaya zvezda*, March 20, 1988.
20. Ibid. In 1989 an informed civilian defense specialist, Vitaly Shlykov, castigated the "Stalinist art of winning by numbers rather than by skill" as practiced by the Soviet armed forces in World War II. Shlykov contrasted poorly trained Soviet pilots (including, he said, leading aces Aleksandr Pokryshkin and Ivan Kozhedub) with the far superior aces of the Luftwaffe, who were "given proper training and used sparingly, being valued for their skill in aerial combat." Interview in *International Affairs*, no. 5 (May 1989): 23.
21. Korotovsky and Frolov, "A Hobbled Initiative."
22. Lieutenant Colonel G. Belostotsky, "Wait . . . a Test Target," *Krasnaya zvezda*, February 5, 1988.
23. Interview with Lieutenant Colonel Vasily Vysotsky, "We Are Rarely in the Air," *Komsomolskaya pravda*, August 7, 1991. A senior captain stated that the Soviet VVS "could not have operated as crisply in the Persian Gulf as did the Americans." He explained: "The overabundance of instructions does not yet allow us to reach their level."
24. Interview with Colonel General A. Borsuk by Colonel V. Seledkin, "To Assume Responsibility More Boldly," *Krasnaya zvezda*, July 12, 1988.
25. Valery Ye. Menitsky, Honored Test Pilot of the USSR, "Flying Skills: The Key to Victory," *Krasnaya zvezda*, May 11, 1989.
26. Ibid. As a case in point, the chief test pilot of the Yakovlev Design Bureau remarked how some Mikoyan pilots had visited one MiG-29 regiment whose pilots were restricted to 6 G in the aircraft (it is designed for normal operations at up to 9.5 G): "And it is like that for many flight parameters. What kind of combat readiness and combat capability can you talk about when a pilot doesn't have any idea of his aircraft's potential?" Interview with Andrei Sinitsyn by Major S. Prokopenko, "The Yak-141: The Aircraft, People, and Problems," *Krasnaya zvezda*, August 17, 1991.
27. Menitsky, "Flying Skills."
28. Colonel (Ret.) V. Uryuzhnikov, "Don't Make the Mistakes of the Past," *Kommunist vooruzhenykh sil*, no. 16 (August 1989): 13–15 (emphasis added).
29. Lieutenant Colonel of Medical Service V. Koslov and Lieutenant Colonel A. Zhilin, "The Pilot in the Combat Training System," *Aviatsia i kosmonavtika*, no. 8 (August 1990): 10–12.
30. Lieutenant Colonel A. Tokarenko, "Testing by Initiative," *Aviatsia i kosmonavtika*, no. 12 (December 1990): 4–5.
31. In a typical venting of such frustration, one VVS captain wrote as early as 1975: "It is all very well that GCI operators should assist us fighter pilots, but one should not rely on their support for everything." Captain A. Potemkin, "Respond to the Situation," *Aviatsia i kosmonavtika*, no. 12 (December 1975): 15.
32. Major General Ya. Yanakov, "From the Retrograde to the Modern," *Aviatsia i kosmonavtika*, no. 1 (January 1992): 2–3.
33. Interview with Colonel General Ye. Zarudnev, "We Must Not Lose Control of the Situation," *Aviatsia i kosmonavtika*, no. 12 (December 1992): 2–3.

7. How Might They Have Done If . . .

1. Raymond L. Garthoff, *Soviet Strategy in the Nuclear Age* (New York: Frederick A. Praeger, 1958), xi.
2. Colonel Mike Press, "The Human Factor: The United States versus the Soviet Fighter Pilot," *Air University Review*, November-December 1986, 76.
3. Barry D. Watts, "Air Warfare: A Comparison of Soviet and U.S. Views" (paper delivered at the Tenth General Working Meeting of the Military Conflict Institute, U.S. Military Academy, West Point, New York, May 4–8, 1987), 18.

8. Russia's Air War in Chechnya

1. That excludes the limited, and largely uncontested, Russian air activity in Tadzhikistan and elsewhere around the southern periphery of Russia following the USSR's collapse.

2. A competent Russian treatment of the Chechen war that drew on many of the sources used in this chapter was published in June 1995 under the lead authorship of N. N. Novichkov, at the time deputy director of the ITAR-TASS Agency for Scientific and Technical Information. For a translation of the chapter on air operations, see *Frontal and Army Aviation in the Chechen Conflict* (Camberley, England: Conflict Studies Research Center, Royal Military Academy Sandhurst, 1995).

3. General Deinekin, under whom Dudayev had served while Deinekin was LRA commander, had temperate words for Dudayev during the early days of the confrontation: "Dudayev was an intelligent commander, a highly qualified pilot—we never put pilots with a poor reputation in charge. . . . Dudayev was quite a good pilot, a good commander, he was known for his concern for people, he was very efficient and dependable." Interview with General Deinekin by Vladislav Listyev on Ostankino television First Channel, December 14, 1994. By the end of March, Deinekin merely noted that Dudayev had commanded an air division "which was no worse than others" and that "the general himself did not shine with any outstanding talent, although he performed meticulous service." Deinekin added that the Muslim world was well aware of Dudayev's bomber division's combat operations against the mujaheddin in Afghanistan and that for this reason, Dudayev "had to change his image." Interview with General Deinekin by Yury Dmitriyev and Nikolai Kishkin, "Air Force Commander in Chief Pyotr Deinekin: 'I Am Prepared to Account for Every Aerial Bomb,'" *Trud*, March 2, 1995.

4. Pavel Felgengauer, "The Chechen Campaign" (paper presented at the Third Annual Conference on Russian Defense Decisionmaking, U.S. Naval Postgraduate School, Monterey, California, November 7–8, 1995), 6.

5. Quoted in Timothy L. Thomas, "The Russian Armed Forces Confront Chechnya: II—Military Activities, 11–31 December 1994," *Journal of Slavic Military Studies,* June 1995, 268.

6. That immediately prompted speculation in Moscow that the Defense Ministry had not planned a tactically sound operation to settle the Chechen problem but instead was suckered into a decision by cabal under pressure from Yeltsin's closest advisers. See, for example, Nikolai Vishnevsky, "Grozny Offered a Dialogue," *Nezavisimaya gazeta,* December 17, 1994. That report called the failed clandestine assault on Grozny on November 26 "manifestly amateurish in nature" and an operation conducted by forces other than regular military, notably the former KGB and the Ministry of the Interior. Many accounts saw the Defense Ministry blindsided by Yeltsin's closest cronies. For a detailed review of events leading up to the invasion and the politics behind them, see Timothy L. Thomas, "The Russian Armed Forces Confront Chechnya: I—Military-Political Aspects, 11–31 December 1994," *Journal of Slavic Military Studies,* June 1995, 233–56.

7. Quoted in John Barron, *MiG Pilot: The Final Escape of Lieutenant Belenko* (New York: McGraw-Hill Book Company, 1980), 68.

8. S. Frederick Starr, "Chechnya: The U.S. Interest," *Wall Street Journal,* December 22, 1994.

9. ITAR-TASS, Moscow, January 11, 1995.

10. Interfax, Moscow, October 10, 1995.

11. Felgengauer, "The Chechen Campaign," 5.

12. Vremya television report, June 28, 1995.

13. See Charles Blandy, "The Battle for Grozny," *Jane's Intelligence Review* 7, no. 2 (February 1995): 53–56.

14. Lieutenant Colonel V. Beltsov, "Air Operations in Chechnya," *Vestnik vozdushnovo flota,* no. 2 (1995): 44–47.

15. Asked where Chechnya got its aircraft, General Deinekin answered emphatically: "Dudayev did not get from the [Russian] air force a single screw, landing gear, or cotter pin, much less a combat aircraft. Chechnya appropriated DOSAAF aircraft and the air defense and Aeroflot flying schools." Dmitriyev and Kishkin, "Air Force Commander in Chief Pyotr Deinekin."

16. See Aleksandr Khokhlov, "Will Dzhokar Dudayev Bomb Moscow?" *Komsomolskaya pravda,* January 17, 1995.

17. Aleksandr Ivanov, "Dudayev Has No 'Air Bridges,'" *Krasnaya zvezda,* March 21, 1995.

Sinitsyn added that those VPVO radar units were as deprived of creature comforts as were any other Russians deployed, noting that they had no tents for heating, no bathing and laundry facilities, no cooks—not even an adequate change of warm underclothing.

18. Beltsov, "Air Operations in Chechnya."
19. Simon Elliott and Alexander Velovich, "Backing Down: Russian Air Attacks on Chechnya Seem to Have Failed," *Flight International,* January 11–17, 1995, 23.
20. Interview with General Pyotr S. Deinekin, "The Air Force between the Sky and . . . the Scandals," *Argumenty i fakty,* no. 12 (December 1994): 8.
21. ITAR-TASS, Moscow, December 14, 1994.
22. See Yulia Kalinina, "Operation 'New Year': Grozny Was Bombed by Diesel Engine Mechanics in Training to Be Pontoon Bridge Builders," *Moskovsky komsomolets,* January 6, 1995.
23. Interview with Colonel General Pyotr S. Deinekin, "Flying in Your Dreams and in Reality," *Rossiiskiye vesti,* August 17, 1995.
24. To dramatize the alleged effectiveness of those strikes, the Russian Ministry of Defense released the following intercepted radio transmissions from rebel forces in the Chechen command post:

> "Cyclone to Panther 1. We're being bombed. They're blowing holes in the building right down to the cellar."
> "Get all the leaders together in the large hall."
> "They're using direct fire against the command post."
> "We need to withdraw our forces to the other side of Sunzha. Otherwise they'll bury us."
> "The second line of defense will be at the Minutka intersection. There are many dead and wounded in the palace. There isn't time to deal with them. We need to get out ourselves. If we don't manage it now, we'll wait until dark and leave."

Another transmission followed two hours later: "Panther 3 to Cyclone. After today's strike, everyone is very badly shaken, in shock. The strikes were very powerful and precise." Quoted in Beltsov, "Air Operations in Chechnya," 44–47.
25. Interview with Deinekin, "Flying in Your Dreams."
26. Reports from Moscow indicated that the pilots of three VVS aircraft ejected successfully but were executed by Dudayev's forces. The reports also noted that the Chechen terrorist Shamil Basayev had shot Russian pilots (none of whom had fought in Chechnya) during his bloody rampage in Budennovsk. Vremya television report, June 28, 1995.
27. Colonel Anatoly Surtsukov and Lieutenant Colonel Sergei Prokopenko, "A Shooting Sky: How Many Years Now Has It Tested the Mettle of the Ground Forces' Helicopter Pilots?" *Krasnaya zvezda,* July 18, 1995.
28. Quoted in Paul Beaver, "Army Aviation in Chechnya," *Jane's Defense Weekly,* June 10, 1995, 79.
29. Surtsukov and Prokopenko, "A Shooting Sky."
30. Ibid.
31. Among the best of the VVS's forward air controllers in Afghanistan were former pilots or navigators who had been removed from flight status for medical or other reasons. See Colonel I. Alpatov, "Forward Air Controller: The Experience of Combat Operations in Afghanistan," *Aviatsia i kosmonavtika,* no. 5 (May 1990): 18–19.
32. See "Chechen Conflict Taught Russia Vital UAV Lessons," *Jane's Defense Weekly,* July 1, 1998.
33. See Michael Specter, "Yeltsin Declares Chechen War Over, and Ousts Four Critics in Military," *New York Times,* January 20, 1995, and Fred Hiatt, "Moscow Debates Intensify Despite Claims of Victory," *Washington Post,* January 21, 1995.
34. See Steven Erlanger, "High Price of a 'Victory,'" *New York Times,* January 22, 1995.
35. Radiostantsiya Ekho Moskvy, August 19, 1995.
36. Interview with Pavel Grachev on Ostankino television, March 31, 1995.
37. See Richard Boudreaux, "Russians Seal Off City, Shell Chechen Civilians," *Los Angeles Times,* December 25, 1995, and "Death Toll Reported at 600 from Fighting in Chechnya," *New York Times,* December 26, 1995.
38. Kalinina, "Operation 'New Year.'"

39. "The Total in Writing: Is Price No Object?" *Obshchaya gazeta,* no. 3 (January 19, 1995): 5.
40. David A. Fulghum, "Chechnya Cripples Russian Aviation," *Aviation Week and Space Technology,* August 7, 1995, 20–21.
41. General Pyotr S. Deinekin, "Where We Are Directing the Flight of Our Birds: On the Air Force's Status and Development Prospects," *Armeisky sbornik,* no. 8 (August 1996): 9–12.
42. Alexander A. Belkin, "The War in Chechnya: Impact on Civil-Military Relations in Russia" (paper presented at the Third Annual Conference on Russian Defense Decisionmaking, U.S. Naval Postgraduate School, Monterey, California, November 7–8, 1995), 17.
43. "Chechnya: They Didn't Stint on the Cost," *Trud,* August 1, 1995.
44. Stephanie Simon, "Russians Offer Amnesty to Chechens," *Los Angeles Times,* December 3, 1995.
45. For more on Lebed's role in shaping the endgame of the war in Chechnya, see Benjamin S. Lambeth, *The Warrior Who Would Rule Russia,* MR-805-AF (Santa Monica, Calif.: RAND, 1996), 98–118.
46. Report by Aleksandr Gerasimov on Moscow television, April 7, 1995.
47. One such allegation was that a Su-27 was downed by a U.S.-made Stinger on November 29, even before the Russian ground invasion had begun. That was doubly implausible, since the Su-27 is a fighter-interceptor, not a ground-attack aircraft. Its restriction to a medium-altitude patrol orbit above 20,000 feet would have kept it well outside the lethal envelope of the Stinger, even if the latter had been available to the Chechen rebels. See ITAR-TASS report, "The Pentagon Checks Whether There Were Stingers in Chechnya," December 14, 1994.
48. Interfax, Moscow, August 19, 1995.
49. Interview with General Pyotr Deinekin, "The Crisis in Military Aviation," *Nezavisimoye voyennoye obozreniye,* February 22–28, 1997.
50. See "Dead or Alive," *Economist* (London), April 27, 1996, 54.
51. ITAR-TASS, August 2, 1995. Cost estimates for the war varied widely. Andrei Illarionov, director of the Economic Analysis Institute, wrote that Russia was spending the equivalent of $60 million a day at the height of combat operations and had exhausted $5 billion by the end of February. ITAR-TASS, Moscow, March 2, 1995. Other sources saw Russia's state coffers being drained by $30 million a day and the operation costing between $2 and $5 billion through early January. See Lee Hockstader, "Chechnya Draining Russian Economy," *Washington Post,* January 9, 1995. The total Russian allocation to defense for 1995 was only $11–$14 billion, barely one-twentieth of the U.S. defense budget.
52. General Mikhail P. Kolesnikov, "Military Organizational Development as an Inalienable Part of the Establishment of Russian Statehood," *Krasnaya zvezda,* September 30, 1995.
53. Interview by Andrei Vandenko, "Pavel Grachev: Yet More Dots over Yet More I's," *Moskovskaya pravda,* August 2, 1995.
54. Michael Specter, "Killed in Chechnya: An Army's Pride," *New York Times,* May 21, 1995.
55. Vremya television report, June 28, 1995. This was despite the persistently abysmal quality of life in the VVS, where more than five thousand flying officers at the time still had no apartment accommodations for themselves or their families.
56. Mark Galeotti, "Decline and Fall: Moscow's Chechen War," *Jane's Intelligence Review* 7, no. 2 (February 1995): 51.
57. Timothy L. Thomas, "Fault Lines and Factions in the Russian Army," *Orbis,* fall 1995, 531.
58. *Aviation Week,* August 7, 1995.
59. Ruslan Ignatyev, "Nonflying Weather Sets In," *Rossiiskaya gazeta,* March 4, 1995.
60. *Aviation Week,* August 7, 1995.
61. See "Russian Air Strategy and Combat Aircraft Production: A Russian Air Force View," in Randall Forsberg, ed., *The Arms Production Dilemma: Contraction and Restraint in the World Combat Aircraft Industry* (Cambridge: MIT Press, 1994), 45.
62. See Benjamin S. Lambeth, "Moscow's Lessons from the 1982 Lebanon Air War," in Air Vice Marshal R. A. Mason, ed., *War in the Third Dimension: Essays in Contemporary Air Power* (London: Brassey's, 1986), 127–48.
63. For detailed amplification, see Benjamin S. Lambeth, *Desert Storm and Its Meaning: The View from Moscow,* R-4161-AF (Santa Monica, Calif.: RAND, 1992).
64. Interview with Major General Yevgeny Nikitenko, "Grozny Is Not the Desert: First Attempts

to Derive Lessons from the Army's Actions in Chechnya," *Krasnaya zvezda*, January 27, 1995.

65. Colonel (Ret.) Vitaly V. Shlykov, "The War in Chechnya: Implications for Military Reform and the Creation of Mobile Forces" (paper presented at the Third Annual Conference on Russian Defense Decisionmaking, U.S. Naval Postgraduate School, Monterey, California, November 7–8, 1995), 12.

66. See "Russian Military Assesses Errors of Chechnya Campaign," *International Defense Review*, no. 4 (1995): 5–6.

67. Interview with Colonel General Ye. Podkolzin, "Don't Cry over the Military! We Have a Military, and Russia Has Defenses! We Were Marginalized," *Sovetskaya Rossia*, February 23, 1995.

68. Interview with Colonel General Mikhail Kolesnikov, "Despite All the Difficulties, the Russian Military Has Stood Its Ground and Remains a Guarantor of Stability," *Krasnaya zvezda*, May 6, 1995. General Kolesnikov worked hard to distance himself from the Chechnya debacle. He kept a low profile, refrained from endorsing the intervention, and generally avoided commenting on it in the press. Such behavior suggested that there was a rift between Kolesnikov and Grachev and that the former was seeking to protect his bona fides with the High Command. On May 7, 1995, Kolesnikov was promoted to the rank of "General of the Army," making him one of only two Russian four-stars at that time and the equivalent of Grachev. A little more than a year later, after placing first in the initial round of the 1996 presidential election, Yeltsin fired Grachev; several weeks thereafter he replaced Grachev with Colonel General Igor Rodionov, the commandant of the General Staff Academy. In the interim, Kolesnikov was appointed acting defense minister.

69. Lieutenant Colonel Valery Veshnikov, "If Flying, Then How to Fly, If Shooting, Then How to Shoot," *Armeisky sbornik*, no. 7 (July 1995): 26–27.

70. Ibid.

71. Steven Erlanger, "Russia's Army Seen as Failing Chechnya Test," *New York Times*, December 25, 1994.

72. Statement to Radiostantsiya Ekho Moskvy, December 23, 1994.

73. Carey Goldberg and Sonni Efron, "Yeltsin Demands Withdrawal Date from Chechnya," *Los Angeles Times*, January 7, 1995.

74. Said one flatly: "There are no area targets to be destroyed by heavy aviation in the theater of operations in Chechnya." Interfax, Moscow, June 2, 1995.

75. Interfax, Moscow, March 3, 1995. See also the interview with General Deinekin, "Official Version: 'We Only Attacked Grozny Military Installations,'" *Trud*, January 17, 1995.

76. Interview with Colonel General Pyotr S. Deinekin, "The Air Force in the Chechen Conflict," *Krasnaya zvezda*, March 17, 1995.

77. Sergei Ovsiyenko, "Low Cloud Cover Screens the Air Force: Commander in Chief Pyotr Deinekin Is Unable to Dispel the Haze over Air Force Actions in the Chechen Conflict," *Rossiiskiye vesti*, January 13, 1995.

78. Interview with Deinekin, "Flying in Your Dreams."

79. Ibid.

80. Pavel Anokhin, "A Military Landing in the Elbrus Region," *Rosiiskiye vesti*, June 6, 1995.

81. Vremya television report, June 28, 1995.

82. Interfax, Moscow, June 1, 1995.

83. Quoted in Carey Goldberg and Sonni Efron, "Russians Suffer 'Crushing' Loss in Rout by Chechens," *Los Angeles Times*, January 3, 1995. The Russian defense reporter Pavel Felgengauer highlighted the fundamental error of letting tank convoys into the city without first sanitizing the area. He noted openly: "It is very strange that the military leadership, primarily General Grachev, as a representative of the military's professionals, could not say 'no' to the politicians." Pavel Felgengauer, "Russia on the Brink of a Catastrophe: The Russian Subunits Which Entered Grozny Have Been Routed," *Sevodnya*, January 5, 1995.

84. See Wendy Sloane, "A Goliath No More: Russian Army Takes It on the Chin," *Christian Science Monitor*, January 13, 1995.

85. One Western account reported that the VVS had targeted Dudayev's family compound in the suburb of Tashkala and Grozny's electric plant but had missed: "Instead, they scored direct hits

on such objects as the muddy back yard of pensioner Yevgenia Pogosyan." Carey Goldberg, "Russia Steps Up Bombing near Chechen Capital," *Los Angeles Times,* December 20, 1994.

86. A major difference was that poor weather in the target area during Operation Desert Storm typically forced a mission abort because of strict rules of engagement prohibiting weapon release unless the prebriefed target could be acquired and positively identified. In Chechnya, the VVS evidently dropped without regard for the possibility of collateral damage.

87. The operation also prompted early recalcitrance from senior commanders on the scene, one of whom, Major General Ivan Babichev, halted his advance and refused to fire on unarmed civilians. See Alessandra Stanley, "Russian General Halts His Tanks in Chechnya in Sign of Uneasiness," *New York Times,* December 17, 1994. General Gromov stated frankly in an interview that the operation was "being handled by idiots." Interview by Livia Kling, "Idiots Are Responsible for This Operation," *Kurier* (Vienna), January 5, 1995.

88. Interview by Aleksandr Zhilin, "Boris Gromov: The Operation Was Prepared in Profound Secrecy," *Moskovskiye novosti,* January 8–15, 1995.

89. Sergei Surozhtsev, "The Legendary Army in Grozny: The Opinion of a Military Expert on the Actions of the Russian Army in Chechya," *Novoye vremya,* nos. 2–3 (January 1995): 14–15.

90. "Letter from Officer X," *Time,* January 23, 1995. One of the Russian generals who quit rather than lead troops into Chechnya later stated that Grachev lacked the courage to tell Yeltsin that his troops were unprepared for the invasion. See Fred Hiatt, "Russian General Assails Defense Minister on Chechnya," *Washington Post,* January 27, 1995. Another account noted that in his previous incarnation as airborne commander, Grachev had been known to try to impress important visitors by ordering his paratroopers to jump in excessively high wind conditions, resulting in injuries on landing. That commentator noted that Grachev's seeming readiness to endorse a half-baked invasion plan merely to please Yeltsin would have been "in character." Reported in Sonni Efron, "Army in Tatters May Threaten Russian Reform," *Los Angeles Times,* February 27, 1995.

91. Interfax, Moscow, February 23, 1995.

92. Quoted in Michael Specter, "For Russia's Army, Humbling Days," *New York Times,* January 8, 1995.

93. Quoted in Steven Erlanger, "Dire Warning to Legislators on Plight of Russian Army," *New York Times,* November 19, 1994. This was contradicted in the same month when Grachev assured Yeltsin that despite all, the armed forces were "fully combat ready and capable of carrying out any task." That rosy picture was sharply contested by a formal protest to the parliament by eleven generals from the Ground Forces' Military Council, headed by Colonel General Vladimir Semenov, complaining that there had not been a division-level training exercise since 1992 and that one-third of the army's helicopters were nonflyable. See Igor Chernyak, "Scandals: Infantry Generals Attack Grachev," *Komsomolskaya pravda,* December 10, 1994.

94. One report indicated that VVS test pilots from Akhtubinsk who delivered precision-guided munitions (PGMs) in Chechnya had been awarded Philips television sets. By comparison, the report said: "General Klishin's ace pilots were usually given a wrist watch—or, at best, a domestically made television set—for testing state-of-the-art aircraft." At the time, Lieutenant General Yury Klishin commanded the State Flight Test Center at Akhtubinsk. See Anton Vasiliyev, "Pilots Given a Television Each for Grozny Bombardments," *Novaya yezhednevnaya gazeta,* January 14, 1995.

95. Beaver, "Army Aviation in Chechnya," 79.

96. Surtsukov and Prokopenko, "A Shooting Sky."

97. Interview on the Moscow Mayak radio network, October 16, 1995.

98. By one account, Colonel General Deinekin was designated "Senior Controller for Air Operations," with the VPVO's commander in chief, Colonel General Prudnikov, subordinated to him as "Controller for Air Defense Support" (see Richard Woff, "Who's Who in the Chechen Operation," *Jane's Intelligence Review* 7, no. 4 [April 1995], 161). Whatever the actual relationship between the two service chiefs may have been, there is no evidence that either was ever actually on site at the operational command center in Mozdok.

99. Interview with Colonel General Ye. Shaposhnikov, "The Air Force Today and Tomorrow," *Aviatsia i kosmonavtika,* no. 8 (August 1990): 2–3.

100. Surtsukov and Prokopenko, "A Shooting Sky."
101. General Charles G. Boyd, USAF (Ret.), "Making Peace with the Guilty," *Foreign Affairs,* September–October 1995, 37–38.
102. Anatol Lieven, "Russia's Military Nadir: The Meaning of the Chechen Debacle," *National Interest,* summer 1996, 24.
103. Interview with General Deinekin by Vladislav Listyev, Ostankino television First Channel, December 14, 1994.
104. See "The Chechen Trap," *Economist* (London), January 7, 1995, 39.
105. Colonel General Pyotr S. Deinekin, "Russia Has Been, Is, and Will Remain a Great Aviation Power," *Krasnaya zvezda,* August 19, 1995.
106. Interview with Colonel General Pyotr S. Deinekin, "Russia Will Not Remain without Wings," *Krasnaya zvezda,* November 5, 1994.
107. Interview with Colonel General Pyotr S. Deinekin, "Pilots Are Always Equal to the Task," *Trud,* August 19, 1995.
108. See Richard Boudreaux, "Chechens Drop Russia Talks after Leader's Death," *Los Angeles Times,* April 25, 1996.

9. Waning Prospects for a New Fighter

1. The first generation of jet fighters was exemplified by the U.S. F-86 Sabre and the Soviet MiG-15. The second generation was led by the U.S. F-100 Super Sabre and the Soviet MiG-19. The third generation was characterized by the U.S. F-4 Phantom, the Soviet MiG-21, and the French Mirage IIIC. The fourth generation, which equip most modern air forces today, is represented by the U.S. F-14/F-15/16/18 class of fighters and the Russian MiG-29 and Su-27. The USAF's stealthy F-22 Raptor, now scheduled to enter service in 2005, is the first of the fifth generation of fighters.
2. *Soviet Military Power: An Assessment of the Threat* (Washington, D.C.: U.S. Government Printing Office, 1988), 82.
3. See Nick Cook, "Soviets to Deploy Two New Fighters," *Jane's Defense Weekly,* July 27, 1991, 132.
4. *Soviet Military Power: 1990* (Washington, D.C.: U.S. Government Printing Office, 1990), 80.
5. See "USAF Promotes MFI to Defend F-22," *Flight International,* April 6–12, 1994, 5.
6. See "USAF Expects Russia to Field Four Wings of Multirole Fighters by 2020," *Inside the Air Force,* April 1, 1994, 3.
7. Conversation with the author in Moscow, September 8, 1993.
8. Lev Chaiko, *Helicopter Construction in the USSR* (Falls Church, Va.: Delphic Associates, 1985), 70–71.
9. Vladimir Ilin, "The Fighters of the 21st Century," *Krylya rodiny,* no. 4 (April 1991): 20.
10. Conversation with the author in Santa Monica, California, November 11, 1988.
11. Interview by Yu. Morozov, "This Is Our Life," *Morskoi sbornik,* no. 7 (July 1992): 43–48.
12. Interview by B. Moseichuk, "We Are Shedding Excess Weight," *Argumenty i fakty,* no. 38 (September 1991): 2.
13. Interview on Radio Rossia, Moscow, September 18, 1991.
14. Quoted in Michael D. Towle, "Stealth Jet Doesn't Overawe Soviet Expert," *Fort Worth Star-Telegram,* June 21, 1991.
15. Conversation with the author in Moscow, September 5, 1993.
16. Colonel A. Krasnov, "Air Combat with 'Ghosts,'" *Aviatsia i kosmonavtika,* no. 7 (July 1991): 4–5.
17. This assumed, of course, that one or the other side would be foolhardy enough to insert expensive stealth fighters intentionally into multiparticipant maneuvering dogfights, with the attendant risk of higher loss rates on both sides because of unobserved shots.
18. The latter, it now seems apparent, was the MiG-29M, an upgraded MiG-29 with a larger wing area and better performance. That aircraft, later redesignated the MiG-33, was turned down by the VVS in favor of air-to-air and ground-attack upgrades of the Su-27.
19. Sukhoi was also reportedly engaged in work on "fundamentally new types of fighters." How-

ever, the firm was said to be concentrating on improving the Su-27. *Krylya rodiny,* no. 4 (April 1991): 21.

20. Interview by Nick Cook, "Soviet Air Chief Pushes for Quality," *Jane's Defense Weekly,* August 10, 1991, 220.

21. Nick Cook, "Advanced Fighters under Flight Test," *Jane's Defense Weekly,* March 7, 1992, 373.

22. Quoted in "Lack of Funds Holds Up Mikoyan's F-22 Rival," *Flight International,* March 10–16, 1993, 5. A flight of Mikoyan's putative new fighter in 1991, only a year after the first flights of the USAF YF-22 and Y-23, would have been unprecedented in Russian fighter development. Hitherto, the pattern of new Soviet fighter design typically featured a lag time of four to five years or more between the initial flights of the U.S. and the offsetting Russian aircraft.

23. In seeming contradiction to those hints from Mikoyan, General Deinekin told German Luftwaffe sources in 1992 that a fifth-generation Russian fighter was *not* in development. See Charles Bickers, "Russians Trying to Veil New Fighter," *Jane's Defense Weekly,* August 22, 1992, 5.

24. See "Lyulka/Saturn Al-41 Ready for Takeoff," *ConCISe,* August 31, 1995, 351.

25. Cited in David Markov, "Russia's Hot New Fighters," *Air Force Magazine,* September 1993, 40.

26. "Les Russes modernisent et visent l'export," *Air et Cosmos,* no. 1467 (April 11, 1994): 33–34.

27. Craig Covault, "Russia Debates Doctrine, Bomber, Fighter Decisions," *Aviation Week and Space Technology,* May 31, 1993, 23.

28. See Douglas Barrie, "Mikoyan Poised to Fly F-22 Rival," *Flight International,* July 13–19, 1994, 12, and Charles Bickers, "Multirole MiG Fighter to Fly This Summer," *Jane's Defense Weekly,* July 16, 1994, 1.

29. Interview with Colonel General Anatoly Malyukov by Piotr Butowski, "Flying in the Face of Adversity," *Jane's Defense Weekly,* April 17, 1993, 15.

30. See Simon Saradzhyan, "Russia Spending Scarce Funds on Futuristic Warplanes," *Radio Free Europe/Radio Liberty Report,* April 22, 1996.

31. Interview with Colonel General Pyotr S. Deinekin by Yelena Agapova, "A Russia without Wings Is Not Russia: It Does and Will Have Them," *Krasnaya zvezda,* August 15, 1992.

32. Interview on Moscow television, September 17, 1992.

33. Colonel General Pyotr S. Deinekin, "Always Ready for Action," *Krasny voin,* August 7, 1993, 3.

34. Interview with Colonel General Viktor Kot, "The Air Force Acquires a New Image," *Krasnaya zvezda,* January 27, 1994.

35. Interview with Colonel General Anatoly Malyukov by Dmitry Grinyuk and Piotr Butowski, "An Unusual Conversation at the Main Staff," *Krylya rodiny,* no. 11 (November 1991).

36. *Krylya rodiny,* no. 4 (April 1991): 21.

37. Interview with Colonel General Pyotr S. Deinekin by Charles Bickers, *Jane's Defense Weekly,* May 7, 1994, 32.

38. Interview with Colonel General Pyotr S. Deinekin by Gennady Lisankov, "Aircraft First," *Rossiiskaya gazeta,* May 5, 1994.

39. Butowski, "Flying in the Face of Adversity," 15 (emphasis added).

40. Specifications and performance details for the Su-35 are presented in Andre Brand, "Le Sukhoi Su-35, un 'vrai-faux' Su-27!" *Air et Cosmos,* no. 1470 (May 2, 1994): 32–34.

41. Quoted in "Lack of Funds Kills Russian Interceptor Program," *Flight International,* November 17–23, 1993, 11.

42. Cited in Yury Mamchur, "If We Preserve the Defense Complex, We Will Preserve Russia," *Krasnaya zvezda,* October 29, 1992.

43. Cited in a Radio Rossia newscast, March 5, 1993 (emphasis added).

44. Interview on Moscow television, April 17, 1993.

45. Ibid.

46. David Hearst, "Military Cuts Put Yeltsin under Threat," *Guardian,* June 15, 1994.

47. ITAR-TASS World Service, December 24, 1993.
48. Conversation with the author in Santa Monica, California, November 11, 1989.
49. Interview with Lieutenant General Vasily Vorobyev, "The Priority Is for Social Programs," *Syn otechestva,* February 14, 1992.
50. Cited in Yury Kovalenko, "The French and Russians Will Build a Helicopter," *Izvestia,* June 12, 1992.
51. Brigitte Sauerwein, "Defense Conversion: Russia's 'Strategic Imperative,'" *International Defense Review,* no. 6 (1992): 734.
52. See Douglas Barrie, "Cuts Put Flanker's Future in Jeopardy," *Flight International,* August 26–September 1, 1992, 15.
53. Cited in Valery Begishev, "The Defense Industry Is Gaining the Upper Hand," *Lesnaya gazeta,* September 19, 1992.
54. Interview with Anatoly M. Petrovich (general director of the Komsomolsk-na-Amure Aviation Production Association), "It Isn't Conversion That Causes Unemployment," *Krasnaya zvezda,* September 30, 1992.
55. Interview with Petrovich by Colonel A. Andryushkov, "We Make the Best Interceptor in the World," *Krasnaya zvezda,* January 13, 1993.
56. Interview with Colonel General Pyotr S. Deinekin by I. Chernyak, "The Man Sitting in Moscow Is Going into a Spin Again," *Komsomolskaya pravda,* March 17, 1993.
57. Bickers interview, *Jane's Defense Weekly,* May 7, 1994, 32.
58. Nikolai Novichkov, "The Russian MiGs Set for Flight Test," *Aviation Week and Space Technology,* January 1, 1996, 21.
59. "U.S. View of MiG-1.42," *Aviation Week and Space Technology,* January 15, 1996, 19. An earlier report, citing as evidence the forward-folding control surfaces of the new Vympel R-77 air-to-air missile, maintained that these reflected an intention for internal carriage and that the missile was expressly developed for Article 1.42, in keeping with a long-standing Soviet practice of designing a new air-to-air missile for each new fighter. See "Waiting for Russia's Stealth Fighter," *International Defense Review,* no. 6 (June 1995): 42.
60. Such posturing also played nicely into the hands of those Russian cynics who maintained that the unofficial state religion was "Skoro Buddhism," a clever derivation from the Russian *skoro budet* (loosely translated as "any day now").
61. Douglas Barrie, "Cold Comfort," *Flight International,* May 31–June 6, 1995, 26.
62. Douglas Barrie and Alexander Velovich, "Russia Faces Procurement Crisis as Air Force Budget Is Slashed," *Flight International,* January 31–February 5, 1996, 22.
63. "Special Report," *ConCISe,* May 18, 1996, 476.
64. Nikolai Novichkov and Michael A. Dornheim, "MiG 1.42 Set for First Flight," *Aviation Week and Space Technology,* January 11, 1999, 436–37.
65. Nikolai Novichkov, "S-37 Test Bed Evaluates New Fighter Concepts," *Aviation Week and Space Technology,* November 10, 1997, 46.

10. From Hard Times to Crisis

1. Anders Aslund, "If the Ruble Goes Under, So Could the Region," *Washington Post,* July 12, 1998.
2. Interview with General Pyotr S. Deinekin, "The Crisis in Military Aviation," *Nezavisimoye voyennoye obozreniye,* February 22–28, 1997.
3. "Statement of the Council on Foreign and Defense Policy: The Present Condition of the Russian Military Is an Imminent Catastrophe," *Nezavisimaya gazeta,* February 14, 1997.
4. Interview with Marshal of Aviation Yevgeny Shaposhnikov, "An Airplane? Good! But It Has to Be a Good Airplane," *Rossiiskaya gazeta,* July 10, 1997.
5. Alexsei G. Arbatov, "Military Reform in Russia: Dilemmas, Obstacles, Prospects," *International Security,* spring 1998, 83.
6. The data in this section are drawn from Sergei Rogov, "Military Reform and the Defense Budget of the Russian Federation" (unpublished paper, 1997). Rogov is director of the Institute of the USA and Canada and a prominent Russian commentator on defense and security matters.

7. Ibid., 3.
8. Paul Mann, "Russians Sound Alarm over Stalled Reforms," *Aviation Week and Space Technology,* May 26, 1997, 65.
9. Nikolai Novichkov and Paul Mann, "Decay Eats at Vitals of Russian Air Force," *Aviation Week and Space Technology,* March 17, 1997, 32.
10. Interview with Deinekin, "The Crisis in Military Aviation." Nor, evidently, were the deserving production entities invariably receiving their due returns on effort, thanks to rampant corruption at all levels of Russia's government-industry nexus. By one report, a recent audit by the Chamber of Accounts, Russia's equivalent of the U.S. General Accounting Office, determined that of a $150 million loan by the Finance Ministry to the Moscow Aviation Production Combine (ANPK) to provide MiG-29s for sale to India, not a single cent made its way to the enterprise to finance the already completed aircraft. Venyamin Sokolov, "The Virus in Russia," *New York Times,* June 1, 1998.
11. Douglas Barrie, "Coming Down to Earth," *Flight International,* August 6–12, 1997, 35.
12. Interview with Lieutenant General Yury Klishin, "In What Will We Take Off into the 21st Century?" *Armeisky sbornik,* no. 8 (August 1996): 45–48.
13. "In Brief, Russia," *Nezavisimoye voyennoye obozreniye,* February 8–14, 1997, 1.
14. "Moscow Airscene," *Air International,* October 1997, 206.
15. Colonel General Vyacheslav Yefanov, "The Big Hopes of Big Aviation: Military Transport Aviation Has No Alternative to Supporting the Strategic Mobility of Russia's Armed Forces," *Armeisky sbornik,* no. 6 (June 1996): 7–9.
16. Piotr Butowski, "Russia's Air Forces Face Up to Their Dilemmas: Part One," *Jane's Intelligence Review* 9, no. 10 (October 1997): 447–52.
17. Ibid.
18. "Strategic Bomber Numbers Cut in Russian Reshuffle," *Jane's Defense Weekly,* April 29, 1998, 13.
19. Nick Cook, "Russia's Air Force Is Down but Not Out," *Jane's Defense Weekly,* March 19, 1997, 23.
20. Barrie, "Coming Down to Earth," 37.
21. Interview with Shaposhnikov, "An Airplane? Good!"
22. Interfax, Moscow, August 15, 1997.
23. Piotr Butowski, "Russia's Air Forces Face Up to Their Dilemmas: Part Two," *Jane's Intelligence Review* 9, no. 10 (November 1997): 503.
24. Pyotr Yudin, "French to Aid Russia's Engine Purchase," *Defense News,* April 6–12, 1998, 12.
25. Igor Khripunov, "Sales Push: Russia Forced to Rely on Weapons Transfers to Asia-Pacific Nations," *Armed Forces Journal International,* October 1997, 72–77.
26. Alexander Velovich, "Russian Air Force Faces Cuts to Save Projects," *Flight International,* September 17–23, 1997, 18.
27. Interfax, Moscow, August 15, 1997.
28. Aleksandr Koretsky, "The Bustle around the Helm: Everyone Wants to 'Run' Military Reform," *Sevodnya,* August 16, 1997.
29. Butowski, "Russia's Air Forces: Part Two," 498.
30. "MFI Maiden Flight Set," *Aviation Week and Space Technology,* February 23, 1998, 23. Even though the putative new fighter was no longer scheduled for series production, Korzhuev added, at least test-flying the reported prototype had now become "a matter of honor" for the company. Piotr Butowski, "Russia's Fighter 2000 Chases Its JSF Rival," *Jane's Defense Weekly,* April 15, 1998, 3.
31. "MiG-MAPO Avionics Upgrades Aimed at Export Customers," *Aviation Week and Space Technology,* December 8, 1997, 35.
32. Interfax, Moscow, December 15, 1996.
33. "Fifth Su-27IB Flies," *Flight International,* January 21–27, 1998, 22. Another combat aircraft said to be still receiving shoestring procurement financing was the Su-25TM, two of which were slated to be delivered to the VVS in 1998 and four more in 1999 for a unit flyaway cost of $8.3 million each. See "Russian Air Force Orders Limited Number of Sukhoi Su-25TMs," *Flight International,* March 24–28, 1998, 17.

34. "S-37 Design 'Experimental,' Says Sukhoi," *Flight International,* November 26–December 2, 1997, 30.
35. Major David R. Johnson, USAF, "Russia's Military Aviation Industry: Strategy for Survival," *Airpower Journal,* summer 1997, 51.
36. Interview with Deinekin, "The Crisis in Military Aviation."
37. Interview on Radiostantsiya Ekho Moskvy, August 15, 1997.
38. Patrick Brunet, "Le MiG 1.42 Sort d l'Ombre," *Air et Cosmos,* no. 1684 (December 25, 1998): 27–29.
39. Ibid., 28.
40. Nikolai Novichkov and Michael A. Dornheim, "MiG 1.42 Set for First Flight," *Aviation Week and Space Technology,* January 11, 1999, 436–37.
41. David Hoffman, "Russia's 'Stealth' Bluff: Rollout of Fighter That Hasn't Been Built," *Washington Post,* January 24, 1999.
42. "World News Roundup," *Aviation Week and Space Technology,* February 1, 1999, 24.
43. Hoffman, "Russia's 'Stealth' Bluff."
44. Vladimir Isachenkov, "Cash Shortage May Ground New Russian Jet," *Seattle Times,* January 20, 1999.
45. David A. Fulghum, "JSF Reflection Is Golf Ball–Sized," *Aviation Week and Space Technology,* February 15, 1999, 27.
46. Brunet, "Le MiG 1.42 Sort d l'Ombre."
47. Hoffman, "Russia's 'Stealth' Bluff."
48. Isachenkov, "Cash Shortage May Ground New Russian Jet."
49. "Appointment Signals Sukhoi-MiG Merger," *Aviation Week and Space Technology,* February 8, 1999, 72.
50. Novichkov and Dornheim, "MiG 1.42 Set for First Flight," 437.
51. Indeed, as perhaps a measure of the desperation that MiG-MAPO may have felt to keep its long-moribund effort alive, some sources in Moscow were said to have averred that Russia was ready to entertain a co-development offer from China, and even to manufacture operational versions of the aircraft for China and possibly India thereafter, whatever interest (or lack thereof) the VVS might have in the dying program. Ibid.
52. Simon Saradzhyan, "New Russian Fighter May Never Take Flight," *Defense News,* February 22, 1999, 22.
53. This implied that even in better days, VPVO aircrews flew no more than 100 hours or so per year, as contrasted with the U.S. norm of 180–240 hours per year.
54. Quoted in *Krasnaya zvezda,* November 29, 1997.
55. "In Brief, Russia."
56. Lieutenant Colonel Vladimir Matyash, "Army and Navy Servicemen Begin the New Training Year amid Hope and Anxiety," *Krasnaya zvezda,* December 3, 1996.
57. Interview with Lieutenant General Vladimir Mikhailov, "A Military Commander and His Establishment: The Fourth Air Army, the Most Powerful Army in the Russian Air Force's Frontal Aviation, Celebrates Its 55th Anniversary This Year," *Armeisky sbornik,* no. 8 (August 1997): 36–38.
58. Interview with Lieutenant General Yury Klishin, "A Wingless Russia Is Not Russia but a Third-Class State," *Krasnaya zvezda,* January 11, 1997.
59. Interview with Lieutenant General Aleksandr Ionov, "It's Too Early to Bury the Air Force," *Krasnaya zvezda,* April 15, 1997.
60. Andrei Matyakh, "We Don't Live On Bread Alone," *Krasnaya zvezda,* February 20, 1997.
61. "The Making of a Disaster," *Sovetskaya Rossia,* December 11, 1997.
62. *United States Air Force Statistical Digest, FY 1997* (Washington, D.C.: Assistant Secretary of the Air Force, Financial Management and Comptroller, 1997), 101.
63. Interfax, Moscow, April 7, 1997.
64. Sergei Babichev, "From Parade Formation to Battle Formation: Even Air Shows Are Becoming a Benefit under Conditions of Fuel Shortage," *Krasnaya zvezda,* September 22, 1995.
65. Interview with Mikhailov, "A Military Commander and His Establishment," 38.
66. Aleksandr Ivanov, "Air Defense Forces' Fighter Aviation Is at a Danger Point," *Krasnaya zvezda,* July 20, 1996.

67. Interview with Mikhailov, "A Military Commander and His Establishment," 38.
68. Interview with Colonel General Igor Kalugin, "Not Demeaning the Prestige of Long-Range Aviation," *Krasnaya zvezda,* March 5, 1997.
69. Sergei Babichev and Sergei Prokopenko, "Will Our Pilots Fear the Aircraft? A Few Comments on the Results of the Training Year in the Air Force," *Krasnaya zvezda,* November 25, 1997.
70. Interview with Lieutenant General Yakim Yanakov, "How to Optimize Expenditures for Training," *Krasnaya zvezda,* July 3, 1997.
71. Novichkov and Mann, "Decay Eats at Vitals of Russian Air Force."
72. Interview with Lieutenant General Yakim Yanakov, "Whom Are We Sending to the Regiments?" *Krasnaya zvezda,* September 13, 1997.
73. Interview with Yanakov, "How to Optimize Expenditures."
74. Interview with Ionov, "It's Too Early to Bury the Air Force."
75. David A. Fulghum, "Russia Bets Big on Foreign Sales," *Aviation Week and Space Technology,* April 7, 1997, 35.
76. Interview on Radiostantsiya Ekho Moskvy, Moscow, June 17, 1997.
77. Interview on Air Force Day, "The Air Force Shield and Air Force Sword," *Rossiiskiye vesti,* August 15, 1997.
78. Lieutenant Colonel Sergei Babichev, "It Is Becoming Increasingly Hard to Maintain Altitude," *Krasnaya zvezda,* January 11, 1997.
79. Novichkov and Mann, "Decay Eats at Vitals of Russian Air Force."
80. First Channel television broadcast, Moscow, March 12, 1996.
81. Alexander Velovich, "Russians Order French Equipment for MiG-ATs," *Flight International,* October 8–14, 1997, 18.
82. Colonel General Anatoly Tarasenko, "Flight Safety Is in Jeopardy," *Na boyevom postu,* October 2, 1997, 2–3. General Tarasenko was the last air commander for the Group of Soviet Forces in Germany (GSFG).
83. After requiring three hours to be jacked up and towed off the runway, the aircraft was repaired to a point where it was able to be flown back to Russia two days later.
84. "Do We Really Need the Russian Knights or Not?" *Krasnaya zvezda,* February 6, 1997.
85. Interview with Ye. Shaposhnikov, "An Airplane? Good!"
86. Babichev, "From Parade Formation to Battle Formation."
87. Interview with General Pyotr S. Deinekin, "Russia Has Always Been and Will Remain a Great Aviation Power," *Rossiiskiye vesti,* May 18, 1996.
88. Interview on Radiostantsiya Ekho Moskvy, Moscow, June 17, 1997.
89. Sevodnya program, Moscow television, May 20, 1997.
90. Igor Semenchenko, "Servicemen Are Still Slaving Away," *Krasnaya zvezda,* February 28, 1997.
91. Rogov, "Military Reform and the Defense Budget," 31.
92. Arbatov, "Military Reform in Russia," 93.
93. Later, in November 1997, Yeltsin promoted General Sergeyev to become the first post-Soviet marshal, prompting one critic to remark snidely: "The first success of military reform—a marshal is appointed." Quoted in Martin Nesirsky, "Yeltsin Moves for Reductions in Armed Forces, *USA Today,* November 26, 1997.
94. Rogov, "Military Reform and the Defense Budget," 37.
95. Steve Liesman, "Russia Appears Serious on Revamping Military," *Wall Street Journal,* March 11, 1998.
96. Martin Nesirsky, "Russia's Armed Forces Seem Close to Collapse," *St. Louis Post-Dispatch,* April 22, 1998.
97. Vadim Solovyev, "The New Defense Minister Becomes a Presidential Team Player within a Month," *Nezavisimaya gazeta,* June 21, 1997.
98. Interview on Radiostantsiya Ekho Moskvy, Moscow, July 17, 1997.
99. Interview with General Pyotr S. Deinekin, "Whoever Is Master of the Sky," *Armeisky sbornik,* no. 3 (March 1997): 6–9.
100. Interfax, Moscow, August 11, 1997.
101. Interview with General Pyotr S. Deinekin, "Who Has Long Been Loading Up the Work?" *Moskovsky komsomolets,* August 3, 1997.

102. Interview with Deinekin, "Whoever Is Master of the Sky."
103. Colonel General Volter Kraskovsky, Colonel General Igor Maltsev, and General Ivan Tretyak, "It Must Be Reorganized, Not Destroyed: There Is No Alternative to Centralized Command and Control of Air Defense," *Nezavisimoye voyennoye obozreniye,* October 3–9, 1997, 4. The authors are the former commander of the missile and space defense forces, the former head of the VPVO main staff, and the former commander in chief of VPVO, respectively.
104. Sergei Grigoryev, "The Current Reorganization Means Destruction: Russia's Air Defense System Must Be Preserved," *Nezavisimoye voyennoye obozreniye,* November 28, 1997, 2.
105. RIA, Moscow, August 6, 1997.
106. Radio Mayak, Moscow, August 31, 1997.
107. ITAR-TASS, Moscow, July 19, 1997. Andreyev added grimly that it was "senseless" to talk about the Russian military's difficulties." He explained, "Enumerating them does not make them disappear."
108. Interview with Colonel General Viktor Sinitsyn, "The Keys to the Skies Are in Reliable Hands," *Armeisky sbornik,* no. 4 (April 1997): 10–16.
109. Major General (Ret.) Valentin Rog, "A New Military Aviation for a New Russia: The Reorganization of the Air Force and Air Defense Forces as a Single Branch of the Armed Forces Is an Objective Regularity," *Nezavisimaya gazeta,* October 15, 1997.
110. See "Russia Combines Military Aviation Units," *Flight International,* July 16–22, 1997, 8.
111. Yevgeny Krutinov, "It Is a Poor Commander Who Does Not Want to Become Commander in Chief," *Sevodnya,* July 7, 1997.
112. "Russia, Belarus Work on Joint AD System," *BMD Monitor,* April 17, 1997, 132.
113. Russian Television Network, Moscow, August 31, 1997.
114. Interfax, Moscow, June 18, 1997.
115. Interview with Major General Nikolai Anisimov, "The Budget Strain Will Ease," *Krasnaya zvezda,* January 9, 1998.
116. Aleksandr Koretsky, "The President Threatens to Pension Off Generals and Marshals: Boris Yeltsin Has Already Discharged Air Force Commander in Chief Pyotr Deinekin from Service and Is Ready to Do the Same with the Defense Minister," *Sevodnya,* December 15, 1997.
117. "Serie noire pour le transport aerien Russe," *Air et Cosmos,* no. 1639 (December 19, 1997): 53.
118. "Multiple Engine Failure Blamed for An-124 Irkutsk Accident," *Flight International,* December 17–23, 1997, 21.
119. "Russian Air Force Grounds Most Planes," *Washington Post,* December 13, 1997.
120. Interview on Russian Television First Channel, Moscow, December 12, 1997.
121. "The Making of a Disaster." Rokhlin went on to implore his Duma colleagues to form a commission to impeach Yeltsin over the sorry state of the VVS. See "Russian Air Force Chief Offers to Step Down," *Aerospace Daily,* December 12, 1997, 392.
122. Koretsky, "The President Threatens to Pension Off Generals and Marshals."
123. Sergei Grigoryev, "The Combined Air Force Will Have a New Commander in Chief: It Was Not Air Disasters That Led to Pyotr Deinekin's Dismissal, but Disagreements in Approaches to Military Organizational Development," *Nezavisimoye voyennoye obozreniye,* December 19–25, 1997, 2.
124. Ilya Bulavinov, "Igor Sergeyev: If I Can't Do It, I Will Leave," *Kommersant,* July 19, 1997.
125. Aleksandr Koretsky, "Almost Darwinian: On Branches and Natural Selection," *Sevodnya,* June 24, 1997, and Russian Television Network "Pulse" program, Moscow, July 21, 1997.
126. Mikhail Urusov, "The General's Crossword," *Moskovskiye novosti,* July 13–20, 1997, 11.
127. Interview on Russian Television First Channel, Moscow, December 12, 1997.
128. Andrew Duncan, "Time of Consolidation for Russia's Military," *Jane's Intelligence Review* 9, no. 10 (October 1997): 455.
129. Interfax, Moscow, May 25, 1997. Attack helicopters during the 1960s were a part of the VVS. They were transferred to the ground forces in 1990 as an independent subunit.
130. Leonid Kostrov, "A Marriage in the Skies: Divorce Is Inevitable," *Obshchaya gazeta,* no. 41 (October 16–22, 1997): 2.
131. Ibid.
132. Interview with Deinekin, "Whoever Is Master of the Sky."

133. Lieutenant General Aleksandr Ionov, "Air Force Reform: It Rests on the 85-Year Experience of Russian Military Aviation," *Nezavisimoye voyennoye obozreniye,* August 9–15, 1997, 1, 3.

134. Ibid.

135. Interview with Deinekin, "The Crisis in Military Aviation," 1, 5.

136. Grigoryev, "The Combined Air Force Will Have a New Commander in Chief."

137. Ilya Bulavinov, "The Air Defense Forces Destroyed the Enemy Commander in Chief and Achieved Total Victory over the Air Force," *Kommersant,* January 21, 1998.

138. Interfax, Moscow, August 11, 1997.

139. Bulavinov, "The Air Defense Forces Destroyed the Enemy."

140. After Kornukov's appointment, one report commented that "Marshal Sergeyev was going to put in a word for Pyotr Stepanovich Deinekin" during a pivotal meeting with Yeltsin on the VVS leadership issue but that in the end, "for some reason [he] said nothing about Deinekin in the Kremlin. Had he changed his mind? Or did someone change it for him?" Sergei Larionov, "Heads Roll in the Air Force: Heroes of the Soviet Union to Get 'Handshake,'" *Moskovsky komsomolets,* January 30, 1998.

141. Bulavinov, "The Air Defense Forces Destroyed the Enemy." One report noted the determination of Moscow's powerful mayor, Yury Luzhkov, to evict military occupants from some of the choicest properties in the city's center, presumably including Pirogovskaya Street. That too could have been a factor behind the move of VVS headquarters from downtown Moscow to the former VPVO headquarters in the Moscow suburban hinterland. Not long after he became mayor in 1992, Luzhkov won an arrangement in which Yeltsin gave the Moscow city government ownership of all federal property within the city limits. See Vladimir Kostrov, "Deinekin and Prudnikov Continue Flying Together," *Russky telegraf,* December 10, 1997, and "From Mayor's Nest to the Kremlin?" *Economist,* April 11, 1998, 38.

11. Toward Uncharted Horizons

1. In a formulation that would have done any Western air power advocate proud, Deinekin once remarked that the Desert Storm air campaign enabled the coalition's leaders "to decide the outcome of the war in a short time, essentially without involving the ground grouping." Interview with General Pyotr S. Deinekin, "Whoever Is Master of the Sky," *Armeisky sbornik,* no. 3 (March 1997): 6–9.

2. Russian Television Network, Moscow, January 20, 1998.

3. "Yeltsin Touts Military Inventory, Troop Downsizing," *Boston Globe,* January 21, 1998.

4. Russian Television Network "Vesti" program, Moscow, January 20, 1998.

5. Interview on Moscow television, January 22, 1998.

6. "Russia AD, AF Merger Set," *BMD Monitor,* March 17, 1998, 95.

7. Yury Golotyuk, "The Kremlin Has Finally Appointed a Commander of Russia's Military Skies," *Russky telegraf,* January 21, 1998.

8. Michael Gordon, "Russian Air Chief Has No Regret on Downing of Korean Jet," *New York Times,* January 24, 1998. See also Alastair Macdonald, "Russian Air Chief Ordered KAL Downing," *Washington Times,* January 23, 1998. Defense Minister Sergeyev later sought to minimize Kornukov's statements, saying that Kornukov "was just executing orders."

9. A. Dyatlov, "While the 'Black Box' Is Still Silent," *Komsomolskaya pravda,* July 7, 1989.

10. In the U.S. case, the core issue in the interservice dispute over the language of Joint Publication 3-09, "Doctrine for Joint Fire Support," related to the USAF concern that the draft document, as written, would allow surface commanders undue authority over air operations in a given area of responsibility. The USAF's inability to reach a resolution of the issue to its full satisfaction in the joint arena was closely akin to Deinekin's failure to prevail with respect to the General Staff's ruling, which, he felt, threatened to undermine his own efforts to make the most of Russia's now-meager fighter potential. On the Joint Publication 3-09 issue, see "Air Force Chief of Staff Plans to Appeal to Army on Fire Support Doctrine," *Inside the Pentagon,* April 23, 1998, 1, and "Military Chiefs Resolve Joint Fire Support Doctrine—for Now," *Inside the Pentagon,* May 21, 1998, 3.

11. For a perspective on the issues at stake in the U.S. case, see Benjamin S. Lambeth, "Bounding the Air Power Debate," *Strategic Review,* fall 1997, 42–55.

12. Alexander Velovich, "Russian Air Force to Be Halved," *Flight International,* February 18–March 4, 1998, 32.

13. Nikolai Novichkov, "Country's Woes Dog Russian Designs," *Aviation Week and Space Technology,* August 3, 1998, 3.

14. "More Air Force Leadership Changes Expected," *Moskovsky komsomolets,* January 30, 1998.

15. Alexander Velovich, "Russian Air Force Chief Overhauls Merger Plan," *Flight International,* February 4–10, 1998, 16.

16. Interfax report in English, June 10, 1998.

17. Interview with Colonel General Anatoly Kornukov by Svetlana Sorokina, Moscow television, June 22, 1998.

18. Mikhail Shevstsov, ITAR-TASS dispatch, March 21, 1998.

19. Velovich, "Russian Air Force to Be Halved."

20. Ilya Kedrov, "VVS and VPVO Integration—'Normal Flight,'" *Nezavisimoye voyennoye obozreniye,* June 19–25, 1998, 1.

21. "Strategic Bomber Numbers Cut in Russian Reshuffle," *Jane's Defense Weekly,* April 29, 1998.

22. Sergei Babichev and Aleksandr Veklich, "A Redistribution of VVS and VPVO Forces and Assets Is Under Way," *Krasnaia zvezda,* March 18, 1998.

23. Interview with Colonel General Anatoly Kornukov on the "I Serve the Fatherland" program, Russian television network, March 29, 1998.

24. Colonel General Anatoly Kornukov, "The Structural Development Theory of the New Air Force: Its Potential Capabilities to Fight for Air Supremacy Could Increase by 25 Percent as a Result of Reform," *Nezavisimoye voyennoye obozreniye,* March 13, 1998, 3.

25. Piotr Butowski, "Bear Successor Will Enter Service after 2010," *Jane's Defense Weekly,* September 9, 1998.

26. "Less Bang for the Ruble," *Defense Week,* January 1 , 1999, 4.

27. Quoted in interview with Colonel General Anatoly Malyukov by Piotr Butowski, "Flying in the Face of Adversity," *Jane's Defense Weekly,* April 17, 1993, 15.

28. Interview with General Deinekin by Vladislav Listyev on Ostankino television First Channel, December 14, 1994.

29. Andrei Baranovsky, "The Russian Air Force Has Nothing to Fly," *Sevodnya,* March 30, 1995.

30. Pavel Felgengauer, "No Professional Military Can Be Foreseen in Russia So Far," *Sevodnya,* May 4, 1995.

31. Interview with Lieutenant General A. Borsuk, "Corrections Are Needed," *Aviatsia i kosmonavtika,* no. 7 (July 1991): 2–3.

32. Major General Yevgeny Korotchenko, "We Need a 21st-Century Military," *Krasnaya zvezda,* June 9, 1993. Another general expressed the same point even more baldly: "Is there a measure of effectiveness of the military which we dream about? Yes, there is. The Gulf war. In forty days, Western professionals routed an Iraqi army built according to the Soviet model, armed with our weapons, and trained by us." Major General Vladimir Dudnik, "Military Reform: Eight Years of Marking Time," *Moskovskiye novosti,* September 13, 1992, 7.

33. Interview with Colonel General Pyotr S. Deinekin, "Who Will Take Up the Sword?" *Krylya rodiny,* no. 3 (March 1993).

34. Interview with Colonel General Pyotr S. Deinekin, "A Time for Decisive Actions," *Aviatsia i kosmonavtika,* no. 1 (January 1993): 4.

Index

absolute funding shortage, constraining Russia's
  fighter ambitions, 153–56
accident rate: mounting because of continuing
  budget crisis, 172–74; situation following Soviet
  era, 27–29
accomplishments of Chechnya air campaign, 132–37
aeronautical rating levels, 61–62
Afghanistan, 96, 100–101, 126
airborne warning and control system (AWACS),
  123, 147
air campaign in Chechnya, 119–32; beginnings of
  candor in self-assessment, 133–37; burdens of bad
  planning, 138–39; costs of, 129–32; disjunctions
  in joint force integration during, 141–42; gaining
  air control during, 123–24; implications of, 142–
  44; key accomplishments of, 132–37; operational
  setting of, 121–22; preparatory moves for, 122–
  23; price of financial starvation during, 139–41;
  problems and lessons from, 137–42; results of,
  129–32; showing limits of air power in irregular
  war, 142; sustained air support to ground operations
  during, 124–29; validation of airlift in, 132–33
air-combat fighter, a new: and constraints on Russia's
  fighter ambitions, 150–56; Russia's interest in,
  146–48; signs of advanced prototype development
  of, 148–50; waning prospects for, 145–56
air control, gaining in Chechnya air campaign,
  123–24
Air Defense Forces. *See* VPVO
air doctrine: evolution of, 34–55; and force structure
  and development plans, 45–55; post-Soviet retrenchment, 35–38; reform plans for, 35–38;
  within the Russian VVS, 40–43
Air Force. *See* Russian VVS; Soviet VVS
airlift, validation in Chechnya air campaign, 132–33
air power, limits of in irregular war, 142
Air Superiority Fighter (ASF), 145

air traffic control, problems with following Soviet
  era, 29–31
Amelko, Admiral Nikolai, 54
Andreyev, Colonel General Vladimir, 103, 178,
  184, 189
Antonets, Lieutenant General Vladimir, 18
Antoshkin, Lieutenant General Nikolai, 63,
  184, 189
Arbatov, Aleksei, 34, 158
Aviation Training Center, 63
AWACS. *See* airborne warning and control system

bad planning, burdens of in Chechnya air campaign,
  138–39
Barkovsky, Colonel Valery, 128
Basayev, Shamil, 128
basing approaches, within the Russian VVS, 44–45
Baturin, Yury, 175
Belenko, Lieutenant Viktor, 56, 120–21
Belyakov, Rostislav, 146, 149–50, 153
Bokov, Lieutenant General Leonid, 167, 169
Borsuk, Colonel General Anatoly, 24, 105, 109, 194
Boyd, General Charles, 142
breakup of the USSR: and CIS military organization,
  14; immediate consequences of, 9–14; impact on
  defense industry, 13–14; problems with air defense
  from, 9–13; and Russian unilateralism, 14
Brezhnev, Communist Party General Secretary
  Leonid, 195
budget crisis, continuing, 190–91; constraining Russia's fighter ambitions, 153–56; depriving operations and support, 167–68; flagging morale from,
  1, 174; immobilizing training, 168–72; impact on
  the Russian VVS, 158–74; mounting safety problems from, 172–74; price of in Chechnya air campaign, 139–41; suspending force development,
  159–67

229